AF830773

The Primordial Dance

THE PRIMORDIAL DANCE

Diametric and Concentric Spaces in the Unconscious World

PAUL DOWNES

PETER LANG
Oxford • Bern • Berlin • Bruxelles • Frankfurt am Main • New York • Wien

Bibliographic information published by Die Deutsche Nationalbibliothek
Die Deutsche Nationalbibliothek lists this publication in the Deutsche Nationalbibliografie; detailed bibliographic data is available on the Internet at http://dnb.d-nb.de.

A catalogue record for this book is available from the British Library.

Library of Congress Cataloging-in-Publication Data:

Downes, Paul, 1970 July 12-
The primordial dance : diametric and concentric spaces in the unconscious world / Paul Downes.
p. cm.
Includes bibliographical references and index.
ISBN 978-3-03-430760-4 (alk. paper)
1. Subconsciousness. 2. Phenomenology. I. Title.
BF315.D69 2012
154.2--dc23
2012026838

Cover image by Aleksandra Jasniewicz

ISBN 978-3-0343-0760-4

Peter Lang AG, International Academic Publishers, Bern 2012
Hochfeldstrasse 32, CH-3012 Bern, Switzerland
info@peterlang.com, www.peterlang.com, www.peterlang.net

For Aleksandra Jasniewicz
and our daughter Eva Downes, with love

Contents

Acknowledgements

I will always be grateful to Nick McDonald, Trinity College Dublin, for his support and advice with this project in its early stages. My thanks also to Aleksandra Jasniewicz for her help with the section on Memling's *Last Judgment* and to Killian O'Rourke, Mater Hospital Dublin, for his comments on aspects of the penultimate draft. I would like also to acknowledge with thanks the support of Fionnuala Waldron and St Patrick's College, Dublin, Research Committee.

Part of chapters 3, 5.2, 5.3, 5.4 and 7.2 first appeared in Downes, P. (2003). Cross-cultural structures of concentric and diametric dualism in Lévi-Strauss' structural anthropology: Structures of relation underlying the self and ego relation? *Journal of Analytical Psychology*, 48, 47–81, © 2003 John Wiley & Sons Ltd. Aspects of chapters 3.1, 8.4, 9.3 first appeared in Downes, P. (2011). Concentric and diametric structures in *yin/yang* and the mandala symbol: A new wave of Eastern frames for psychology. *Psychology and Developing Societies*, 23 (1) 121–53, © 2011 Sage Journals.

Parts of chapters 5 and 9.2 are based on Downes, P. (2013). Developing Derrida's Psychoanalytic Graphology: Diametric and Concentric Spatial Movements. *Derrida Today*, © 2013 Edinburgh University Press, which can be found at: http://www.euppublishing.com/joural/drt. Parts of chapters 11.3 and 11.4 initially appeared in, Downes, P. (2010). Schema structure-content relativity. *Cybernetics and Human Knowing*, 17 (3), 7–43, © 2010 Imprint Academic Journals, while chapter 11.2 is based on an earlier, more expanded version: Downes, P. (2006). Newtonian space: The 'blind spot' in Newell and Simon's information processing paradigm. *Cybernetics and Human Knowing* 13 (3), 25–55, © 2006 Imprint Academic Journals.

My thanks to the National Museum of Art, Architecture and Design, Oslo, for permission to reproduce Edvard Munch's *The Scream*; to Österreichische Galerie Belvedere, Vienna, for Gustav Klimt's *The Kiss*; and the National Museum, Gdansk, for Hans Memling's *Last Judgement*.

Figures and Tables

PART I

Setting the Stage for the Primordial Dance

CHAPTER 1

Introduction

A silent axis of the unconscious world rests largely undiscovered. A task of this book is to bring the contours of these poles to the fore. To breathe life into this scrutiny of the primordial in relation to the unconscious, a key question needs to emerge and be interrogated: *Is there a spatial-phenomenological structure, of a primordial unconscious dimension, influencing human experience?* Response to this core question requires development of a wide range of philosophical, psychological and anthropological insights. It requires a framework that is more than being merely the sum of the parts of phenomenology and psychoanalysis. A radical recalibration of these terrains is being sought.

This questioning of spatial structures in a domain of the unconscious brings the potential to uncover fundamental, overlooked, primordial projections in experience, observations and truth claims. It offers an approach to deconstruct ideological blind spots. Awareness of potential projected structures is also an important condition for engagement with wider modes of experience, as part of personal and cultural development, and for opening from states of repressed structural experience. The abdication of our potential spaces for experience need not continue.

Proposing candidate spatial structures of the unconscious provides not only a concretization of understanding but also engages with the development of publicly defensible criteria for interrogation of the unconscious, as part of an interpretative scientific approach. In response to this core question, a specific central argument this book seeks to address is that: *A primordial spatial relation of diametric-concentric interaction exists as a dynamic, a priori structure and is projected into empirical realities of systems of experience, including systems of the unconscious.* This primordial dance between concentric and diametric spaces needs to be uncovered.

An initial setting the stage for the different parts of this inquiry into the proposed primordial dance requires elucidation of key concepts such as, concentric and diametric space, primordiality, a spatial-phenomenology and dynamic, *a priori* structures. Understanding of primordiality, in particular, needs to be refashioned from associations with the term that distract from the current argument. A spatial-phenomenological understanding of concentric and diametric projected spatial structures requires clarification of its relation to at least some previous accounts of phenomenology in philosophy and the social sciences. In doing so, the issue of developing an approach, if not method, for a spatial-phenomenological inquiry is to be articulated. Apprehending concentric and diametric spaces as dynamic, *a priori* projections requires an amplification of Heidegger's violent reconstruction of Kantian conceptions of *a priori* truths to challenge an *a priori* domain of static abstractions. This amplification seeks to address key lacunae in Heidegger's reconstruction. Understanding of the unconscious world is taken, for current purposes, to involve repression but also to go much further into unconscious systems of relation in dynamic spatial terms. In order to engage with this broader understanding of the unconscious world, a number of areas in psychology that are key for a spatial-phenomenology are to be reconstructed in terms of their hidden unconscious aspects.

A diametric dualistic spatial structure is one where a circle is split in half by a line which is its diameter, or where a square or rectangle is similarly divided into two equal halves (see Figure 1). In a concentric dualistic spatial structure, one circle is inscribed in another larger circle (or square); in pure form, the circles share a common central point (see Figure 2).

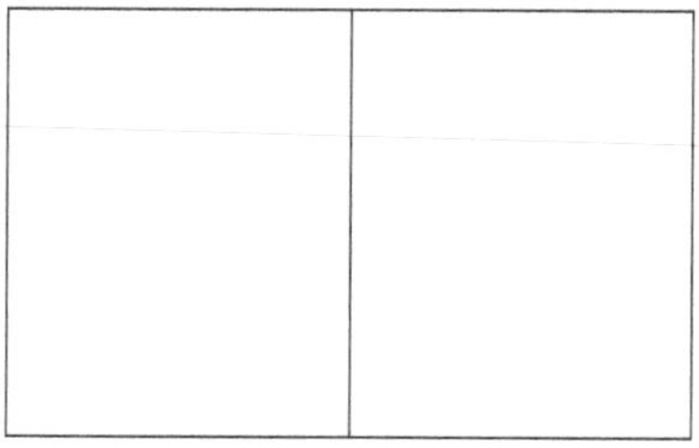

Figure 1 Diametric Dualism

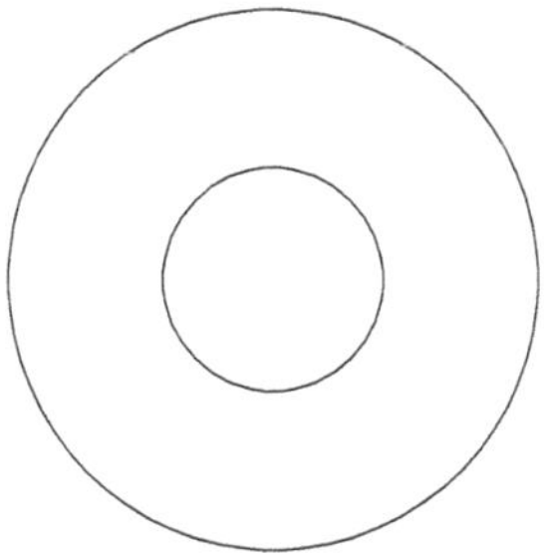

Figure 2 Concentric Dualism

1.1 Dimensions of primordiality

How can a primordial dance even be possible? Is this primordial dimension not a chimera? Primordiality must be not be tethered to a conception of the 'primitive' lost in the mists of history. A focus on concentric and diametric spaces in terms of a primordial dimension requires a shift towards spatiality and away from linear historical time, as the key site of primordiality. This is not to scythe away ancient historical dimensions from understanding of the primordial but rather to instate and invigorate a concrete spatial understanding.

Primordiality is a multifaceted concept and it cannot be assumed that various aspects of an understanding of primordiality are complementary with each other. That concentric and diametric spaces can give expression to diverse meanings of primordiality and in doing so, offer an integration of these dimensions for a domain of primordial experience and truth claims, is to be argued for. It is posited as a question, rather than an assumption, as to whether any such site for primordiality offers a unity between its diverse strands.

What is meant by primordiality can be unfolded in many distinct, though often complementary ways. It can involve a focus on the primordial as experience in the early years of a child, as a cross-cultural truth, as ancient historical excavation and as a more fundamental truth or experience.

Primordiality as a more fundamental truth or experience imputes the need for clarification of the criteria for such claims to be more fundamental. Other important conceptions of primordiality include the possibility of a truth and experience prior to socially constructed realities. Such a primordiality would require a level of relation prior to language itself, a dimension of private experience, that is not to be conflated with private language. It expresses a transcendence, or at least direction towards transcendence, of socio-historically conditioned truths, that is not a sheer reduction to abstract essences. Primordiality as an axis of space, as an interaction between diametric and concentric spaces, needs to be considered in relation to all of these dimensions.

Understanding of primordiality can be facilitated by a number of other related conceptions of Heidegger, Derrida, Gilligan, Jung and Freud. Heidegger views a primordial truth as being concerned with a potential unity within experience,[1] as a dimension that is not reducible to simple subjectivity of experience. Primordiality is envisaged as providing a direction towards a unity, as a unifying process, that does not equate with a totality governing all aspects of experience. This primordial direction of unity and holism for experience is to be firmly distinguished from an abstract unity that filters difference. As a unifying direction, primordiality must embrace difference as an inclusive unity. A primordiality as unity invites escape from the frozen compressed unity of categorization and eschews a grounding in abstract, categorial essences.

Perhaps the simplest example of primordial experience in the sense of being a unifying direction for experience, and which is also a fundamental experience, is that of sleep. The integrating functions of sleep are a direction towards gathering a unity for experience. And as a unity within experience and a unifying process, it is to be distinguished from a claim for experiential totality; sleep as a primordial experience does not invite

1 See also Richardson (1974, p. 74), Brooke (1991, p. 96). Heidegger (1929) highlights 'an essential distinction' between 'comprehending the whole of beings as such and finding oneself in the midst of beings as a whole'. The former is 'impossible in principle' (p. 99).

an implication that it is to take over all experience. Sleep and dreams are one road to primordial experience, though it is not envisaged that they are the royal road to a concentric pulse of relation.

Other features of a quest for a more primordial truth from the vantage point of Heidegger include the need to go beyond Cartesian splits between mind and body, reason and emotion, self and world, as well as beyond reliance on the limited schema of causal explanation. This is not to oppose a primordial truth search with science. There can be avenues for their compatibility, though to find such pathways, the void in the heart of empiricism needs to be confronted. Another aspect to primordiality, resonant with Heidegger (1927),[2] is an interrogation of *a priori* truths. These *a priori* truths need not be spliced completely apart from the empirical, or what Heidegger calls ontical realm, as their traces may be projected into this realm of 'appearances'.

Building both explicitly and implicitly on Heidegger's work, Derrida questions primordiality with regard to 'origins' that he deconstructs as not being fundamental. This includes causal origins and constructs such as 'experience'. He seeks prior traces and challenges the primordiality of basic assumptions in Western thought, including a Platonic bias towards visual metaphors of knowledge. Derrida problematizes the visual, aural, haptic metaphors and assumptions pervading accounts of truth, in his excavation of the absent, the unsaid, the unthought in truth claims. Such a questioning of primordiality for truth and experience invites a skepticism regarding truth claims based on a core or centre that excludes the margins.

While primordial experience may enter perceptual and cognitive realms, these are not being argued to be its source. Primordial experience is being argued to commence as a preperceptual mode of experience. Both Heidegger and Derrida share a rejection of the primordiality of truth claims based on the construct of the individual subject; this Cartesian *cogito* sought a foundation for truth and experience in the self-reflection of an isolated individual subject. Derrida especially seeks movement away

2 As Henrich (1994) highlights, a Kantian *a priori* is radically different from Heidegger's ontological reconstruction of Kant.

from a preoccupation with false certainties of foundations or grounds, though Heidegger (1927) is committed to a fundamental ontology in his primordial truth search. At first sight, it is difficult to conceive of a role for Derrida in a primordial truth search for a more fundamental level of relation, except as an antithetical foil. However, this view of Derrida's deconstruction as a tearing away of grounds in a quasi-nihilist fashion will be seen to be an oversimplification of his much more nuanced position that leads to a reconstruction of truth claims.[3]

A primordial search for a more fundamental truth needs to resist and modify premature, flattened static grounds. Derrida conceives of difference as being more originary than traditional grounds, though itself not being a traditional ground. An inquiry into the primordial that embraces the different truth concerns of early Heidegger and Derrida invites a reconstruction that goes beyond traditional conceptions of foundations and grounds, whether causal or otherwise. Primordiality is envisaged as a more fundamental relation, intimately associated with experience. The tensions and resonances with Derrida will need to be explored.

Though Gilligan does not engage directly in examination of primordiality, a number of themes in her work have implications for this issue. Her emphasis on a relational subject in an ethic of care challenges traditional Western Cartesian assumptions of an isolated, abstracted subjectivity. Yet Gilligan's earlier work in particular appears mainly concerned with deconstructing any perceived primordiality of universal truth claims, such as those of Kohlberg's stages of moral reasoning. Her concern with contextualism in order to challenge premature universalizing claims also reaches into her later work. She challenges Erikson's universalist claims for adolescence as a stage of growth into separation and independence. This challenge to abstract universalism can also be interpreted as paving the way for other different kinds of primordial experiences and truth claims. Another sense

3 For example, Derrida (1995) states, 'I have constantly insisted on the fact that the movement of deconstruction was first of all affirmative – not positive, but affirmative. Deconstruction, let's say it one more time, is not demolition or destruction' (p. 211).

of primordiality can be construed as emerging from Gilligan's later work, in particular. This is as an authenticity of experience, of a lost experience or voice that is viewed as prior to and more important than cultural forces that gloss over such voice. Search to uncover this loss of voice offers some resonance with Heidegger's account of authenticity as primordiality.[4] This more primordial connective experience, lost to awareness, also offers an interplay with Heidegger's view of primordiality as a unity within experience, or unifying direction.

A Jungian approach to primordial experience and truth ultimately investigates a domain, not simply of myths across diverse cultures, but of a space prior to myths in his proposed central archetype of the collective unconscious. Much of his concern is with integration of the unconscious and personal experience, as a primordial direction of unity for experience. Primordial experience, expressed through primordial images, tends to challenge and unseat a prematurely grounded level of experience. Jung characterizes this as the integration process between the self and the ego, adapted to an external world. Primordiality for Jung involves a recentering of experience rather than a Derridean rejection of centres. Freud tends to engage with primordiality at the levels of early childhood experience and ancient cultural patterns. Yet his later, underdeveloped and frequently misunderstood accounts of the life and death drives begin to postulate another idea of primordiality, as a more fundamental level of influence on structures of the unconscious.

For current purposes, the main aspects of the argument regarding primordiality are for it as:

a) a more fundamental truth or experience;
b) an *a priori* structure projected into empirical observations and texts;
c) a direction of unity for experience, thereby challenging Cartesian splits between mind and body, reason and emotion, self and world;

4 However, Heidegger's (1927) terrain also envisaged a dimension of *inauthentic* structures as being primordial.

d) an authenticity of experience;
e) a truth and experience prior to socially constructed realities;
f) a cross-cultural truth;
g) being beyond the limited schema of causal explanations.

These avenues for questioning of primordiality may not necessarily be related to each other. Can the proposed spaces of diametric and concentric relation help provide a unity to the truth search for primordiality?

Primordiality as a) is a weaker version of the claim for b), as a) seeks only the more primordial rather than the primordial as such. The focus of much of the book is on a) and engages with b) on the issue of the existence and meaning of the projected structures in empirical observations and texts. However, it is predominantly in section D of the book that interrogation of the meaning of these projected structures in relation to an *a priori* truth, is taken up. Primordiality as d) is a special case of a claim for primordiality as c). Primordiality as e) and f) are strongly related. Primordiality as c) to g) pervades different chapters, with varying degrees of emphasis.

Primordiality as f), as a cross-cultural or transcultural truth, is an extremely important concern, though the argument provided here is very much a preliminary one. This is especially so, given that the main thinkers examined, Gilligan, Freud, Heidegger, Jung, Derrida and Lévi-Strauss, as well as Laing, are all from the Western hemisphere. An ethnocentric critique focusing on whether constructs are Western-biased, and thus, do not pertain to wider cultural contexts, is one lens within a crosscultural critique; a crosscultural critique additionally adopts a concern with resistance to cultural conditioning, as part of a search for dimensions of a more primordial, unifying experience. Thus, primordiality as f) is strongly related to c), d) and e). Primordiality as experience in the early years of a child is investigated as a dimension of primordiality a) and c) here.

Primordiality as ancient historical excavation is less obviously a domain of relevance to this argument. Concerning primordiality as ancient prehistory, the whole tenor of this book is not seeking for some retrieval of the past *ab initio*. It is neither a quest for emulation nor preservation of the past; it is not a quest for primordiality as a nostalgia for the mythical origins of a spatial experience that we have lost from the past. Neither is it an attempt to employ an understanding of primordiality in terms of a primitive ancient state of being. Such a conception of the 'primitive', excised from history as the counterpoint to a modern civilization, is well recognized in anthropology as being seeped with a Western colonialist bias towards the 'other' (Brickman 1993). Primordiality is not to be reduced to a recapitulation of the archaic or 'primitive'. It requires apprehension through a framework that avoids such colonialist pitfalls, while also eluding a tendency to excise the past. A shift is needed in the axis of primordiality to further apprehend the primordial as a placing out of joint, as a displacement in space, more than as a displacement in linear time.

What has been soldered together as primordiality requires a remelting. This includes the implicit or explicit primordiality of universal, exclusive and causal truth claims, cognition of a Cartesian subject and identification of the primordial in linear time as the primitive ancient historical. In the jargon of postmodernism, a primordial truth claim is not a 'metanarrative' (Lyotard 1984). Primordiality is not a quest for an overarching story. It is not reducible to a cognitive worldview but is examined as conditions of possibility framing experience and understanding. It does not purport to exclude a wide variety of other truths and experiences. It is recognized that truth claims are relative to the underlying goals of such truths, at different levels of description for the respective, plural domains of relevance. Primordial structures of differential relation are not for all contexts of relation; this is not a totalizing claim for ubiquity. A relational focus on traces of concentric and diametric structures requires avoidance of the Scylla of a hegemonic universalism and the Charybdis of a flat relativism. Yet there is a need to go further than simply a questioning of the primordial, to engage also in a primordial questioning. This requires a truth standard and framework more fundamental than that of traditional science. This questioning requires a more primordial quest.

CHAPTER 2

A Spatial-Phenomenological Approach

What series of steps can be taken to pave the way for the movements of the proposed primordial dance? Investigation of diametric and concentric spaces of relation as primordial spatial-phenomenological structures requires a somewhat compressed introduction to key aspects of a spatial-phenomenology. As illustrated in Table 1, these key aspects all pertain to primordiality in at least some of its various senses a)–g).

Table 1 Key aspects of a spatial-phenomenology in relation to primordiality

Blind spots in the spatial assumption structure of a text	Primordiality as: a) a more fundamental truth or experience
Need to develop spatial structural criteria for priority of some modes of experience and truth	Primordiality as: a) a more fundamental truth or experience, c) a direction of unity for experience, d) a more primordial authenticity of experience, g) beyond causal explanations
Narratives of lived experience in phenomenological accounts	Primordiality as: c) a direction of unity for experience, d) a more primordial authenticity of experience, g) beyond causal explanations
Going beyond ethnocentrism	Primordiality as: e) a truth and experience prior to socially constructed realities, f) a cross-cultural truth
Dynamic *a priori* structures of diametric and concentric space	Primordiality as: b) an *a priori* structure projected into empirical observations and texts, e) a truth and experience prior to socially constructed realities, f) a cross-cultural truth

2.1 A search for blind spots in the spatial assumption structure of a text to uncover a more fundamental primordial truth level

A spatial-phenomenological interrogation takes as its Archimedean point,[1] a questioning of potential concentric and diametric spatial projections. This is combined with scrutiny of other hidden and explicit spatial preunderstandings, projected into the assumption structure of a given text. It is not being sought to produce a spatial-phenomenological method as such but more a spatial-phenomenological approach, as frames for understanding and experience.

This investigation can include, but is by no means confined to, discourses on spatial themes directly addressed in a given narrative account. As a search for the foundational limits of a text, a spatial-phenomenological approach engages with what Heidegger (1927) calls basic concepts, 'Basic concepts determine the way in which we get an understanding beforehand of the area of subject-matter underlying all the objects a science takes as its theme, and all positive investigation is guided by this understanding' (p. 30). Basic concepts are necessary conditions for framing the understandings of an issue, though they may themselves be resting on spatial assumptions as conditions of possibility.

If there is to be a primordial axis of space, prior to empirical truths and yet in some way interacting with domains of relevance for empiricism, this implies consideration of these spatial dimensions as at least being a void, a void in the heart of empiricism. This spatial blind spot or void is to be understood literally. Luhmann emphasized the blind spot (1994) or 'a kind of invisible space' (1995, p. 25) excluded from the awareness of an observer in science and the consequent need for 'second order observation:

1 This is with reference to understanding, as distinct from a starting point in experience of such spatial-phenomenological structures. The 'how' question, namely, how to engage in further experience of these spatial-phenomenological structures is beyond the scope of this book.

an observation of observations' to examine this blind spot (Luhmann 1995, p. 3).[2] Yet for such textual caesura, Luhmann is invoking space as a metaphor and not literally.

A focus on blind spots in textual edifices invites the further step of interrogating the spatial projections through such blind spots. Empirical observation is laden with theoretical assumptions and is a selective filter of relevant features for observation. This is well-recognized in philosophy of science. It does not make the empirical truth claims false but limited in their explanatory scope. Consideration of the void in empiricism goes further than these issues. It treads pathways beyond what is eased out of consideration in the chiselled construction of a conceptual edifice, where affective aspects supporting value-judgments are occluded. It is more than simply being a negative limiting condition but is a starting point for a more primordial inquiry.

This inquiry interrogates projection, not simply of random experiences, affects or images but of a distinctive spatial structure. It is proposed that there is a fundamental projected spatial structure to be uncovered through the roots of empirical observation. This spatial projection is one that absorbs a range of emotional states within its projected structures. In this sense, it is the void in the *heart* of empiricism, a space that incorporates feeling. This spatial-relational understanding of the roots of empiricism is not antiempirical. The void can be integrated with empiricism through a spatial-phenomenological approach to engage with a more primordial understanding to which empiricism can contribute. Examination of texts of empirical observation is to uncover the aspects of the void in the heart

2 In a jurisprudential context, Hart's (1961) positivism identifies a blind spot in legal argument and legal systems of authority as the 'rule of recognition', namely, that norm underlying other derivative norms, which itself is not subject to rational reconstruction in terms of legal rules but is rather mere convention. Kelsen's (1945) positivism similarly postulates a basic norm, a *Grundnorm*, which provides an interpretative leap to the creation of other norms in a legal system, through an act of will rather than a conclusion from a premise by an intellectual operation. Again this can be termed a blind spot in legal interpretative logic.

of its empirical claims and to open a different space of diametric and concentric interaction.

This spatial-phenomenological inquiry involves excavation of not only the existence of such spatial projections in a given text or set of empirical observations (which obviously is itself also a text). It also requires exploration of the meanings of the existence of such a spatial-phenomenological projection in any given context. Though the existence of a common spatial-phenomenological projection offers a unifying feature across diverse contexts, the significance of this projection is multifaceted and diverse for each given context. It is not a search for a single story; rather it is a projected assumption structure for diverse, potentially infinite narratives. As a dynamic projective space, it is interactive with the contextual materials rather than a static frozen appendage to them. This spatial-phenomenology is not simply a phenomenology of space but a phenomenology *through* space.

It is a question less of spatial-phenomenology being in Husserlian fashion 'to the things themselves', though Husserl's 'things' immediately accessible to experience are much wider than physical things or empirical facts. Rather, spatial-phenomenology is a movement 'to the spaces themselves' underlying not only entities and human experience, but wider structures of the unconscious beyond the traditional Western constructions of the human subject. If Husserlian phenomenology is preoccupied with an intentionality that presupposes an object for intention, a spatial-phenomenology interrogates the spatial backgrounds, presupposed not only in intentionality, but prior to intentional experience of a conscious subject. Though spatial-phenomenology may include cognition, its spatial-phenomenological structures are projected prior to cognition (and subjectivity).

Heidegger's (1927) radical reconstruction of Husserl's phenomenology in *Being and Time* sought a more primordial or originary phenomenology and is of more immediate concern for the purposes of a spatial-phenomenology.[3] For Heidegger, phenomena are not essentially subjective, nor are they the inner contents of conscious representations in a referential relation to the outer objects making their appearance in or through them. A Heideggerian focus on uncovering phenomena concealed, or partly revealed in appearances, excavates the spatial projections already appearing in the text as displaced, hidden, glossed over phenomena. These phenomena are, nevertheless, at least in some way, manifested in the appearance of the text. A 'levelling down' of the hidden phenomena leads to an appearing 'in disguise' (Heidegger 1927, p. 59). A spatial opening is thus sought, to uncover the more primordial truth of the phenomena. This interactive space between hidden phenomena and appearances is to be a more dynamic relation than the static traditional distinction between form and substance. Much of Heidegger's (1927) argument rests on the uncovering of a set of structures, where some aspects are treated as prior to others, through a series of relations in a structural whole – a structural whole that was itself never quite manifested as a concrete spatial projection. In the absence of a clearly visualized spatial structure or holistic set of structures, much of Heidegger's account falls away into an argument merely by authority.

These spatial projections go beyond a mere recategorizing. It is not simply a reconstruction of categories that is sought, but also a more dynamic movement beyond the static categorial as such. Heidegger (1927) sought to develop what he termed *existentialia*, in contrast to a categorial mode.

3 This is not to deny at least some significant continuities between aspects of Husserl's phenomenology and that of a spatial-phenomenology resonant with Heidegger (1927). For example, Moran (2007) highlights the following aspects of Husserl's 1925 lectures published as *Phenomenological Psychology*, 'According to Husserl, there is always a "pregiven world" as the backdrop of experience. World is the "all-inclusive abiding ground of existence" ... It has its own universal *a priori*, essential structure, which includes the spatial and the temporal but also much more ... It is grasped pre-theoretically and pre-predicatively' (p. 147). This is largely indistinguishable from Heidegger's own position, once a modification is made to view the *a priori* not so much as a universal structure and truth totality for all experience, but rather as a structure for primordial experience which is a unity or unifying process within experience.

Philipse (2007) states that 'Since these categories allegedly are inadequate for understanding our human mode of existence and its temporal structure, Heidegger sets himself a double task: a "destruction" of traditional categories by showing why they are inadequate, and a "construction" of a system of new categories for ontological self-understanding, the so-called *existentialia*' (p. 174). However, this account does not give sufficient emphasis to this need for a change beyond the categorial *per se*.[4] Perhaps Philipse intended to convey the dynamic aspect through the notion of such reconstructed categories being part of a wider temporal system. What is sought in a spatial-phenomenological approach is not so much a space for play *within* the categorial.

The active process of a spatial-phenomenological projection frequently amounts to an unseating or recalibration of basic concepts and categories founding a given conceptual edifice. This is not a recipe for homogeneity of implications and consequences through this refluidation of the roots of a tradition or context of inquiry. As a dynamic projective space of concentric and diametric structures, it invites change to contextual foundations, thereby bringing reconstruction of meaning in its field of contents.

In terms of primordiality as a unity or unifying process, concentric and diametric spatial projections involve a discourse on a direction of unity for experience that does not suppress or deny fragmentation. It is a unifying process *after* fragmentation. It is not seeking to exert a dam to

4 Heidegger sought a dynamic temporal unifying background, prior also to Kantian conceptions of *a priori* categories. Kisiel (1993) also refers to categories of being, when discussing an aspect of Heidegger's development prior to *Being and Time*. Discussing the text of Heidegger's Summer Semester Lectures 1923, he states that they provide 'the context in which Heidegger for the very first time mentions, albeit in passing, those innovative and tradition-breaking categories of being called "existentials", meant there to articulate the most unique and highest possibility latent in the facticity of being human' (p. 398). Kisiel (1993) comments that 'the ways-to-be as characters of being seem ... to be straightforward expressions ("categories") less prone to the jargonizing that the existentials have become ... What did "ex-sistence" give him that "to be" did not?' (p. 397). Apart from a stronger connection to lived primordial experience, they also offer a development in going beyond the merely categorial.

buttress against an ineluctable fragmentation. In existential terms, interaction between projected spaces of concentric and diametric relation is a discourse of potential unity for experience and meaning which not only accommodates meaninglessness. It requires this initial loss of meaning in the unseating of the oblivion of falsely (or at least, prematurely) grounded experiences and understandings.

The simplification in any process of categorization is well-recognized in a number of domains. Categorization itself as a simplification and filtering process is emphasized both in cognitive and social psychology (Rosch 1978; Tajfel 1978) and in claims to deconstruct categories as primordial essences (Sayer 1997). The need to go beyond a deductive approach based on categories of understanding is also acknowledged in the interpretative approach of legal reasoning that, at times, seeks a more active balancing of principles in constitutional legal texts than what Tribe (1988) describes as a static categorical definitions approach. Concentric and diametric spatial interactions need to be understood in a more dynamic sense than as static reified categories. A spatial discourse is needed to dance out of the Procrustean bed of the categorial.

Much of this quest for a spatial-phenomenology operates through a Heideggerian lens from his early *magnum opus*, *Being and Time*, though not his subsequent work.[5] Yet in doing so, this same blind spot and unthought in early Heidegger's work also needs to be brought to the fore, through examination of diametric and concentric spatial projections in his text. Though Heidegger does not employ the term 'unconscious', it can be interpreted as a feature of his work, once a view of the unconscious is broadened beyond that of the individual human subject. In doing so, the *a priori*-empirical relation, as well as that between being and human beings needs further elucidation.

5 Heidegger subsequently abandoned his search for temporal structures of transcendence. However, Malpas (2008) argues for the continuity of Heidegger's spatial concerns across early, middle and late phases of his work. While there are a range of distinct phases even within Heidegger's early work (Kisiel 1993), for current purposes, early Heidegger will be taken to mean up until 1927, when he published *Being and Time*.

It is being argued that an interrogation of the spatial unthought in Heidegger (1927) is highly consistent with his early phase of thought seeking fundamental structures of being. This is without necessarily committing to an argument that this proposed spatial-phenomenological reading of Heidegger was directly intended by that author. An argument for a high level of consistency with early Heidegger's text in uncovering the unthought blind spots must be firmly distinguished from an interpretative approach that exploits silences in a text, to import alien schemata and which in doing so, tends to filter major aspects that are contrary to such schemata. Whether for interpretation of the work of early Heidegger or others, interrogation of unthought blind spots is not a *carte blanche* for an interpretation of empty logical possibilities. It builds on implications and directions meaningfully manifested already in the thinker's text.

Heidegger's phenomenology sought to investigate ontological structures. These structures of being evade simple description, as they are caught within the descriptive limits of language as to what being 'is'. Heidegger's questioning of being in his primordial truth search does not call a spade a spade. Heidegger's 'spade' is neither a static abstract symbol on a card, nor a concrete instrument that digs sand. However, a spatial-phenomenology of concentric and diametric spatial projection offers a concretization of this primordial search that, at least in its visual manifestations and experiential implications, is amenable to ordinary language, while avoiding reduction to simple slogans, prescriptions or assertions.

Derrida, unlike Heidegger, explicitly engages with terms and language of the unconscious. Derrida's spatial interrogation pertains to a more elusive domain than that of basically static images underpinning language; this spatial domain is irreducible to simply cognitive structures shaping everyday intentional practices and engages with concerns regarding an unconscious space of repression. In opening up a quest for a more dynamic and elusive spatial domain, Derrida (1978) introduces his distinctive concept of *différance*, which he suggests is 'a new kind of question about metaphor, writing and spacing in general' (p. 199), 'The thinking of difference can neither dispense with topography nor accept the current models of spacing' (p. 204). He relates concerns with differential relation to those of both space and time. *Différance* involves a linguistic attempt to fuse spatial and temporal concerns, gathering together an association of *différer*, to differ in space, with deferral, i.e., to delay or postpone presence. Derrida (1978) expressly relates conceptualizations of space to language and thought, 'Does the fact that language can determine things only by spatializing them suffice to explain that, in return, language must spatialize itself as soon as it designates and reflects upon itself?' (p. 16).

A spatial-phenomenological approach fundamentally shares a Derridean concern to expose dynamic spatial movements in the construction of a text and to engage in a broadening of Freudian repression. It differs from Derrida through this specific interrogation of projected structures of differential relation, namely, concentric and diametric spaces. These projections pave a path through a deconstruction of blind spots to a reconstruction. It might be objected that any such projections are a kind of bias of presence, an assumption of a continuous hidden substance standing under appearance, that Derrida accuses as being assumed in terms such as experience, grounds, origins, primordiality and being – and which early Heidegger (1927) especially invokes.[6] This concern will need to be addressed in this proposed spatial-phenomenology to analyse how diametric and concentric spaces do not succumb to a simple presence as 'substance' in the structures – and to resist treatment of primordiality as simple presence.

This is not to conflate Heidegger's aim of the destruction of traditional ontology in *Being and Time* with Derrida's textual goals of deconstruction. There are differences in early Heidegger's search for a primordial truth of being and Derrida's assault on textual assumptions. However, these differences are not cavernous ones, at least for the arguments of Derrida that search for an entirely other text and for a future psychoanalytic graphology,

6 Derrida (1974) relates his own search to Heidegger's, envisaging that his conception of difference is more primordial or originary than the understandings of early Heidegger, though in doing so, Derrida requires a different understanding of the primordial or originary, 'The ontico-ontological difference and its ground … in the "transcendence of Dasein" … are not absolutely originary. Difference by itself would be more "originary", but one would no longer be able to call it "origin" or "ground", those notions belonging essentially to the history of onto-theology, to the system functioning as the effacing of difference' (p. 23).

such as in *Writing and Difference*, and *Archive Fever*. Derrida's focus in deconstruction theory is on amplification and critique of spatial assumptions underlying basic concepts such as origins, centres, causality, subjectivity, traces of memory in repression etc. He postulates a future graphology or spatial understanding of the unconscious, stating that Melanie Klein's work perhaps leads the way.[7]

If an opening up of another domain of relevance for science is to occur, it must challenge a traditional conception of space as being merely metaphorical. Derrida is himself searching for a level prior to the literal-metaphor opposition. A spatial-phenomenological approach will also be applied to Derrida's own work, where it engages with accounts of the unconscious as a system of repression wider than a Freudian one. This approach is not so much as a deconstruction of his textual concerns but as a reconstruction of them regarding key terms, such as trace, erasure of the trace and *différance*.

As early as 1920, Heidegger employed the term 'deconstruction' (*Abbau*), 'Exactly in this wanting-to-become-free from an ungenuine, non-primordially appropriated tradition this philosophy is always obligated to the continuing existence of what it "deconstructs" [*abbaut*], not fortuitously but for primordially philosophical reasons' (p. 3). Heidegger (1920) is explicit that his deconstruction of the categories of being in traditional ontology is for the purpose of a clearing towards a primordial level of truth, where 'the destruction is ... actually closer to the primordial' (p. 142). Though the goals of Derrida's deconstruction are at times less clear, Derrida has frequently reiterated that his project is an affirmative one of developing an entirely other text. Nevertheless, Derrida would question a conception of truth as primordial, at least in the sense sought by early Heidegger. The question arises as to whether an investigation of concentric and diametric projections, as part of a primordial truth search, necessarily requires acceptance that these are primordial structures? Three different

7 Derrida (1988/1990) offers a similar promissory note, not only in relation to Freud, Klein and the unconscious, but also for Heidegger, stating that *Being and Time* '... is still waiting to be really read. There are still enormous reserves in Heidegger's text left for further interpretations' (p. 146).

kinds of claim can be distinguished here for a spatial-phenomenology of diametric and concentric projections. The weak claim is that they are simply an approach to provide a critical deconstruction, for example, of ideology, without themselves offering a more primordial truth goal. The strong claim is that they facilitate a deconstruction of blind spots for the purpose of a primordial, or more primordial truth goal. A stronger claim again is that they also offer an *a priori*, primordial truth level. It is recognized that the stronger the claim that is being made, the higher the burden of proof for such a claim in a spatial-phenomenology.

Heidegger's (1927) words also require interpretation reflexively, as encompassing his own inquiry into a primordial, ontological truth for structures of being which he envisaged as a science, 'The real "movement" of the sciences takes place when their basic concepts undergo a more or less radical revision which is transparent to itself. The level which a science has reached is determined by how far it is capable of a crisis in its basic concepts' (p. 29). The spatial-phenomenological argument in this book engages in a proposed revision of a range of basic concepts of the unconscious and subjectivity, both in psychology and philosophy. The ones focused upon are: Gilligan's precognitive frames for her ethic of care and logic of justice modes of moral reasoning, Freudian repression and later Freud's life and death drives, Jung's central archetype of the collective unconscious, Derrida's trace and erasure of the trace in an unconscious system or text, Heidegger's being-in, *Angst*, care and transcendental horizon of temporality, classical cognitive science's concepts of the 'schema' and problem search in space, and Johnson and Lakoff's image schemata, in what they call second generation cognitive science. Though some of these basic concepts do not explicitly advert to a conception of the unconscious and may initially even seem to eschew the relevance of unconscious structures, nevertheless, their common hidden spatial assumptions will be opened up, to expose an unconscious domain of relevance. Though these basic concepts may *prima facie* appear to differ in even radical ways, it is being argued that they all project a *common* blind spot regarding concentric and diametric spaces. This common blind spot is the primordial spatial unconscious of their accounts on the unconscious.

2.2 The need to develop spatial structural criteria for priority of some modes of experience and truth as being more primordial

A spatial-phenomenology through concentric and diametric spatial projections needs to tread along pathways not yet provided for in phenomenology. Though Heidegger (1927a) sought to emphasise his phenomenology as a method, as distinct from a technique (§5), this remained largely underdeveloped in his work.[8] Kisiel (1993) observes that between 1919 and 1929, Heidegger 'vacillated between the two poles of whether philosophy is to be the primal science or no science at all' (p. 17). The poverty of Heidegger's method has been perhaps most forcefully criticized by Tugendhat (1967). He emphasizes the lack of criteria for privileging as primordial in any Heideggerian truth claims, whether for disclosure of being or for preference of a dimension of experience as being authentic. A conception of phenomenological *truth* requires further justification and criteria than those offered by Heidegger (1927a), in his treatment of phenomenology as the name for the method of ontology (§5).

As well as setting out a range of relations within purportedly primordial structures, Heidegger (1927) sought to relate these to other aspects treated as derivative and unprimordial. While *Being and Time* refers to an array of affective terms like: *Sorge, besorgen, Affekt, Affektion, Gedrücktheit, Einfühlung, Missmut, Freude, Lebenssorge, Stimmung, Hoffnung, Wunsch, Fürsorge, Angst* (care, concern, affect, affection, depression, empathy, ill-humour, joy, the cares of life, mood, hope, wish, solicitude, anxiety), only

8 Although Heidegger's phenomenology adopts deductive inferences, in Malpas' (1997) words, 'the interpretation is not as such an axiomatic or deductive structure' (p. 12). However, MacQuarrie's (1977, pp. 185–6) characterization of Heidegger's project as relying mainly on insights attained in states of anxiety, rather than on deduction, is too subjectivist a reading and neglects the formal, structural aspects of Heidegger's concerns. Derrida (1995) views his own deconstruction theory as 'reducible neither to a method nor an analysis (the reduction to simple elements …)' (p. 83).

some are viewed as giving expression to and existing through a primordial holistic structure. For example, Heidegger (1927) suggests that empathy is not primordial but derivative from this holistic primordial structure that includes a prior connective level of 'being-with' (p. 162). Specific existential states, which encompass affective dimensions, are viewed as being part of a primordial spatial structure, whereas others are treated as being indirect and derivative, in relation to this prior structure. Being derivative, they are purported to be lacking in primordiality. Without elucidation of this primordial structure in spatial terms, it is difficult for Heidegger (1927) to ascertain criteria for how certain affective states and truth claims are primordial, and others are not.

Development of an argument for primordiality of particular experiential states clearly rests on further illumination of this structural whole, as a structure – and specifically, as a spatial structure. Through development of this structural whole as a concrete projected primordial spatial structure of concentric and diametric spaces, a spatial-phenomenological approach seeks to develop criteria for how certain truth claims and experiential modes can be prioritized as being more primordial than others. They are conceptualized as being more primordial in a spatial structural sense, to inform understanding of primordiality in the senses a) to g) in section 1.1. While Dostal (2006) states that 'it is hard to envisage what shape an ontology based as much on spatiality as temporality would take' (p. 144), the spatial-phenomenological approach of concentric and diametric projected structures to develop such an ontology is not, however, seeking an equiprimordial relation between space and time. An initial concentration on dynamic spatial structures paves the way for the prior primordiality of a temporal directional movement, to be discussed in chapter 10. It is a priority of a temporal transcendental horizon consistent with early Heidegger (1927).

Laing's (1959) phenomenological approach in psychology was influenced by Heidegger's *Being and Time*, both directly through appropriation of terms such as 'being-in-the-world', and also indirectly, *via* a Sartrean existentialist influence.[9] Mitchell's (1974, p. 240) critique of

9 Heidegger (1949) explicitly rejected Sartre's (1943) subjectivist reading of *Being and Time*.

Laing's phenomenological approach in psychology reveals a tension in Laing's goals of developing a science of experience (envisaged by Laing as a totalization), a politics of experience and a mystical pursuit of transcendental experience. While Laing (1959) relies on a conception of a 'true' self to contrast with a 'false' self in his account of schizoid phenomenology, criteria for privileging one experience as true and another as false are largely left veiled. Again there is a need for spatial-phenomenological criteria for privileging some modes of experience. A claim for primordiality of experience as being more fundamental or more unified requires (spatial structural) criteria. A spatial-phenomenology is not a science of all experience as a truth totality claim. Nor is it the museum of a social science importing a limited, artificial domain upon which humanity can vainly seek to exert prediction and control.

Spatial structural criteria for a more primordial truth offer a truth-conception in relation to an experiential unity or unifying direction. This unifying direction projects a primordial truth. The spatial structural criteria emerge from the spatial structures themselves as projections. Investigation of projections into a text is at a range of interconnected levels: a) explicit spatial themes, b) concentric and diametric spatial projections and inferences from their relations, c) the assumption structure of a text in spatial terms, d) necessary and supportive background spatial conditions for framing understanding.

2.3 A different, complementary phase to the narratives of lived experience in phenomenological accounts

Lived experience is the pulse and first phase of phenomenological description in psychology and sociology. This is a vitally important listening process to the experience of self and other. Phenomenology in this relational tradition is an attempt to perceive the world as it appears to the individual through shared dialogue. This involves an epistemological commitment to the validity of the lived experience of individuals, as an important truth in itself, whether or not it corresponds with an 'external' reality.

A spatial-phenomenological focus on structures of experience and the unconscious operates through a different phase from a phenomenological seeing, listening and gathering of lived experience. Though they are complementary, it is important to keep firmly separate the phenomenological description, from the subsequent interrogation of spatial-phenomenological projections into the text of this lived experience. A related point on the importance of not letting the voices of those giving their accounts of experience become drowned out by, nor mediated through, the filters of the researcher, has been emphasized in phenomenological approaches in sociology. Thus, Gould et al. (1974) highlight the importance of clear separation between descriptive accounts and subsequent interpretation. The need for distinct phases between phenomenological description and analysis has been reiterated in the contexts of a phenomenological approach to health psychology for heroin addicts (Downes 2003a) and educational psychology for inner city, urban youth (Ivers & Downes 2012).

A phenomenological approach of uncovering hidden, often marginalized, voices can be centrally ascertained, in the work of Laing (1959), with individuals experiencing psychosis, together with that of Gilligan and her colleagues on voices of adolescent girls being displaced and undergoing a loss of relation in a patriarchal culture. For Gilligan's implicitly phenomenological concerns, the girls are 'at risk for losing touch with what they know through experience' (Taylor, Gilligan & Sullivan 1995, p. 4). Though not couched in terms of primordiality, the emphasis on lived experience in the approaches of both Laing and Gilligan gives expression to conceptions of authenticity and its loss. Whereas Laing (1968) famously refers to that estranged integration called normality, Taylor, Gilligan & Sullivan (1995) document Oliva's 'fight for a "real relationship"', beyond 'the seeming inauthenticity of her mother's niceness' (p. 84) and elsewhere, interpret 'a defense against genuine intimacy and an obstacle to authentic relationship' (p. 159). Similarly, Brown & Gilligan (1992), explore 'the desire for authentic connection' (p. 5), for 'authentic', 'genuine', 'resonant', 'real' relationships (pp. 40–1) and loss to 'the ground of felt experience' (p. 128). These experiential preoccupations all presuppose that some kinds of experience are to be privileged as being more important than others. They invoke an implicit conception of primordiality as a ground for experience, as a unifying, authenticity of experience. Gilligan and her colleagues appear to base the criteria for privileging these experiences on an intuitive appeal.[10] A spatial-phenomenology can illuminate such criteria.

Both Laing (1982) and Gilligan (1982; 1990) develop aural metaphors for truth to challenge a Western Platonic visual tradition associating knowledge with sight. They share a search for a more authentic voice, allied with a conception of repressive forces for such an authentic, lived experience in Western society. Brown & Gilligan (1992) conclude that they have learned about 'the power of beginning with girls' voices' (p. 232). At no stage do Gilligan (1982, 2011), Gilligan et al. (1988), Brown & Gilligan (1992), Taylor, Gilligan & Sullivan (1995) expressly locate their work on lived experience, care and voice in a phenomenological tradition. One reason for this may be a suspicion of drawing upon a theoretical attitude that distracts from lived experience. This may also be because of an emphasis given by Gilligan to aural truth metaphors and to distinctively female voices, in contrast, for example, to Heidegger's construal of the Greek *logos* of phenomena as a letting be seen (though in a more nuanced sense than the purely visual), in what can be construed as a basically patriarchal tradition. Gilligan (2011), in her review of her work, almost thirty years later, again 'calls for a new way of speaking, a change in the very terms of the conversation' (p. 14). She interprets Freudian free association as a listening process that privileged women's voices, as a precursor of this new way of speaking (once Freudian thought is disentangled from the Oedipus complex, in particular). To distinguish Gilligan's concerns from what she might characterize as a patriarchal phenomenological tradition, there is a need to characterize a research focus on this initial phase of lived experience as a *relational* phenomenological approach of description and interpretation. Gilligan (2011) could also be construed as questing for a reconstruction of aspects of Freud's work as

10 Brown & Gilligan (1992) offer a description of a feature of 'more' authentic relationship as a becoming 'more willing to voice conflict and openly disagree' (p. 224).

being a relational phenomenology. Such a relational phenomenology would also centrally embrace the concerns of Laing.

Though these interpersonal, relational phenomenological approaches in psychology offer analysis through the mediated account of the researcher, nevertheless, they strongly endeavour to let the qualitative research accounts of the subjects speak for themselves, often in direct quotes. Mitchell's (1974) characterization of the enduring value of Laing's work on psychosis as being its phenomenological descriptions, more than its analysis, is testament to the importance of at least some distinction between these levels, 'The advantage of a phenomenological method is not that is gives us a new analysis, but that it offers perfect phenomenology: after reading Laing's studies we understand much better the internal characteristics of the nuclear family' (p. 285).

It is to be acknowledged that even the descriptive features of the phenomenological narratives of Laing and Gilligan are constructed. Mitchell (1974) highlights the excision of the role of the father in Laing's accounts of familial relations for the aetiology of psychosis. However, just because narrative accounts are necessarily constructed and implicate a subjective theory-ladenness on the part of the narrator, this does not require the conclusion that such constructions are either false, misleading or incapable of sustaining a more fundamental or primordial truth. Uncovering of a pattern of relational difference between concentric and diametric spaces in a phenomenological narrative does not prove that the observer was factually 'correct' in his or her description of a particular individual's psychological state or experience. It is not a proof at the level of correspondence between word and world, at the classical Aristotelian level of truth as correspondence. It is a constructed truth of lived experience that may offer pathways into exploration of spatial projections, underlying such experience.

Psychoanalytic narratives may also describe lived experience emerging from an interpersonal dialogue, though analysing this constructed dialogue further for its insight into unconscious structures. Freud's (1900) accounts of dreams offer an example of a phenomenology as lived experience, documented somewhat separately from a subsequent level of interpretation. Whereas Laing's phenomenological emphasis on communication patterns deemphasized the role of unconscious influences, a spatial-phenomenological approach reinserts the primacy of unconscious systemic interactions into a phenomenological analysis. A phenomenological concern with lived experience needs to be reconciled with unconscious structural systemic relations influencing such lived experience and potentially conscious to such lived experience.[11] Laing (1961) perceives a contradiction between phenomenological concerns with experience and an apprehension of what he construes as a psychoanalytic confusion of levels through 'unconscious experience'. While this contradiction can be partly resolved through characterization of unconscious experience as potentially conscious experience, there is again a need to recognize that examination of unconscious relations is a different level from phenomenological description. However, distinguishing different levels does not require a Laingian view that these levels are in contradiction. A spatial-phenomenological approach explores their interplay. This spatial-phenomenological interrogation of Freudian repression endeavours to offer directions for experience that are not simply freedom from repression; it also seeks to provide an account of freedom for experience. This freedom for experience is to enter the hospitable spaces that envelop us in the deep. It is a reclaiming of a world of depth from a postmodernist *écrasement*.

Any argument for a distinct phase to focus on spatial structures of experience, subsequent to engaging directly with lived experience, is not to advocate a subsequent structural interrogation that is largely remote from experience. Heidegger, even prior to *Being and Time*, was very much concerned to reach a dimension of life, rather than reification, in the structures of experience he sought to uncover. Kisiel (1993) provides the following account of Heidegger's search, in his Winter Semester 1925–26 course, for a 'preintuitional substructure', 'to get at a deeper structure of presence, immediacy, and givenness than the structure of immediacy offered by intuition' (p. 400). This concern with immediacy of lived experience

11 This approach is largely resonant with Stolorow (2007, 2011) and Brooke (1991, 2009) who have sought a reconciliation between Heidegger and psychoanalysis, and Heidegger and Jung, respectively.

must also be held throughout for a spatial-phenomenology, in questioning continuities between experiential structure and content.

While Heidegger (1927) also sought a primordial structure prior to intuition, concentric and diametric spatial projections can, nevertheless, be construed as being framing intuitions. However, in doing so, it is not to reduce concentric and diametric spaces solely to the level of the intuitional (or subjective presence). Any such characterization of concentric and diametric spaces as intuitions is to, thereby, understand them not as fundamental grounds but as provisional projected structures of a prior primordial level.

2.4 The need for a primordial cross-cultural phenomenology to go beyond ethnocentrism

Said's (1978) excoriating critique of an abstract essentialism in the construction of 'Orientalism' by Western thinkers can be interpreted as a phenomenological concern for genuine engagement with a person's lived experience. He emphasizes the need for the voice of the individual, 'It seems a common human failing to prefer the schematic authority of a text to the disorientations of direct encounters with the human' (p. 93), 'Orientalists are neither interested in nor capable of discussing individuals' (p. 154). His is a phenomenological appeal to lived experience to challenge the grey nets of the 'dehumanized thought' (p. 108) in abstraction. Said (1978) offers a phenomenological assault on the stasis of categorization and its removal from historical context and a life-flow, 'the Orient as being always the same, unchanging, uniform, and radically peculiar object' (p. 98), with no discussion of 'the living, contemporary Orient' (p. 98). It is this shift from experience to static categorization that is central to his phenomenological critique, 'It would be converted from the consecutive experience of individual research into a sort of imaginary museum without walls, where everything gathered from the huge distances and varieties of Oriental culture became categorically Oriental' (p. 166).

Said's (1978) call for a critical deconstruction of abstract, ethnocentric categorization resonates with the first proposed level of phenomenological description. Yet he recognizes that this alienating categorization process of rendering a person as the 'other' is itself a projection, 'Once we begin to think of Orientalism as a kind of Western projection onto and will to govern over the Orient ...' (p. 95). In doing so, this invites a further level of examination of the dimensions to such projections, including spatial dimensions. Said (1978) also acknowledges the need for an understanding that not only deconstructs manipulative projections, but also thwarts repression, 'Perhaps the most important task of all would be to undertake studies in contemporary alternatives to Orientalism, to ask how one can study other cultures and peoples from a libertarian, or a nonrepressive and nonmanipulative, perspective' (p. 24). This again invites a renewed questioning of the processes of projection, repression and reification that a spatial-phenomenological approach seeks, while alerting to the dangers of treating spatial projections as abstract categories or essences. Said would presumably be wary of any primordial truth claim for spatial projections lest they become reduced to the stasis of abstract categories or essences.

A spatial-phenomenological approach is resonant with Teo & Ferraro's (2003) concerns to expose 'ethnocentric intuitions' in psychology and beyond. They highlight ethnocentrism in psychology as a form of theory-laden intuition underlying observations. They seek to challenge the neutrality of such intuitions. Focusing on Western ethnocentrism, Teo & Ferraro (2003) build on a Kantian conception of intuition as guiding interpretation of constructed facts. Besides racism and researchers' prejudices as two explicit manifestations of ethnocentrism, another involves exclusion or disregard of non-Western views, or in their assimilation without a reconceptualization of the psychological framework. In this type of ethnocentrism, it is assumed that Western psychological conceptualizations are superior. Teo & Febbraro's (2003) conception of intuition is drawn from Kant. By implication, this invites a focus on *spatial* intuitions and ethnocentrism.[12]

12 Teo (2008) describes the avenues and scope for interpretation of empirical data as 'the hermeneutic surplus of interpretation' (p. 51). In these terms, it is the

For a spatial-phenomenology, intuition needs to be interpreted in spatial terms and in a broader sense than Kantian intuition, to encompass emotion and dynamic movement between spaces of intuition.

This ethnocentric critique focusing on whether constructs are Western-biased, and, thus, do not pertain to wider cultural contexts, is one lens within a cross-cultural critique. A cross-cultural critique additionally adopts a concern with resistance to cultural conditioning, as part of a search for dimensions of a more primordial, unifying experience.

Heidegger's (1927) phenomenological approach is well-recognized as being vulnerable to an ethnocentric critique.[13] Kisiel's (1993) valuable account of the genesis of *Being and Time* identifies distinct phases of development of Heidegger's thought, with little evidence of Heidegger's interrogation of wider sources than in Western culture, in those earlier phases. This is not, however, to deny strong resonances in Heidegger's thinking with a wider ambit of concern, beyond his declared aim of the destruction of the (Western) history of ontology and trenchant critique of Cartesian thought. Parkes (1987) explores resonances between Taoist thought and Heidegger (1927), to thereby challenge a view 'in some of the secondary literature' (p. 107) on Heidegger, that treats Asian ideas as only being in harmony with Heidegger's later work. Parkes (2006) suggests that Heidegger's contact with a number of Japanese philosophers in the 1920s may also have fostered Taoist and Zen Buddhist influences directly upon *Being and Time*.[14] May (1996) speculates that prior to *Being and Time*,

---

spatial-hermeneutic surplus of interpretation which requires a specific cross-cultural questioning, as a key part of an ethnocentric critique in a spatial-phenomenology.

13 For example, pragmatist Rorty (1991) comments that *Being and Time* is 'most charitably' interpreted as an account of 'Western Dasein, rather than as an account of the ahistorical conditions for the occurrence of history' (p. 41). Guignon (1983) similarly questions whether Heidegger can offer 'the horizon' for the understanding of being, instead of 'a particular cultural horizon as embedded in a particular language' (p. 211).

14 Parkes (2006) suggests '... the conclusion is unavoidable that Heidegger was less than generous in acknowledging how much he learned from the East Asian tradition' (p. 107). May (1996) identifies a range of East Asian influences in Heidegger's later thought, though not directly on *Being and Time*. Stambaugh (1987) explores resonances between Taoism and predominantly Heidegger's later work, while Zimmerman

Heidegger may, however, have been influenced by Buber's (1910) *Zhuangzi* giving expression to Eastern understandings of silence. Similarly, Kotoh (1992) emphasizes Eastern features of Heidegger (1927) regarding silent discourse as primordial experience, 'this emphasis on silence distinguishes Heidegger from the mainstream Western tradition' and 'brings him close to oriental thinking based on silence' (pp. 40–2).

In a spatial-phenomenology silence is not merely a pruning of sound. It is not simply a dearth of voice, a void, the sound of one hand clapping. It is the breath to fill the voice. Nor is silence merely a passive, somewhat mysterious, contrastive reference point, as it is for James (1890) in his description of thunder existing not by itself, but against an interactive background of silence that it requires to be heard. A silent space for primordial experience needs to emerge as an active force – not simply as a sheer nothing, nor a passive other. And as an active force, it is not simply a background wallpaper, nor part of the furniture. It is to rearrange not only the furniture. The silent storms alter also potentially the very shape of the room and house. The silence is foundational for experience.

A concern with ethnocentrism is accentuated for Heidegger's later work, after *Being and Time*, that largely moved away from phenomenology and which relied on an arbitrary privileging of the German and Greek languages in his etymological search for being. Later Heidegger (1966/1990) conceived of 'the special inner relationship between the German language and the language and thinking of the Greeks' (p. 63). Heidegger's sympathies towards nazism, in the 1930s and subsequently, are well documented, incontrovertible and abhorrent.[15] Whether described as giving expression to a parochialism (Malpas 2008), nationalism, 'a one-sided use of ancient Greece' (Mizoguchi 1987, p. 198) or tendencies towards nazism, there is a clear need to firmly distinguish this ethnocentrism in middle and later

---

(2006) examines some limited parallels between Buddhism and again Heidegger's mostly later thought, perceiving a common concern with nondualism.

15 See, for example, Ott (1993), Farias (1987/1989), Neske & Kettering (1990), Safranski (1998), Stolorow et al. (2010) for accounts of Heidegger's unforgiveable Nazi sympathies.

Heidegger from a spatial-phenomenology.[16] A broadening of a primordial truth search is required for a spatial-phenomenology to embrace cross-cultural truth concerns. In doing so, the avowed Eurocentrism of Heidegger's later work that moved away from phenomenological concerns renders it as being outside the Pale of a spatial-phenomenological approach. Similarly, Heidegger's propensity to rely on etymological sources for a purported primordiality based on German and Greek languages provides fallow ground for a cross-cultural primordial truth search in a spatial-phenomenology. That language and etymology are not as central to early Heidegger of *Being and Time*, is noted by Levinas (1986/1990, p. 152), while Kockelmans (1972, p. xii) and Sallis (1992) also highlight the lesser prominence given to the role of language in *Being and Time* compared with Heidegger's later work.

A spatial-phenomenology gives expression to early Heidegger's transcendental project, abandoned by him in his later thought. In doing so, a scrutiny of spatial dimensions is being brought to the fore. Yuasa (1987) suggests that 'discoverable at the base of the Eastern philosophical tradition is the idea of space-consciousness as more important than time-consciousness. To put it conversely, there is a tendency in the Western philosophical tradition to regard time-consciousness as more important than space-consciousness, and therein to locate the core of ego-consciousness. Herein lies one of the historical reasons for this difference in sensitivity between East and West' (p. 172). Through a topological reading of Heidegger's early, middle and later work, Malpas (2008) advocates a conception of place as 'a historical and topographical heritage' that though articulated for particular places, nevertheless attempts a thinking of being that 'goes beyond any such place' (p. 314). While being in strong agreement with Malpas regarding the central and neglected role of space in *Being and Time*, the emphasis of this proposed spatial-phenomenological reading is less on one of the role of 'place' [*Platz, Ort*] in Heidegger.

16 A spatial-phenomenological connection, explored in subsequent chapters, between Gilligan's background frames for moral reasoning and Heidegger's (1927) search for structures of being in his ontological project engages with a significant and much noted gap in Heidegger's work in relation to a conception of ethics, which, nevertheless, does not simply reduce ontology to ethics.

2.5 Dynamic *a priori* structures of diametric and concentric space

Primordiality as an *a priori* truth is the strongest claim identified for primordiality (claim b). The deduction of purportedly pure *a priori* concepts of the understanding is central to Kant's *Critique of Pure Reason*. Kant's pure concepts of the understanding or categories are applied *a priori* to objects, as aspects of an argument that subjective conditions of thought can have objective validity. He sought to challenge the Lockean view that there was nothing in the intellect that was not previously in the experience of the senses, by arguing for prior forms which did not come by experience, but through which experience was acquired. With these purportedly transcendental forms, Kant (1781) seeks the '*a priori* conditions of a possible experience in general' which are 'at the same time conditions of the possibility of objects of experience' (A111). This search for *a priori* conditions requires questioning, for Heidegger, of the kind of subjectivity and objectivity involved in such conditions.

Assumed by Kant's dependence 'dogmatically' (Heidegger 1927, p. 45) on a Cartesian conception of an isolated subject, this subject-object framework is challenged by Heidegger's ontological reformulation of the *a priori* for his structures of existentiality. Heidegger is questioning the kind of reality of these *a priori* concepts that goes beyond such subjectivity. In place of what Heidegger construed as a Kantian vacillation between understanding of the *a priori* in either psychological or logical terms, Heidegger sought a phenomenological interpretation of this *a priori* through an understanding of the primordial structure of Dasein, literally, being-there or being-here. Dasein is, at least in *Being and Time*, a pre-subjective structure of experience of self that is prior to the dichotomy of subject and object.

A spatial-phenomenological focus seeks to uncover concrete spatial dimensions of this *a priori* structure of existence, while sharing with Heidegger a conception of such structures as being dynamic, though not simply reducible to linear, historically changing processes. Heidegger broadens *a priori* structures, *via* Fichte and Lask, to incorporate more affective and not simply rationalistic, dimensions of experience in Kant. This affective broadening resonates with a spatial-phenomenological conception of these *a priori* structures as being unconscious. However, the unconscious spatial structures traverse pathways beyond the unconscious as simple subjectivity.

A key distance from Kant which is evident in the proposed spatial-phenomenological framework of dynamic projected structures of concentric and diametric spaces, is that space and time are viewed as being fundamentally interconnected, unlike Kant's assumption that they are separate from each other. Space is not being taken to be simply flat and Euclidean as Kant presupposed. Well-known different meanings of a Kantian *a priori* further need to be distinguished. A Kantian *a priori* can mean *inter alia*:

(i) what is presupposed in all our experience;
(ii) that which is not derivable from particular senses;
(iii) logical necessity;
(iv) conditions that are not amenable to experience;
(v) conditions that are not revisable by experience.

A debate is not being entered into as to whether primordial dynamic space is presupposed in *all* our experience and is thereby *a priori* in sense (i). The dynamic spatial interaction proposed between concentric and diametric structures is argued to be *a priori* in the sense of being presupposed in all our *primordial* experience. In other words, *a priori* concentric and diametric relations are being examined as dynamic, spatial necessary conditions for primordial experience, though not necessarily for all experience. It will be argued that concentric and diametric structures *can* be experienced. They are potentially immanent in our experience.[17] While

17 Thus, they are not transcendent in Kant's sense here. The dynamic *a priori* role of concentric and diametric spatial structures of relation fits neatly into neither Kant's treatment of knowledge as transcendent, nor transcendental. Transcendent knowledge is not a possible object of experience. Transcendental knowledge amounts to the necessary conditions of our experience. Similarly, as necessary conditions of

this can include our everyday experience and empirical senses, this is not a claim that these spatial structures are ii) derived from particular senses, nor from everyday experience. With regard to a possible claim for dynamic *a priori* structures of concentric and diametric space as being that of iii) logical necessity, there are well-recognized difficulties in making such a strong claim.[18]

What is being sought here is an understanding of the role of a specific, dynamic *a priori* spatial structure as a projective logic. It is as a logic of concentric and diametric structures projected into texts. This is as part of a spatial-phenomenological questioning of the prior necessary and supportive spatial conditions for a text. Spatial projections in texts need to be exposed even when they appear to be neutral. An appearance of neutrality can be unmasked to reveal particular spatial commitments. This argument does not necessarily logically preclude other specific candidate spatial structures from being relevant to primordial projections, in its claim for the primordiality of these specific concentric and diametric spatial projections.

In relation to a projective logic for spatial structures, it is notable that Kant (1781) conceives of space and time as being *both* a priori and projected into empirical experience:

> Even space and time, however pure these concepts may be of all that is empirical, and however certain it is that they are represented in the mind purely *a priori*, would nevertheless lack all objective validity, all sense and meaning, if we could not show the necessity of their use with reference to objects of experience. Their representation is a mere schema, always referring to that reproductive imagination which calls up the objects of experience, without which objects they would be meaningless. The same applies to all concepts whatsoever. (A195)

---

primordial experience – and not necessarily all experience – it cannot be flatly stated that concentric and diametric structures are transcendental in a Kantian sense.

18 Such a strong claim for transcendental arguments is persuasively argued by Körner (1967) to be impossible, in principle, as it would need to demonstrate that all other possible alternatives to a particular *a priori* aspect have been excluded. Obviously, necessary conditions in a logical argument need to be distinguished from necessary conditions for causality.

Kantian structures include forms of sensibility, categories, schemata relating concepts to images and percepts, while involving applications of the categories in the principles of pure understanding. As an *a priori* intuition Kant conceives of space as a precognitive dimension which may also be manifested in empirical experience, including cognition.

A priori structures are being conceptualized as being able to engage with primordial experience; this is not a Kantian quest for a 'pure' domain of reason, as an island beyond such structures of experience. Acceptance of primordial spatial structures as not being revisable by experience, as a feature of their being *a priori* structures, is to be distinguished from the related claim of Kant that *a priori* conditions are independent of experience,[19] or not amenable to experience. It is being argued that concentric and diametric primordial spatial projections are amenable to experience but not revisable by experience, beyond their mutual interaction and interchangeability.

The dynamic concentric and diametric spatial structures are being examined as projected into empirical appearances. There is at least some loss through this projective process. It is not necessarily a complete loss, as some dimensions of the phenomena are constituted by the appearance, in at least a displaced, crushed, compressed form. For the Heidegger of *Being and Time*,[20] there is not an absolute split between an *a priori* level and its projection into the empirical.[21] Kisiel (1993) summarizes early Heidegger's (1920) position in his Summer Semester course on the phenomenology of intuition and expression, 'Is the opposition of absolute-relative, apriori-

19 As Anderson (2010) highlights, Kant (1787) is forced to acknowledge some ways that *a priori* cognition might have to rely on experience, at least indirectly.

20 Lafont's (2007) characterization of 'the core assumption of Heidegger's interpretation of the ontological difference, namely, that there is an absolute and permanent dichotomy between two different kinds of knowledge (ontic and ontological) and their respective kinds of truth' (p. 117), basically portrays a later position of Heidegger that would be more resonant here with a Kantian *a priori*.

21 Heidegger (1927) does envisage a relation between ontology questions and scientific ones, though it remained seriously underdeveloped, 'the question of being aims … at ascertaining the *a priori* conditions *not only for the possibility of the sciences* … but *also* for the possibility of those ontologies themselves which are prior to the ontical sciences and which *provide their foundations* …' (p. 31) (my italics).

history, irrational-rational, really a genuine one? Placing the schema itself in question and perhaps dissolving it is to be realised with the help of critical destruction, a basic aspect of the phenomenological method' (p. 125). For Heidegger (1927), 'the structure of existentiality lies *a priori*' (p. 69). His search, for 'not just any accidental structures, but essential ones' (pp. 37–8), engages with a challenge to each of these diametric oppositional categories of absolute-relative, *a priori*-history and irrational-rational.

Postulating an *a priori* structure of care as (ontologically) prior to reason, Heidegger offers a violent reconstruction of a Kantian *a priori* possibility of knowledge. Heidegger seeks to broaden Kant's focus beyond a foundation for the positive sciences and beyond a problem of judgment; he constructs the key problem around understanding *a priori* structures of being. Moreover, care is a broader conception than intentionality. Heidegger's shift is from a narrow conception of reason to a broader one of 'being' that includes a conception of a range of affective dimensions, such as anxiety. However, the structural and spatial dimensions of care, as an *a priori* structure, remained significantly underdeveloped.

This care structure is envisaged, by Heidegger, as encompassing key spatial dimensions; it needs to be uncovered and amplified in its spatial-phenomenological dimensions for a further understanding of primordiality and *a priori* structures. This requires much stronger development of the structural relationship between space (and time) and unconscious affective dimensions than that developed both in Kant and even Heidegger's *a priori*. In doing so, understanding of the unconscious as both *a priori* and projected into human experience requires development.

Blattner (2007) makes the point that 'Heidegger does not offer sufficient justification for the conclusion that the regional ontologies specific to individual sciences are *a priori* disclosable, therefore, properly philosophical. Rather, his argument can only reach so far as to conclude that the very broad ontologies of the large-scale regions of being analyzed in *Being and Time* ... are *a priori*, hence philosophical' (p. 18). The spatial-phenomenological approach being adopted throughout this book can in many ways be read as an engagement with this caesura in Heidegger's work regarding justification of ontologies pertinent to (though not merely specific to) individual sciences, such as psychology. It is being argued that the unfolding of this concrete proposed primordial structure of diametric and concentric space at the level of a regional ontology can pave the way to Heidegger's further level of a fundamental ontology and investigation of a reconstructed *a priori* level of understanding.

Johnson (1987) challenges the purity of a Kantian *a priori* domain of reason beyond experience through a focus on image schemata that he connects to bodily experience. This search will be seen to offer much resonance with a spatial-phenomenological approach. Johnson's (1987) challenge to an abstract *a priori* realm offers some resonance with Heidegger's reconstruction of a Kantian *a priori* in phenomenological terms, away from Cartesianism. While Johnson's (1987) focus on image schemata treats these forms as expressions of embodied experience, Heidegger's *a priori* truth search enters a somewhat different level of primordial experience and one which is not reduced to simply subjective experience, whether bodily or otherwise.

Jungian conceptions of the unconscious operate mostly within a traditional Kantian framework for its proposed archetypal structures and primordial images of the collective unconscious. Jung postulates an *a priori* level of the archetype *per se* and an empirical level of its manifestation. He operates a projective logic for the unconscious, as well as a spatial one, to the extent that the archetypal structure is an image. A significant expansion of this projective logic, compared with Kant's narrow framework for experience, is that Jung engages with a much wider, affective experiential realm. It is notable that Jung offers one specific, spatial candidate structure – the mandala – as being the central archetype of the collective unconscious, prior to other primordial images and archetypes. This mandala structure is a concentric spatial one, typically as a circle inscribed by a square. However, the spatial-phenomenological dimensions to this mandala structure have remained highly limited, both in an *a priori* and empirical sense, throughout Jung's whole *oeuvre*.

Understood in terms of projection, concentric and diametric spaces are claimed to be a holistic *a priori* structure of being that is subsequently projected into experience, feeling, cognition, and behaviour, as well as into systems and texts. This projection process not only breaks and fragments the holism of these projected structures, it brings a displacement and loss to this dynamic structural whole. However, this loss is not only occurring through the projection process but is somehow central also to this dynamic, *a priori* spatial structure.

The basic argument being put forward here is for a double loss in projection entwined with a potential revitalization. Firstly, concentric spatial phenomena are the lost, displaced, compressed structures found in diametric spatial projections. The buried spaces of concentric relation have been twisted into diametric relations. Secondly, both concentric and diametric spatial projections are themselves lost, displaced and further compressed in empirical texts. The concentric-diametric spatial interplay offers a spatial structural account of this unconscious hidden movement as a primordial process – as a primordial dance.

It is not being sought to repair a broken bridge to the primordial. It is not a matter of finding a pathway across the river. There is no primordial aboveness as abstraction from the flow. The primordial dance involves immersion in the river flow.

CHAPTER 3

Participants in the Primordial Dance: Diametric and Concentric Space

3.1 Primordiality as a cross-cultural truth: A preliminary review of the cross-cultural prevalence of concentric and diametric spatial structures

An empirical cross-cultural argument for projections of concentric and diametric space is not directly pertinent to refutation of an *a priori* argument for such structures, at least through a traditional Kantian view of *a priori* truths. However, it is relevant to an argument for primordiality, in the different, though related, sense of primordiality as a cross-cultural truth, in order to challenge ethnocentrism. This initial cross-cultural argument also supports another argument for the primordiality of concentric and diametric spaces as a dynamic interactive unity. An argument for the cross-cultural relevance of concentric and diametric spatial projections requires further steps to establish that these are crossculturally meaningful for lived experience.

Jahoda's (1982) cross-cultural, anthropological review concludes that 'the simplest and at the same time most common type of symbolic classification ... is the dual one'. (p. 251). Resonant with Osgood (1979), Jahoda (1982) recognizes that the Chinese classification of *yin/yang* is 'perhaps the best known case' (p. 251) of fundamental bipolar oppositions. A key vantage point for highlighting the cross-cultural prevalence of concentric and diametric spaces is the work of structural anthropologist, Lévi-Strauss. He explored physical structures within and across different cultures, as well as mythological systems, to uncover not only examples of concentric and diametric structures but also initial steps to understanding their mutual relation.

Lévi-Strauss (1963) cites a range of examples of the concentric spatial opposition observed by different anthropologists. These include: the village plan of Omarakana in the Trobriand Islands, published by Malinowski; the Baduj of western Java and the Negri-Sembilan of the Malay peninsula, observed by de Jong; the village of the Winnebago tribe observed by Radin and an archaeological finding in the Lower Mississippi Valley. The consensus view of anthropologists is that Malinowski was more sensitive than Lévi-Strauss to local context, as the former spent more time living in the native culture (e.g., Leach 1970, 1982). Thus, the fact that the concentric opposition observation in the Trobriand Islands comes from Malinowski, and not Lévi-Strauss directly, strengthens its evidential reliability.

Concerning the Lower Mississippi Valley, Lévi-Strauss (1963) emphasizes that concentric structures are genuinely ancient structures, 'We are therefore dealing with a type of [concentric] structure which in America extends far back into antiquity, and whose later analogues were to be found in pre-Conquest Peru and Bolivia and … in the social structure of the Sioux in North America and of the Ge and related tribes in South America' (p. 143). This latter structure, however, was not simply bipolar but 'forming six concentric octagonal figures' (p. 143).

Concentric structures can be found also in Islamic, Japanese, Russian, Chinese, Jewish, Celtic, African, ancient Greek and Estonian contexts, while Jung locates the concentric mandala structure in Buddhist, Hindu and Christian traditions.[1] An example of concentric structures from Iran is the 'talking tree' bowl, the tree being a symbol of the 'Fount of Life' (Melikian 1998). The 'talking tree' inside the inner concentric circle was according to the 'Book of Kings' (*Shah-Nameh*) seen by Alexander the Great in his search for the 'Fount of Life' (Melikian 1998). Leidy (2008,

1 Terms such as 'Islamic' or 'Christian' contexts are a major simplification of the complexity occurring within these contexts. Similarly, it is important to acknowledge diversity in Jewish contexts, such as Rabbinical, Sabbatian, and Kabbalistic ones, as well as Talmud (Bakan 1958).

p. 124) observes that one of the earliest painted examples of a (concentric structured) mandala known to exist is the Womb World mandala or *Garbhadhatu* (*Taizōkai*), in Kyoto, Japan, from the second half of the ninth century. Though without expressly making a connection with the mandala structure, Likacheva (1981, pp. 144–5) observes that the structure of Russian orthodox churches is designed in concentric fashion, as a circle surrounded by a square. Likewise, Hellberg-Hirn (1998, pp. 22–3, p. 37) highlights the concentric structured dimensions pervading Russian symbolism.

Jung (1936/1985) highlighted the cross-cultural prevalence of the concentric primordial mandala symbol in Buddhist and Chinese contexts, though with a particular emphasis on the quaternity dimension of the four corners of the outer square of the mandala:

> Just as the stupas preserve relics of the Buddha in their innermost sanctuary, so in the interior of the Lamaic quadrangle, and again in the Chinese earth-square, there is a Holy of Holies with its magical agent, the cosmic source of energy, be it the god Shiva, the Buddha, a bodhisattva or a great teacher. In China, it is Ch'ien – heaven – with the four cosmic effluences radiating from it. (p. 252)

Similarly, he noted that 'in the Western mandalas of medieval Christendom, the deity is enthroned at the centre, often in the form of the triumphant redeemer, together with the four symbolical figures of the evangelists' (Jung 1936/1985, p. 252).

The Chinese Taoist *yin/yang* (see Figure 3) is an example of two basically concentric dualisms (the light within the dark half and the dark within the light half). These concentric halves can be smoothly separated from each other and are located within a frame that is basically that of a diametric structure.[2]

2 The ancient Chinese saying, *'tien yuan, ti fang'*, heaven round, earth square, referred to by Volk (1995), helps draw attention to the fact that the two halves of *yin/yang* are not squares, as in a typical diametric structure but include a curved, round dimension; the dividing membrane between both halves is curved and not simply linear. This does not limit the diametric feature as the two halves can be separated from each other. However, it does imply that there is a directional movement towards a circular more concentric state, away from the starting point of the diametric structure.

Figure 3 *Yin/Yang*

Suler (1991) recognizes *yin/yang* as inviting 'a balance of diametric processes' (p. 21). The diametric frame is seen as key to the notion of balance in *yin/yang*. The interplay between light and dark takes places against the background interplay between concentric and diametric spatial structures, as part of an overall structural whole.

In Jewish art and archaeology, Strange (1995) highlights the concentric structures of the 'Decorated Stone Dome of the Hulda Gates' (p. 68) and the Zodiac from the Central Panel of the Mosaic floor of the Beth Alpha synagogue (p. 100). Stones at Cashel Aenghus, the House of the Love-God, at Newgrange in Ireland, provide an example from Celtic culture of concentric spirals on their surface. Moreover, Nichols (1990) describes a Druidic grove at Woodhenge, near Stonehenge, in England, the concentric structured 'house of the Great Mother', 'structured as a temple', where 'by the orientation one could read it that the midsummer sun was to enter the secret cells – the inner circles – of the moon' (p. 39). Oslisy's (1996) research with the Bradshaw Foundation has observed the Lindili Site Rock art of Central Western Africa. Located 8km south of the cultural area of Kongo Boumba, more than twenty figures are engraved on its rock surfaces. They comprise of circles including a chain of eleven concentric circles, together with meandering lines. He also observes the Kongo Boumba sites with their numerous concentric circles, motifs that can also be found in the decorations of the ceramics of the Okanda tradition in the same area, from the second century BC; almost all motifs in the the Kongo Boumba art are circles, spirals, concentric circles, lines of circles arranged chain-like,

It invites a contrast between a diametric position and a more concentric directional process.

and dissected circles. Concentric structures are acknowledged in aspects of ancient Greek thought. A conception of concentric space is evident in Plato's *Timaeus*, while Kerenyi (1976) highlights frescoes in ancient Cretan art as interwoven spirals (p. 95) and 'a classical picture of this procession which originally led by way of concentric circles ...' (p. 96). In Western culture, such a concentric spatial structure influenced Dante, *via* Plato, for the spatial background in his *Paradiso*. Kriiska et al's (1997, pp. 30–1) excavations of the Stone Age settlement site and ruin of the stone cist grave of the Early Metal Age in Kasekula, Estonia, reveal concentric structures (see also Vedru 1997 for similar findings in Estonia). Moreover, Mandel (1984) highlights 3,000-year-old ring-graves (*kivikirstkalmed*) in Muuksi, Vohma and Kasekula, Estonia, which have a concentric structure. This concentric structure contrasts with the later (*tarandkalmed*) graves from the third to fifth centuries in Jaagupi, Estonia, which have a diametric structure. Mandel (1984) notes that from the twelfth century at Kaku, in Saaremaa, Estonia, the circular, concentric structure of the burials vanishes.

The contrasting structural relation of diametric spatial opposition has also been observed cross-culturally, by Lévi-Strauss (1962): he notes that examples of diametric dualism 'abound' (p. 135), citing specific tribes in North and South America. Moreover, the simple 'subjective' (Leach 1965/2000, p. 111) everyday cross-cultural oppositions between 'good' and 'bad' are structured in a diametric oppositional way. The diametric good-bad opposition also underlies myths such as those of the Shuswap, which treats the owl as a cannibalistic monster in contrast to the Kutenai, which treats the owl as a benefactor (Lévi-Strauss 1973, p. 261). The Janus-face of two heads looking in diametrically opposite directions is well-known in Greek mythology.

Kagan (1989, p. 94) criticizes Piaget for generalizing Western A/Non-A logic, a logic based on an assumed separation between A and Non-A, so that A and non-A are in a basically diametric structural opposition. Historically, the Western world has followed the logical principles of Aristotelian philosophy. This logic is based on the law of identity which states that A is A, the law of contradiction (A is not non-A) and the law of the excluded middle (A cannot be A *and* non-A, neither A *nor* non-A). Aristotelian A-Non-A contradictions presuppose a diametric spatial structure of opposition in that A and Non-A are assumed to be basically separate. Diametric opposition, as the basic schema for Western logic, can be strongly associated with a Western priority for diametric over concentric structures of relation. Can a discourse on diametric projections offer a domain of wisdom that does not so much exclude, as subsume, the logician?

Diametric spatial structures of opposition emerged in Conquergood's (1994) three-year ethnographic portrayal of how male teenage street gangs in Chicago divide into diametric structured opposition, even though there is no tangible reason for the content of these oppositions such as ethnic, socio-economic, racial or regional differences. Observing that 'there are hundreds of gangs in Chicago, but all of them align with one of two Nations: People or Folks' (p. 204), Conquergood (1994) emphasises that 'the division between the two Nations, People and Folks, is absolutely arbitrary and constructed' (p. 207). He cites Scholes' (1985) conception of the binary opposition of diametric dualism as violence – and in similar vein to structuralist linguists Saussure and Jakobsen – this violence of division is viewed as being embedded within communication in Western culture, 'The most basic and most violent acts of differentiation are those that divide a field into two opposed units. This sort of "binary opposition" ... is fundamental to the phonemic nature of speech and is deeply embedded in all Western thought' (p. 112).

In terms of cross-cultural pervasiveness and a cross-cultural truth, the bipolar concentric and diametric structures are arguably more important than other types of opposition. They can be said to be the building blocks or constituent parts of more complex structures. This position is expressed, by Lévi-Strauss (1981), 'Of course, all mythemes of whatever kind, must, generally speaking, lend themselves to binary operations, since such operations are an inherent feature of the means invented by nature to make possible the functioning of language and thought' (p. 559).

An example of the binary opposition, as the building block or constituent element of a more complex structure of symmetry, is that of the triangular pyramid exhibited in the Mandan and Hidatsa hunting rituals. There Lévi-Strauss (1973, p. 249) refers to 'symmetrical relations', in effect, diametric structured inversions within the more complex structure of opposition. Similarly, the structure of a spiral cycle to express the forms of marriage for the Australian tribe, the Wikmunkan (Lévi-Strauss 1969, p. 209) is itself a content which can be incorporated within a more elemental, diametric binary structure of inverted symmetry.

This initial cross-cultural review of concentric and diametric spaces by no means purports to be a comprehensive one. It needs to acknowledge the diversity of contexts of observations of projected structures of concentric and diametric spatial relations, such as in myths, social structures, rock art, temples, graves, group rituals and processes, and Western logic. This diversity includes historical diversity in time, ranging from myths from ancient times up to current day observations of group processes. Gergen (1994) raises an important issue regarding a potential confirmation bias in the process of selectivity in empirical observation:

> In the same sense that case histories furnish such an immense array of material that virtually any theory of development may be sustained, cultural history offers such a welter of developmental exemplars that investigators may select as needs or interests dictate. In effect, whether a theory appears to be confirmed or falsified importantly depends on the tactics of observational selection. (p. 163)

These initial steps for an argument that concentric and diametric relation are primordial as cross-cultural projected structures, relies not only on their observation by a diverse range of independent observers, across a wide vista of cultures historically.

The goal of an empirical argument here for the cross-cultural prevalence of concentric and diametric structures of relation is not to assert totalizing truth claims for these structures as factual universals. Rather, it is to emphasize that these structures of relation are potential realities and illustrations of a widespread propensity for such spatial structural projections, as part of a cross-cultural truth for a primordial spatial interrogation; their empirical expression illustrates not only their potential expression but invites investigation of their role as projections and as structures of displaced, partial projections of phenomena. An emphasis on potential rather than simply factuality recognizes that, even if concentric and diametric structures are not historically observable in a given culture, this does not mean that could not potentially be an expression of that culture. Gellner (1981) makes this basic point regarding the more static notion of explanatory schemata, 'The existence of explanatory schemata which apply to some human societies only, if such schemata exist at all, need not be attributed to the non-universality of some human element, but only to the specificity of some forms of social organization, which however remain open to all human populations in similar circumstances' (p. 19).

Concentric spatial structures are a feature of at least some Eastern and Western cultures. Although an association of diametric spatial relation with Western thought and logic is evident, it is overly simplistic to conclude in diametric oppositional fashion that a concentric spatial projection is necessarily more Eastern, and a diametric spatial projection is necessarily more Western.[3] Nevertheless, concentric structures offer a particular resonance and association with Eastern traditions.

3.2 Primordiality as a dynamic unity: Dynamic interplay of concentric and diametric spatial structures

One level of argumentation for primordiality is as a unity or direction of unity for experience. A condition for spatial structures to be relevant for such an understanding of primordiality is that they can offer (i) a dynamic, directional feature and (ii) be in some way part of a structural whole. It is these dynamic relational features to concentric and diametric spaces that need to be uncovered for their primordiality as a unity or unifying direction. It is not being argued that the establishment of such a dynamic interactive relation is proof of primordiality in this sense, as a further argument would be needed for how these structures engage with experience and primordial experience as a unifying direction.

3 Neither is an argument being made, for current purposes, that a concentric space has been historically lost or covered over in Western thought and experience. Taylor (2007) argues for the flattening of conceptions of time as being linked to a distinct era in Western thought, the eighteenth century.

A purportedly key distinguishing feature of concentric and diametric spaces, observed by Lévi-Strauss (1973), is that they tend to co-exist in 'functional relation' (p. 73) and not simply in isolation. This echoes the structuralist insight that meaning resides in relational difference rather than in a single term. They are structures of relation as part of a system of relations. Being mutually interactive, at least potentially, they are observed as structures *of* relation but also structures *in* relation. Lévi-Strauss recognizes that they are are fundamentally interlinked, so that an increase in one is compensated for by decrease in the other. They express a dynamic compensatory quality – a relational and temporal quality that appears to be missing from other cross-cultural, symbolic structures. Concentric and diametric structures are also fundamentally dynamic movements that can be examined as processes of projection. They are potentially dynamic, spatio-temporal models of relation. Thus, they are not to be viewed as simply static images or symbols, but more as opposing directions of spatial relation in dynamic tension. As spaces bestowed with movement, concentric and diametric structures are far from being frozen Apollonian images.

This relational aspect *between* concentric and diametric spaces brings a level of dynamism for both of these structures which is not captured within other anthropological symbolic representations, such as a triangle (e.g., the triangular schema of life-death-dream in Central Australia, Lévi-Strauss 1963, p. 237), the five point star dividing the feudal cycle of marriage for the Kachin of Burma (Lévi-Strauss 1969, pp. 248–9) or diamond in Navajo art (Witherspoon & Peterson 1995). Moreover, even if other symmetries[4] or structural oppositions can be shown to have relevance to a psychological or primordial truth claim, this does not of itself invalidate the importance of concentric and diametric structures as a potential cross-cultural discourse. This would rather require further analysis of concentric and diametric spaces to justify their primordiality as a fundamental ground.

The holistic interplay within *yin/yang* requires further explication for its concentric and diametric structures. In *yin/yang*, the small realm of light

4 Other more complex symmetries or oppositions than Lévi-Strauss' conceptions may also have psychological relevance (Maranda 1972, p. 342).

in the larger dark realm and dark in the larger light realm suggests movement from light to dark and *vice versa*. In the dark realm there is a directional force towards light and in the light realm there is a directional force towards darkness.[5] As with an interplay between concentric and diametric structures, *yin/yang* includes not only a bipolar relation but also implies a directional process of change to some degree. It is not simply to be viewed as a static symbolic structure. The two halves of *yin/yang*, in other words, the diametric frame within which the two concentric relations are located, express one way that concentric and diametric structures can be related. On this view, concentric and diametric spaces are subsumed as part of *yin/yang* and are therefore not more primordial than *yin/yang*.

Significantly, in Chinese culture, *yin/yang* was conceived as a product of a prior process – a prior *concentric* process. The Chinese initial world egg myth is described by Wilhelm (1977), whereby 'the separation of heaven and earth out of the cosmogenic egg is almost uniformly the first act of this process of creation' (p. 191). The egg is itself a concentric structure and Wilhelm's (1977) quotation from an ancient Chinese text indicates that this concentric egg structure was viewed as a preceding state from which *yin/yang* emerged, '[In the beginning], heaven and earth were in the state of chaos [*hun-tun*], which was shaped like an egg … After 18,000 years heaven and earth split apart, the *yang*, being limpid, formed heaven, the *yin*, being turbid formed earth' (Wilhelm 1977, pp. 191–2). This concentric egg background, prior to *yin/yang*, invites the implication that interplay between concentric and diametric relation is not simply reducible to being elements of *yin/yang* but is in some way a prior background to *yin/yang*.[6]

5 There is also an implication within *yin/yang* that movement in the light *direction* within the dark *realm* (and in the dark *direction* within the light *realm*), allows for the reverse process, namely, that the dark *realm* itself is not simply a *positional* state but is also a *directional* one. Likewise, the predominantly light *realm* is itself also a *directional* movement within itself and not simply when it is immersed as the minor quality in the dark realm.

6 Suler (1991) also focuses on interplay with a background relation for *yin/yang*, emphasizing its blank background, 'There is one final duality … The figure is drawn on a

This argument for a primordial cross-cultural spatial discourse operates at a different level of description from relevant truths and lived experiences contextually meaningful solely for a specific culture. It is complementary to an ethnographic focus operating simply internal to the constructed meanings of a given cultural context, through a pluralistic view of many relevant levels of description of human experience and behaviour for psychology, anthropology and beyond. These different levels depend on the particular goals for questioning, underlying each level and paradigm (see also Gergen 1994).

It must also be accentuated that any investigative lens to uncover diametric and concentric structures does not require Lévi-Strauss' assumptions that ancient societies are basically unchanging and without historically changing and politically meaningful discourses (what Lévi-Strauss 1962, 1963 described as 'cold' societies in contrast to modern 'hot' societies of historical change). Brickman (1993) summarizes a range of trenchant anthropological critique of Lévi-Strauss' structuralism as drawing up a binary opposition between ancient, primitive, unchanging societies and modern, historically changing ones, 'Any actual intercultural communication would require both parties to recognize they inhabit, simultaneously, the very same historical time; yet most modes of anthropological discourse have been predicated on the distance maintained by representing the anthropological other as in the past' (p. 138). The concern for current purposes is not so much to emphasize concentric and diametric spaces as existing in the past but rather to highlight their key role in current individual and societal experience – as primordial spatial structures of current, dynamic experience. Whereas Brickman (1993) exposes the need for 'the deconstruction of the anthropological trope that placed this subject in a timeless primitivity in the first place' (p. 139), a further step towards such deconstruction is to highlight the contemporary relevance of such ancient structures of relation. They are not to be consigned to a museum of the static space and time of the 'primitive'.

---

blank page; it arises from a contentless background, from emptiness. A creative tension exists between form and formlessness' (p. 22).

It is their reanimation that is of interest for a more developed understanding of their primordiality as projected structures. Any traditional invocation of concentric and diametric structures as being part of a mysterious, passive other of the East (which Brickman 1993 aptly associates with parallels of the rendering of the female as the passive, mysterious other, *via* de Beauvoir's *The Second Sex*, 1949) needs to acknowledge the shift of vantage point, in relation to concentric and diametric spaces for current purposes. Rather than placing them in passive fashion as a static background 'other', their reanimation is precisely for the purpose of emphasizing their active role in contemporary, cross-cultural experiences. They are a potentially active structural force that can be susceptible to rational interrogation and meaningful to lived experience. They offer a discourse of displacement in space that itself needs to be rescued from being displaced back into linear historical ancient time; flattening of this space occurs through its compression into linear history. Concentric and diametric spaces must not become shredded into the stasis of an ancient time, fashioned both from and into linearity.

Despite reliance on diverse sources, a significant limitation to the observations of Lévi-Strauss is that he purports to take a neutral, 'birds-eye' view of the role of these concentric and diametric structures in a given society. This absolutist vantage point requires deconstruction with regard to the colonial, historically constructed and economically sustained privileged position of the Western observer outside the particular social arrangements under interpretation (Said 1978; Brickman 1993). Thus, a major omission in Lévi-Strauss' accounts of concentric and diametric spaces in a given culture is the absence of the direct voices of the people themselves, so that they could give direct accounts of the constructions of meanings from their multifaceted perspectives. As Culler (1975) highlights, structuralism tends not to be concerned with meaning for individuals (p. 59, p. 269). Rather than necessarily invalidating these interpretations as being alien to the shared meanings of a given culture, this process dimension invites a necessary suspicion of Lévi-Strauss' views requiring further investigation.

It is important to accentuate that in a spatial-phenomenological approach, the relations between concentric and diametric spaces are not being derived empirically, even though traces of their projections are apparent from empirical observation. Implications of the relations between concentric and diametric spaces can be ascertained, in principle, as an *a priori* argument regarding the entailments of their relative differences. Lévi-Strauss' account of diverse empirical observations of concentric and diametric structures is but one small part of his structural anthropological project; this project is open to a number of criticisms. The spatial-phenomenological argument being developed here is not one that requires commitment to accepting other aspects of Lévi-Strauss' work.

A claim is not being made that the relational differences between concentric and diametric spaces are qualities that are in some way essential or intrinsic to either structure, considered as individual isolated structures, abstracted from the context of their mutual relation. This is not an attempt to find static categories which cohere. Rather concentric and diametric spatial structures are conceived as being in rhythmic interaction.

The epistemological commitments underlying Lévi-Strauss' cross-cultural observations of concentric and diametric structures require modification for a spatial-phenomenology. Lévi-Strauss' reliance on an analogy between the structure of myths and that of structural linguistics has been strongly questioned (Caton 1987). While his epistemology is drawn from linguistics, this does not require that the cross-cultural observations of concentric and diametric structures, and their relative differences, be confined to examination only from a paradigm drawn from linguistics. Arguably, it was the very cage of this paradigm that prevented Lévi-Strauss from expanding upon the proposed existential, phenomenological aperture of these structures.

These ancient structures *of* relation *in* relation share with language the feature of being a transsubjective system of relations. However, as a discourse of implication this does not make the spatial structures reducible to a linguistic system. The examination of them here is to develop a position beyond Lévi-Strauss, rather than simply echoing his fundamental assumptions. Suler (1991) makes a related point in relation to Taoist models:

> This style of thinking in images is quite different than the verbal modes that dominate western cognitive styles. Language tends to represent experience in an abstract, logical, objective and linear fashion. However, imagery – a sensory-perceptual composite

> construction – has two distinct advantages: it more efficiently captures the emotions of an experience, and it more efficiently encodes the multiple, complex meanings of the experience. (p. 19)

However, images such as concentric and diametric spaces can go beyond a rational-affective dichotomy to reveal a discourse of implication that incorporates both reason and emotion. It is a more fundamental discourse of implication than simply a 'style of thinking' or one which treats such spaces in static terms. Developing Granet's (1934) description of the *tao*, as 'the rhythm of the space-time structure', Stambaugh (1987) recognises that 'Taoism is basically outside the Aristotelian categories of predication (example: *yin* and *yang* cannot be pinned down either as substances or as forces)' (p. 90).

The contours of the proposed primordial dance between cross-cultural, concentric and diametric spaces invite a focus on relations *between* both structures. This relational movement requires the development of a spatial discourse of implication with regard to their mutual differences. Like Wordsworth who crossed the Alps without realizing it, Lévi-Strauss opened up a discourse of relation between concentric and diametric structures, without apprehending the potentially wider scope of this spatial discourse, as it becomes transferred to more primordial and affective contexts of relation.

3.3 Features of the primordial dance: Relations between concentric and diametric space

3.3.1 First entailment of the relative differences between concentric and diametric spaces: Assumed connection and assumed separation

A key relative difference between diametric and concentric spaces, overlooked by Lévi-Strauss' empiricism, is ascertainable in principle. It is evident that the inner and outer poles of concentric space are fundamentally attached to each other, unlike in diametric space; both concentric poles coexist in the same space, and thus, the outer circle overlaps the space of the inner one. The outer circle surrounds and contains the inner circle. The opposite that is within the outer circle or shape cannot detach itself from being within this outer shape. Similarly, notwithstanding that the outer circle or shape can move in the direction of greater detachment from the inner circle, it cannot, in principle, fully detach itself from the inner circle in concentric relation (even if the inner circle becomes an increasingly smaller proportion of the outer). Full detachment could conceivably occur only through destroying or altering the form of the other pole, by a violence akin to the Massagetes, who had the habit of cutting up their parents and eating the pieces. It can be concluded that full detachment could occur only through destroying the very concentric structure of the whole relation itself.

In contradistinction, in diametric space both oppositional realms are basically detached and can be further smoothly detached from the other. These conclusions operate for both structures, whether they are viewed as being two-dimensional, or three-dimensional. A concentric space assumes connection between its parts and any separation is on the basis of assumed connection, whereas diametric space assumes separation and any connection between the parts is on the basis of this assumed separation. As structures in relational difference, this contrast is a relativistic one of degree. Concentric and diametric spaces thus can be seen to offer contrasting structures of differential relation.

D'Aquili (1975) notes the Cartesian commitments of Lévi-Strauss to uncovering mental structures; it may have been these very commitments to rigid Cartesian dichotomies which led to Lévi-Strauss' blind spot for this key entailment that concentric relation challenges such dichotomies and is more connective than diametric relation. A Japanese cultural context offers an exploration of the entwinement between the spatial and the relational. Kimura (2005) emphasizes that the Japanese words *uchi* (inside) and *soto* (outside) express a characteristic cultural ethos, where *uchi* (inside) is exactly equal to that of one's family or group. Morioka (2007) suggests that 'the idea of inside/outside is not only a radical essential category of cultural characteristics, but [is] also universal' (p. 193). Yet a diametric outsideness is an assumed separation that is radically different from the assumed connection of the outside pole to the inner pole of concentric space. Inner and outer need not necessarily be diametrically framed but may also be concentrically framed. The Japanese concept of *ma* can signify the space between one thing and another and can also be used for understanding of human relationships (Kimura 2005; Morioka 2007). Concentric and diametric spatial structures invite application to relations between self and other, thereby entwining the spatial and relational, as with the Japanese concept *ma*.

According to Roberts (2002), in his introduction to *The Odyssey*, 'anti' is a more nuanced term in ancient Greek than its modern diametric oppositional usage:

> Chapman [in his translation of *The Odyssey*] was alive to ambiguities in the word; in Greek αντι (anti) means both to be worth the same as and 'over against, opposite' (the latter sense is the one that has come down into English). In fact Chapman read antitheon as both god-like and anti-god and translated it according to his sense of the context. (p. xv)

Again, this offers a view of differentiation between poles that is a more nuanced one than the assumed separation of diametric relation. A concentric space furnishes a thread of assumed connection, a like-ness, coexistent with a differentiation. In contrast, for diametric space, in Bachelard's (1964) words, 'simple geometrical opposition becomes tinged with aggressivity' (p. 212).

While these relative differences between concentric and diametric spaces may be observed empirically, it is vital to recognize that these inferences are *a priori* entailments. They are not being derived from empirical examples; the examples are simply illustrative. The inferences are of relative priority, a necessity of relative priority. It is fully recognized that transcendental, *a priori* arguments are, as Körner (1967) exposes, always vulnerable with regard to the strong Kantian claim for their necessity.[7] A claim for

7 Kant reconstructed the term transcendental from the context of scholastic logic and metaphysics, in his focus on necessary *a priori* truths independent of experience.

necessity cannot exclude a myriad of other possible circumstances. It is not being argued that the relative differences between concentric and diametric structures meet a strong Kantian claim for absolute necessity. Rather, it is a specific contextual necessity of relative priority.

This weakness in *a priori* truth claims for necessity resonates with a related (though different) poverty in the referential claims of the hypothetico-deductive method, highlighted by Gergen (1994). There is a necessary looseness of the link between hypothetical construct and observation:

> [...] if there is no transparent or necessary linkage between the languages of science (scientific description and explanation), on the one hand, and scientific observation on the other, then it is difficult to sustain the traditional empiricist argument that the facts of the world drive or determine the propositions that come to stand as 'scientific knowledge'. (Gergen 1994, p. xiii)

That there is a necessary leap from observation to hypothetical construct can be illustrated, for example, by the jumps from observation of 'recall' to that of 'long-term memory' and a 'schema' organizing long-term memory. The latter are inferred from the fact of the observed recall.

A vertical level of *a priori* entailments of the relations between concentric and diametric spaces is to be clearly distinguished from the horizontal level of the referential relation between these spatial structures and their projections in empirical texts. The horizontal, empirical referential argument here for concentric and diametric structures is one of consistency but not logical necessity as entailment, as it cannot be ruled out that many other structures, spatial or otherwise, give expression to either of these manifestations of assumed connection or separation in a specific empirical context. There is a necessary loss in meaning in an inference that an empirical example of assumed connection gives expression to concentric spatial projections and assumed separation gives expression to diametric spatial projections, respectively. Yet this loss between hypothetical construct (concentric and diametric spatial projections) and their operationalization (assumed connection and separation) is very much a part of the scientific hypothetico-deductive method.

An example of the limited scope of this empirical reasoning process can be taken from the cognitive science area of deduction. Johnson-Laird

& Byrne (1991) attempt to show that people tend to reason deductively with mental models rather than formal logic rules. This is strictly speaking, an argument at the relativistic level. This relativistic level is that x (mental models) is a better explanation than y (formal logic rules), rather than simply x *is*. They state that, 'no amount of data, of course, can pick out one theory against all comers. Infinitely many theories are compatible with any finite set of observations. But, our problem is simpler: it is to decide amongst three possibilities' (p. 194), namely formal rules, content-specific rules and mental models for deduction. It is this jump from observation to infinite possible hypothetical constructs that Gergen (1994) is highlighting as a key limit to traditional empirical methods. Johnson-Laird and Byrne (1991) seek to resolve this problem by selecting between three purportedly mutually exclusive alternatives, in seeking grounds for preference of one hypothetical construct over another.

Similarly, it is to be recognized that the empirical claim for assumed connection and concentric spatial relation, and assumed separation and diametric spatial relation, is at a relativistic level that one operationalization is more an expression of one spatial structure than the other one. It is their relative, relational differences that are being focused upon as referential inferences regarding these spatial structures. A strength of such referential inferences is that the spatial structures are visible and provide more concrete grounds for such publicly justifiable inferences than in relation to purely abstract hypothetical constructs. An argument for the 'presence' of such spatial projections in empirical observations or other texts is strengthened if more than one of the relational entailments can be consistently uncovered in the texts. This brings empirical coherence across the *a priori* entailments.

The argument for a referential relation between concentric and diametric structures and the respective entailments of assumed connection and separation is a stronger one than simply that of consistency and concreteness. While other spatial structures or abstract concepts may also be linked with assumptions of connection and separation, concentric and diametric spatial structures are arguably more basic and elemental spatial structures than other ones which might provide such consistency. Furthermore, concentric and diametric spatial structures offer scope for a dynamic interplay between these spaces, in a way which may not be available to other static spatial models that are not so firmly conceptualized as being part of a unified whole. Other spatial models would need to preclude the possibility that they are merely more complex versions of this basic opposition between concentric and diametric spaces. While parsimony of explanation is far from being a conclusive ground for preference of specific hypothetical constructs over others, it is this combination of being a more parsimonious explanation, with being a more dynamic, interactive and also basic structure of spatial relations,[8] that provides other grounds for preference of a referential relation between concentric and diametric spaces and assumed connection and separation, respectively.

Another key basis for preference of this referential relation, is that as relative differences, a vital directional dimension to assumptions of connection and separation is embraced. They are positional structures relative to each other, rather than in an absolute spatial sense. They are also relativistic, directional projections. In other words, their operationalizations would be meaningless without the counterpole; it is a *relation* that is being operationalized, a directional relation (whether towards an assumed connection or separation). The issue is not so much one of uncovering a 'substance' but rather a dynamic relationship.

A more radical way to conceive of the inferences of concentric and diametric spaces in a text is less to focus on proof of whether they are already 'in' the text or observed phenomena. Rather it is to start from the vantage point of the observer/interpreter and ask the question as to how these concentric and diametric spatial projections of the observer/interpreter impact upon and affect the meaning of the text. The concern here is primarily one of projective significance for the contextual materials. It is less a preoccupation with authorial intentionality. This is a focus on the theory-laden, spatial blind spots in the observer/interpreter's account of empirical observations or other texts; these spatial blind spots necessarily involve a projection of some discourse on space which requires uncovering.

8 See also, Culler (1975) on a 'structurally much more satisfying explanation' as consisting of a few 'basic elements' rather than a large number that becomes 'an arbitrary array' (p. 249).

Entailments of concentric and diametric spaces are candidate starting points for such an interrogation.

3.3.2 *Second entailment of the relative differences between concentric and diametric spatial relation: Symmetry as unity and mirror image inverted symmetry*

Lévi-Strauss (1973) explicitly relates diametric structures to mirror image inversions between both diametric poles. He describes 'symmetrical inversions' (p. 247) in Mandan and Hidatsa myths:

> [...] these myths are diametrically opposed ... In the Mandan version ... two earth women who are not sisters go to heaven to become sisters-in-law by marrying celestial brothers. One who belongs to the Mandan tribe, separates from an ogre, Sun, with the help of a string which enables her to come back down to her village. In revenge, Sun places his legitimate son at the head of the enemies of the Mandan, upon whom he declares war. In the Hidatsa version ... everything is exactly reversed. Two celestial brothers come down to earth to be conceived by human beings and born as children. Sun's sister, an ogress, is joined with an earthborn character by means of a string. She makes him her adopted son and puts him at the head of the enemies of the Hidatsa. (Lévi-Strauss, 1973, p. 250)

He reiterates a view of diametric opposition as expressing qualities of inverted symmetry, when contrasting the myth of the Thompson and the Coeur d'Alene with that of the Chilcotin (Lévi-Strauss, 1973, p. 262). Echoing a view of diametric symmetry as 'transformations which sometimes result in the meaning being turned inside out' (p. 260), Lévi-Strauss (1973) invokes descriptions of myths framed by an understanding of their relation as involving a mirror image:

> One often observes ... that mythological systems after passing through a minimal expression, recover their original fullness on the other side of the threshold. But their reflection is inverted a bit like a bundle of light rays entering into a camera obscura through a pin-point opening and forced by this obstacle to cross over each other. The same image seen rightside-up outside is reflected upside-down in the camera. (pp. 259–60)

Strictly speaking, a mirror image is plane symmetry rather than the line (or point) symmetry of diametric space. Nevertheless, plane, line and point symmetry all accommodate a view of symmetry as reversal or inversion, as in diametric space. While Lévi-Strauss (1970, p. 31) acknowledges the need for greater precision within his use of terms such as symmetry,[9] it was a key concept in much of his work (e.g., Lévi-Strauss 1963, 1970, 1973). He developed an argument for inverted symmetry in relation to diametric structures, through contrast with concentric ones.

While Lévi-Strauss (1963) related diametric structured, mirror image symmetry to myths and sought 'unconscious' (p. 58) structures, he did not integrate this with an examination of this structure's relevance to wider emotions, beyond a recognition of affect underlying attributions such as good and bad.[10] This is despite, not only Jung's well-known preoccupation with emotion, the unconscious and myths, but also Freud's (1916–1917) explicit account of resistance and repression in similar terms of a kind of inverted symmetry:

> Every mental process ... [except external perception] exists to begin with in an unconscious stage or phase ... it is only from there that the process passes over into the conscious phase, just as a photographic picture begins as a negative and only becomes a picture after being turned into a positive. Not every negative, however, necessarily becomes a positive; nor is it necessary that every unconscious mental process should turn into a conscious one. (p. 295)

Freud's underlying vision here, echoing also Freud (1910a, pp. 25–7), is that meaning is, as in Lévi-Strauss' words, 'turned inside out'.

9 Culler (1975) argues that the inversions between myths in different cultures are less convincing than those from related cultures, highlighting the danger of arbitrary preselection and omission (pp. 50–5).

10 The Freudian influence on Lévi-Strauss' structuralism is well known (see e.g., Lewis 1977, 1985; Rossi 1974). Nevertheless, without disagreement, Lévi-Strauss (1970, p. 11) cites Ricoeur's (1963) characterization of his work as emphasizing Kantian rather than Freudian concerns with unconscious structures, so that Lévi-Strauss is comparable to 'Kantism without a transcendental subject' (Ricoeur 1963, p. 24).

The diametric spatial mirror image inversions, of 'us' versus 'them', is a pervasive theme of Said's (1978) trenchant dissection of the Eurocentrism in constructs of Orientalism, with implications for both psychological and anthropological understanding. Thus, Said (1978) challenges the '"We" are this, "they" are that' (p. 237) and 'the advanced/backward binarism so centrally advocated in late-nineteenth-century Orientalism' (p. 207). He asks 'whether there is any way of avoiding the hostility expressed by the division, say, of men into "us" (Westerners) and "they" (Orientals)' (p. 45). The naturalness of the diametric spatial projections that 'channel thought into a West or an East compartment' as 'binary opposition' (p. 46) is critically deconstructed, 'the language of Orientalism ... brings opposites together as "natural," it presents human types in scholarly idioms and methodologies, it ascribes reality and reference to objects (other words) of its own making' (Said 1978, p. 321).[11] Said's (1978) deconstructive critique of inverted symmetry projections implies the need for a further questioning of this evaluative structure, 'the culturally sanctioned habit of deploying large generalizations by which reality is divided into various collectives: languages, races, types, colors, mentalities, each category being not so much a neutral designation as an evaluative interpretation. Underlying these categories is the rigidly binomial opposition of "ours" and "theirs", with the former always encroaching upon the latter' (p. 227). Concentric structured projections offer a different pathway for modification of diametric projections.

Concentric spatial structures of relation are not a symmetry as inversion. Rather they offer a different symmetry as unity, where the line or axis of symmetry brings the same pole rather than a mirror image pole in diametric structures.

11 Said (1978) again points to the role of diametric inversion framing Eurocentric classifications, 'as Renan's whole treatise on the Semitic branch of the Oriental languages goes very far to show, is comparative: Indo-European is taken as the living, organic norm, and Semitic Oriental languages are seen comparatively to be inorganic. Time is transferred into the space of comparative classification, which at bottom is based on a rigid binary opposition between organic and inorganic languages' (p. 143).

It might be objected that a framework of concentric and diametric structures amounts to a reification of truth claims through the very positing of structures. However, they are not reifications but relations. They are structures *of* reification and of directional movement from reification. They embrace the reified in a process towards its potential dissolution. This framework does not wash its hands of reification; it is not a diametric split of assumed separation from reification. Though neither is it a causal history of a reification, where such reification manifests itself.

Montesquieu's (1749) *dictum* that it would be *un très grand hasard*, if laws from the context of one country could be translated successfully to another, is an injunction towards recognition of the almost organic contextualism of a system of meaning, which may dry up when *déraciné* and applied elsewhere.[12] This rebuttable presumption of contextualism and non-transferability is important to engage with at different levels of understanding concentric and diametric relations. The question arises as to whether Lévi-Strauss' cross-cultural observations of structural arrangements of place, as a discourse of communication, can also extend beyond contexts of myth, to a wider opening of the relational differences between these structures of relation – to include existential and unconscious affective contexts of meaning. It is *un très grand hasard* that these relational differences between concentric and diametric spatial structures can illuminate an existential, meaningful discourse of lived experience and a discourse of the unconscious and of ontology.

3.3.3 Third entailment of the relative differences between concentric and diametric spaces: Foreground-background interaction versus noninteraction

Another feature of diametricity, contrasted with concentric space, is highlighted by Lévi-Strauss. He argues that self-sufficiency and a split relation

12 Kahn-Freund (1974) exposes the strengths and weaknesses of Montesquieu's contextualist caution.

to the outside environment is a general quality of diametric structures and systems, 'In a diametric system ... virgin land constitutes an irrelevant element; the moieties are defined by their opposition to each other, and the apparent symmetry of their closed structure creates the illusion of a closed system' (Lévi-Strauss, 1963, p. 152). While this makes sense for the immediate example given for social structures, it is not yet clear if non-self-sufficiency and orientation to the outside environment is a general quality of concentric as opposed to diametric relation, as Lévi-Strauss (1963) claims:

> [In concentric relation] The system is not self-sufficient, and its frame of reference is always the environment. The opposition between cleared ground (central circle) and waste land (peripheral circle) demands a third element, brush or forest – that is, virgin land – which circumscribes the binary whole while at the same time extending it, since cleared land is to waste land as waste land is to virgin land. (p. 152)

Lévi-Strauss rejects closure for concentric structures, by implying that the relation of the background to both poles of the dualism is governed by the relation within the dualism itself, i.e., 'cleared land is to waste land as waste land is to [background] virgin land'. The mode of relation to the background is not extraneous to the respective modes of relation within the poles themselves. Thus, as the concentric poles are in assumed connection to each other, they are also in assumed connection to the background; and this assumed connection to the background resists closure within the concentric structure. In contrast, diametric structures' relation to their own poles is one of assumed separation which then maintains an assumed separation with the background.

There is minimal interaction between the structural poles of diametric relation and the background space (i.e., virgin land). Diametric structures' relation to their own poles is one of a mirror image division, which then maintains a cleavage from the background that becomes closed off. Moreover, diametric and concentric structures are dynamic processes as much as structures. Thus, a diametric structure tends to impose a diametric process in its interaction with the background, whereas a concentric structure initiates a concentric relation with the background. In this sense of involvement with the background, concentric relation is not a self-contained structure. There is a closer proximity between background and foreground within concentric relative to diametric space. In comparison, diametric space is a much more closed structure – closed off from the background. There is greater closure in a diametric spatial structure relative to a dis-closure process of relative opening in concentric spatial relation. A variant of the entailment of relative closure for diametric structures is that they bring decreased permeability (transparency) relative to the increased permeability (transparency) of concentric structures.

A preliminary case can be made that a closed focus on foreground causal factors – to the neglect of background factors such as necessary and supportive conditions and their spatial assumption structure – is a cognitive process and intuition that reveals a Western bias, with regard to perception and thinking. For example, cross-cultural research on perception highlights the tendency of US participants to prioritize foreground over background dimensions (Nisbett et al., 2001). Masuda and Nisbett (2001) presented realistic animated scenes of fish and other underwater objects to Japanese and Americans and asked them to report what they had seen. The first statement by American participants usually referred to the focal fish ('there was what looked like a trout swimming to the right'), whereas the first statement by Japanese participants usually referred to background elements ('there was a lake or pond'). Japanese participants made about 70 per cent more statements about background aspects of the environment. In a subsequent recognition task, Japanese performance was weakened, by showing the focal fish with the wrong background, thereby, indicating that the perception of the object had been intimately linked with the field in which it had appeared. In contrast, American recognition of the object was unaffected by the wrong background. Resonant with this cross-cultural interrogation of background, Miller (1984) observed an increased causal attribution to background context rather than dispositional factors for an Indian-Hindu sample compared with an American one. Meaning dependent on the background relation to foreground has thus been recognized at different levels of analysis in cognitive psychology, with regard to perception and attribution.

Projection of spatial-phenomenological structures opens up this neglected background spatial domain, which tends to get glossed over in Western culture. A systemic focus on background necessary and supportive spatial conditions for the foreground causal factors can be construed as a challenge to this Western cognitive bias towards the foreground and causality as a foreground factor.

It must be reiterated that these empirical illustrations of the entailments of the relative differences between concentric and diametric structures must not distract from acknowledgment that these entailments are a priori inferences, as a necessity of relative priority, a necessity of relative differences in these spatial structures of difference. Thus, a cautionary note must be asserted as to inducing other inferences with regard to concentric and diametric structures from empirical examples. The entailments of the relative differences between concentric and diametric spaces do not derive from empirical examples. They are at a vertical a priori level that is not to be conflated with a horizontal empirical referential level. This vertical a priori level is not an anthropological nor psychological empirical level of questioning, despite the extraction of examples of these relative differences from these domains.

PART II

Spatial-Phenomenology: Interpersonal and Intrapsychic Dimensions

CHAPTER 4

A Spatial-Phenomenological Reinterpretation of the Relational Subject in Gilligan's Ethic of Care

4.1 Diametric and concentric spatial frames for moral choice: Assumed separation and assumed connection

Prior projected spatial structures silently pervade Gilligan's insights into moral reasoning, as being governed by distinctive, precognitive modes of relation. In her classic work, *In a different voice*, Gilligan (1982) highlights assumptions of separation and connection between self and other, as framing different conceptions of reasoning for moral choice. However, these assumptions have been interpreted in spatial terms in a somewhat rudimentary fashion, as a 'hierarchy' and a 'web' of relationships. For Gilligan (1982), 'the images of hierarchy and web inform different modes of assertion and response: the wish to be alone at the top and the consequent fear that others will get too close; the wish to be at the center of connection and the consequent fear of being too far out on the edge' (p. 62). For a spatial-phenomenological reinterpretation of Gilligan's work, there is a need for further excavation of these unconscious frames in spatial structural terms.

Gilligan's (1982) qualitative research in a United States cultural context highlighted two contrasting relational states framing moral reasoning. It is these prior relational states or frames that can be interpreted in spatial terms as projected intuitions. One relational state is an *assumed connection* between self and other in an 'ethic of care'. She contrasts this with an abstract, hierarchical impersonal 'logic of justice' approach, based on a prior relational state of *assumed separation* between self and other. Gilligan (1982) contrasts two eleven-year-old children's modes of relation:

> To Jake, responsibility means *not doing* what he wants because he is thinking of others; to Amy, it means *doing* what others are counting on her to do regardless of what she herself wants ... she, assuming connection, begins to explore the parameters of separation, while he, assuming separation, begins to explore the parameters of connection. (p. 38, italics in original)

These assumptions of separation and connection give paradigmatic expression to the first entailment of the relative differences between diametric and concentric spaces. The contrasts between the frames of assumed separation in a logic of justice and assumed connection in an ethic of care offer direct correspondence with projected diametric and concentric spatial structures, respectively. Diametric and concentric structures are necessary spatial-relational conditions for framing the two different modes of Gilligan's moral reasoning process.

As characterized by Gilligan (1982), assumptions of separation are rooted in Kohlberg's moral choice and reasoning. Kohlberg (1976) distinguished preconventional, conventional and postconventional morality, to reflect a purported growth in moral understanding from an individual to societal to universal point of view. Gilligan's (1982) well-known critique of Kohlberg's stages of choices exposed the assumption of Kohlberg's moral reasoning as being in relation to an abstract other, 'abstract[ing] the moral problem from the interpersonal situation, finding in the logic of fairness and objective way to decide who will win the dispute' (p. 32). It is this abstraction from relationship that is a diametric spatial projection gluing together this whole logic of justice framework.

Whereas an ethic of justice is characterized as emanating from an assumption of formal equality, that everyone be treated the same, Gilligan (1982) portrays an ethic of care as resting on 'the premise of nonviolence – that no one should be hurt' (p. 174). Gilligan (1982) perceives the two views of morality as 'complementary rather than sequential or opposed' (p. 33), while retaining a tone of criticism of the logic of justice approach, 'But this hierarchical ordering (treated as an impersonal conflict of claims) with its imagery of winning and losing and the potential for violence which it contains, give way ... to a network of connection, a web of relationships that is sustained by a process of communication' (p. 32). The concentric spatial intuition founding relation and connection is a supporting condition for a projection of non-violence. The legalistic logic of justice mode of reasoning arises as a breakdown of the relational and interpersonal mode of care and concentric assumed connection; winning and losing in adversarial decision-making are diametric structured mirror image inversions that a concentric assumed connection moves away from. This aspect of hierarchy as prioritization of one abstract right over another again gives expression to a diametric spatial inverted symmetry between winning and losing.

In the hypothetical problem of Heinz's dilemma, devised by Kohlberg as one of a series to measure moral development in adolescence, a man considers whether or not to steal a drug he cannot afford to buy in order to save the life of his wife. As described by Kohlberg (1976), Jake responds to this dilemma based on a balancing of competing rights to life and property. For Gilligan (1982), Jake's logic of justice reasoning applies a solution appropriate to a generalized other to the specific context of the individuals in the problem. The abstract other of a diametric spatial assumed separation between self and other[1] invites, what Teo (2008) describes as epistemological violence in the construction of otherness; it allows the other to be viewed in terms of deficits (Spring 2007; Downes & Gilligan 2007), or at least as passive and deanimated of individuality (Said 1978). Abstraction is not only a depersonalization and reification; it is a construction of other for the pragmatic purpose of a legal system founded on power for its efficacy.

The otherness of the other is constructed through the assumed separation of abstraction. Depersonalising the other paves the way for this other to be treated in pragmatic instrumental terms as a means not as an end (though it does not necessitate such a treatment, it is not a sufficient condition for such a treatment). With abstractive principles (e.g., the right to life versus property), a person becomes a mere object beholden to the implementation of this abstraction. On this view, the pharmacy owner

1 The abstract, generalized other (Gilligan, 1982; Benhabib, 1987) underlying Kohlberg's logic of justice for choice would presumably be traced by Hegel (1830–31) to the Roman 'abstract ego, which must be distinguished from individual idiosyncrasy' (p. 279) in the construction of impersonal legal rights.

in Heinz's dilemma is treated instrumentally like an object, if an abstract balancing of rights results in the stealing of his property.

For Gilligan (1982), the communicative process required to ascertain the psychological needs of various individuals embedded in a moral dilemma requires an individual, contextual focus of 'response' (p. 19), rather than a formal and abstract kind of communication. This offers much resonance with a phenomenological listening to a person's lived experience. It is an attempt to go beyond a category-based mode of reasoning. A category based approach, pervading the logic of justice discourse as priority based on rights, tends to lack the subtlety to adapt to the unique individuality of each person's psychological needs. As a woman, quoted by Gilligan (1982), states, 'Sometimes the hierarchies are good, as long as you look at them by themselves but they fall apart when you try to impose them on your decisions. They are not organised somehow to deal with life decisions and it doesn't allow much room for responsibility' (p. 126). A mode of lived experience is appealed to that is not amenable to meaningful interpretation through static categories defined in advance. This perspective echoes somewhat the gap between the logic of justice in law and that of life and living systems, acknowledged by Kahn-Freund (1977) in labour law, where he viewed law as being in a certain sense a secondary force in human affairs. Yet a significant background shift is occurring here in Gilligan (1982), from a more past based reliance on static categories in a logic of justice to a more present based relational interaction. This temporal shift also invokes a spatial shift in the framing intuitions. And as necessary spatial conditions for the framing of the moral reasoning approaches, this spatial shift goes beyond mere spatial metaphor.

Gilligan (2011) envisages an ethic of care as 'a relational ethic, grounded in the premise of interdependence. But it is not selfless' (p. 23). A concentric relational space allows for a conception of assumed connection as interdependence, while also retaining some boundaries between the poles, so that one is not reduced to the other, as with selflessness. A concentric projected spatial-relational identity retains a sense of self in its connection with another, while also challenging diametric oppositional identities.

For Gilligan (1982), an ethic of care is associated with a world of relationships, where an awareness of the connection between people gives rise to responsibility for one another, 'a perception of the need for response' (p. 39); it is a perception of the world as an 'expanding network of connection' (p. 39), where conflict is mediated 'personally through communication in relationship' (p. 29). Choice as an interpersonal relational dialogue with a concrete other is based on an assumption of a concentric spatial-relational connection between self and other. Gilligan (1982) claims this different voice is 'associated' (p. 2) with a female moral reasoning, neglected by Kohlberg's earlier work.

Gilligan (1982) contrasts the approach of 'Jeffrey' and 'Karen' to a moral dilemma: 'Both children deal with the issues of exclusion and priority created by choice but while Jeffrey thinks about what goes first, Karen focuses on who is left out' (p. 32).[2] Karen's approach is an inclusive one of concentric structured assumed connection rather than a diametric spatial assumed separation from the person who is left out. Karen's reasoning serves to avoid a diametric splitting in relation. The assumed connection of concentric inclusion invites more celebration of difference and diversity than a diametric structure of exclusion. The assumed separation of the detachment in the justice perspective facilitates 'the failure to attend to need' (Gilligan & Attanucci 1988, p. 82).

While Gilligan (1982) treats both moral modes as complementary, and as giving expression to contrasting spatial metaphors of network and hierarchy, Tong (1989) criticizes Gilligan for failing to offer a conceptual bridge between her two modes. Building on observations of Gilligan & Attanucci (1988) and Johnston (1988) regarding a capacity of US adolescents to switch between both modes, Gilligan (1988a) offers a spatial

2 This inclusive, relational concern with not leaving someone out is also a theme in Gilligan's later work, involving interviews with preadolescent girls, such as eleven-year-old 'Lauren's' account, 'We were in a group ... and after all the ideas were given, Nina says, you haven't heard [my] argument and Ellen goes, well, who cares, let's do this anyway ... I go, "Excuse me, you forgot somebody, and she has a good idea"' (Brown & Gilligan 1992, p. 84). Brown & Gilligan (1992, p. 167) observe that 'the generosity and openness that we saw in ten and eleven-year-old girls when they created spaces for their own and others' voices tend to give way in these twelve and thirteen-year-olds to self-protection' (p. 167) (see also Gilligan 1988a, p. 9).

model of their relation drawn from Gestalt psychology, which keeps both modes categorically distinct:

> The two moral voices ... denote different ways of viewing the world ... As in the ambiguous figure which can be perceived alternately as a vase or two faces there appear to be two ways of perceiving self in relation to others, both grounded in reality, but each imposing on that reality a different organization. But as with the perception of the ambiguous figure, when one configuration of self emerges, the other seems to temporarily vanish. (pp. 8–9)

More recently, Gilligan (2011) briefly invokes 'a psychological continuum leading from separateness to connectedness' (p. 31). The importance of a focus on background conditions of relation is also recognized by Kasworm (1984), who further assails the 'lack of specificity' of the 'key concept' (p. 248) of 'network' for Gilligan's ethic of care. Beyond a general view of holism and reductionism as being complementary approaches to any problem, and a conception of a network of relation as a two-way process rather than a shortcircuiting and splitting of communicative relation, there is a limited framework, or ontology, to relate both modes of moral reasoning. Concentric and diametric spaces can contribute to this background relation in a dynamic sense to allow movement and interaction.

Gilligan (1982) is explicit in her claim that a fundamentally new understanding is being offered for moral reasoning through her ethic of care and that its core insight is that of connection and interdependence, 'This ethic ... evolves around a central insight that self and other are interdependent ... [and] focuses on the dynamics of human relationships and dissipates the tension between selfishness and responsibility through a new understanding of the interconnection between other and self' (p. 74). Interpreted in relation to precognitive, background spatial frames, Gilligan's (1982) claim is very much supported by an understanding of this significant shift from a diametric spatial structure of assumed separation in 'formal and abstract' relation (p. 19), to a concentric spatial relation of assumed connection. While many others have also highlighted the key role of framing a problem in psychology (Schön 1993; Reddy 1993), law (Tribe 1990) and philosophy of science (Kuhn 1962; Feyerabend 1988), Gilligan's (1982) key insight is that these frames are structured intuitions or modes of relation as assumed connection and separation, respectively. Gilligan's pivotal contribution can be taken further for a psychological domain of problem framing through fundamental primordial spatial structures of relation, as concentric and diametric structured preunderstandings and precognitive projections.

Concentric and diametric projections offer candidate primordial conditions for contrast, interaction and movement, as systemic relations between the different ethical modes. Concentric and diametric spatial projections, in potentially dynamic interaction, provide evidence that a fundamental, primordial distinction exists in experience between care and justice. Moreover, they give a more primordial, fundamental framework of understanding and relation than Gilligan's (1982) spatial metaphors of network and hierarchy. These necessary conditions for framing modes of moral reasoning are unconscious in the sense of being precognitive, more primordial in the sense of being more fundamental, and as necessary conditions and structures of relation, they go beyond mere construal as metaphors in spatial terms. They offer a broadening of subjectivity, as Gilligan's relational subject is immersed in wider projected structures of relation, as experiential spaces of concentric and diametric relation framing the ethical modes. Gilligan's (1982) specific relational paradigm shift[3] represents an important step in the critique of Western abstraction as a mode of diametric spatial thinking, based on an assumed separation between not only self and other, but also self and world. Gilligan has instigated a subtle, yet significant, phenomenological shift, whereby ethical reasoning is an expression of primordial experiential states. Her work furnishes not only a different voice but a different space.

A concentric structured spatial projection for experience and frames for understanding brings a care mode of assumed connection, and its corollaries of inclusiveness, nonviolence and capacity for relational interaction. A concentric projection is an assumed connection that resists the violence

3 Gilligan's (1982) uncovering of precognitive structured frames for problem solving are significant contributions, beyond simply an advocacy of a more relational ontology, as in, for example, Buber's (1923) I-Thou relation, Levinas' (1969) 'face' of the other. See also Freeman (2011) on resonances between feminist thought and Heidegger (1927) regarding a relational mode.

of a breaking into diametric oppositional poles of assumed separation. A diametric structured spatial projection brings a mode of assumed separation between self and other, and mirror image inverted symmetry between winning and losing a dispute.

Concentric and diametric spaces are proposed to be fundamental projections underlying experience as horizons of understanding for the framing of ethical reasoning. As modes of primordial experience giving rise to an ethic, they are cross-culturally relevant structures and potentially dynamic in their interaction with each other in experience. As cross-culturally relevant conditions, in potentially dynamic interaction, the projected structures serve to distinguish the more primordial framing level from the subsequent, culturally constructed, cognitive-affective working out of the ethics, mediated through these prior projections. The cultural cognition process instantiates the frames, in various ways, that may differ across different cultures.

Recognition of the core projected structures underlying Gilligan's ethical modes is a step towards freeing Gilligan's work from charges of being specific to North American culture. Gilligan's (1982) methods have been queried, *inter alia*, by Tong (1989, p. 166), on the grounds that she needed to be more attentive to racial, class and individual differences, in addition to her focus on gender.[4] The projected concentric spatial intuition underlying the assumed connection of ethic of care offers an important bridge beyond a diametric structured thinking, associated with Western thought. Although Gilligan's (1982) work offers an important spatial shift for a primordial, cross-cultural psychology, there are a number of issues that also need to be confronted as part of this process.

Key aspects of a spatial-phenomenology for an ethic of primordial relational being prior to and extending Gilligan's ethic of care

The argument, for current purposes, is that there is a need for a prior, more primordial level to Gilligan's relational pragmatism in her ethic of care, a

4 A wider sampling that included African, Hispanic and Asian Americans was addressed in Gilligan & Attanucci's (1988) empirical research on care and justice modes.

level that engages further with concentric and diametric structures, through a spatial-phenomenological focus. This prior level is to be uncovered as one of primordial relational being, at an intrapsychic level of relation. This primordial relational being for an extended ethic of care is in a spatial-structural sense and engages with primordiality as: a unifying direction for experience, an authentic dimension for experience, a level prior to socially constructed truths, a cross-cultural truth and a more fundamental experience and truth.

Table 2. Key aspects of a spatial-phenomenology for Gilligan's (1982) ethic of care and logic of justice in relation to primordiality

Diametric and concentric spatial frames for moral choice: Assumed separation and assumed connection	Primordiality as: a) a more fundamental truth or experience, g) beyond causal explanations
Beyond relationship as a socio-cultural conditioning in Gilligan's relational pragmatism	Primordiality as: c) a direction of unity for experience, d) a more primordial authenticity of experience, e) a truth and experience prior to socially constructed realities
A questioning towards a primordial, cross-cultural extension of an ethic of care	Primordiality as: c) a direction of unity for experience, d) a more primordial authenticity of experience, f) a cross-cultural truth

Three interrelated issues are explored for the significance of this prior spatial-phenomenological level. This prior level is needed to engage with:

Argument (i) The vulnerability of Gilligan's relational pragmatism to conditioning by a socio-cultural logic that cannot be assumed to be benign in a 'soft relativism' (Taylor 1991);

Argument (ii) That Gergen's (2000) characterization of Gilligan's ethic of care as the basis of a postmodern relational morality for a fragmented interpersonal relational self illuminates a) a problem of the penumbra between categories of care and justice and b) the need for a framework of dynamic, spatial projections underlying care and justice. A third issue is raised, in preliminary fashion, as a question more than argument (iii): To what extent can some Eastern perspectives develop a meaningful discourse in terms of concentric and diametric spaces, as part of an ethic to resist socio-cultural realities perceived as illusory?

These intertwined issues do not seek to deny the existence of Gilligan's ethic of care but rather to extend its projective concentric structured intuition to wider domains of relation. It is recognized that these arguments are far from being definitive proofs of a prior level of experience to Gilligan's relational pragmatism. They are to pave to way for further interrogation of spatial-phenomenological levels of the unconscious at an intrapsychic level, and regarding primordiality as relations of authenticity and a unifying direction for experience, examined in later chapters. Moreover, this provides only an initial step in the critique of a unitary subject or self, whether this subjectivity is deconstructed through a postmodernist lens or one of spatial-phenomenology.

4.2 Beyond socio-cultural conditioning in Gilligan's relational pragmatism: Towards a primordial relational being *via* Taylor's ethics of authenticity

Argument (i) The vulnerability of Gilligan's relational pragmatism to conditioning by a socio-cultural logic that cannot be assumed to be benign in a 'soft relativism' (Taylor 1991).

To draw out this contrast between a relational pragmatism and a primordial relational space of being in an extended ethic of care, there is a need to highlight this pragmatism in Gilligan (1982). Viewed by Gilligan (2011) as 'a human ethic' in a democratic society, in contrast to a 'feminine ethic' in a patriarchal culture (p. 22), the contextual relational appeal of Gilligan's (1982) ethic of care is a pragmatic approach that focuses on ends and not just means. It allows for consequences, plus a process that is not reduced to its consequences. It may at first sight appear that eleven-year-old Amy's assumed connection challenges a pragmatic mode of reasoning, given that it invites a risk and vulnerability that Heinz's wife may die without receiving the medicine, if the pharmacist does not consent to her interpersonal appeal. However, Amy does, nevertheless, invoke a pragmatic reference point through her envisaged consequence that Heinz may go to jail for stealing and he would not be in a position to mind his ill wife, 'If he stole the drug, he might save his wife then, but if he did he might have to go to jail, and then his wife might get sicker again, and he couldn't get more of the drug, and it might not be good' (Gilligan, 1982, p. 28). Gilligan's (1982) analysis of Amy's perspective is that it is focused on 'the effect that theft could have on the relationship between Heinz and his wife' (p. 28). It is a different pragmatic focus as to consequences on relationships.[5] Gilligan (1982) emphasizes that its 'central tenet' is one of 'nonviolent conflict resolution' (p. 30).

As Gilligan (1982, p. 10) highlights, Piaget (1932) observes that girls have a more 'pragmatic' attitude towards rules, 'regarding the rule as good as long as the game repaid it' (p. 83). Echoing a patriarchal, chauvinism of Freud (1925) on the superego, Piaget treats such a legal sense as less developed in girls than boys and as an example of a dimension that is central for moral development. In contrast, Gilligan (1982) reframes such pragmatism

5 A logic of justice also relies on pragmatic dimensions. Based on a balancing of competing rights to life and to property, the logic of justice reasoning applies a solution for choice which is mediated through an abstract domain of relevance for a generalized other, in anticipation of future consequences to the individuals in the problem scenario. The pragmatic consequences to the individuals affected by the choices to be made influence the substantive balancing process being considered in the abstract domain of relevance (of rights to life versus property). There is a reciprocal interaction between the abstract domain of the impersonal other and the pragmatic consequences of the decision.

as being a relational, contextual truth that challenges static categorization. Gilligan (1982) observes that Amy's response is an attempt to go beyond formulaic categories or schematization, 'To the question about conflicting responsibilities, Amy again responds contextually rather than categorically, saying "it depends" and indicating how choice would be affected by variations in character and circumstance' (p. 38).

Gilligan's (1982) description of a woman Ruth's response to this dilemma again brings to light a pragmatic focus on consequences:

> Heinz's decision to steal is considered not in terms of the logical priority of life over property ... but rather in terms of the actual consequences that stealing would have for a man of limited means and little social power. Considered in the light of its probable outcomes – his wife dead, or Heinz in jail, brutalized by the violence of that experience and his life compromised by a record of felony – the dilemma itself changes. (p. 101)

It becomes framed as a 'collision between two lives, formerly conjoined but now in opposition, where the continuation of one life can occur only at the expense of the other' (Gilligan, 1982, p. 101). The contours of Gilligan's (1982) relational pragmatism for choice operate against the backdrop of a concentric spatial intuition of assumed connection between self and other, including stresses upon sustaining such connection.

An ethnocentric critique focusing on whether constructs are Western-biased, and, thus, do not pertain to wider cultural contexts, is one lens within a crosscultural critique; a crosscultural critique additionally concerns resistance to cultural conditioning, as part of a search for dimensions of a more primordial, unifying experience. An important and neglected port of call for a cross-cultural critique of the relational pragmatism of Gilligan's ethic of care is its vulnerability to being conditioned through a specific socio-cultural logic. A range of contexts can be highlighted where choices based on assumed connection between self and other, choices based on friendship and influenced by relational pragmatic dynamics, can lead to choices injurious to self and other (Downes 2009a). The group dynamics of peer pressure have long been recognized as an important factor of youth engagement in crime (Sutherland, 1939). Though Gilligan (1988a) contrasts 'submission' in friendship (p. 18) with connection, it is not self-evident how

Gilligan's ethic of care and relational dimension can be distinguished from the interpersonal relational dynamics of loyalty, connection and friendship, a peer pressure particularly associated with adolescence, for key, real world, moral choices.

Other examples in different cultural contexts than the US, where an interpersonal relational focus in reasoning for key life choices has led to decisions injurious to self and other, include human trafficking in the Baltic States. There some of the female trafficking victims were documented as being tricked into decisions to travel by supposed friends (Downes et al., 2008). Similarly, phenomenological accounts of the lives of twenty-seven Russian-speaking, male heroin addicts in Estonia point to the key role of friends in facilitating the engagement in addiction to heroin (Downes 2003a). This was less through deception than for human trafficking, but more through a simple association with cultural conformity and other pressures of social identity, mediated by the social marginalization of Russian-speakers in areas of Estonia (Downes 2007). Though not to deny the benefits of relational connection,[6] there are also dangers in a process of trust and assumed connection. This shift away from a defensive ethic to an ethic of care is not one bereft of *Angst*. A Freudian critique would also point to the need for a focus on unconscious dimensions to trust and choice, recognizing the capacity of the conscious mind for self-deception in motivations for choice. None of these concerns pertain to a questioning of the existence of a relational ethic of care in wider cultural contexts, but to consequences of its application in diverse contexts.

The problems here, however, are more than simply the pragmatic ones of dangers of relation, as distinct from loss of relation. The difficulties are not only that relational pragmatism may often not be itself pragmatic, i.e., where detrimental consequences to self are affected and effected by a relational concern with the consequences of choice for relationship with

6 Drawing upon Gilligan's (1990) critique of Erikson's (1968) conception of identity through independence, benefits of such relational processes of assumed connection and trust, for example, between son and mother, were also highlighted in the cultural context of Estonia, for many of the Russian-speaking male heroin addicts in Downes (2003a).

another. The additional concern is how a socio-cultural logic of conditioning manifests itself, in the dialogical process of communication and relationship extolled by Gilligan, in her ethic of care as purported 'webs of protection' (Gilligan 1988b, p. 156). Social influence cannot be assumed to be benign, even at a dialogical level between self and other, quite apart from the way groupthink paves its way into attitudes and behaviour.

Where are the resources in the self to resist a flattening conformity to a sweeping cultural logic for choices that may be detrimental to the person's own well-being, as well as destructive for others? A lack of resources to challenge cultural conformity brings a dearth of resistance to becoming, what Garfinkel (1967) terms a cultural dope, namely, a consumptive slave to cultural forces in choice and motivation. The individual becomes processed into conformity with the cultural matrix of taken for granted assumptions (Downes 1993; Downes & Downes 2007), what Nietzsche (1872) terms 'the lie of culture which poses as the sole reality' (p. 48). At least for some individuals' experiences, there may frequently be a need to challenge the habits of mind, heart, body and language, tattooed upon a culture. Some psychologists, like Erikson (1968), would additionally claim such a counterpoint is the task of each rising generation. In contrast, postmodernist positions tend to carefully – and not so carefully – prune even the possibility of resistance to fashions of sociocultural conditioning dessicating human experience.

Limits to this relational pragmatism include those for pragmatism more generally, namely, that its goals and values for useful, helpful moral decisions (in relationship with others) tend to be framed within the context of a common consensual cultural or subcultural logic (Downes 2003b, 2004, 2009a). It offers little to resist the sweep of such cultural or group logic. Like minds trained to polish flowers, its consequences are not useful; pragmatism turns against itself, at least as a liberatory force. This applies both to a logic of justice concern with pragmatism and arguably, *a fortiori* to the relational pragmatism of Gilligan's ethic of care, concerning its susceptibility to a consensual, subcultural logic conditioning.

A further variant of this socio-cultural critique of Gilligan's relational pragmatism can be inferred from Taylor's (1991) identification of contemporary (Western) relational ethics bringing dangers of a pure subjectivism of trivial choices. Taylor (1991) identifies these modes of experience as where personal 'identity crucially depends on my dialogical relations with others' (p. 48).

For Taylor, the contemporary Western culture of 'authenticity' tends towards soft relativism, what Heidegger (1927) would term, mere '"subjective" discretion' (p. 270). This subjectivism of values leads to a position that 'things have significance not of themselves but because people deem them to have it – as though people could determine what is significant, either by decision, or perhaps unwittingly and unwillingly by just feeling that way' (Taylor 1991, p. 36). Taylor characterizes this culture of authenticity as involving a fusion of historical antecedents, including Cartesian interiority and, *via* Rousseau, a romantic expression of an inner nature. For a primordial cross-cultural truth, Gilligan's ethic of care needs at least some further distinction from these Western cultural forms of life. Gilligan (1988) expressly raises concerns about moral relativism, and her ethic of care is committing to core conceptions of nonviolence, inclusiveness, connection and relational communication as response to another's need. Elsewhere, Gilligan (1986, p. 326) criticizes a conflation of care with feeling. A spatial-phenomenological reinterpretation of Gilligan's ethic of care similarly needs to go beyond subjective relativism.

Rather than simply rejecting a process of cultural conditioning towards subjective authenticity, Taylor (1991) raises the question as to how an ethic can be drawn from these modes of experience. He recognizes that these cultural dimensions may be displacements of a prior, more significant, mode of experience. Taylor (1991) interprets this ethic as a contemporary ethic of authenticity. For this search for authenticity of experience to be developed into an ethic, Taylor (1991) views it as needing to challenge a soft relativism which 'implicitly denies the existence of a pre-existing horizon of significance, whereby some things are worthwhile and others less so …' (p. 38).[7] Allied with this search for a preexisting horizon of significance,

7 A charge of relativism applies to contextualist approaches generally, as Amaya (2011, p. 325) highlights, in the related context of legal justification. Amaya (2011) puts forward 'a nonfoundationalist conception of legal justification … [which] denies

Taylor (1991) acknowledges the challenge to socio-cultural conditioning through convention in an authenticity that 'demands a revolt against convention' (p. 65).

It is this spatial-structural dimension of concentric and diametric relation that is a key dimension in distinguishing this proposed primordial relational being, from the subjective relativism of what Taylor (1991) describes as alienated, trivial forms of ethics of authenticity, emerging in contemporary Western culture. These forms are viewed as deriving from what he treats as an ideal of an ethic of authenticity. There are some resonances between a primordial search and Taylor's (1991) conception of authenticity as relational and as a search for wholeness, 'self-truth and self-wholeness are seen more and more not as means to be moral, as independently defined, but as something valuable for their own sake' (Taylor 1991, pp. 64–5). However, a focus on spatial-phenomenological projections, as structures of experience and as necessary conditions for framing experience and choice, goes beyond traditional oppositions such as ideal-real, subjectivity-objectivity. As a background spatial projection at the level of framing truths and experience, this is to be distinguished from the subsequent level of cognition and action that concretizes such framing intuitions in a given context. Unconscious spatial frames and constructions of reality adopted for cognition are different levels of understanding. This view of prior primordial structural intuitions shares, with Taylor (1991), the need for some criteria or reference point beyond sheer, raw subjective relativism for choice. The reference point being offered here is not an abstract ideal but rather a structure of primordial experience, as concentric and diametric spaces of assumed connection and assumed separation, respectively. This primordial level offers a discourse on criteria for experiential wholeness, while offering structures of experience that need not be reduced to traditional understandings of subjectivity.

---

that there is any set of propositions which provide the foundation upon which the justification of the rest of the factual and normative propositions in law depends' (p. 323). Gilligan's relational ethic of care can be construed as a challenge to the dichotomy between a foundationalist and nonfoundationalist approach to moral reasoning.

Gilligan's later work engages with dimensions of loss of assumed connection in intrapsychic, as well as interpersonal, experience. Significantly, there is a specific recognition of the need to challenge Western cultural assumptions and conventions of experience that negate other spaces for experience. Thus, Gilligan (1990) highlights the tensions between female adolescent experience and a Western logic based on rigid dualisms:

> The either/or logic that Gail was learning as an adolescent, the straightline categories of Western thinking (self/other, mind/body, thoughts/feelings, past/present) and the if/then construction of linear reasoning threatened to undermine Gail's knowledge of human relationships by washing out the logic of feelings. (pp. 18–19)

Here Gilligan (1990) is, in effect, seeking a non-Western mode of experience that challenges diametric spatial intuitions. Elsewhere, Gilligan's work describes what amounts to a diametric structured, mirror image inversion between voice and silence as a feature of repressive cultural communication, 'Girls in the study live in a territory between voice and silence: If they continue to speak from their experience they may find that their voice is out of relationship, too loud, off key. If they remain silent they are in immediate danger of disappearing' (Taylor, Gilligan & Sullivan 1995, p. 202). Connection in relationship is envisaged as a pathway out of such fragmentation.

Diametric spatial structures of mirror image inversion are also adverted to by Brown & Gilligan (1992), for girls 'at the edge of adolescence', where 'what feels and seems unloving to girls is often called love; what feels and sounds mean or cruel in women is often covered by sweetness and called "sweet" or "nice"' (p. 160); they characterize this diametric split in spatial terms as 'the wall' of 'relational impasse' (p. 161). Again an explicit tension with Western culture is invoked for a twelve/thirteen-year-old girl 'Jennifer' who moves 'into the sea of Western culture and a profound psychological loss' (Brown & Gilligan 1992, p. 180). This Western culture is viewed by Gilligan in terms of a diametric spatial splitting, 'The either-or framing (selfish or selfless, self or relationship) marks an inner psychological split or division. Taking on moral language, girls take in the dichotomies of a culture which splits good from bad women and divides the selfish from the selfless' (Brown & Gilligan 1992, p. 177). Diametric spatial projections of assumed separation impinge upon experience and language. On Gilligan's (2011) account of 'patriarchal splits and hierarchies' (p. 24) across a range of her work, there are strong grounds for further investigation of the meanings of diametric spatial relations as being a structural expression of patriarchal cultural processes and projected realities constructed in people's lives (see also, Scales 1986/1996, p. 1053).

A subtle, somewhat understated, shift of emphasis appears to have taken place between Gilligan's earlier and later work, concerning care, voice and assumed connection. Whereas her earlier work envisages a relational pragmatism in the different voice of her ethic of care, her subsequent framework shifts more towards a consideration of relational authenticity as a way of being (which offers some resonance with Taylor's ethic of authenticity). While both early and later Gilligan involve a concentric structured projection to frame the respective relational approaches, the pragmatic concern with consequences on relationships gives way, somewhat, to the contours of an intrapsychic dimension, combined with interpersonal relation. The pragmatic dimension is more susceptible to being considered a product of Western cultural conditioning than the later intrapsychic aperture that will be seen to offer resonance with aspects of some Eastern traditions. This later relational authenticity concern, as a dimension of a relational way of being, also proffers a trenchant critique of Western cultural processes, evinced as alienating girls through their being out of relation to themselves and others.

Movement beyond diametric splits invites a different concentric spatial intuition of assumed connection at an intrapsychic level (and not simply at the interpersonal level of *In a different voice*). This invites challenge to internalization of diametric projections at an intrapsychic level of relation. Excavating the concentric spatial projection underlying the interpersonal relation of Gilligan's ethic of care is a key mediating step towards a concern with ethics and intrapsychic relation going beyond Gilligan's purportedly key term, 'network'. There is a need to extend the domain of concentric relational interactions beyond the interpersonal to the intrapsychic.

In terms of being an unconscious, precognitive, concentric spatial intuition framing choice, Gilligan's (1982) work may offer a step forward towards finding common ground with some Eastern projections of concentric modes of relation. However, in other ways, Gilligan's (1982) contextualism hardly transcends a distinctive Western tradition. For example, the Greek sophists offered similar visions of truth as mutable, contextual and pragmatic, a contextualism extolled as well by the Western thinkers, Vico, Voltaire, and Montesquieu (Kelly 1992). Moreover, even within a logic of justice, the English common law tradition, for example, has long recognized the need for equity, i.e., more flexible contextual principles of interpretation than the general common law category interpreted in a literalist fashion as the letter of the law. It is the concentric relational dimension of assumed connection more than the contextualist, pragmatic aspect of Gilligan's ethic of care that offers distinctive innovation of insight and scope for development of a cross-cultural understanding. Though not expressly aiming to do so, Gilligan's work offers both a phenomenology and a spatial-phenomenology; it is a phenomenological account of lived experience and a spatial-phenomenology of concentric and diametric structures of primordial relation.

4.3 Extending some postmodern implications for Gilligan's relational pragmatism: Necessary spatial conditions in Gergen's saturated self

Argument (ii) Gergen's (2000) characterization of Gilligan's ethic of care as the basis of a postmodern relational morality for a fragmented interpersonal relational self illuminates a) a problem of the penumbra between categories of care and justice and b) the need for a framework of dynamic, spatial projections underlying care and justice.

Gergen's postmodern relational pragmatism is particularly aware of the need for cultural sensitivity and the dangers of hegemonic, prematurely universalist truth claims in a fast-changing global society, where observed truths may simply be stories as cultural snapshots in historical time (Gergen

1973, 1992, 1994a, 2000; Gergen et al., 1996). Gergen (2000) envisages Gilligan's conception of a web of relationships and bonds of caring or assumed connection as being 'extended to form the basis for a postmodern, relational view of morality, in which moral decisions are viewed not as products of individual minds, but the outcome of interchange among persons' (p. 168). For Gergen, a relational self tends to replace essentialized versions of self; relationships create and recreate personal identity. Gergen (2009) continues this move beyond a conception of self to argue for relational being, beyond even a relational self, where the relation itself is more fundamental than the separate self.

Gergen (2000) observes the disjunction between different contexts of self, where 'through an array of newly emerging technologies the world of relationships becomes increasingly saturated. We engage in greater numbers of relationships, in a greater variety of forms, and with greater intensities than ever before' (p. 79). A multiplicity of selves is viewed, at times, by Gergen (2000), through the spatial metaphors of fragmentation and saturation of self:

> This fragmentation of self-conceptions corresponds to a multiplicity of incoherent and disconnected relationships. These relationships pull us in myriad directions, inviting us to play such a variety of roles that the very concept of an 'authentic self' with knowable characteristics recedes from view. The fully saturated self becomes no self at all. (p. 7)

Gergen (2000) terms this disconnection within the self as 'a multiphrenic condition' (p. 80). Nevertheless, Gergen (2000) also celebrates a view of multiplicity of selves as opening 'an enormous world of potential' (p. 17), echoing Lyotard's (1984) wonderment at the diversity of postmodern selves.

One concern here regarding Gilligan's ethic of care, raised indirectly by Gergen (2000), is a need for understanding some kind of unity or at least potential unifying direction of self making the choices in relation to self and other. In diverse contexts, with multiple kinds of relationships, commitment to a relational, pragmatic contextualism for moral choice brings a dizzying array of dispersed self-other relations. Gergen (2000) treats this 'postmodern consciousness' as the beginning of 'the erasure of the category of self' (p. 170). Gergen aptly construes Gilligan's (1982) ethic of care in terms of an extension into relational, postmodern pragmatism. Yet in highlighting these implications for a fragmented self, there is a need to acknowledge the difficulties of such a fragmented contextualism, not only generally, but also specifically for an ethic of care.

Gergen's (2000) lens of fragmentation of the self, through which Gilligan's ethic of care can be interpreted as a postmodern relational morality, invites spatial implications that impinge upon the ecological validity of the hypothetical problem dilemmas that Kohlberg relied upon and Gilligan reinterpreted. Focus on a fragmented self, in a diverse range of relational contexts, tends to move the avenue for interpretation of Heinz's dilemma away from an assumed connection predominantly between the narrator/self (as Heinz) and the owner of the pharmacy (as other). It invites an opening of the background space of the moral dilemma to consider a range of relationships for Heinz, what Gergen (2000, p. 174) terms a postmodern 'plethora of selves' that would need to be engaged with, through this proposed ethic of care, assumed connection, approach.

In the hypothetical dilemma as constructed, there is nothing provided on the attitude of Heinz's wife herself. Her voice and perspectives are kept in a passive role, at least, by Kohlberg. Gilligan (2011) refers to 'the active role she [Amy] accords the unnamed wife in the decision making' (p. 34), where Amy suggests that Heinz and his wife 'should really just talk it out and find some other way to make the money'. Yet this partial voice for the wife assumes that her position is not one where she wants Heinz to steal the drug at all costs; Amy has already taken that option away from her, before the dialogue would commence. An authentic, relational dialogue for an ethic of care would presumably need to start from a perspective of where a person is at, rather than where someone thinks they 'should' be at; Amy shortcircuits this relational process at least to some degree. A relational ethic needs to include a shift away from a generic outcome focus, identified in advance.[8] The dilemma becomes accentuated if his wife is beseeching

8 See also Downes (2007a) on the need to move beyond a generic outcomes focus in relational contexts of education. That a generic outcomes focus in a reasoning process relies upon culturally constructed assumptions of conventionality is a corollary of

Heinz to steal the drug or do anything to get it to save her life. Further, there may be Heinz's wife's brothers, sisters, parents or also children, who are aware of this issue, in a transfer of this dilemma into a naturalistic context. Many of them may also be anxiously demanding Heinz to act to obtain the drug, through whatever means.

While Gilligan (1982) constructs Amy's response to Heinz's dilemma as one of a responsive, relational ethic of non-violence, it is possible to interpret a refusal of Heinz of his ill wife's requests, her own families' voices and their children's agonized cries for action as itself being, not only a non-relational response to their declared voices and needs – but as also being a refusal that could be construed as a psychological violence to his wife and even to some of these other people. The ethic of care as non-violence may turn against itself, once a moral relativity is accepted between physical and psychological violence.[9] Gilligan's construction of an ethic of care may turn here into a somewhat arbitrary privileging of an injunction against physical violence over psychological violence.

Heinz's wife may construe his non-violence to the pharmacist, as a psychological violence towards herself. There are some good grounds for challenging an assumed privileging of rejecting physical violence over psychological violence in an ethic of care, so that the ethic of care as non-violence turns against itself. Any such attempted privileging, in Cartesian

what Marmor (2001) would term 'the condition of efficacy', namely, that 'there is no point in following a conventional rule that is not actually followed by the pertinent community' (p. 210). The pertinent community is culturally variable. Marmor's conventional rules here refer not to legal rules but to a prior level of the rule of recognition in Hart's (1961) positivism.

9 This relativity is not to advocate a strong social constructionist view that violence is itself solely a social construct. Part of Gilligan's (1982) difficulty concerns Mill's (1869) liberal injunction for an ambit of freedom that is delimited by the principle of not doing harm to others. Once Mill's harm is expanded beyond physical harm, the scope for interpretative dilemmas in moral reasoning amplifies possibly exponentially. Yet Gilligan's implicit diametric split between bodily and psychological violence/harm risks the reimportation of a Cartesian division long rejected, even in many legal systems, which do give recognition to psychological harm, such as nervous shock.

fashion, of a diametric splitting projection between psyche and body, needs to be cognizant of international research on bullying in schools; psychological dimensions of bullying are frequently recognized as being at least as harmful as physical bullying (van der Wal et al., 2003). Passivity can also be seen as a violence, for example, regarding bullying as exclusion. In similar vein, the damaging psychological effects of authoritarian teaching, though not violent physically, has been observed to play a key role in motivating harmful early school leaving (Fingleton 2004; Downes & Maunsell 2007). Laing & Esterson's (1970) accounts of the psychological violence associated with exclusion of one scapegoated member of the family in authoritarian modes of family systemic communication is also testament to the profound effects of a purely psychological violence.

It is clear that Gilligan (1982) does recognize a psychological violence in her ethic of care with regard to a concern that nobody is left out.[10] However, its relative weighting against physical non-violence is somewhat elided, as this would reintroduce a balancing process that challenges somewhat the purity of a distinction between a logic of justice and ethic of care. A recurrent problem here is the background conditions of relation between the two moral reasoning approaches.

Gilligan's ethic of care can salvage this ethic of non-violence dimension, if it is construed in dynamic, directional terms as a projection, a concentric structured spatial projection onto relationships and situations. As a projected state, it does not mean that this ethic necessarily succeeds in being carried out in a no-win situation of least violence or harm in the decision to be made (on this broader view of non-violence, as psychological and physical). The person tries for such non-violence, in his/her concentric spatial projection of assumed connection. However, the situational environment may be a diametric structured space of split alternative paths that both resist such a concentric spatial projection. It is not simply a contrast between intention and effect or consequence. This is not merely an ethic

10 Her later work encompasses 'explosive', 'fracturing' 'relational conflicts' (Brown & Gilligan 1992, p. 124), while Ward's (1988) empirical classification regarding care, justice and violence observes psychological violence.

of good intentions of non-violence, where, in T.S. Eliot's words, in 'The Hollow Men', 'between the idea and the reality ... falls the shadow'. As a precognitive mode of concentric assumed connection, it is a background taken for granted assumption. The relational state of concentric spatial projection of assumed connection cannot be inextricably tied to pragmatic consequences, upon which the person may have highly limited influence. It is a separate element in the synthesis constructed by Gilligan in her ethic of care. These elements may, even often, be associated and in interplay, but the relational assumed connection and the pragmatic are different levels in any such association. It is not a 'not-caring' about consequences; it is rather a not being able to control directly these consequences, in what Gilligan elsewhere describes, as 'the danger in authentic encounters' (Brown & Gilligan 1992, p. 56). A problem of the penumbra between the two ethics, treated as categories, can be seen as one feature of this recurrent problem concerning elucidation of the background conditions of relation between both aspects.

Treating a logic of justice and an ethic of care in positional terms, as purely distinct categories,[11] rather than as dynamic projected directions of spatial intuitions framing reasoning approaches, also invites a disturbing implication. This implication is that a logic of justice approach operates a radical split separation between self and other – rather than a relativistic diametric spatial separation compared with a concentric assumed connection of care. This radical split between self and other would invite dangerous implications for such a bereft-of-empathy reasoning process, without connection to those involved in the application of the 'logic'; the logic of justice then becomes redolent of a radically disconnected, inhuman technocratic analysis, such as that provided, for example, in the portrayal by Nicholas (1961) of Roman law, including laws of slavery, as 'a thoroughly scientific subject' (p. 1). A radical excision of empathy is poor recipe for a human logic of justice.

11 See also Gilligan (1988a, p. 8). That the proposed categories of care and justice are distinct does not preclude that they can be simultaneously invoked (Johnston 1988; Gilligan & Attanucci 1988) for a given problem.

There is a need to go beyond a background ontological relation of a diametric spatial split or assumed separation between an ethic of care and logic of justice treated statically as categories. The penumbra between the categories challenges their very categorial state. Gilligan's later work offers a critique of positional truths pertinent to this penumbra problem:

> Our effort to find ways of speaking about human experience in a manner that resounds its relational nature and carries the polyphony of voice, as well as the ever-changing or moving-through-time quality of the sense of self and the experience of relationship, has led us to shift the metaphoric language psychologists traditionally have used ... from an atomistic, positional, architectural, and highly visual language of structure, steps and stages to a more associative and musical language of movement and feeling ... (Brown & Gilligan 1992, p. 23)

This critique, resonant with a focus on dynamic spatial directional projections, needs to be applied additionally to her earlier position that advocated a more static, diametric categorial distinction between a logic of justice and ethic of care, even when both are brought together as joint approaches to problem solving.

Significantly, Ward's (1988) empirical finding of an 'integrated reasoning mode', in a US sample of fifty-one urban adolescents, observes that 'the call for setting limits on violence is different, and it raises the importance of determining whether the interwoven justice and care concerns are a different form of moral thinking' (p. 197). Ward (1988) acknowledges, 'Initially it was thought that there would be only the categories of justice and care or uncodable ... Two additional categories of responses were offered in the students' judgments of real-life violent events' – both and integrated (p. 191). Though the number of responses in this integrated mode is not stated, Ward's (1988) evidence for this interwovenness challenges a categorial view for Gilligan's ethic of care and logic of justice. Rather than treating this evidence as an unexplained exception to the categorial distinctions, it supports a directional view of care and justice as dynamic spatial projections of experience.

Gilligan's (2011) more recent suggestion of a continuum between connection and separation invites, by implication, some important loosening of strict categorial boundaries between the two kinds of ethical reasoning processes. Entering this penumbra between categories, they can thus become directions of reasoning more than positions of reasoning. This view of an ethic of care as a projected, directional relational process, as distinct from a relational position, moves away from a position of a specific outcome as being assumed to take place as part of the relational process. In other words, Amy's outcome of no stealing to take place is but one within a relational process. From this directional approach, it cannot be excluded that a decision to steal is not a relational act, i.e., from the perspective of the dialogical decision between Heinz and his wife, it may be interpreted as a relational act. While the relational and the pragmatic coexist in Gilligan's (1982) ethic of care, they do not necessarily coexist for a relational approach to occur. A relational direction is concerned with consequences but not necessarily governed by consequences. In any move from an ethic of care as relational pragmatism to one as relational authenticity as part of a primordial relational being, outcomes are anticipated but not predetermined. It is this domain of relevance between relational pragmatism and relational authenticity that is, at least partly, occluded in Gilligan's work.

Another implication needs to be encountered for this opening of the space of the background relationships. As the web of relationships becomes more diverse, the construal of a motivation as an ethic of care loses an absolute vantage point. There is no birds-eye view for determination of a motivation as an ethic of care. It becomes partial to the perspective of the interpreter. In this decentering of an abstract vantage point, there is no one to one correspondence between self and other for the key role of interpreting assumed connection. The fragmented self, other and external observer as narrator may all have different perceptions, regarding whether an assumption of connection or separation has occurred in a given instance across the range of relations with relevant actors as others, constructed as having relevant voices for a dilemma. Among the network of contextual interactions, a global construct of care may struggle to emerge. And even a majoritarian consensus is problematic. This is part of a postmodern turn for Gilligan's (1982) ethic of care, implicit in Gergen's (2000) account of a saturated, fragmented self, where 'coherence and contradiction cease to matter', 'as the category of the individual person fades from view' and 'consciousness of construction becomes focal' (p. 170).

Another illustration of the need to deconstruct a diametric categorial distinction between an ethic of care and logic of justice is an implication of Lyons' (1988) interviewee's account. As a variant of the commitment to a non-violence, Lyons (1988) describes a forty-six-year-old female lawyer (presumably in a North American context), whose 'ultimate principle for resolving moral conflict', through an ethic of care, was to work out '"the least painful alternative for all the people involved"' (p. 31). This approach is understood, by Lyons (1988), as meaning 'to see the situation in its context, to work within an existential reality and ensure that all persons are understood in their own terms' (p. 32). This relational process dimension of care is, however, in this example, also a *balancing* of conflicting needs and rights. It involves a both/and approach. This is a both/and that challenges the categories internally, as distinct from a both/and approach to adopting each category for a given problem, as observed by Johnston (1988). It is both a relational and balancing process, as part of the one process, that again undermines the categorial purity of care and justice modes. Furthermore, it relies on a questionable objectivism and quantification for pain, in its understanding of 'least painful alternative', that stills the possibility of a deconstruction of a birds-eye vantage point.

This issue of the decentering of an abstract vantage point is also relevant for a background spatial systemic focus on a dynamic system of relations, within which such frames for moral reasoning take place. A filtering from consideration of some relationships compared with others for an assumed connection is a problematic assumed separation from the relevance of their needs and voices. Necessary spatial conditions uncovered as blind spots include the spatial closure of the network of relations among which projections onto 'Heinz' are to operate, in an assumed connection between self and other. This implicit spatial closure means that a wider network of voices for engagement with, in an assumed connection, gets silently suppressed.

4.4 Towards a primordial, cross-cultural extension of an ethic of care

(iii) To what extent can some Eastern perspectives develop a meaningful discourse in terms of concentric and diametric spaces, as part of an ethic to resist socio-cultural realities perceived as illusory?

Gergen et al. (1996) highlight the need to develop a stronger cross-cultural focus in psychology. Beyond the obvious ethnocentric, methodological concerns with a sampling reliant on US subjects, from what Woodiwiss (2003) describes as 'one of the most culturally distinctive societies in the world' (p. 108), the question arises as to whether the content of Gilligan's ethic of care is limited to Western culture.[12] Gilligan's qualitative research approach was less concerned with representativeness than with allowing a different voice and aspect of experience to come to the fore.

A *prima facie* case has been established that the cross-cultural spatial intuitions framing Gilligan's logic of justice and ethic of care offer a defence against critique that Gilligan's modes are, what Teo & Febbraro (2003) would term, Western ethnocentric intuitions. Identifying concentric structural frames for an ethic of care is an argument for the cross-cultural relevance of such projected structures, embracing at least some Eastern contexts. This argument needs more development to examine whether such concentric and diametric spatial structural projections can be relevant to lived experience in some Eastern traditions.

At the outset, this very questioning of Western ethnocentrism must recognize its acute limitations here. These limitations go beyond simplistic constructed categories of East and West that import the danger, highlighted by Said (1978), of being a Western projection onto Eastern cultures as a counterpole. Any characterization of thought as Eastern is a

12 Sharma's (2006) acknowledgement of the genetic fallacy of rejecting human rights from an Eastern perspective simply because this paradigm originated from Western culture is also applicable to Gilligan's ethic of care. Yet there can be other grounds for modification of both frameworks from Eastern perspectives.

major oversimplification and does not acknowledge differences between and within Indian, Chinese, Japanese traditions, as well as other Asian contexts. Asia is obviously far from being a homogenous single region, given its immensely complex, diverse number of states, religions, communities, languages and cultures. Other concerns with such a questioning, raised by Said (1978), include the employment of essentialist abstractions to describe a culture, the lack of attention to the detail of individual voices and everyday lived reality, as well as a propensity for selective fragments as a simplification of the complexities of lived experience. These dangers would be accommodated through a phenomenological focus on the first phase of phenomenological description described earlier, if individual voices and experiences were given expression from diverse 'Eastern' contexts. The fragments raised here are denuded of such a level of interrogation.

This account does not aim to offer a comparative analysis of Asian systems such as Hinduism, Buddhism, Jainism, Confucianism, Yoga, Taoism and Zen Buddhism. Aspects of Buddhist and Hindu conceptions will be mainly examined here, together with Taoist insights, in this preliminary questioning, even concerning these traditions. As Inada (1990) recognizes, 'Alone among the great systems of Asia, Buddhism has successfully crossed geographical and ideological borders and spread in time throughout the whole length and breadth of known Asia' (p. 91).[13] Whereas Buddhism originated in India, Zen Buddhism emerged in East Asia as one of the products of Chinese culture after contact with Indian traditions.

Focus here is not on all or representative modes of experience in diverse Eastern contexts but rather on certain kinds of experience concerned with an inner unity, with meditative experience, with resistance to socio-culturally constructed truths.[14] Many of these illustrations of traditional Eastern

13 This is by no means to deny the obvious resonance with Gilligan's ethic of care of, for example, Confucianism's concept of humanity (*jen*) as 'not a mere abstract concept, but one that extends concretely throughout the whole of sentient existence' (Inada 1990, p. 92).

14 It is also a broadening of moral questions to include ones of how to live a meaningful life, what Taylor (1989) characterizes as a moral preoccupation with 'how am I going to live my life' (p. 14), as an ethic of authenticity (Taylor 1991).

perspectives rely on a host of assumptions that may be meaningful for a given cultural context but also require fresh justification for many Western perspectives and for a cross-cultural, as distinct from 'Eastern', or regional psychology.

A conception of choice as meditative experience, where the mind is to be emptied, is a challenge to Western conceptions of choice as cognition and as pragmatism. In Hindu and Buddhist traditions, *sadhana* is roughly translatable from Sanskrit as 'means to completion or perfection'. Bhattacharyya (1999) provides an account of *sadhana* in terms of a process of liberation through inner transformation, as 'a means whereby bondage becomes liberation' (p. 174). Bondage to worldliness is to be overcome through dispassion and nonattachment. The goal of *sadhana* is to reach a dimension of spiritual realization, which includes enlightenment, pure love (*prema*) and liberation from *samsara*, the cycle of birth and death. An Eastern vision here is of a liberation from certain modes of attachment or connection, as part of a journey towards a more primary connection of *prema*. It is associated with a capacity to resist more illusory forms of attachment in moral choice and in *samsara*. Yet this is not to reject other kinds of assumptions of connection in Buddhism, such as compassion (*karuna*), which, as Inada (1990) observes, literally means 'passion for all' (p. 101).

Gyatso (2001) observes that Buddhism contrasts *samsara* with liberation, 'To attain liberation, we need to abandon self-grasping, the root of *samsar*a, by attaining a special wisdom directly realizing emptiness, or selflessness'; he refers to the need 'to escape from *samsara* by abandoning its cause, self-grasping. This wish is renunciation' (p. 64). His account of Buddhist thought continues, 'perfection cannot be found in *samsara*. *Samsara* promises much but can never deliver real satisfaction. It is not possible for impure, transient objects to provide the lasting joy we seek' (p. 71). On this view, '*samsara* pleasures are shortlived and ensnare us if we become attached to them' (Gyatso, 2001, p. 72). As Mehta (1987) observes, *Śamkara* summons 'This tree of *samsara*' that 'must be torn out from its very roots. Alone in pulling it out lies the fulfilment of life's purpose' (p. 20).

Erricker (1995) gives a Buddhist account of *nirvana* as enlightenment or awakening, 'It is an awakening to the way things truly are, and an extinguishing of the ignorance that fetters us to continual rebirth in the realm of *samsara*, which we can translate as motivation by desire, ignorance and aversion' (p. 19). Desire and aversion in *samsara* are clear diametric spatial oppositions as mirror image inversions. *Samsara* is a state of being trapped within these oppositions. Erricker (1995, pp. 54–5) observes that Buddhist teaching on samsaric existence is depicted visually in the 'wheel of becoming'. At the centre of the wheel are the three driving forces, ignorance, desire/greed and aversion represented by a pig, cockerel and snake. Erricker (1995) continues, 'Beyond this maya (the repeated movement of creativity and destruction) lie peace and happiness, untouched by death and rebirth (which are simply movement of momentous change in the samsaric cycle ...)' (p. 57). The further diametric mirror images of creativity-destruction, death-rebirth are part of the structure of *samsara* which is to be moved beyond according to Buddhist thought. A prior space is to be sought between change and stability.

Allied with the diametric mirror image space of desire and aversion, ignorance is given expression within a diametric spatial structure, through development of the third entailment of the relative differences between concentric and diametric spaces, namely, foreground-background noninteraction in diametric spatial structures. Desire and aversion operate in a closed structural relation to wider background environmental stimuli. This closure and noninteraction with background is an ignorance of such stimuli, a filtering of connection with such background. The dominion of diametric spatial projection brings an ignorance of all that is not locked within the closed, mirror image space of desire and aversion.

For Taoist traditions, Parkes (1987) observes 'the predominance of Taoist imagery about wandering above and beyond the dust and grime of worldly affairs and their concern with not being bound by things' (p. 126). This offers much resonance with a Buddhist movement beyond illusory *samsara*. While acknowledging the importance of opposites in Taoist thought, Rajneesh (1979) also notes that,[15] 'Lao-Tse says that there is one state in nature, however, when we do not consider the opposites at all.

15 Parkes (1987) observes that Taoism challenges anthropocentrism and offers an affinity with nature that is largely lacking in Heidegger's existential-phenomenology.

That is the highest state. He calls it *Tao*. *Tao* is the state of one's nature when we are not aware of either good or bad. When we do not even know what it is to be good and what it is to be bad, that is the supreme tranquility' (pp. 411–12). This invocation of a state of experience beyond the diametric structured, mirror image oppositions of good and bad also invites acknowledgement of the possibility of a unity within experience. In his commentary on the *Tibetan Book of the Great Liberation*, Jung (1939) also perceives that 'natural wisdom' goes beyond diametric oppositions, as it is 'undefiled by evil' and 'unallied to good'. However, he cautions that if brought to a Western context, such wisdom would be reduced to being mere liberation from moral considerations.

These examples from some Eastern traditions challenge the perceived illusion and *samsara* of diametric spatial oppositions between pleasure and affliction, and categorizations of a domain of experience through the lens of good and evil. They are part of a mirror image diametric relation that is treated as illusory, compared with a prior, more fundamental level of reality and experience. Categorizations of good and evil are retrospective to a prior meditative level of experience, where the mind is emptied of categories.

This diametrically structured level of experience is frequently contrasted with a mandala-structured level of experience that is concentric. Choice and motivation as a meditative experience involves some dimension of shifting away from a diametric *samsara* level to a concentric mandala level. In doing so, the very understanding of choice itself may require substantial change. In meditative experience, choice and motivation are shifted towards a renewed concentration on a precognitive level of experience; this emptying in meditation is not reducible to choice as cognition. Choice is now more at a structural level to experience than concerned with pragmatic external world consequences. It is an experiential restructuring, modifying diametric spatial intuitions towards an interaction with concentric spatial intuitions – primarily at an intrapsychic level. This does not mean that external world consequences are not relevant. Dalal & Misra (2010), for example, explicate an 'Indian psychology' as being concerned not only with inner transformation, but also with external world realities. Rather it raises a question whether the process dimension, the 'how' of choosing, requires a restructuring of experience – and whether that choice is not reducible simply to pragmatic terms of consequences.[16]

Another relevant dimension to explore concentric structured experience of assumed connection is *samadhi*. *Samadhi* is a Sanskrit term to denote a state of intense concentration or absorption of consciousness induced by complete meditation. This term is used by both Hindus and Buddhists to describe a non-dualistic state of consciousness in which the experiences of the subject become one with the object. The etymological meaning is derived from the root 'sam' (together or integrated), 'a' (towards), and 'dha' (to get, to hold). Thus, the literal meaning can be interpreted as developing integrity, wholeness or truth. Assumed connection here implies a wholeness of self, an integration as part of a wider capacity for concentric structured experience.

Kvaerne (1975) treats the relationship of *sadhana* to the concentric structured mandala as follows:

> [...] external ritual and internal sadhana form an indistinguishable whole, and this unity finds its most pregnant expression in the form of the mandala, the sacred enclosure consisting of concentric squares and circles drawn on the ground and representing that adamantine plane of being on which the aspirant to Buddhahood wishes to establish himself. The unfolding of the tantric ritual depends on the mandala; and where a material mandala is not employed, the adept proceeds to construct one mentally in the course of his meditation. (p. 164)

Liberation here is conceived as being through movement towards concentric structured experience, through a concentration on concentric patterns.

16 Mulla & Krishnan (2008) identify two dimensions of Karma-Yoga, namely, sense of duty or obligation towards others and an absence of desire for rewards; the latter dimension offers a clear challenge to pragmatic assumptions of choice led by consequences. Karma-Yoga differs from conventional Western models of motivation reliant on an individualistic-hedonistic bias and which are largely based on cognitive calculative processes (Shamir 1991) or diametric mirror image, positive/negative reinforcements in behaviorism. Regarding Taoist perspectives, Parkes (1987) also highlights that Taoists 'particularly abhor the division of things into the instrumental categories of the useful and the useless' in their 'rather idiosyncratic praise of uselessness' (p. 117).

Viewed in light of these initial, fragmented Eastern perspectives, Gilligan's ethic of care develops a core insight for concentric structured experience as a spatial frame of assumed connection, *prema* or wholeness. However, it needs to be taken further to distinguish connection or attachment to limited samsaric features of reality in a given culture, from a more primordial concentric connection of attachment. This more primordial experiential connection brings with it an implication of a detachment from the purportedly illusory and samsaric. Interpersonal relation of assumed connection between self and other, as a frame for moral choice, brings the danger of displacement into an illusory connection – and requires a prior intrapsychic relation or state of being of concentric structured experience.

This conclusion, however, requires the caveat that wholeness, as non-dualism, is not directly equivalent to concentric dualistic structures, even though both go beyond a state of non-diametric dualism (Downes 2010). Parkes' (1987) words are somewhat apposite, 'In Taoism, the movement of transformation is the opposite of the Platonic one: rather than concentering the soul in preparation for the ascent to unity with the Absolute, one de- and ex-centers the self to allow it to merge in all directions with the formlessness of tao' (p. 126). This Taoist approach also gives expression to a view of living in harmony with nature, with 'numerous passages in the Taoist texts describing a primeval condition' extolling a return to nature (Parkes 1987, p. 129). It is notable that non-dualism itself imports a diametric dualistic split between a unity and an illusory external world, in seeking a withdrawal from the illusory. Somewhat in contrast, a concentric dualism invites a modification of the 'illusory', samsaric diametric structured dualistic world; while concentric relation and non-dualism both invite a simplicity and unity, concentric relation does so through interacting and engaging with aspects of complexity to potentially modify its defensive diametric structures. While it has not been established here that such projections succeed in their goal of detaching from a purportedly illusory, samsaric external culture and attachment to material objects, it is a goal of such concentric projected states of experience that concentrate on emptying and growth of the self (and relinquishing of the ego).

It is evident that from these Eastern perspectives, a question of transformation arises as being from a diametric spatial intuition and structure of experience towards, at least at times, a concentric spatial intuition and structure of experience. This requires a further intrapsychic, phenomenological process. This goes further than simply the concentric structured assumed connection, at an *interpersonal* level, between self and other, in Gilligan's ethic of care. Another prior relational state of being is needed. Gilligan's (1982) interpersonal focus for assumed connection is a limited domain of projection of a concentric spatial intuition for experience and choice. In a moral relation between self and other, a construct both of self and the structures of experience underlying the self are presupposed. Gilligan's ethic of care and logic of justice, founded as they are on projected spatial intuitions of concentric and diametric relation respectively, are expressions of particular existential, phenomenological states of being. Moreover, from some Eastern perspectives, there are other possibilities for states of being, in which to project concentric structured spatial relations. In doing so, other approaches to morality, choice and experience can unfold.

This is not to deny a distinctive logic of justice focus in some Eastern terms, including what Leary (1990) describes as 'development of an authentic Asian approach to human rights' (p. 25). Diametric spatial structures are also envisaged as being primordial structures of relation, even if associated more with Western culture. Sharma (2006) attempts to develop an abstract, logic of justice discourse more resonant with Eastern traditions, and summarizes the following perspective:

> Human rights are Western in the sense that the concept of human rights evolved in the West with the citizen as its primary referent rather than a human being. The citizen is a human being but if we take the human being as our starting point then our perspective on human rights shifts kaleidoscopically to reveal a different configuration (p. 260).

Any such ethnocentric critique of the logic of justice approach in Heinz's dilemma would regard the division between civil and political, and social and economic rights – Aristotle's commutative versus distributive justice – as a Western biased construct. It is a division already unseated somewhat in, for example, the legal system in Mumbai, India, which recognizes a justiciable 'pro-poor right to housing' (Hohmann 2010, p. 183), as an aspect of the right to life. Hohmann (2010) acknowledges this as a radical shift in human rights discourse. Viewing Heinz's dilemma beyond a narrowly US cultural context would also require more cognizance of the international right to enjoyment of the highest possible standard of health (UN Special Rapporteur 2005, 2006; Downes 2007, 2008). Another avenue for interpretation of Indian culture in terms of diametric spatial structures of assumed separation and hierarchical mirror image relations is that of its caste system, described in Donnelly's words (1990), as 'separate, exclusive, mutually repelling groups … integrated into a hierarchic order …' (p. 66).

While a detailed account of contexts where an ethic of primordial relational being may be more appropriate than a logic of justice or an unextended ethic of care is outside the scope of this book, there is at least one domain of contrast that is important to advert to for current purposes. Whereas a logic of justice approach is very much a rule-following, or at least, principle-following one, and an ethic of care focuses more on the relational process dimensions with connective assumptions of inclusiveness and nonviolence, a primordial relational being embraces, especially, the level of rule or principle-generation.[17] It engages with the process of construction of the criteria for rules, principles and relationships. In this sense, it also offers a challenge to conventional cultural conditioning. Just as it is not being proposed that a more primordial truth is a truth totality, it is not being claimed that a rule-generation (or construction of criteria) mode for new frameworks of understanding ethical reasoning can be blandly applied to all contexts of conflict or moral dilemmas. This is not to be a recipe for an anarchic individualism, nor for a relationality that seeks only relation to self and not other, community and world.

17 Marmor (2001, p. 205) distinguishes between conventional rule 'coordination' functions and 'constituting' rules in discussing legal conventionalism underlying a rule of recognition for a legal system. This echoes the importance of distinguishing these two levels in a different context.

A spatial-phenomenological approach has been employed to interrogate the background spatial conditions of possibility, as blind spots underlying Gilligan's ethic of care and logic of justice. In doing so, it has focused on different, though strongly related, aspects of this background assumption structure, a) specifically on concentric and diametric spatial projections in this framework, b) on necessary spatial conditions as blind spots framing conceptualization, and c) on spatial themes in the content of Gilligan's theory and in Gergen's suggested extension of it to a postmodern relational pragmatism.

CHAPTER 5

A Spatial-Phenomenological Reinterpretation of the Psychoanalytic Subject in Freudian Repression and Early Childhood Experience

Introducing this spatial-phenomenological framework for psychoanalytic subjectivity, a wide range of key features across the Freudian corpus are addressed. These include repression, projection, obsessional neurosis and the dual drive theory. These psychoanalytic concepts can be recast in light of this spatial model of diametric and concentric relations. Relating this spatial-phenomenological reinterpretation to Freud's death and life drive is with a view to offering an alternative avenue into his much criticized and even derided later work. Freud's life and death drives are far from being 'nonsense upon stilts', to adapt Bentham's famous condemnation of natural law theories.

A spatial-phenomenological reconfiguration extends to other aspects of early childhood experience, largely resonant with Freud, such as Winnicott's transitional objects and Bowlby's attachment theory. While Freud's concerns with psychosis were much more limited than his interrogation of neurosis, a number of phenomenological accounts of psychosis, from a range of thinkers, will be argued to provide further evidence of the centrality of this axis of diametric and concentric spatial structures to the unconscious world. In a spatial-phenomenological reinterpretation of the psychoanalytic subject, a search for primordial structures in an unconscious system of relations needs to tread along pathways prior to causal explanations.

Influential objections to Freud's empirical causal claims will now initially be considered. In Lear's (2009) words, the preoccupation with efficient causes as the only acceptable scientific level of explanation in psychoanalysis has 'plagued the discipline throughout the last century'

(p. 1314). Moreover, it has distracted from key insights of Freud, in his later work especially, with regard to space and postmechanistic perspectives.

5.1 Key limitations in critique of Freud's causal-temporal claims

Argument: That (i) a range of well-known empirical objections to Freud's causal claims ignore that such objections are limitations to empirical truth claims generally and not only Freud's specifically and (ii) this highlights a need to shift empirical and conceptual focus onto spatial systemic background conditions for causal claims in psychoanalysis to interrogate projections.

During the past century, commentary on Freud's work has been marked by a preoccupation with the causal claims of Freud rooted within a temporal axis of consideration of the role of prior childhood trauma due to sexual origins in subsequent symptom formation. The first part of this chapter will argue that discourse on Freud's causal claims in relation to time has given rise to simplistic critique of Freud's position and requires recognition of more complex systemic concerns.

Grünbaum's (1986) interrogation of Freudian causality leads to his critique of the Freudian position as follows: if symptom B exists and antecedent A of a trauma is also known to exist, it is still not logically possible to infer that A *caused* B. For instance, he observes that 'confirming the prior occurrence of the trauma does not show that it was a cause of the *Rat Man*'s obsessions' (Grünbaum 1986, p. 227). Twenty years later, Grünbaum (2006, p. 272) reiterates this objection to Freud's causal inferential relation in *Rat Man*. Freud's claims for a childhood sexual etiology of subsequent trauma experienced in adulthood is not, as Grünbaum is at pains to highlight, an empirical observation but a theoretical leap between putative disjunctive events in time. Grünbaum's position is a rehearsing of the psychological commonplace that correlation is not cause. Nevertheless, Wallace (1989) while recognizing Grünbaum's 'constricted vision of science' (p. 525) in his defence of psychoanalysis against Grünbaum, concludes that 'Grünbaum's blows against the clinical testability of analytic hypotheses are most telling in the area of ... putative causal linkages between patterns of childhood experience and adult psychopathological and characterological constellations' (p. 518).

Grünbaum (1986), however, overlooks the fact that his argument here is merely an implicit rehearsal of Hume's (1777) more general critique of causal relations between A and B. Hume argues that this causal relation is conventional and habitual rather than a necessary or logical one. This is the case for any causal claim. As Bhaskar (1989) notes, there is a distinction between causal laws and empirical invariances; scientific experimental activity can only establish the pattern of events of the empirical invariances and the causal law is a further step beyond direct observation. Thus, it is the category of causality employed by both Freud and Grünbaum which leads to this logical problem; this is an inbuilt limitation to empiricism itself, more than simply Freud's constructions of it.

As highlighted earlier, Gergen (1994) expounds on a related point for the context of social psychology, when highlighting the theoretical leap between any given hypothetical construct and its empirical operationalization; the pathway back from the observed operationalization to the hypothetical construct is by no means a self-evident one. There may be multiple, even infinite, possible hypothetical constructs consistent with any given empirical operationalization. The leap across the gap in observation is a limitation built in to causal explanation; it is a constraint upon an empirical science of psychology, as well as upon Freudian conceptions of this envisaged by a hypothetical construct of past trauma and its operationalization through later symptoms in the adult. Sherwood's (1969) critique of the hypothetico-deductive method is that it cannot be applied to aspects of Freudian reasoning 'without either committing one to laws which are psychologically false or else trivializing the original explanation' (p. 239). Yet this critique requires further expansion. It is not simply that the hypothetico-deductive empirical method applied to psychoanalysis is the problem, but rather this very method itself is extremely limited, at least in the social sciences.

When asking if Freud's 'psychoanalytic edifice' (p. 257) is relevant to the twenty-first century, Grünbaum (2006) frames his analysis of causality through what he characterizes as Freud's inference that the therapeutic removal of neurotic symptoms is produced by the cathartic lifting of the patient's previous ongoing repression of the prior traumatic memory. Grünbaum (2006) codifies this claim of Freud's 'Therapeutic hypothesis' as follows, 'Lifting repressions of traumatic memories cathartically is causally relevant to the disappearance of neuroses' (p. 269). Yet Grünbaum (2006) envisages a lifting of repression as an all or nothing event rather than as an ongoing process. He relies here on a rigid dualistic conception of causal relevance, in contradistinction with a lack of causal relevance.

This tendency to overlook background necessary or even simply supportive conditions for the cause to 'work' is criticized in Mill's (1872) challenge to a clearcut distinction between causal and non-causal states, 'It is seldom if ever between a consequent and a single antecedent that this invariable sequence subsists. It is usually between a consequent and the sum of several antecedents the concurrence of all of them being requisite to produce, that is, to be certain of being followed by the consequent' (p. 327). Mill noted that very often one antecedent is termed the cause, the other antecedents being conditions. Intervention models that 'work' causally have hidden necessary contingent conditions, without which the more obvious causal elements could not have occurred, just as striking a billiard ball to hit another presupposes the necessary condition of gravitation. Causes necessarily operate within a background of supporting conditions that are structured sources of the cause's efficacy. It is precisely these conditions that Rutter (1985) argues have been frequently overlooked within developmental psychology:

> it is commonly but wrongly assumed that a significant main effect in a multivariate analysis means that that variable has an effect on its own. It does not. What it means is that there is a significant main effect for that variable, after other variables have been taken into account: that is not tantamount to an effect in the absence of all other variables. (p. 601)

Another possibility is that particular background necessary or supportive conditions may simply be missing and that if they were present the intervention would have causal impact.

Echoing Mill (1872) and Rutter (1985), there is a need to go beyond a narrow and flawed 'magic bullet' cause, as envisaged by Grünbaum (2006), to focus on necessary and supportive conditions for causal relations in the removing of repression. Freud (1925, p. 34) already recognized this through giving force to the role of instinct and phantasy in mediating effects from external causes (as well as emphasizing their own substitutive, independent, predominant causal role in neurosis). While Grünbaum (1986) does distinguish between necessary and sufficient conditions, and explores what he terms Freud's 'Necessary Condition Thesis' (NCT), he does not apply with full force the implications of this wider interrogation of the role of background conditions in any putative causal explanation.

Grünbaum (1984) criticizes Habermas' (1972) view that therapeutic progress can 'overcome' an aetiologic linkage by dissolving it. Grünbaum (1984) denigrates the coherence of this view as 'the instantiation of a causal connection cannot possibly also qualify as the dissolution of this linkage' (p. 11). Yet once again this criticism rests on Grünbaum's limited conception of the roles of necessary background conditions underlying a causal relation. As Buzzoni (2001, p. 148) highlights, Habermas' (1972, p. 257) suspension or dissolution of a causal linkage, 'depends on the lack of an essential condition', just as a match can fail to light because it is damp; absence of or change to a necessary condition constitutes the possibility in principle of modifying a causal sequence. The supporting or necessary conditions can be viewed as a potentially dynamic background spatial relation influencing, 'overcoming' (Habermas 1972, p. 271), or even 'dissolving' the underlying the causal relation.

Another reason why Grünbaum (2006) falls into the trap of a magic bullet causal explanation, for catharsis and repression, is that he places undue emphasis on memory of a past trauma as a cognitive event to be recalled, without sufficient recognition of the need for an affective integration of that relived experience. Though at times he does acknowledge affect (Grünbaum 1984, pp. 180–1; 1986, p. 224) to supplement cognition in relation to Freudian memory, this relative neglect of affective dimensions is further evident from Grünbaum's framing of the following question:

> Just what is the *ratio* of the forgetting of distressing experiences to their recall, and what other factors determine that ratio? Freud gave no statistical evidence for assuming that forgetting them is the *rule* and remembering them is the exception. Yet, as we can see, his theory of repression is devastatingly undermined from the outset if forgettings of negative experiences do not greatly outnumber rememberings statistically. After all, if forgetting is not the rule, then what *other* reason does Freud offer for supposing that when distressing experiences are actually forgotten, these forgettings are instances of genuine repression because of affective displeasure? (Grünbaum, 2006, pp. 267–8)

Cognitive recall of a repressed experience is not equivalent for Freud to an engagement to 'work through' (Freud 1914c, pp. 155–6) the repressed experience, as Grünbaum assumes here; the lived emotional experiential dimension is factored out of Grünbaum's equation. This may be somewhat unsurprising, given Fisher & Greenberg's (1977, p. 348) survey of the general neglect of Freud's conception of 'working through' in research dealing with therapy given the 'insight' label. However, Grünbaum additionally overlooks the implications of Freud and Breuer's explicit statement in the *Preliminary Communication* (1893) of their classic work, *Studies on Hysteria*, that 'Recollection without affect almost invariably produces no result' (1895d, p. 6).

In his attempted assault on Freud's causal explanations of repression, Grünbaum imposes a quantitative statistical schema onto memory and experience, as though these can be simply reduced to bits and pieces of information to be subsequently recalled. Grünbaum's question here has neither a right nor wrong answer; it is meaningless, as it fails to recognize the constructed dimension to memory and experience, and that such experience is not simply a discrete event. This point at issue is reminiscent of Derrida's (1997) denigration of Lévi-Strauss' (1955) view that 'the sum of … knowledge' in the Western world prior to 'the invention of writing and the birth of modern science' has gone 'up and down' rather than having 'a steady increase' (p. 129). Derrida (1997) incisively asks 'What is a quantity of knowledge' (p. 129) and states that Lévi-Strauss' assertion is neither true nor false but simply meaningless; it has no construct validity. The parallels with Grünbaum's quest for a Freudian quantity of memory and experience are obvious. It is somewhat surprising that Grünbaum's position overlooks these constructed dimensions, given that at least an implication of his frequent emphasis on the 'contamination' of psychoanalytic facts by the analyst's suggestions is, as Frosh (2006, p. 53) notes, a recognition that what occurs between analyst and analysand is a constructive process.

A related issue here, in examining the need to go beyond conceptualization of removal of repression as a discrete event and a 'magic bullet' cause, is to envisage the unconscious and repression in systemic terms more than the rigid causal terms of much of the past century. Skinner's radical behaviorism has also been seen to elude empirical observation for complex systems, despite its rhetorical claims to scientific rigour. As Rachlin (1984) highlights within behaviorism, the pattern of determination by conditioning is more complex than a single one to one correspondence between a behaviour and a consequence:

> It would seem to be an important task for psychology to determine what the (overt behavioral) criteria are for the use of mental terms, how they change with circumstances, how they interact with one another. Before doing this job, it may be necessary to widen the conception of the operant, as originally advanced by Skinner, from a single discrete event (such as a lever press) to a complex pattern of events that may occur over days and weeks and (consequently) to alter the notion of reinforcement from contiguity between a pair of discrete events (response and reward) to more complex correlations that have meaning only over an extended period. (p. 567)

This widening of the operant to a complex pattern of events within a system highlights the complex conditions of feedback and the problem of interpretation of feedback. It is simply an application to the context of behaviorism of Quine's (1961) well-known critique of Popper's (1959) discrete event falsification in science,[1] as ignoring the complex systemic interaction of

1 Popper (1959) advocated that a scientific theory cannot be confirmed as 'true', but can only be falsified, i.e., proven false, by an experiment. Quine (1961) highlighted that an individual experiment, in other words, a discrete event, is insufficient to render a theory false and that interpretation of the consequences of a given experiment involves

observations and theory. In other words, a single event can provide limited scope for interpretation in a dynamic and complex system.

Without seeking to invoke or extol behaviorism as a scientific ideal for psychology, it is nevertheless evident that the dynamic and complex system of the unconscious and its repression processes require a scrutiny which similarly accommodates a systemic level interrogation, rather than merely a discrete causal event focus pursued by Grünbaum (2006). Breger (2009) highlights that this wider focus was already held by Freud and Breuer (1895d):

> Freud and Breuer made clear that, although one can speak of a trauma as if it is a single entity, more typically a series of related events have a cumulative effect. The cases in *Studies* [on Hysteria] certainly bear this out; behind the psychological disturbance of most of the patients lies a complex group of traumatic and conflict-laden occurrences and relationships that cannot be reduced to a single event. (p. 74)

It is evident that the debate regarding the empirical status of psychoanalysis needs to move forward to systemic concerns.[2] It has partially done so through characterization of the unconscious as a language system (Lacan 1968; Habermas 1972); however, a language analogy is not the only system level focus possible for apprehending the Freudian unconscious. A spatial-phenomenological systemic discourse of dynamic interaction between diametric and concentric spaces is also possible.

A further issue in relation to Freud's empiricism which has been superficially explored by some of his critics[3] is his understanding of theory-

---

a more complex analysis of a system of relations between observations. There is not a one to one correspondence between an empirical observation and falsification of a truth claim.

2 See also Fisher & Greenberg (1977, p. 10) and Wallace (1989, p. 524) on a movement from monotraumatic causal focus to a total pattern of life events, experiences and relationships and Downes (2009) on wider systemic dimensions to concentric and diametric space.

3 Though not Grünbaum (1986, p. 218), on this point, who aptly criticises Ricoeur's (1981) hermeneutic interpretation of Freud, for overlooking the need for interpretation within observation.

ladenness projected into observation underpinning causal claims. The twentieth-century high watermark for psychology, of a theoretical *tabula rasa* or blank slate, was Watson's (1914) behaviorism. Such assumptions of non-theory ladenness in observation of brute facts is an outmoded philosophy of science. Theory-ladenness seeped into observation is well recognized in philosophy of science (e.g., Duhem 1905; Kuhn 1970; Feyerabend 1988) and requires further critique in the practice of psychology (Gergen 1982; Follesdahl 2001; Teo 2008). It is notable that Freud, already in 1915 (p. 117), acknowledged that observations are theory-laden and further interpreted theoretically.

Against this backdrop, some of the prominent criticisms of Freud's empirical psychology can be understood as giving insufficient recognition to the limitations of interpretation free observation in psychology. Thus, for example, Storr (1997) indicts Freud for relying on his personal experience as a source and frame for his psychoanalytic theories. This may be understandable as a criticism of Freud's imaginative though flawed theoretical reconstruction of Leonardo da Vinci's dreamworld (Wohl & Trosman 1955) and Freudian male chauvinism, reaching its zenith in examples of interpretation such as the *Dora* case (Moi 1981; Stadlen 1989). Storr, nevertheless, fails to acknowledge Reichenbach's (1938) well-known and important distinction in philosophy of science between hypothesis generation and justification. Recourse to personal experience is appropriate for the former though not the latter. Similarly, Sulloway (1979) trenchantly assails Freud's work for hiding the theory-ladenness seeped into its observations and causal claims, '... he ... sought to portray his discoveries as rooted in empiricism and in so doing, emphasised his debt to his clinical materials and to the psychoanalytic method, not to theoretical ... inspirations' (p. 443). However, a theoretical *tabula rasa* of non-theory ladenness advocated by Storr and Sulloway is facile for the latter part of the twentieth century and was successfully avoided by Freud in the first part of that century.

An argument is needed to move on from the somewhat sterile methodological puritanism of debates on causality and time in relation to psychoanalysis, to a more intense apprehension of cross-culturally meaningful spatial and systemic understandings of Freud's work on the unconscious. These methodological critiques of Freudian causality have not so much been fishing in the dark. Without an interrogation of prior spatial systemic background dimensions, they have been fishing in a forest without water.

5.2 Projection of the diametric spatial structure in obsessional neurosis: Inverted likeness, assumed separation and non-interaction with background stimuli

In making the case for diametric and concentric spatial structures as primordial projections that are the unthought, blind spot in Freud's search for unconscious structures, primordiality is being specifically envisaged as a more fundamental truth or experience, a unifying direction for experience, a cross-cultural truth, as well as being prior to causal levels of explanation. Amplifying insights regarding cross-cultural spatial structures of concentric and diametric relations can facilitate expansion of the scope of the Freudian unconscious beyond Western culture.

The illustrative examples here for a spatial-phenomenological reinterpretation of repression and obsessional neurosis, require recognition of a number of empirical limitations in Freud's work. These include the small number of Freud's actual case studies provided to substantiate his theories, as well as the clinical weakness that many of his patients did not actually improve after his analysis with them. Another key limitation is that these cases of obsessional neurosis are usually from only one gender, as Freud tended to associate obsessional neurosis with males (Appignanesi & Forrester 2005, p. 189). However, as Appignanesi & Forrester (2005, p. xiv) acknowledge, Freud did seek to go beyond a view of hysterical neurosis in gender terms, where hysterical neurosis had traditionally been associated with female examples.[4] Hysterical neurosis was considered by Freud to be

4 Hysteria disappeared from the DSM III classification in the 1970s and was broken into a variety of diagnoses such as borderline personality disorder, anorexia, multiple personality disorder, psychosomatic illness.

the conversion of repressed pain into a bodily symptom, in contrast to obsessional neurosis, which was the conversion of repressed pain into obsessional ideas and repetitive ritual behaviours. Such a Cartesian division between conversion through body or mind is a limited one, with or without the early Freudian gloss that recollection of an early sexual experience was one of revulsion and fright in hysteria, in contrast to that of pleasure accompanied by reproach in obsessional neurosis. Despite a range of limitations in Freud's work, the baby must not be thrown out with the bathwater in dismissing key insights which are available from evidence Freud presented.

Though given more extreme emphasis by Klein (1946; 1948), repression as a process of splitting or assumed separation is a central feature of Freud's understanding. Freud (1914) describes his framework at the end of the Breuer period, 'I looked upon psychical splitting itself as an effect of a process of repelling which at that time I called "defence", and later, "repression"' (p. 11). Freud (1940) also explores a 'splitting of the ego in the process of defence' discussing 'a rift in the ego which never heals but which increases as time goes on' (p. 276). Splitting or assumed separation is, for Freud (1923), not simply an outcome but also a process associated with repression, 'The repressed is only cut off sharply from the ego by the resistances of repression' (p. 24). The assumed separation of diametric spatial structures gives expression to a key feature of repression as a splitting process; diametric space can be considered both a structure and a dynamic process of inducing assumed separation in its movement as a projection.

Freud's (1912–13) discussion of obsessional neurosis similarly observes a denial of 'hostile feelings against the dead loved one', and a 'contrast between conscious pain and unconscious satisfaction over the death that has occurred' (p. 61). This ambivalence highlights a diametric structural feature of inverted symmetry projected within repression of experience and behaviour. Freud's (1916–17) account of resistance and repression in terms of an inverted symmetry has already been observed. Such a pervasive mirror image symmetry is central to Freud's accounts of obsessional neurosis. In a well-known case of obsessional neurosis, *Wolf Man*, Freud (1926) strongly emphasizes the interplay of two diametrically opposing states, 'In following up a single instinctual repression we have thus had to recognize a convergence of two such processes. The two instinctual impulses have been overtaken by repression – sadistic aggressiveness towards the father and a tender passive attitude to him – form a pair of opposites' (p. 106). The passive orientation is a mirror image of the active one involved in aggression, while the tender attitude towards the father is a mirror image of the sadistic attitude. Each is both an instantiation of a repressive principle and a denial of the other repressive principle. Freud goes so far as to recognize that repression is itself divided into two conflicting processes. He extends this dualistic structure, in effect, making it a general feature of obsessional neurosis, 'The symptoms belonging to this [obsessional] neurosis fall, in general, into two groups, each having an opposite trend. They are either prohibitions, precautions and expiations – that is, negative in character – or they are, on the contrary, substitutive satisfactions which often appear in symbolic disguise' (Freud, 1926, p. 112).

The reaction to prior trauma tends to impose a diametric opposition of a repressive split between trauma and reactive prohibition, precaution and/or expiation. This can become an active feedback loop as the process of establishing further diametric relations invites another cycle of reactive prohibition, precaution and/or expiation. This further diametric relation to the reactive prohibition is substitutive satisfaction – a mirror image of the prohibition. Referring to 'ever greater room to substitutive satisfaction at the expense of frustration' (p. 118), Freud (1926) expresses the diametric oppositional structure underlying obsessional neurosis, 'In the crudest instance the symptom is diphasic: an action which carries out a certain injunction is immediately succeeded by another action which stops or undoes the first one even if it does not quite go as far as to carry out its opposite' (p. 113).

Acceptance of the diametric mirror image structure underlying the emotions and behaviour of the *Wolf Man* is not contingent upon accepting that his anxiety of being devoured by a wolf was a substitute for the idea of castration by the father (Freud 1926, p. 108). The diametric structure to understand emotions and behaviour is logically independent of a) the Oedipus complex, b) castration anxiety as 'a prime motivator' (Fisher & Greenberg 1996, p. 119) implied by the Oedipus complex, c) acceptance or otherwise of the presence of castration anxiety in *Wolf Man*.

In his comments on Freud's *Rat Man* case of obsessional neurosis, Sherwood (1969) implies that this inverted symmetry insight of Freud challenges conventional Western logic: 'And why should the patient have felt such remorse at the father's death if he hated him? It is items like these which present at least a *prima facie* incongruity' (p. 222). Freud traverses beyond Western A/Non-A logic with mirror image structures of ambivalence.

This underlying diametric structure and process is also evident in the famous example of obsessional neurosis and separation anxiety which Freud (1920) observed through his grandson Ernst's game of *fort-da*, disappearance-return. Freud (1920) describes a boy 'greatly attached to his mother' who 'had an occasional disturbing habit of taking any small objects he could get hold of and throwing them away from him into a corner, under the bed, and so on ...' (p. 14). He continues:

> I eventually realized that it was a game and that the only use he made of any of his toys was to play 'gone' with them. One day I made an observation which confirmed my view. The child had a wooden reel with a piece of string tied round it ... What he did was to hold the reel by the string and very skillfully throw it over the edge of his curtained cot, so that it disappeared into it, at the same time uttering his expressive 'o-o-o-o'. (Freud 1920, p. 15)

Freud agreed with the boy's mother that the child's utterance meant 'fort' ('gone') and noted that, 'He then pulled the reel out of the cot again by the string and hailed its reappearance with a joyful "da" ["there"]. This, then was the complete game – disappearance and return' (p. 15). The game of disappearance-return is an example of reversal expressing diametric structured behaviour and experience. This mirror image reversal is not a cancelling of one pole by the other, both coexist in an uneasy tension.

A further diametric spatial dimension emerges from the repetition of this game. Freud's (1920) assessment of the function of repetitive play was as follows:

> in their play children repeat everything that has made a great impression on them in real life, and that in doing so they abreact the strength of the impression and ... make themselves master of the situation ... As the child passes over from the passivity of the experience to the activity of the game, he hands on the disagreeable experience to one of his playmates and in this way revenges himself on a substitute. (pp. 16–17)

According to Freud (1920), the child compensated himself for the instinctual renunciation he had made in allowing his mother to go away without protesting 'by himself staging the disappearance and return of the objects within his reach ... The child cannot possibly have felt his mother's departure as something agreeable or even indifferent' (p. 15). Turning his experience into a game, 'At the outset he was in a passive situation – he was overpowered by the experience; but by repeating it, unpleasurable though it was, as a game, he took on an active part' (p. 16). Freud (1920) envisaged the function of repetitive play as the child becoming an active 'master of the situation' (p. 16), through repeating that which had left a significant emotional impression. Disappearance-return, combined with a reversal from passivity to being in active control, are examples of inverted likeness expressing diametric structured behaviour and experience.[5]

Yet this spatial process underlying the compulsion to repeat goes beyond the mirror image inversion feature of diametric structures. The ritual repetition of the *fort-da* game of disappearance-return is a projective imposition of this play structure onto a complex background of possible alternative activities or experiences. This repetition places a separation from the (unpleasurable) background stimuli through concentrating attention on the closed system of the game (i.e., the *only* use made of *any* toy was the repeated game of disappearance and return). The repetition brings a static fixed interaction with the background. This very separation from the background unpleasure (of the mother's absence) through the closed system of the repeated game is a feature of diametric rather than concentric structured experience. It is a radical lessening of interaction with the background stimuli.

While this function of lessened interaction with background stimuli is not necessarily the only function of repetitive play generally,[6] the feature

5 Sincoff (1992) has observed that subjects who score highest on repression scales are statistically more likely to adopt judgments dividing reality into diametric oppositions between good and bad. In effect, they project a diametric spatial structure onto the world, constructing mirror image inversions.

6 Piaget (1962), for example, highlights the repetition involved in children's practice play.

of noninteractive, assumed separation between the diametric pattern and its background resonates with Freud's economic dimension to anxiety also for traumatic neurosis, 'in the experiences which lead to a traumatic neurosis the protective shield against external stimuli is broken through and excessive amounts of excitation impinge upon the mental apparatus' (1926, p. 130). Such diametrically structured experience launches a greater barrier against external background stimuli than concentrically structured experience. This diametric spatial projection to narrow background stimuli through repetitive behaviour is an active process exerting its dominion as a compulsion and is not only a defensive structure. Freud (1926, p. 153) directly relates a compulsion to repeat with the fixating factor of repression.

While Freud (1920) describes the repetitive action of Ernst's game as an expression of obsessional neurosis, he later acknowledges anxiety as direct separation anxiety from the mother (Freud 1926). Resonant also with Anna Freud, Bowlby's (1973) neo-Freudianism would examine the play of this child as an expression of (pre-Oedipal) separation anxiety leading to a defence of detachment to deal with the pain of loss of the attachment object.[7] This invites interpretation of Freud's (1920) view of Ernst's game in the light of his later (1926) emphasis. Expressions of diametric oppositional structured experience and behavior thus include (i) the inverted likeness involved in the structure of the child's game, (ii) the disconnection from background stimuli through repetition expressing a closed structure imposed upon the background, and (iii) the tendency towards detachment or assumed separation from the mother frequently observed in young children as a reaction to loss.

This diametric feature of non-interaction with background stimuli offers a direct structural expression of another key feature of Freudian

7 Separation anxiety 'disorder' is the only anxiety disorder specific to childhood according to the American Psychiatric Association (APA 2000). Freud's obsessional neurosis is a broader pattern that can be associated with a range of clinical level disorders, such as generalized anxiety disorder, specific phobia, social phobia, posttraumatic stress disorder, panic disorder, obsessive-compulsive disorder (OCD), as well as separation anxiety disorder. However, a distinctive emphasis of Freud is on the sexual origins of obsessive, reactive to trauma, neuroses.

repression, namely, withdrawal of cathexis (Freud 1926, pp. 92–3). Freud (1926) envisages this withdrawal from engagement of cathexis as being a repressive defence against anxiety. The ego seals itself off from further interaction with libido or external stimuli. Diametric splits from interaction with background stimuli offer a spatial account of a loss of energetic interaction, as part of a structural projection bringing severe restriction of energy flow. This withdrawal feature of repression pervades other accounts in Freud's work. Freud (1926) also observes a phenomenon of 'isolation' in obsessional neurosis:

> When something unpleasant has happened to the subject or when he himself has done something which has a significance for his neurosis, he interpolates an interval during which nothing further must happen – during which he must perceive nothing and do nothing. This behaviour, which seems strange at first sight, is soon seen to have a relation to repression. (p. 120)

Again this projected diametric spatial structure seals off interaction and change to behaviour and in an extreme form brings this paralysis in isolation; it is resonant also with Freud's (1920) emphasis on decathexis and the Nirvana Principle, as a reduction in stimuli to zero tension.

Freud (1896) described the obsessive ideas and rituals of an eleven-year-old boy to resist the memory of being sexually abused by a servant girl in a paradigmatic case of obsessional neurosis. Among other actions, the boy would only sleep if the bed was pushed against the wall, three chairs exactly had to stand by the bed, pillows were placed in a particular pattern and he was allowed to kick his legs out a certain number of times and then lie on his side. These repetitive behaviours correspond to Freud's (1920) account of prohibitions, precautions and/or expiations as a frustrative reaction to the prior trauma rather than the further phase of substitutive satisfaction. The boy's repetitive behaviour was an attempt to place a diametric opposition of assumed separation between his current situation and the memory of the sexual abuse which took place in the same bed. He was to lie on his side rather than in the position where he was abused; the pillows were to be placed in a different way from their position at the time of the abuse. The other measures were to create the feeling of distance through a diametric relation between his current state and that of future danger of abuse. Again the repetition and narrowing of possible behaviours into a ritual brings a static fixed diametric interaction of closure with the background environment.

This diametric spatial projection is amplified by the inversion of the passivity of the boy's role as the victim and his active role in his ritual actions. It is a mirror image of controller-controlled. Freud's suggestion that in obsessional neurosis frustration is replaced by satisfaction implies the danger of the process of victim turned abuser highlighted in much research on the victim-abuser cycle in sex abuse (e.g., Lane 1997; Prentky et al 1989), though studies by Widom (1996) and Williams (1995) observe that this danger is not simply a direct one without other mediating factors.

Although repetition and inversion are key features of play generally (Lancy 1980, p. 472), in obsessional neurosis these elements may be distinguished simply by the difference in degree of repetition and frequency of inversions.[8] A view of diametric spatial structures as projections of ego defences would emphasize a continuity between features of repetition and inversion in ego formation generally, and obsessional neurosis as an extreme within this process (Downes 2003). Similarly, mirror image inversions in dreams are well recognized by Freud (1900) as not necessarily being related to pathology, as they are prevalent in birth-dreams, and 'contrariwise', 'just the reverse' dreams (p. 526, p. 439). Once again, a spatial logic or discourse is implied. Freud's (1900) own famous dream of Irma's injection displays this mirror image structure. In the words of Appignanesi & Forrester (2005):

> The dream is populated by two sorts of character: there are the female patients and there are male doctors; there are characters representing a self-reproach and there are characters representing self-justification ... Not a single person cited either in the dream or in Freud's associations falls outside the two categories of doctor and patient; even Freud's brother, who lends Breuer his pallor and clean-shaven chin, appears in the associations because 'we had news a few days earlier that he was walking with a limp owing to an arthritic affection of his hip'. (pp. 118–19)

8 See also Kernberg (2009) on trauma, repetition and reversal.

As Appignanesi & Forrester (2005) highlight, 'Each element is paired off: the dream is a list of self-justification closely linked to a list of self-recrimination. The logic is that of the talion, with self-justification canceling out self-recrimination. And the wish-fulfilment of the dream is embodied in the representational "triumph" of the self-justificatory elements' (p. 118). The wish-fulfilment dimension is the victory of one diametric pole over its mirror image.

Again and again the silent systemic space of diametric relations manifests itself. It is not merely a passive backdrop but an active organising principle of the unconscious shaping the movement of different garbs of appearance. Development in experience is a movement in excess of diametric spatial structures that are bound within the restricted domain of a mirror image relation and desiccated relation to background stimuli. The question arises as to whether diametric spatial relations are a circumscribed part of another wider spatial mode of relation? Concentric spatial relation offers a different potential spatial direction, as a modification of diametric space. It is neither of unlimited experiential possibility, nor simply a defiance of the limitations of the restricted space of diametric relations.

A shift from defensive structures of repression requires engaging with a movement from the closure of diametric spatial structures of non-interaction with background, towards more concentric structures of relational engagement. However, concentric spatial relation is not a horizonless opening. It is not an opening out into simple abstraction of general possibility; it resists the truncation of diametric spatial relation and yet is itself a space for concrete possibilities and not simply general, haphazard unlimited possibility. Viewed in terms relative to diametric relation, it is an expansion, an amplification of interaction with background stimuli of possibility. Openness and closure are relative terms to be interpreted against the backdrop of such concentric and diametric spatial structures. These spatial structures open an alterity in the core of the pleasure principle itself and provide a discourse on systemic relations underlying Freudian mirror image repression and movement from this repression.

A question arises as to whether this diametric spatial structural view of projection, as a primordial process of the unconscious in obsessional neurosis, is supported by Freud's own understanding of projection. Can Freudian projection be interpreted in primordial, structural, nonreactive to repression terms? A tension between primary and defensive projections can be seen to pervade Freudian conceptions of projection. Though not reducible to simple wish-regression (Freud 1907, Freud/Jung letters, p. 61), Freudian projection is usually treated as a 'variety of repression' (Freud 1907, Freud/Jung letters, p. 40). A typical view of Freudian projection is exemplified by Sulloway's (1979) position that, for Freud, projection is fundamentally viewed as a defence (pp. 101–2) and von Franz's (1980/1992) reference to Freud's inclination to the 'assumption that only repressed material is projected' (p. 369). Projection is thus, from these vantage points, treated as a reactive distortion of reality through the process of repression.

A wider framework for projection also emerges from Freud's work. Freud (1911, pp. 67–8) refers to secondary repressions which operate together with primary, organic repression. It is only within this realm of secondary repressions that projection is treated as a secondary defence (see Sulloway 1979, p. 384). Nevertheless, elsewhere Freud (1912–13) does transcend a view of projection as simply a 'defensive procedure' (p. 61). He explicitly states that projection is also a primary process, 'But projection was not created for the purpose of defence; it also occurs where there is no conflict. The projection outwards of internal perceptions is a primitive mechanism ...' (Freud 1912–13, p. 64). This view would in principle accommodate diametric and concentric structural projections as a primary process.

At first glance, later Freud seems to reject a role for projection in obsessional neurosis. Freud (1926) states that there is 'no trace of projection' (p. 128) in obsessional neuroses as the source of fear is from the superego. However, this later rejection of projection for obsessional neurosis is a rejection of projection at the content level (affect/image/idea) only.

While Freud's view of projection tends to examine projection from a content perspective of what is projected (i.e., image, affect or delusional idea), Freud (1912–13) does conceptualise projection in paranoia in bipolar/dualistic structural terms, 'The pathological process in paranoia ... makes use of the mechanism of projection ... The typical case of such a conflict is one between the two members of a pair of opposites – the case of an ambivalent attitude, which we have examined in detail as it appears in someone mourning the death of a loved relative' (p. 92). He subsequently generalizes a dualistic structure to projection beyond the context of paranoia to that of consciousness and the unconscious, 'When we, no less than primitive man, project something into external reality ... we are recognizing the existence of two states ... the existence of unconscious mental processes alongside the conscious ones' (p. 94). Thus, it must not be overlooked that Freud accommodates a more structural (dualistic) examination of projection.

This proposed shift of emphasis and vantage point to the unthought, blind spots in Freud's work concerning space, is not a matter of dismantling stone by stone, Freud's elaborate edifice that concentrated on past events in linear time. It is a reconstruction through a logical extension of Freud's own concerns. Consistently explicated across a range of (albeit male only) cases relating to obsessional neurosis, Freud's implicit spatial discourse is clearly more developed for diametric space rather than movement from this space towards concentric spatial projections.

5.3 Primordiality as a more fundamental experience: Early childhood projections of concentric space for transitional objects

In contrast to Freud's descriptions of children's play and rituals, Winnicott (1971) highlights 'transitional objects' and 'transitional phenomena', such as a cuddly toy or tune. This opens a pathway to a different underlying projected structure than diametric space. Winnicott (1971) suggests that, 'The [transitional] object represents the infant's transition from a state of being merged with the mother to a state of being in relation to the mother as something outside and separate' (pp. 14–15). As a transition in time, it is not yet within the frame of an external other, nor reducible to a state of non-differentiation from the 'me' or the mother. It is for Winnicott (1971), 'the place in space and time where and when the mother is in transition from being (in the baby's mind) merged in with the infant and alternatively being experienced as an object to be perceived rather than conceived of' (p. 96).

Winnicott highlights a transitional object as being a more subtle experience than the diametric framed mirror image one of 'me' and 'not-me'. The transitional object is different from 'me', yet still in an assumed connection to 'me', as 'a tendency on the part of the infant to weave other-than-me objects into the personal pattern' (p. 3). Separation on the basis of assumed connection is a key concentric spatial feature. Winnicott (1971) seeks to describe a structure which incorporates difference within identity, 'The use of an object symbolizes the union of two now separate things, baby and mother, at the point in time and space of the initiation of their state of separateness' (pp. 96–7). The outer pole of a concentric relation is in an assumed connection of unity with the inner pole, while also including a space of separation from the inner pole. This aspect of the child's relational world locates the child in the inner circle, with the transitional object in the outer circle as the transitional state before a diametric opposition between the child and objects to be perceived as external. The concentric structure offers a model for understanding of Winnicott's description of 'the separation that is not a separation but a form of union' (p. 98). Winnicott (1966) explicitly characterizes this in spatial terms as 'a potential space' (p. 371) – a space 'in relation to a feeling of confidence' (p. 371) for the baby, a space of assumed connection as 'trust' (p. 372). These concentric spatial projections are indirectly supported by Kellogg's (1979) findings that the concentric structure of mandalas (along with sunschemas) are basic designs which young children typically employ in their first attempts at human figure drawing.[9]

Winnicott (1971) explicitly contrasts the transitional object with Klein's (1934) 'internal object'; the transitional object is neither internal nor external (p. 9), fitting into neither of these diametrically framed alternatives. He links ego formation to assumed separation, thereby implicitly supporting a view of diametric spatial structures as constitutive of the ego, 'As soon as there is the ego organisation available, the baby allows the object

9 The developmental aspect of such concentric images produced by children was discussed by Fordham (1994, p. 22, p. 45) based on his empirical observations (see also Downes 2003).

the quality of being not-me or separate' (1971, p. 80). Winnicott (1971) appropriately describes the use of the transitional object or phenomena as a 'paradox' (p. xii); this 'intermediate area of experience between the thumb and the teddy bear, between the oral eroticism and the true object-relationship' (p. 2) is paradoxical within a diametric structured Western tradition, reliant on a clearcut division or assumed separation between subject and object.

Unlike Klein (1934; 1946), who relies on this subject-object dichotomy to frame a conception of internal objects, Winnicott seeks a level prior to this diametrically framed logic. Referring to a burgeoning 'objectification of the object' (p. 80) and recognition of it as 'an entity in its own right' (p. 89), the assumed separation between object and the child herself/himself is a later aspect of the temporal sequence of establishing capacity for relation (Winnicott 1971). The concentric structured capacity for relation expressed in the transitional object is later superceded to some degree by the diametric structured relation necessary for objectification.

Ernst's game described by Freud (1920) and the rituals of the older sexually abused boy (Freud 1896) involved projections of diametric oppositional structures. This contrasts, at least initially, with the transitional object which involves projections of concentric relational structures. Given that Winnicott (1971) treats the transitional object as a 'defence against anxiety' (p. 4), the question arises as to the parallels and differences in the styles of the children's play or repetitive behaviour as responses to anxiety. Though Winnicott locates the transitional object within the child's experience ranging with 'wide variations' (p. 4) between four and twelve months, he observes that the transitional object has relevance for older children, 'Patterns set in infancy may persist into childhood, so that the original soft object continues to be absolutely necessary at bed-time or at time of loneliness or when a depressed mood threatens. In health, however, there is a gradual extension of range of interest ...' (p. 4).

A notable difference between the game of disappearance and return in the child observed by Freud (1920) was a certain hostility towards the object, so that Freud interpreted Ernst's behaviour as an act of revenge. In contrast, the transitional object is in some way a soft object or phenomenon of affection. Though Winnicott (1971) observes a role for repudiation (p. 47) of the transitional object in the process of objectification, its presence or possession is 'vitally important to the infant for use at the time of going to sleep ...' (p. 4). It is an object the child desires or is attached to. Ernst's behaviour exemplifes, what Lancy (1980) would describe as, a 'play complex' of 'manipulative play' (p. 475). Fordham (1994, p. 94) also elucidates the contrast between transitional objects and libidinal and aggressive objects.

For the eleven-year-old boy (Freud 1896), the positioning of objects around his bed was a procedure to establish assumed separation from the trauma of previous and anticipated sexual abuse. His relation to the objects in or surrounding the bed did not include a desire for their possession but rather their relocation. In contradistinction, the continuing need for the transitional object in times of anxiety as the child gets older is an attempted regression to the earlier concentric structured relational state. Nevertheless, at an extreme, this regression moves into a repetitive, ritual behaviour that becomes an enactment of a diametric mode of relation. While the transitional object can stay the same, the mode of relation undergoes a change as the person moves from infant to child, so that the attached concentric mode of relation to the object is transformed into use of the object as a static fixed structure to bring separation from unpleasant background stimuli. This creates a pseudo or 'distress ego' (Neumann 1973, pp. 74–7), articulated for young trauma victims, as well as for some aspects of Winnicott's 'false self' (Winnicott 1977, p. 50); this appears diametrically structured but is nevertheless unstable to stress and frustration. Winnicott (1971) highlights the temporal dimension in experience of the transitional object, 'the infant's journey from the purely subjective to objectivity ... the transitional object (piece of blanket etc) is what we see of this journey of progress towards experiencing' (p. 6). This dimension of time allows for objectification of the transitional object, so that the relation to it changes spatially from a concentric to a diametric structured projection.

5.4 Primordiality as a more fundamental experience: Early childhood projections of concentric and diametric space underlying attachment bonding

Bowlby shared, with Freud and Winnicott, a preoccupation with the importance of early childhood experience for later personality development. He developed Freud's separation anxiety through focus over time on the effects of the quality of early childhood attachment between a primary caregiver and a child. Attachment in children is viewed as involving an emotional long-lasting bond that a child forms with a caregiving adult. Security of feeling of attachment for the child is understood as the adult attachment figure(s) being sensitive and responsive to the child's needs, as well as being consistently available. Where there is a lack of responsive care, children are perceived to form insecurely attached relationships with their primary caregiver.

A spatial-phenomenological reinterpretation of attachment theory gives expression to concentric projected structures of relation as being ones of assumed connection between self and other, between child and primary caregiver, in attachments of secure relation. A concentric spatial relation provides for separation on the basis of assumed connection and a more open interaction with background stimuli. On this view, the assumed separation of a split relation in diametric spatial structures offers a basic projection for relations of insecurity of attachment. To develop a capacity for attachment, change from diametric spatial experience is needed.

Bowlby's basic framework was refined by Ainsworth to identify two kinds of insecure relationships, namely, avoidant and ambivalent (Ainsworth et al., 1978). These developments can also be construed as giving direct expression to different entailments of a basic diametric spatial-relational projection. Children displaying *avoidant* attachment tend to hide their negative emotions, to engage in neutral interactions with their attachment figure and to minimize his or her importance as a source of comfort (Main & Solomon 1986; Cassidy 1994). Avoidant attachment is a kind of retreat into a strategy of self-reliance, associated with consistent rejection by the attachment figure. It is a defence against further rejection. Avoidant attachment is a direct expression of the third entailment of the differences between diametric and concentric spatial projections, namely, that this diametric projected structure engages in a reduced interaction with background environmental stimuli. It is combined with the first entailment of assumed separation as a diametric spatial-relational experience between the child and his/her minimizing of the importance of the caregiver.

Children displaying *ambivalence* of attachment are observed to be fearful and combine a heightening of negative emotions with increased dependence on the attachment figure, in a search for the attention of the inconsistently available caregiver (Cassidy & Berlin 1994). In this projection of a relational space, there is an interchange between a diametric split of assumed separation and hostility to the caregiver, with a concentric assumed connection to the caregiver. Yet this is itself a diametric spatial projection, as a process of division itself *between* concentric and diametric modes of relation. This diametric opposition between concentric and diametric projected spatial-relational states is itself an experiential projection at a different level; it occurs so that these spatial projections are not continuous in experience but rather split from each other. Movement between both aspects is not so much a continuum as a rupture. The diametric mirror image of this kind of ambivalence occurs between the concentric and diametric spatial structures of experience; it does not preclude another kind of ambivalence that is a mirror image predominantly *within* a diametric spatial structure, as occurs in another type of insecure attachment.

This third type of insecure attachment was observed by Main & Solomon (1986), namely, disorganized attachment. Children with disorganized attachments tend to lack a coherent, organized strategy to cope with distress in the presence of their caregiver. In their review of the attachment literature, Brumariu & Kerns (2010) cite a range of studies that observe such disorganized attachment in children as showing:

> contradictory, bizarre, and incoherent behaviours as an expression of experiencing a paradoxical situation: the caregiver is at the same time a source of apprehension and the secure base ... Three groups of disorganised attachment have been identified, two

> of which manifest role reversal with the caregiver: controlling-caregiving, including children who focus on guiding and entertaining the parent; controlling-punitive, including children who manifest hostile behaviors toward the parent ... (p. 178)

Again this reveals a diametric spatial projection underlying insecure attachment. Here a range of role-reversals as diametric mirror image inversions are observed, typically within a diametric structure. Thus, concentric-diametric ambivalence as a mirror image between both spaces, in what is termed ambivalent attachment, needs some distinguishing from a predominantly within-diametric spatial ambivalence. Nevertheless, a common spatial structure of experience underlies all of these insecure attachment relations, it is the dominion of diametric spatial projections. In contrast, security of attachment brings the different concentric spatial projection underlying experience and relation.

All of this uncovering of proposed primordial spatial projections underlying early childhood experience of relation with a primary caregiver is logically independent from a range of associated claims for attachment theory. The uncovering of these unconscious, primordial structures of relation – primordial in the sense of being fundamental and as a direction towards experiential unity – does not imply that the primary caregiver be the mother,[10] nor require a specific kind of family structure. Neither does it necessitate acceptance of the somewhat questionable method of Ainsworth's Strange Situation Procedure to investigate attachment security of an individual child. This Strange Situation Procedure is arguably culturally biased (White & Woollett 1992), limited in ecological validity, insensitive to individual temperamental differences, and out of tune with sensitivities of young children to physical environment and even to the voice tone and accent of the adult. As unconscious structural projections, the diametric and concentric spaces are precognitive, though they may also

10 See, for example, Burman (1994) for an account of chauvinistic gender role assumptions built into the work of at least early Bowlby and also Winnicott, though not Winnicott's explication of transitional objects, or Bowlby, once 'mother' is broadened to primary caregiver.

be projected into different domains of affective, cognitive, perceptual, and interpersonal conscious experience.[11]

Insecurity of attachment is being viewed as a loss or need for further establishing of concentric spatial modes for affect and relation with a primary caregiver. This rupture gives rise to accentuated diametric structured spatial relation for affect and as a primordial projection onto a primary caregiver. This is not equivalent to a maternal deprivation theory of early Bowlby, or its ideal-object variant, in Green's (1983) focus on the death of a mother-image. However, it does share Green's search for a structural dimension. Concentric structured experience arguably concretizes Green's (1983) concerns with 'the dead mother from a structural point of view' (p. 144), this 'structural function' (p. 145), where the person's love is 'mortgaged to the dead mother' (p. 158) – an experiential death though the actual mother or primary caregiver may be still alive. The assumed connection in experiential affect and relation to a primary caregiver is construed not in gender terms but in structural spatial-relational terms; the need for a connective, nurturing, sensitive, responsive and consistent relationship with a primary caregiver, however that manifests itself in diverse cultural contexts, is a need for concentric structured experience and relation. It is a focus on concentric deprivation, as distinct from maternal deprivation. This concentric deprivation is different from a mother image or archetype, though it is in assumed connection with it and the mother image may often be a pathway into the exploration of the concentric structure and dynamic.

The distinctive dimensions of avoidant, ambivalent and disorganized attachment are all part of a common spatial structure of experience – diametric spatial projection – as a common projected space underlying insecure attachment. This commonality of space brings the implication that therapeutic work on the slow unseating of this projected space needs

11 Some attempts to apprehend differences of attachment bonding adopt semi-projective techniques, such as picture response procedure and story-stem narratives (Bretherton, Ridgeway & Cassidy 1990). Concentric and diametric spatial interactions offer a further step for the development of such projective approaches, including for therapies that engage at a preverbal level such as art, play, and drama therapies, as well as for verbal therapies.

to embrace movement across all the entailments of diametric projection, and not only the dominant ones, such as foreground-background non-interaction and assumed separation for avoidant attachment, and mirror image inversion for disorganized attachment. As well as a holism in the potential interaction between diametric and concentric spatial projections, there is also a holistic dimension *within* the different dimensions to diametric space, as a primordial space.

A spatial-phenomenological approach to understanding unconscious projections in terms of diametric and concentric structures, brings a shift of emphasis. This reorientation is from the hazards of memory reconstruction of events in early childhood to a more present-based focus on the psychic constellations as spatial structures for movement in experience. This movement involves an interplay between diametric and concentric primordial spaces, frequently developing an opening to concentric spatial dimensions in a reconstruction from diametric spatial projections, in at least some contexts of experience. Underlying structures of primordial experience are not 'caused' as such. They invite relevance of the historical-causal within a present and future focused approach on progress, as movement within these diametric structures towards a concentric structured experiential trajectory that would allow for their interplay, as part of a growing experiential flexibility.

It is important also to emphasize that a focus on systemic relations of concentric and diametric projected structures occurs at a wide range of systemic levels, and not only the intrapsychic or familial. Analysis at these levels certainly does not preclude other examination and critique of wider systems impacting upon a child's experience. It invites a questioning at these other system levels as well. It must also be reiterated that a spatial-phenomenological focus is less directly engaged with the linear historical causal level of explanation, in its attempt to uncover dynamic structures of interactive relation. This is not to render linear causal issues irrelevant, but rather to treat them as a different level of description, a different kind of truth claim and as one pathway into primordial spatial concerns in the unconscious.

CHAPTER 6

Projections of Diametric Oppositional Structures in the Phenomenology of Psychosis

To reiterate, the three features of diametric spatial structures highlighted as entailments of their relative difference with concentric space are: assumed separation, mirror image symmetry (inverted likeness), and foreground-background non-interaction. In addition to uncovering these projections in obsessional neurosis and early childhood experience, it will now be argued that these are all projected structures underlying the phenomenology of psychosis. In doing so, differences from obsessional neurosis will need to be identified. As pervasive dimensions relevant to psychotic experience, these structural projections can especially be traced throughout the works of Laing, Freud, Klein and Eigen. There is a notable consensus across their accounts of lived experience in schizoid and schizophrenic phenomenology that is relevant to a spatial phenomenology. This consensus does not include within its scope Freud's earlier work on paranoia in women that sought to relate experience back to what he called the primal scene, the scene of parental sexual intercourse. This proposed causal relation was one Freud subsequently rejected.

This phenomenological consensus and focus is different from an aetiological consensus. While some of Laing's later work can be accused of romanticizing schizophrenia as a journey of authentic experience in an inauthentic society (e.g., *The Politics of Experience* 1967), nevertheless, Laing's (1959) earlier work, *The Divided Self*, remains a vital phenomenological account of schizoid states and starting point for interpretation in a spatial-phenomenological exploration. Early Laing (1959) emphasized the need for a humanistic approach interacting with the person's lived experience. This phenomenological uncovering of key features of lived experience of those with schizophrenia is not necessarily contrary to genetic aetiological aspects to schizophrenia. It is a different level of explanation.

6.1 Uncovering the first entailment of the relative differences between concentric and diametric spaces: Assumed separation of diametric projection in experience of psychosis

Laing's (1959) portrayal of schizoid phenomenology implicitly highlights the first entailment of diametric relative to concentric space, namely, the assumed separation built into projection of diametric structures. He refers to 'a persistent scission between the self and the body' (p. 78). This radical assumed separation between self and body is termed the 'Unembodied self'. This diametric structure of assumed separation between self and body is a constant theme in *The Divided Self*. It occurs in schizoid experience where, 'The body is felt more as one object among other objects in the world than as the core of the individual's own being ... Instead of being the core of his true self, the body is felt as the core of a false self which a detached, disembodied, "inner" "true" self looks on at ...' (Laing 1959, p. 69). Again, 'The individual's being is cleft in two, producing a disembodied self and a body that is a thing that the self looks at, regarding it at times as though it were just another thing in the world' (Laing 1959, p. 162). This theme of 'depersonalisation' (p. 32) is reiterated by examples in Laing and Esterson (1970), such as 'Maya', 'she experienced herself as a machine, rather than as a person' (p. 16).

The exaggerated attempt at detachment from the body parallels an exaggerated separation from interpersonal communication. The pervasive interpersonal mode of relation[1] is also a diametric one of assumed separation

1 See also, Modell (1999) on André Green's 'dead mother syndrome' as bringing great difficulties in *being with* the other.

between self and other, 'He avoids social anxiety by never really *being with* others. He never quite says what he means or means what he says ... He makes friends with people he does not really like and is rather cool to those with whom he would "really" like to be friends. No one, therefore, really knows him or understands him' (Laing 1959, p. 114). The schizoid state is a forcing into accentuated diametric structures of relation due to inability to successfully establish the concentric modes of relation in addition.

Eigen's words in *The Psychotic Core* (1986) reiterate that the psychotic state is unable to resolve problems of synthesis and separation, 'We enter circle after circle. Some speak of a "separation which is not a separation" [Milner], a "separation which is a form of union" [Winnicott], a state in which I, undifferentiation, and the other are interwoven ... The psychotic stumbles on this complexity and is pummeled by it' (p. 162). Eigen (1986) continues, in effect, echoing Laing's accounts, when observing that, 'It is too easy for unity to become obliterating fusion or separation to become autistic-paranoid isolation' (p. 163). Concentric and diametric structures offer concrete cross-cultural primordial models of this spatial thematic of synthesis and separation.

Klein locates a schizoid mode of entrenched assumed separation in early childhood, where the 'splitting' involved in the 'paranoid-schizoid position' (1946) occurs in the first three or four months, 'the mechanism of splitting ... [is] one of the earliest ego-mechanisms and defences against anxiety' (Klein 1946/1997, p. 6). Klein's view of splitting is implicitly endorsed by Laing (1959), 'The splitting is not simply a temporary phenomenon ... It is, on the contrary, a basic orientation to life ... [having] emerged from the early months of infancy with this split already under way' (p. 79). Laing (1959) characterizes this split as a fundamental ontological insecurity, in other words, a diametric projection of assumed separation as a primordial state of being. Laing and Esterson (1970) express this assumed separation as loss of trust, in the experience of 'Lucie', 'I can't trust what I see. It doesn't get backed up. It doesn't get confirmed in any way – just left to drift' (p. 43).

Just as diametric spatial projection is a dynamic process of assumed separation, and not simply a fixed structure, Klein envisages splitting as a process of reaction to a fundamental sense of anxiety. This splitting is viewed as being central to later schizophrenia, 'the early ego splits the object and the relation to it in an active way, and this may imply some active splitting of the ego itself ... the primary anxiety of being annihilated by a destructive force within, with the ego's specific response of falling to pieces or splitting itself, may be extremely important in all schizophrenic processes' (Klein 1946/1997, p. 5).

A diametric splitting process in ego formation is *pre-verbal*. Klein's location of these splitting experiences in early childhood experience, prior to a time when the child's language is developing, brings a consistency with the view of diametric and concentric structures as pre-verbal structures of relation. Moreover, a view of diametric structures of relation, such as splitting, as being part of development of the ego complex generally and not being simply a pathological process, is a perspective echoed by Klein, 'The processes of splitting off parts of the self and projecting them into objects are thus of vital importance for normal development, as well as for abnormal object-relations' (Klein 1946/1997, p. 9).

While, for Klein, the diametric splitting process may be expressed through 'objects', such as the infant's internalization of the mother's breast, the diametric relation is not just to objects but also to the infant's own relation to its ego. Diametric splitting of objects brings a diametric splitting of the ego which, if 'excessive' (Klein 1946/1997, p. 11), is viewed as leading to at least some forms of schizophrenia. Klein states, 'If states of splitting and therefore of disintegration, which the ego is unable to overcome, occur too frequently and go on for too long, then in my view they must be regarded as a sign of schizophrenia' (Klein 1946/1997, p. 10). This diametric splitting process can take place as an experience of the relation of the ego to itself in time. Time becomes fractured into diametric spatial splits in experience.

The trauma of loss of continuity, through bringing a diametric mode of assumed separation to experience in time, also resonates with subsequent accounts in developmental psychology. These include including Laing's conception of early ontological insecurity, Bowlby's insecurity of attachment in the early years, as well as Winnicott (1967):

> Trauma implies that the baby has experienced a break in life's continuity, so that primitive defences now become organized to defend against a repetition of 'unthinkable anxiety' or a return of the acute confusional state that belongs to disintegration of

> nascent ego structure. Madness here simply means a break-up of whatever may exist at the time of a personal continuity of existence. (p. 97)

Klein, as with Laing, emphasizes the appalling feeling in psychosis that 'everything seems to be dead' (1946/1997, p. 21). There is an assumed separation from life, in what Bollas (1999) describes as the 'false or mutant self' (p. 101). Klein gives a further account of this radical disconnection, 'Patients with schizoid features may say: "I hear what you are saying. You may be right, but it has no meaning for me". Or again they say they feel they are not there. The expression, "no meaning" in such cases does not imply an active rejection of the interpretation but suggests that parts of the personality and of the emotions are split off' (Klein 1946/1997, p. 19). Jung (1907) observes a 'characteristic lack of *emotional rapport*' (p. 74), while Laing (1959) reiterates, '... the schizoid individual depersonalises his relationship with himself. That is to say, he turns the living spontaneity of his being into something dead and lifeless by inspecting it. This he does to others, as well, and fears their doing it to him' (p. 112).

Eigen's (1986) conclusion from his clinical observations implicitly echoes Klein's and Laing's accounts:

> For the psychotic individual, the natural interweaving of self and other may turn into a terrifying sense of dissolution or invasion. Correlatively, the natural division between self and other may become a desparate walling-off process ... boundaries between aspects of the self (e.g., between and within mental ego and body ego) break down and become rigid in highly distorting ways. It is as if mental space itself undergoes a serious deformation, so that whatever appears in such 'space' is affected by shifts in the deformed space. (pp. 32–3)

The fragmentation of the contents of experience is through the structure of the background space. However, it is better conceived not in Cartesian terms of a 'mental' space but more broadly as a psychic space or structure of relation in a spatial-phenomenological sense. The splits in the background space are that of a diametric process bringing increased assumed separation within dimensions of experience. The dominion of diametricity stays alive and kicking.

6.2 Uncovering the second entailment of the relative differences between concentric and diametric spaces: Mirror image inverted symmetry of diametric projection in experience of psychosis

Laing (1959) refers to 'the basic defence ... in every form of psychosis' as 'the denial of being as a means of preserving being'; in other words, 'The schizophrenic feels he has killed his "self" and this appears to be in order to avoid being killed. He is dead, in order to remain alive' (pp. 149–50). The underlying phenomenological structure is of diametric opposition between being active and passive – as well as between life and death – where one pole is a mirror image of the other.

The diametric structured active/passive symmetry in schizophrenic experience is also highlighted by Laing (1959), in passages such as the following, which rely on intuition as much as his observations from dialogue, 'at some point those very dangers most dreaded can themselves be encompassed to forestall their actual occurrence ... To turn oneself into a stone becomes a way of not being turned into a stone by someone else' (p. 51). The inverted likeness underlying compensatory opposition is described in his discussion of 'Peter': 'From his earliest days he had been haunted by the sense of being nobody ... Yet at the same time he felt he was someone with very special, with a special mission ...' (Laing 1959, p. 133).

Eigen (1986) treats such megalomania, combined with self-deflation, as central to Freud and Jung's perspectives on schizophrenic experience:

> Both Freud and Jung took megalomania as their key phenomenological entrée to the psychology of psychosis. It is most impressive to witness human beings who believe they are God or who see devils and still more shocking to discover and begin to come to grips with just how inflated one is in one's secret (or not so secret) self. Jung detailed the oscillations in psychosis between inflation and deflation, since megalomania and the severest self-depreciation always go together. (p. 54)

Eigen (1986) highlights the diametric inversions underlying psychosis:

> The same basic polarity Jung described in his work with schizophrenics, the swing from self as god to worm, provides the core material of therapeutic work. One can see in this sado-masochism (Freud), inferiority-superiority or power complexes (Adler), top-dog-little-dog (Perls), and so on. However, all of these are made more forceful by drawing on an underlying sense of divinity or diabolism. (p. 83)

There is a need, however, to distinguish oscillation between opposing diametric poles in the inverted symmetry of obsessional neurosis, from the diametric polarity of inverted poles in psychotic states. The question arises as to what is different in the inverted symmetry of schizoid experience compared with obsessional neurosis, while also recognizing significant relation between both.[2] Inversion of opposites in obsessional neurosis is *within* a diametric structure of ego experiential relation. In contrast, for psychosis, the diametric opposition is also *between* concentric experience and diametric structured ego experience. In psychosis, the diametric ego structure seeks dominion over the concentric dimension; the diametric ego process eats into and begins to overwhelm the concentric process of experiencing.

Contrasting modes of experience include an attempted ego-transcendent concentric relation and a corruption into what may be experienced as a 'devil-like' state of 'sinning' against the soul through entering the diametric ego level of experience. A key task in psychosis is to reorientate the diametric oppositional split between concentric and diametric experience into a concentric background relation of assumed connection and interaction between both. This is not to rule out dimensions common with obsessional neurosis as also occurring on top of this prior background split, so that inverted symmetry also occurs within the ego oppositions.

Eigen (1986) emphasizes the pervasiveness of reversals, in other words diametric structured inverted symmetry, in psychosis:

2 See also, longitudinal studies in psychiatry which have found that adolescent males with neurotic disorders are more likely to develop schizophrenia years later (Weiser et al, 2001), and that neuroticism increases the risk for subsequent onset of psychotic symptoms (Krabbendam et al, 2002). For a review suggesting that neurosis frequently contributes to the subsequent development of psychotic symptoms, see Freeman & Garety (2003).

> The movement from destruction to stability is but one of a series of reversals at work in psychosis. Self-other and mental self-body self provide endless material for the work of reversal. Freud noted that reversal is an elementary operation of the mind, one of the earliest defenses, *perhaps preceding defenses*. In particular, he called attention to reversals of subject-object (turning against the self, turning against the object) and reversals of affect (love turning into hate into love into hate). (p. 216, my italics)

The diametric relation in psychosis occurs not merely at the level of defences within the diametric structured ego but also at a prior level, namely, the imposition of a diametric relation itself between the diametric ego and concentric dimension. This places a rigidly diametric background of non-relation between diametric and concentric structures of experience. Eigen (1986) aptly invokes a concern with space and time, 'In psychosis, reversal may spin everything out of existence or bring life to a standstill ... The space and time we take for granted falls away or was never properly constituted' (p. 217). The assumed connection underlying concentric structured experience falls away or is never properly constituted in psychosis. The taken for granted concentric spatial mode of experiential relation is undermined.

For Klein (1946), 'object-relations exist from the beginning of life, the first object being the mother's breast which to the child becomes split into a good (gratifying) and bad (frustrating) breast; this splitting results in a severance of love and hate' (Klein 1946/1997, p. 2). Klein is somewhat one-sided in ignoring connective, life-giving, concentric dimensions to early childhood experience and in postulation of a synthesized (yet basically diametric) ego developed from birth. Her examination of projections is most pertinent for psychosis. This projected diametric division between a good and bad breast involves not simply a splitting process, but also an inverted symmetry between opposing poles of good and bad, of idealization and persecution, 'Idealization is bound up with the splitting of the object, for the good aspects of the breast are exaggerated as a safeguard against the fear of the persecutory breast ... idealization is thus the corollary of persecutory fear' (Klein 1946/1997, p. 7). Klein's (1946) diametric structured framework is not only of 'good' and 'bad' breast but also relies on the diametric space of assumed separation underlying the subject-object dualism to characterize the breast as an 'object'. Acceptance of this framework does not preclude acceptance also of a potential concentric mode of assumed connection to the primary caregiver. This would resonate with Winnicott's (1971) concerns, noted earlier, for a mode of experience prior to the differentiation between 'me' and 'not me' in early childhood, and as an aspect of secure attachment.

Eigen's (1986) account of a man hospitalized in his early twenties for four months, due to a psychotic breakdown, is a vivid example of this diametric structure of inverted symmetry between opposing poles in schizophrenic phenomenology:

> Carl loved God, but was horrified at his demands. If he followed God's voice he would die. If he followed the devil he would go to hell. Both threw him into panic, doubt, and resistance. He did not want to believe he saw devils, nor did he want to believe he heard God. He searched for some way out, trying to find some way to discount the claims made on him. But the claims were being made and these presences possessed a power and vividness that nothing else could compete with … He went back and forth between God and the devil's way, caught in a steady state of vacillation. (p. 94)

Being horrified at God's demands suggests that the voice of 'God' was from beyond Carl's immediate ego level will.

While in hospital, Carl 'saw my own I falling apart in front of me. My ego was breaking into so many fragments. The breaking went on and on until little was left but crushed powder in blackness' (Eigen 1986, p. 95). The vacillation between 'God' and 'the devil' threatens the ego, in contrast to obsessional neurosis, where the diametric mirror image helps reinforce the ego. Eigen (1986) continues:

> he heard the devil in God's voice, and saw both his father, himself and much more in the devil. The idea that not God, but the devil had been speaking to him from the inside, as well as impinging on him from the outside, led to the profound awareness of just how godless he had become and how easy it was to misjudge spirits. In time he had to confess to himself that he was not capable of telling God from the devil or either from his father or his own ego. The voices and visions he heard and saw were complex amalgams of all of these and much else as well. (p. 95)

The basic shift in structure of experience occurring here is that from a diametric relation of inverted symmetry and assumed separation between God and the devil, to a *yin/yang* type of structure of experience, where the devil is contained in God and God is contained in the devil. In other words, *concentric relations begin to emerge within the diametric frame of the God-devil opposition*. The shift is that there is no longer simply a diametric split between the attempted ego-transcendent, concentric self structured experience of 'God' and diametric compression of ego experience into the 'devil'. Experience is no longer a confinement within the restricted spaces of the diametric mirror image structures.

Two of the reversals expressing inverted symmetry of diametric opposition in Freud's (1911/2002) Schreber case of psychosis[3] are also arguably largely consistent with obsessional neurosis. These reversals can be viewed as operating largely within the diametric ego structure itself, rather than beyond the ego. These inverted symmetries are in Freud's (1911/2002) words, 'Before he was inclined towards sexual asceticism and was a doubter with respect to God, while after the illness had taken its course, he became a believer in God and devoted to voluptuousness' (p. 21):

> the tone of the emotion turned into its opposite; the individual now hated and feared as a result of his persecution was once loved and admired. The persecution established by the delusion serves above all to justify the patient's emotional transformation ... his attitude towards him has in the meantime *diametrically* changed. (p. 32) (my italics)

This second example of inverted symmetry is an example of *both* Klein's (1946, 1948) persecutory and depressive anxiety, a distinction which she recognizes as not being clearcut. For Klein, persecutory anxiety relates predominantly to the annihilation of the ego, while depressive anxiety concerns the damage done to internal and external loved objects by the subject's destructive impulses. Klein's distinction also has relevance for distinguishing the role of diametric projection in obsessional neurosis and psychosis. Modes of experience which go beyond the ego,[4] threaten and/or

3 Freud's Schreber case is based on Schreber's writings rather than on Freud's direct engagement with him.

4 Jung (1907) emphasizes *dementia praecox* (the name coined by Kraepelin, for what was subsequently termed schizophrenia, by Bleuler) as involving processes outside the dominion of the ego, 'The ego-complex is ... no longer the whole of the personality; side by side with it there exists another being, living its own life and hindering and

defy the ego and which contribute to a diametric split between ego experience and a concentric mode of relation enter the realm of psychosis. Those inverted symmetries which tend to focus on internal or external objects (e.g., the father in the *Wolf Man*, the wooden reel of Ernst) are already within the diametric framed experience of the subject-object dualism; they are not yet reaching the level of concentric structured experience beyond the ego. Thus, more is needed for them to operate beyond the realm of obsessional neurosis.

This difference in the *function* of the diametric relation of inverted symmetry is important in distinguishing the diametric inversion of psychosis from that of obsessional neurosis. The function of the diametric structure in obsessional neurosis is to *preserve* the ego, whereas in psychosis this function is itself reversed and the diametric structure serves to *annihilate* the ego. In other words, at a background level a further diametric structured reversal occurs between obsessional neurosis and psychosis – a reversal of the very function underpinning the diametric spatial structural organization. In response to the failure of concentric structured experience to emerge in a stable fashion, the reactive diametric structures of inverted symmetry in psychosis serve the function of seeking to threaten or destroy the diametric ego. The diametric process begins to further split the ego itself. In contrast, the diametric inverted symmetries of obsessional neurosis provide the function of maintaining the diametric ego. Diametric structured inversion is involved in internalized objects in neurosis to preserve the integration of the ego.[5]

---

disturbing the development of the ego-complex, for the symptomatic actions often take up a good deal of time and energy at its expense' (p. 47). Further referring to 'the ego-complex and the autonomous complex' (p. 64) in schizophrenia, 'the complex occupies a relatively independent position in regard to the ego-complex – a vassal that will not give unqualified allegiance to its rule' (p. 45), Jung (1907) goes on to state: 'But if the complex remains entirely unchanged, which naturally happens only when there is very severe damage to the ego-complex and its functions, then we must speak of *dementia praecox*' (p. 68).

5 Recognition of this process serves to provide a bridge to the different mirror image conception of Lacan (1949). This link is to the extent that a function of Lacan's mirror image is to provide the individual with relief from the intensity of fragmenting

The functions themselves of the respective diametric inversions in psychosis and neurosis are in a diametric oppositional relation to each other, though this does not mean that one cannot be transformed over time into its opposing other. Both reversals are as defensive modes a withdrawal into an increasingly more restrictive spatial structure underlying and governing experience. Diametric structures of mirror image reversals provide a corralling of flows of energy. A danger implied by Freud's neglected spatial system is that experience and the unconscious become colonized by repressive diametric spatial structural projections. The respective functions of the diametric inverted symmetries in psychosis and obsessional neurosis are mirror images of each other.

Another example of a series of diametric structured reversals, described by Freud in the Schreber case, is the 'combination of reverential subordination and rebellious resistance ... found in Schreber's relationship to his God' (p. 40). This chain of reversals includes Judge Schreber as being on a mission from God as redeemer of the world, God becoming a persecutor and Schreber mocking God. It is significant that Freud accepted that the diametric structured inverted symmetry underlying Schreber's megalomania was secondary to his primary experience of transformation into a female:

> He takes himself to be called to redeem the world and to restore to it its lost bliss. But he can only do this if he has first transformed himself from a man to a woman ... The essential prerequisite of his mission of salvation was his transformation into a woman. This is not to say that he wished to be thus transformed; it was rather a case of an imperative, grounded in the World Order, which he could ill escape, even if he would personally much rather have remained in his honourable masculine station in life ... the transformation into a woman (emasculation) was the primary delusion, which was at first adjudged to be an act of grievous impairment and persecution and came to be related to the role of Redeemer only on a secondary level. (Freud 1911/2002, pp. 9–11)

---

internal impulses through the boundedness and apparent stability of the mirror image, even though that image is a specious one involving, for Lacan, a deception of the individual through investment in a spectral image. For Lacan, the mirror image is a kind of substitute formation to bring a binary coherence to potentially fragmented elements of the ego.

This primary experience is prior to his ego will. It invites restructuring away from diametric splits between male and female experience, so that female experience can be contained within the experience of the male in concentric fashion (or the male within the female). This experience of transformation into a woman threatened the diametric spatial structure of Schreber's defences. Schreber's failure to develop a concentric relation between his diametric structured ego experience and a potentially transformative feminine dimension was an incapacity to integrate ego and beyond ego levels of experience – and involved a displacement away from concentric structured experience.

Encrustation of experience within a diametric spatial process and this marginalization of concentric spatial experience took the forms of a series of reversals and splits into heightened diametric ego experience (see also Freud 1911/2002, p. 39, on Schreber's splits into 'upper' and 'lower' God, and 'upper' and 'middle' Flechsig). The diametric structure of megalomania was reactive to the primary experience of a quest for concentric mode of experience. The failure to establish a concentric mediating state beyond the ego is a key feature of schizophrenic experience. Without this concentric structured mode of experience, the ego becomes dangerously split in psychosis, whereas a rigid diametric structure of experience in obsessional neurosis tends to solidify and constitute the ego.

A diametric structural level for projection in psychosis is complementary to a content level of projection often focused upon by Freud for schizophrenia. Freud (1894) refers to 'hallucinatory' defences (pp. 58–60) where the 'flight into psychosis' occurs as the ego is unable to reject both the incompatible sexual idea and its accompanying libidinal affect, without also rejecting a substantial part of reality. Offering another projection of content level, Freud (1896, pp. 184–5) suggests that paranoia entails projection of the incompatible idea onto the external world, thereby giving rise to the sense of persecution, delusions and accentuated distrust of other people.

What emerges here from these phenomenological accounts is not only two levels of diametric spatial structured experience (in obsessional neurosis and psychosis) in the unconscious; a clear implication is that a consistent chain or system of diametric structured spatial relations pervades the unconscious. It is evident that diametric spatial features are inextricably entwined with repressed, reactive to trauma, features of the unconscious as a system. The variable life histories' causal effects produce a system level response in the unconscious of a diametric structured spatial background for experience in both obsessional neurosis and psychosis, though with different functions for each diametric process.

The danger is that experience becomes colonized by diametric spatial structural projections. Freud recognizes that these diametric structured reversals are problematic and in need of working through for change. Diametric spatial relations are a structure and a dynamic process within the unconscious as a system. Moreover, these diametric relations are a feature of diverse cultures in their myths and social structures. There is an obvious need for research to examine clinical experience from diverse cultures regarding the prevalence of this diametric structured experience of mirror image symmetry.

6.3 Uncovering the third entailment of the relative differences between concentric and diametric spaces: Foreground-background interaction and non-interaction in experience of psychosis

In phenomenological accounts of psychosis, the extreme attempts at detachment from the body and interpersonal communication are paralleled by an exaggerated attempt at detachment from the background 'landscape' for fear of merging with it. Non-interaction between foreground and background is a feature of diametric more than concentric spatial structures. Yet the interaction of concentric structures with their background needs to be distinguished from a fear of fusion with or drowning in the background stimuli. The phenomenology of a boundary-less interaction with the background and need for strategies to cope with this interaction for schizoid experience, is highlighted by Laing (1959). He describes a patient's 'magical camouflage to help her over her anxiety', when she was twelve years old:

> It struck me that if I stared long enough at the environment that I would blend with it and disappear just as if the place was empty and I had disappeared. It is as if you get yourself to feel you don't know who you are or where you are. To blend into the scenery so to speak. Then you are scared of it because it begins to come on without encouragement. I would just be walking along and felt that I had blended with the landscape. Then I would get frightened and repeat my name over and over again to bring me back to life, so to speak. (Laing 1959, p. 110)

Laing comments that, 'selfconsciousness comes to be relied upon to help sustain the individual's precarious ontological security' (p. 112). This view can be seen to gain sustenance also from Freud's (1911/2002) account of Schreber's 'compulsion to think' to avoid God's withdrawal (p. 44), as well as from other examples.[6] The person's name is one path to construct a diametric spatial identity which separates the person from the 'landscape' or background. Selfconsciousness helps to keep her separate from the background environment, 'Our little girl blended with the landscape. Now, someone who only too easily blends with other people ... and is frightened of losing his identity thereby, uses his awareness of his self as a means of remaining detached and aloof' (Laing 1959, p. 112).

A willed selfconsciousness or detachment from the background is her reactive strategy of diametric projection to the terror of engulfment by background stimuli. She is unable to obtain a middle state of assumed connection to the background, while still being distinct from the background 'landscape'. Her inability to maintain a concentric structured mode of relation to self and background forces the strategy of exaggerated, willed diametric separation from the background. The schizophrenic state requires an extreme reaction against being merged with the background; this reaction

6 Jung (1907, p. 87) also highlights 'compulsive thinking' in schizophrenia, while Laing (1959, p. 109) also offers another example of schizophrenic fear of engulfment by background stimuli, provided by Dooley (1941), 'One of her patients said: "I forgot myself at the Ice Carnival the other night. I was so absorbed in looking at it that I forgot what time it was and who and where I was. When I suddenly realized I hadn't been thinking about myself I was frightened to death. The unreality feeling came. I must never forget for a single minute. I watch the clock and keep busy, or else I won't know who I am."'

is through construction of a detached diametric ego, spliced away from the background.

A further pertinent example of the ambivalent relation to separation from background is given, in Laing's (1959) words, 'There is something final and definitive about an act ... [which a person with schizophrenia] regards with suspicion. Action is the dead end of possibility. It scleroses freedom. If it cannot be utterly eschewed, then every act must be of such an equivocal nature that the "self" can never be trapped in it' (p. 87). Action places a clear separation from the background multiplicity of possibility and carves out a distinct structure on a different plane of reality from possibility. The pervasive problem is the lack of a concentric mediating state relating with the background, so as to facilitate movement to and from a diametric relation to the background. The experiential flexibility is lost.

The failure to furnish a concentric structured state mediating between a diametric spatial mode of being and the background environment is most clearly articulated in the following account, by Laing (1959), regarding 'James':

> when walking on a summer evening in the park alone, watching the couples making love, he suddenly began to feel a tremendous oneness with the whole world, with the sky and trees and flowers and grass – with the lovers too. He ran home in panic and immersed himself in his books. He told himself that he had no right to this experience, but more than that, he was terrified at the threatened loss of identity involved in this merging and fusion of his self with the whole world. *He knew of no halfway stage between radical isolation in selfabsorbtion or complete absorbtion into all there was.* He was afraid of being absorbed into nature, engulfed by her, with irrevocable loss of his self; yet what he most dreaded, that also he most longed for. (p. 91, my italics)

The halfway stage between an identity of horizonless monism and a diametric detached relation of self is a concentric mode of relation. What he dreads is what he also longs for; again, it is evident that this is an inverted likeness expressing diametric structures. The diametric opposition between a connection with the background wholeness and identity of a detached self is further expressed, in Laing's (1959) words, 'His longing is for complete union. But of this very longing he is terrified, because it will be the end of his self ... He does not conceive of a dialectical relationship' (p. 92).

He lacks a transitional mode of being of concentric structured experience, where connection includes difference.

Eigen (1986) further illustrates fusion with the background flood of stimuli, for an individual experiencing psychosis, 'Things raced, leaped out at me. It was as if I were being attacked by the sight and sound of things. There was a heightening of everything, a glistening, a landslide. Things went faster and faster and angles were sharper … It all had this incredible speed yet was so endless. Not that there wasn't any time. It's just that time stood still it went so fast' (pp. 125–6). This extreme is of attempted connection with background stimuli and consequent invasion by this background. In this experience, the person has moved out of diametric structured experience but his/her concentric structured experience is insufficiently established as a mode of relation with the background stimuli.

Eigen (1986) describes a contrasting state of 'mindlessness' in psychosis:

> I felt I was under water. Things were thick, heavy, in slow motion. It was like yawning and stretching for a long time but it didn't feel good … At first I tried to shake the numbness off but it spread through me and took me over. I was like a lizard without feeling. I knew it was a protection and would go away. But it didn't. I was paralyzed … My eyes closed for long periods and I saw dark masses, black, amorphous clouds. I felt them with my eyes open. A nowhere forever. I remember thinking, 'I'm going away'. Now I think I tried to vanish and couldn't quite make it – yet came very close. (p. 126)

This passage illuminates the experience of the insulation of diametric structured experience from its background stimuli. A mode of disconnective relation occurs which seals off the individual from external background stimulation. The person retreats in the extreme into their 'box', while threat to this boxed mode of existence opens up a Pandora's box of defences. The lubrication of experiential movement is lost with the demise of concentric spatial relation.

Decathexis, namely, withdrawal of energy from or loss of interest in objects, is described by Eigen (1986) as 'perhaps the most formidable of all defenses Freud described' (p. 104). It this background filtering of interaction in withdrawal of cathexis 'sent out by the ego' (p. 153), as a detachment from external world stimuli, that Freud (1924) associates in particular with psychosis. Eigen (1986) succinctly portrays Freud's (1914; 1926) decathexis in psychosis:

> Freud noted that this withdrawal is accompanied by an increased cathexis of the ego, expressed in megalomania. Thus, the energy that is withdrawn from objects is invested in the ego … He subsequently realized that decathexis may be more extreme, and that psychic energy may be withdrawn from all life feeling, including the I-feeling. The psyche may so deplete and collapse into itself that it approximates a 'return' to an inorganic (insensate) state. Freud depicts this as a death wish, a dying-out of investment. As long as one is in life and desirous, one is in danger of and vulnerable to pain. Absolute decathexis is absolute painlessness, which, in phenomenological terms, represents a loss of vitality and affective coloring, a self-deadening, a dropping out of psychological and possibly even biological existence. (p. 105)

Movement from the diametric relation of severance from background stimuli in the zero state mindlessness is to the other extreme of immersion in a sea of stimuli over which the individual has no control. The individual has not yet established a concentric mode of relation, namely, a locus of experience which allows for engagement and relation with the background stimuli, without fusion and drowning in them. Without the concentric mediating state to interact with the background, a fundamental defence of a closed diametric state splitting from background stimuli occurs, what Eigen (1986) describes as 'mindlessness'. The person's experience turns to an extreme of stone in its assumed separation from others and from background stimuli. Experience is literally petrified.

Eigen's account of mindlessness in psychosis as a diametric split from background stimuli resonates with Laing's (1959) account of schizoid experience as including implosion into a vacuum, 'This shut up self,[7] being isolated, is unable to be enriched by outer experience and so the whole inner world comes to be more and more impoverished, until the individual may come to feel he is merely a vacuum' (p. 75). He or she hates, envies or attacks a sense of aliveness or complexity of experience, in order to mini-

7 See also, Jung (1907) on 'negativism' in *dementia praecox* including where 'the negativistic catatonic shuts himself up completely, so that for the moment at least there is no means of penetration' (p. 89).

mize the pain of feeling. Laing and Esterson (1970) describe 'Claire' who was 'usually listless: she appeared to be empty' (p. 61), while for 'Maya', 'change disturbed her precarious sense of identity "I don't know how to deal with the unexpected. That's why I like things neat and tidy. Nothing unexpected can happen then"' (p. 29). In mindlessness, diametric structured experience severs from the animation of relation to background stimuli; the complexity of the dynamic background is frozen into a deanimation.

This diametric structured mindlessness is what Green would term 'blank psychosis' (Donnet & Green 1973). Green (1999) highlights the direct relation between the lack of foreground-background interaction, inverted symmetry and assumed separation in blank psychosis; this provides further implicit support for a unified underlying structure of diametric relation to psychosis, 'in "blank psychosis" I described a triangular situation in which, in fact, instead of having a father and mother, we have two objects: the omnipotent malevolent one, and the weak benevolent one. So it is one split in two.' (p. 54).

Eigen (1986) implies that hallucination and mindlessness are diametric mirror image inversions of each other, 'In the most severe cases, hallucination and mindlessness may seem to intersect as the subject approaches zero. It would appear, though, that when there is not even enough energy for hallucination, the subject collapses into an obliterating and final mindlessness' (p. 125). Eigen (1986) further explicates this diametric inversion:

> hallucinatory activity can be used as a defense against a deeper mindless moment. Rena's restless rotation of imagery kept her confused, but alive ... Her psychosis took the image-filled form it did, precisely because she was so afraid of losing her mind. In a sense, hallucinatory agitation was a madness that defended against a more profound madness, one loss that warded off another ... It was something rather than nothing, a leap or fall into another level of existence. The very act of hallucinating made her stand out from life. (p. 307)

Blankness of disconnection from background stimuli, mirror image symmetry exemplified through malevolence/benevolence, as well as omnipotence/weakness, are immersed in a common structure of experiential relation with that of the assumed separation of splitting. Eigen (1986) characterizes inversions as extremes of chaotic fusion with background and a sealed compartmentalized state of diametric relation, which empties from background interaction:

> I do not believe the issue of whether chaos or emptiness is more basic is resolvable. I suspect that assertion of primacy is a matter of temperament. Emptiness refers to a passive aspect of human experience, chaos to 'mindless' activity. Either may be vividly life-enhancing or deadening. One moves back and forth between chaos and emptiness, between more or less activity and passivity. (p. 129)

The schizophrenic failure to trust in concentric structured experience, or lack of development of concentric structured experience in early childhood, leaves him/her without the experiential resources to adopt a strategy beyond extremity of a) a horizonless monism with the background stimuli or b) excessive diametric split and withdrawal from background. The locus of schizophrenic experience drowns in a background swamp or suffers the desiccation of extreme diametric relation.

Laing (1959) cites Boss' (1957) account of a dream heralding psychosis, where the dreamer being engulfed by fire highlights the loss of concentric structured experience through the extinguishing of the concentric structured fire:

> A woman of hardly thirty years dreamt at a time when she still felt completely healthy, that she was afire in the stables. Around her, the fire, an ever larger crust of lava was forming. *Half from the outside and half from the inside her own body could see how the fire was slowly becoming choked by this crust.* Suddenly she was *entirely outside this fire* and as if possessed beat the fire with a club *to break the crust and to let some air in*. But the dreamer soon got tired and slowly she (the fire) became extinguished. Four days after the dream she began to suffer from acute schizophrenia. In the details of the dream the dreamer had exactly predicted the special course of her psychosis. She became rigid at first and in effect encysted. Six weeks afterwards she defended herself once more with all her might against the choking of her life's fire, until finally she became completely extinguished both spiritually and mentally. Now for some years, she has been like a burnt out crater. (p. 162, my italics)

The diametric projection of being half-outside and half-inside the concentric structured fire was part of the process of encrustation. As the diametric relation to the fire reached a level of assumed separation from the concentric fire, the woman tried to break through the crust; she tried to break through the diametric structural split from the background fire. The sealed mode of relation from background in diametric structures brought the crust of solidity through which she tried to desperately penetrate but to no avail. The diametric structure had gained dominion over, engulfed and extinguished the concentric fire. The concentric self of the fire was forced into a diametric relation to the person's bodily ego. The diametric background split between concentric space and ego, fire and body, was expressed through the solidified crust and was pivotal to the dream-phenomenology of the psychosis.

It bears reiteration that this uncovering of diametric and concentric spatial structures of the unconscious, underlying obsessional neurosis, early childhood projections and attachment, and psychosis, is not a reification of the experiential fire of the heart's primordial structures. It is to challenge the encrusted or rusted bars of diametricity, to bring change and growth in experience. Only through excavation of the rusted bars through the spaces of the heart is it possible to engage in movement from disengaged, diametric splits in experience.

A common spatial discourse of the unconscious has been seen to be at play, both for early childhood spatial projections in attachment styles and transitional objects, and for later experiences of obsessional neuroses and psychosis. Causal inferences of continuity of such projected structures from early childhood to adolescence or adulthood assume a basic stability in the projected space rather than an interactive dynamic potential for experience. A potential dynamism would bring movement from, for example, predominantly diametric spatial structures of experience towards concentric spatial structures. More than a questioning that simply seeks to 'prove' these stabilities of projected structures across linear temporal dimensions in the lifespan, a spatial-phenomenological questioning would examine how the shifts from diametric to concentric spatial structures of experience can be promoted and facilitated at various different system levels, both for the individual and wider contexts. It would also question the desirability and dangers of such shifts in certain contexts.

The existence of the primordial spatial structures in a given context is a somewhat different question from the meaning or significance of these structures for that context. The early childhood attachment context is one where the desirability of concentric spatial relations as secure attachment and the undesirability of diametric structured spatial relations as insecure attachments is evident. An interplay between both primordial experiential spaces is a capacity that is less desirable in childhood than it may become in adulthood. It is less obvious whether the movements from diametric structured defences in obsessional neurosis and psychosis, and towards concentric structured openings for experience, is always desirable for a person's life situation. Gilligan's later work has, as already seen, emphasized the loss of such concentric structured experience of assumed connection in adolescent girls. Gilligan's narrative resonates with a view of loss of concentric fire bringing the soot of diametricity for a more opaque, repressed experiential disconnection and withdrawal.

The discourse concerning diametric and concentric spaces provides a key reference point for understanding fundamental intrapsychic movements and growth, as maps for experiential change. A further step is required here concerning the question of the desirability of movement from diametric to concentric spatial structures. This step needs to interrogate the background dimension of the relation *itself* between concentric and diametric spatial projections. The relation itself has already been highlighted as a key distinguishing factor between a spatial-phenomenology of psychosis, compared with obsessional neurosis. It is this background relation to the foreground projections of concentric and diametric structures that enters the territory of Freud's incomplete and much maligned, life and death drives. Is this background relation itself comprehensible in terms of concentric and diametric spaces?

Until this point, all of the excavation of concentric and diametric projected structures have operated largely within an assumption of a self-contained individual human subject. This assumption comes into question in the next investigations of these primordial spatial structures – for Freud's life and death drives, Jung's collective unconscious, Derrida's movement beyond what he portrays as Freud's logocentric repression, and Heidegger's ontological structures of being. In doing so, these offer bridges not so much to postmodern concerns but to what can be characterized as a primordial spatial-phenomenology beyond structuralism.

6.4 A spatial-phenomenological reinterpretation of Freud's *Eros* and *Thanathos*

The need to excavate a background spatial domain

It has been argued that a consistent chain or system of diametric and concentric space pervades the unconscious world. Until now a diametric and concentric spatial system of relations has been seen to operate at the level of individual intrapsychic and interpersonal experience, whether pertaining to obsessional neurosis, early childhood projections or psychosis. Yet this framework, confined to the contours of the individual psychoanalytic subject, is an anthropocentric one. A more primordial truth search is required to explore the background dimensions themselves to diametric and concentric spaces. These background dimensions have been touched upon, specifically for the phenomenology of psychosis, regarding the mode of relation that occurs *between* diametric and concentric spatial projections. Exploration of this background relation is facilitated by later Freud's search for background life and death drives, in a movement beyond anthropocentrism, for an understanding of the unconscious.

A spatial-phenomenological reinterpretation of Freud's life and death drives needs to make explicit that this background domain is, even on Freud's own terms, precausal, prelinguistic and prior to his id-ego-superego structure for the unconscious. That this is clearly so, for Freud, has tended to be lost from view through the glosses on the life and death drives supplied by some commentators. This spatial-phenomenological reinterpretation of *Eros* and *Thanathos* builds on the analysis of diametric spatial projections already observed for obsessional neurosis and psychosis, with regard to key features of Freud's death drive, namely, a) the Nirvana principle of not merely tension reduction but ultimately of elimination of tension, combined with the compulsion to repeat, and b) a drive to destruction as an active process. Further uncovering of these diametric spatial dimensions requires discussion of the relation between concentric spatial projections and a life drive – a life drive much less explicated by Freud than his death drive.

The need for a prior background to diametric and concentric spatial projections also arises from an implication of the uncovering of concentric and diametric projections in early childhood attachment, whereby secure attachment is a concentric projection of assumed connection and insecure attachment (in its various manifestations) is a diametric projection. At this level of early childhood experience, the diametric spaces of insecure attachment are directly understood as being as a lack of concentric spaces of secure attachment. They arise as an absence of concentric relation, as a *privatio boni*. At this level of early childhood projections, diametric spatial structures appear not so much as an originary structure nor as an active drive, but more as a reactive structure to historically malleable external circumstances and relationships. A prior background is needed if diametric spatial structures, especially, are to be interpreted as being primordial as active processes. Additionally this background is implicated if both concentric and diametric structures are to go beyond simply an anthropocentric perspective, to be primordial spaces for life and death. Identification of this proposed prior background to concentric and diametric spaces is also important for distinguishing how diametric spatial structures are necessary as part of ego development, and yet can also be an aspect of a death drive.

It is being argued here that diametric space is intimately linked with the death drive, especially the dynamic process dimensions to diametricity, in contradistinction from its static, positional structural dimensions. With regard to the life drive, it is being argued that it is consistent with concentric spatial projections, once some clarifications to Freud's understanding are accommodated.

This background domain for the life and death drives is envisaged by Freud as being prior to his id-ego-superego structure and prior to a causal schema. This is evident from Freud's work, though not always from commentators on his work. Later Freud (1937) explicitly locates a prior source of resistance to recovery, not in the ego, but in 'some alterations of a rhythm in development in psychic life' (1937, p. 242). This alteration renders relatively impotent the distinction between ego and id (1937, p. 241), with Freud (1923) characterizing the id as 'under the domination of the mute but powerful death instincts ... but perhaps that might be to undervalue the part played by *Eros*' (p. 59). The life drive was conceived by Freud, in 1920, as a fusion of sexual and self-preservation instincts.

Eigen (1996) aptly describes this background relation of the death drive as a process prior to the ego and superego, as well as id, 'This alteration characterizes the foundations of psychic life. It cannot be localized, pinned down. It is structural and atmospheric; it taints the very "space" and "air" in which the psyche moves and breathes. It means something more than a deformation of the id or a warp in the instinctual life' (p. 15). This background atmosphere prior to the ego is for Freud a death *drive*, and not simply instinct emanating from the id, despite Sulloway's (1979) view which emphasises the biological influences of Freud and treats the death 'instinct' as 'firmly implanted within the id' (p. 414). Sulloway (1979) argues that it is a 'changed conception of instinct' to a 'directional-historical view' (p. 407). However, Bettelheim (1982) highlights that the term 'instinct' is a mistranslation of Freud's term *Triebe* and that life and death *drive or impulse* is a better translation. Recognition of this facilitates the removal, or at least distancing, of the life and death drive from the biological and instinctual realm.[8] The death drive is not to be reduced simply to the level of biology.

In carving out a background domain for the dual drives, this also bypasses objections to the life and death drive based on assumptions of it as an instinct. An array of such objections have been postulated, redolent of a sort of theoretical shudder (Monzani 1989), even within psychoanalysis itself. These objections include that: the life and death 'instinct' is anachronistic and biologically nonsensical (Storr 1972; Mizen 2003), modelled on inappropriate physicalist analogies (Penrose 1931; Kapp 1931), insufficiently empirically grounded and nebulous in conception (Fromm 1977), or more intemperately, even in moral terms, as being 'gratuitously

8 As Appignanesi & Forrester (2005, pp. 218–19) note, Sabina Spielrein's initial proposal of the life and death drive in 1908 was criticized by Freud as being a biological and insufficiently psychological emphasis. Freud's rejection of biological reductionism in 1935, long after his postulation of the life and death drives, is also evident in Freud's comments on a paper by Carl Muller-Braunschweig, as cited by Appignanesi & Forrester (2005, p. 431), echoing Juliet Mitchell.

desolating' (Midgley 1988, p. 547), 'perverse poetry' and a 'schizoid delusion' (Holbrook 1971, pp. 76–8).

In seeking to move beyond the pleasure principle in 1920, Freud initiated a shift in focus onto a background domain. The contours of this background have been only partially excavated by Freud himself. Sulloway (1979) observes the need for a broader understanding of Freud's life and death drive than as traditional 'mechanistic' (p. 407) instinct, of pleasure as simple tension reduction. This key broadening of Freud's own paradigm, beyond mechanistic causal type explanations, is a significant departure and paves the way for a spatial-phenomenological focus. The dual drives can give rise to a shift of emphasis away from a past primitive temporal background, criticized as being replete with colonial assumptions of the primitive other (Brickman 2003). It invites focus on an ongoing, prelinguistic, *spatial* background tension. This intensified spatial focus for psychoanalysis is not simply reducible to Freud's earlier topographical models but is also conceptually prior to them.

Though a spatial-phenomenological inquiry is an interpretative approach, its concern with the background space of the life and death drives requires a distancing from hermeneutic interpretations of psychoanalysis. The hermeneutic approaches of both Ricoeur (1981) and Habermas (1972) place extreme reliance on the role of language as pivotal to the unconscious. As Grünbaum (1986) rightly recognizes, this reduction of a Freudian unconscious to language, or a language system, is a distortion of the preverbal dimensions to the Freudian unconscious. This preverbal dimension pertains not only to early childhood experience, but also to the life and death drives. Habermas (1972) concentrates on Freud's (1900) dream interpretation, in developing the centrality of a Freudian hermeneutic approach to recovery of the textual meaning of a dream, hidden even from the dreamer. On this view, a depth hermeneutics disturbs everyday language games and causality is conceptualised as a meaning structure (Habermas 1972, p. 272). Yet Habermas (1972) assumes that depth is a displacement from surface, that the private language of psychoanalysis is a distortion and deformation (p. 255) of the fundamental starting point of the public in communication. It neglects how change in time needs to occur in the everyday public discourse of a culture. This is tantamount to a reversal of Freudian priority of depth over surface, and though a largely coherent logical framework, it is a significant distortion of a Freudian vision of the unconscious.[9] Moreover, such a focus on language as such, as distinct from a spatial discourse, is far from an extrapolation from later Freud's dual drives theory.

Language is treated as the pivotal starting point for knowledge construction in hermeneutic rereadings of psychoanalysis and in postmodernism generally. However, the life and death drives are processes assumed by Freud to be prior to and independent of language and language systems. To neglect this point is to cloud the dual drive theory in further obfuscation by the secondary literature. Resonant with Schopenhauer on this theme as with many other issues (Young & Brook 1994), Freud's (1920) interrogation of a teleology underpinning life came to a tentative conclusion that 'the aim of all life is death, and looking backwards, that inanimate things existed before living ones' (p. 38). This form of inertia, which he viewed as inherent in organic life, thereby preceded even mental life and harked back to an earlier ancient state. A significant implication of Freud's *Eros* and *Thanathos* is that the binding and fragmenting aspects, together with their claimed ancient origins prior to human existence, require the conclusion that these are prelinguistic forces or patterns of relation. Caropreso & Simanke (2008) offer a similar argument for the view that the ancient origins of the life drive must, if to be genuinely ancient, precede the historical manifestation of sexual behaviour as a means of reproduction.

While the life and death drives have provided a framework to support Kleinian theory, and more recently Eigen's (1996) clinical experiential

9 Other criticisms of a hermeneutic reworking of Freud's paradigm include Grünbaum's (2006) indictment that a hermeneutic approach offers little innovative predictive power for a psychology of the unconscious, while Wallerstein (1990) views a hermeneutic approach in antithetical terms to a science of psychoanalysis, treating it as a 'cul-de-sac' (p. 6). Alford (1987) highlights that there is no profound and unalterable source of opposition to society within Habermas' (1972) system in his rereading of Freud, while noting that Habermas (1972) ignores early childhood experiences prior to language as he has no category for them. In contrast, a spatial-phenomenological discourse directly reinterprets early childhood projections in spatial terms.

accounts of psychic deadness and psychosis, another avenue for critique of Freud's later work is Foucault's argument that an important dimension to Freud's death drive, sadism, is quite a recent socio-historical construct. Foucault's charge is that, 'Sadism is not a name finally given to a practice as old as Eros; it is a massive cultural fact that appeared precisely at the close of the eighteenth century, constituting one of the great conversions in the Western imagination – unreason transformed into the delirium of the heart' (Foucault, 1972/2006, p. 361).

Acceptance of Foucault's position would undermine the ancient primeval force of a Freudian conception of *Eros* and *Thanathos*. Yet here Foucault misinterprets an important anthropological distinction between linguistic and cognitive categories (as well as between linguistic categories and precognitive experience). Berlin's (1978) comments on ethnobiological classification illuminate this point, 'although a name may be an unambiguous indicator of a category [in a given culture], absence of a label does not necessarily imply absence of a category' (p. 12). The cultural naming of sadism cannot be equated with prior historical, prelinguistic diametric structural inversions concerning power and sexual experience – of mirror image movement from activity-passivity, pleasure-pain, masochism-sadism – associated with the death drive.

The Nirvana principle and the compulsion to repeat

Freud's economic principle regulating the anxiety of traumatic neurosis is a key pillar of his later thought paving the way for his Nirvana principle of zero tension, expressing the death drive. These economic and Nirvana principles are expressions of diametric spatial structures. The economic principle of reducing tension and stimuli to experientially manageable levels is part of a theoretical movement in psychoanalysis which goes beyond the pleasure principle, as a different dimension to unconscious processes. Freud's (1926) economic dimension to the anxiety of traumatic neurosis observed a process of lessened interaction with background stimuli, as a defensive barrier against excessive stimulation.[10] A barrier against external background stimuli is established. The trauma brings an extremity of stimuli that is met with the structural simplification of a reduced emotional apprehension of the world. This diametric structured dimension of an economic, reduced interaction with background stimuli has been highlighted already for Ernst's repeated game of *fort-da* (Freud 1920) and the ritual behaviour of the sexually abused boy's bedtime defences (Freud 1896). The schematizing process of filtering experience is an economic function underlying regulation of emotional experience. This clear narrowing of interaction with external environmental stimuli occurs as part of a schematization process exhibited in Freud's economic principle, that is extended as part of the death drive.

The Nirvana principle is a more extreme version of the economic principle, in its radical sealed disconnection from background stimuli. Such a diametric insulation from background gives expression to Freud's adoption of the Nirvana Principle that is 'entirely in the service of the death instincts ... whose aim is to conduct the restlessness of life into the stability of the inorganic state' (Freud 1924, pp. 159–60). It seeks to reduce to 'nothing' or at least keep 'as low as possible, the sums of excitation which flow in upon it' (Freud 1924, p. 159). This principle of tension reduction and elimination of stimuli to the level of inorganic death placed the Nirvana principle at the centre of his putative death drive. As Caropreso & Simanke (2008) amplify, for Freud (1924), the pleasure principle would only be activated when attached to stimulation arising from the processes of the repetition compulsion. In other words, the Nirvana principle undergoes a

10 Fromm (1942) expands on the implications of such an economic filtering principle regulating emotional experience through his concept of choice as being constrained by a fear of freedom. Another feature of the death drive, as destructive social group processes of masses in identification with a grandiose and aggressive leader (Freud 1921c), is outside the scope of this chapter. Nevertheless, this diametric spatial projection of reduced interaction with background stimuli, in an economic principle giving rise to fear of freedom that brings a vacuum of conformity, is an obvious starting point for spatial-phenomenological interrogation of this dimension of the death drive.

'modification in living organisms through which it has become the pleasure principle' (Freud 1924, p. 160). The sealed disconnection from background stimuli is a diametric structural feature of decathexis bringing movement towards a state of tranquility in the Nirvana principle. Movement out of such diametric structured decathexis invites a need to liven the grief of unbecoming.

The Nirvana principle of movement towards zero tension is viewed by Freud as being modified by the pleasure principle. Thus, there is at least some connection between the death and life drives, given that the pleasure principle is treated by later Freud as being part of a wider life drive. The question thus arises as to what could the diametric spatial process of mirror image inversion and sealed disconnection from background be modified towards? Building on Freud, any spatial structural life drive must be one which interacts with the death drive in some manner, rather than simply serving to replace it. Viewed as a rhythm (Freud 1937), this implies an interplay between a background diametric spatial relation in its dance with another spatial counterpole.

An emptying of animated experience as decathexis and a split from background stimuli has been highlighted already as a diametric spatial, phenomenological feature of psychosis. Eigen (1986) treats this extreme desiccation of schizophrenic 'mindlessness' as an expression of the Nirvana principle in the death drive:

> Whatever the current status of Freud's concept of psychic energy, decathexis, death drive, and his mythic-mechanistic metapsychology, the psychological realities he pointed to are crucial. He attempted to deal with a tendency to numb or deaden oneself by postulating an urge to return to a zero point. In effect, the subject commits a kind of psychological suicide by emptying or denuding experience, by becoming inanimate. More than a return to the womb and primary narcissism, it is an undoing of all psychic aliveness and all that might keep one in existence. (p. 105)

The denuding of experience in the death drive – the decathexis through a sealed disconnection from background stimuli – gives succour to the view that the diametric structured split from its background relation is a product of a diametric process that corresponds to Freud's *Thanathos*. The sealed disconnection from background stimuli is a diametric structured feature of decathexis and the Nirvana principle. Significantly, it is a feature which is shared with the compulsion to repeat, another aspect highlighted by Freud for the death drive.

Freud (1920) hypothesized that the function of repetition compulsion antedated the pleasure principle. The diametric spatial projection underlying repetitive rituals and play has already been observed as involving mirror image inversions and noninteractive withdrawals of energy or cathexis from background environment stimuli. Concentrating attention on the closed system of the game or ritual involves a repetition, characterised by Freud as a compulsion to repeat, which brings a static fixed interaction with the background. Conceiving of the rituals of repetition compulsion, as being prior to the pleasure principle and as an aspect of a background death drive, invites a realm for diametric spatial projections as a discourse prior to the purportedly causal dimensions operative in the pleasure principle.

In carving out a background domain for this postulated death drive, Freud (1920) envisaged it as involving 'an urge inherent in organic life to restore an earlier state of things' (p. 36). This central feature of the death drive, a compulsion to repeat as a conservative drive to return to an inorganic state of the past, is also amenable to a spatial structural view. This occurs where diametric spatial projection is recognised as an inorganic mode of relation through its severance of relation between itself and its background. Envisaged as a structural projection, the diametric space is both a structure and a dynamic process imposing itself upon its environment. Projection is itself a conservative return to a prior state of affairs, namely, to the projected structure itself. Through projection, this diametric spatial structure both repeats itself and engages in a diametric process of turning relations into diametric structures. Diametricity craves return to closure. The diametric process is an attempted return to the origin of the diametric structure; it is a spatial movement towards a static, inorganic diametric structural relation. This movement is under the dominion of diametric structured spatial projections dictating to the unconscious, as an excess within the unconscious system of relations.

The spatial structure of projection can thus be seen to encompass a key feature of the death drive, namely, the compulsion to repeat. In doing so, this highlights how projection needs to become for Freud a primary process, even prior to repression, and not simply reactive and subsequent to repression. This also raises the issue of whether, as a projection, concentric structures are in some ways implicated in a death drive, or at least compulsion to repeat, and not simply as a life drive. It invites exploration of different kinds of death processes as part of experiential life in death and death in life.

An active drive to destruction and two different kinds of death

Destructiveness of self and other has already been partially explored for aspects of neurosis and psychosis concerning diametric structures, especially with regard to splitting and projection of assumed separation. Freud did not equate all destructive behaviour due to aggression as emanating from the death drive. He envisaged that aggression related to frustration and thwarted desire may be due to a conflict between the pleasure and reality principles.

Fromm's (1977) critique of Freud's death 'instinct' questions any necessary link between Freud's Nirvana principle and a tendency to destroy. Fromm (1977) asks, 'But is this slow decrease of life-force the same as destructiveness? ... is there any evidence or even reason for this identity of the tendency to cessation of all excitation and the impulse to destroy?' (pp. 598–9). The diametric structural feature of disconnection of interaction between diametric structures and background stimuli provides a primordial structure to link Freud's Nirvana principle and the compulsion to repeat, as key elements of the death drive. Furthermore, the process of assumed separation underlying diametric structures, i.e., the splitting in diametric relation, gives expression to the impulse to destroy and unites the impulse to destroy with the common primordial structure of diametric space governing the Nirvana Principle and the compulsion to repeat. The diametric structural relation exemplifies the unity of the elements of the death drive, questioned by Fromm (1977).

At the core of Freud's later theory is a preoccupation with spatial structural features of *uniting* and *binding*. This turn within Freud's work towards a spatial concern with interpretation requires a spatial-phenomenological focus. It envisages that the chain of causes identified by Freud exist against a background relation of necessary conditions, including a background spatial condition of diametric structured space. The chain of causes operates within an atmosphere of diametric spatial conditions that may be a malleable structure of relation. Movement from diametric spatial structures and processes would require a counterpole of a different spatial relation associated with *Eros* – a more connective, uniting spatial structure and process. Moreover, change to such background spatial conditions facilitating causal chain relations may serve to remove supporting or necessary conditions for causal relations.

For Freud (1923), 'the main purpose of *Eros*' is 'that of uniting and binding' (p. 45). He continues, 'by bringing about a more and more far reaching combination of the particles into which living substance is dispersed, aims at complicating life and at the same time … at preserving it' (Freud 1923, p. 40). It is important to emphasize that the process of assumed connection in concentric relation is not any or all kinds of binding. Diametric spatial projection provides an example of another structure of binding, even though it is a structure of assumed separation within that which is bound; the opposites in diametric relation are bound together, though in a less intimate way than in the assumed connection of concentric relation. For concentric relation, the *quality* of binding is pivotal.

Freud (1924) recognizes that the destruction or 'disintegration' involved in the death drive brings 'a state of inorganic stability (relative though this may be)' (p. 163). In other words, an inorganic stability – as a kind of binding – occurs in the death drive, as well.[11] As Sulloway (1979) observes, 'when Freud equated the repetition compulsion and its motive, the death instinct, with Fechner's principle of stability, he was actually merging several aspects of Fechner's original doctrine' (p. 404), namely, 'absolute', 'full' and 'approximate stability'.[12] As destruction or disintegra-

11 See also Fromm (1977) on the 'confusion' which 'apparently arises' regarding the death drive 'because of the ambiguity of the words "stability" and "constancy"' (p. 629).

12 Sulloway (1979) observes that Fechner (1873, pp. 25–41) defined three different forms of stability as follows: *Absolute stability* in which there exists no energy or movement in a given system (this corresponds to Freud's state of Nirvana), *full stability* where parts of the whole are animated by completely regular movements,

tion into an inorganic state is a form of binding itself, Freud's life and death drives are not simply reducible to a diametric opposition between binding and destruction at the level of foregrounded structures of concentric and diametric relation. A concentric, more fluid, binding is a different relation of binding to the more compressed, binding process of a diametric solidity.

A spatial-phenomenological reinterpretation of Freud's *Eros* as a uniting and binding makes a clear distinction between concentric and diametric kinds of bound structures. It is logically independent of the hook of Fechner's theory of stability onto which Freud originally used to pin his nascent theory. Yet if uniting or binding is a central principle of *Eros*, the question arises as to whether a spatial-phenomenological approach simply modifies this central principle, or whether this principle operates with fuller force at a background level to the relation between concentric and diametric projections?

This background dimension emerges also from Klein's view of *Thanathos*. Klein follows Freud, not only regarding use of symbolism from the body (e.g., breast) in understanding stages of childhood development, but also in giving emphasis to the death 'instinct' as a key source of anxiety, 'The first form of anxiety is of a persecutory nature. The working of the death instinct within – which according to Freud is directed against the organism – gives rise to a fear of annihilation, and this is the primordial cause of persecutory anxiety' (Klein 1952/1997, p. 48). Klein (1948/1997) locates the anxiety underlying the diametric process of splitting into 'good' and 'bad breast' as forming 'the core of the superego' (p. 32). This inverted symmetry or reversal also occurs within the Freudian and Kleinian *ego*. She views 'the good internalized breast and the bad devouring breast' as 'Representatives within the ego of the struggle between the life and death instincts' (Klein 1948/1997, p. 32). Though Freud and Klein differed on the developmental timing of these processes, for both of them, the death drive is the background against which diametric structures of experience within the ego and superego emerge – including experience such as splits

---

approximate stability where parts of the whole return to approximately the same position at rhythmical intervals.

within the ego. This transpersonal death drive is prior to the level of the diametric structured ego; the diametric structured ego and superego is but one expression of this diametric structured process of the death drive.

Both life and death drive processes involve a conception of spatial alteration bringing differences in connection and separation. This diametric spatial background is being highlighted as a key supporting condition for interpretation of causal effects upon the unconscious. For a change process away from an experiential state governed by repression and the death drive, a shift is required in the background spatial conditions underpinning an individual's experience. Time is limited as an explanatory phenomenon as the question of antecedent causes in time becomes the more complex one of interaction between causes and supporting conditions in a system of relations. Repression and the death drive arguably occur, not only across time, but through a displacement of relation in the space of the unconscious system.

If a background dimension is needed to explicate the life and death drives, it must be prior to both the id-ego-superego tripartite structure and the foreground spatial projections of concentric and diametric relations, where concentric projections involve those observed for secure attachment and transitional objects. Expressing this background dimension in spatial-phenomenological terms, the question arises as to whether the background relation between diametric and concentric projected spaces is *itself* a diametric one of assumed separation between both projected spaces, or one of assumed connection and interaction as a concentric background relation?

To develop this further, the following phenomenological account, from a Jungian analyst, will be used as a point of contrast. With regard to concentric structured experience, Von Franz (1975) provides a narrative concerning a woman on the brink of hospitalization for psychosis who dreamed of an egg with a voice saying 'the mother and the daughter':

> I … went off telling her all the creation myths and of how the world is reborn from a world egg. I said that this showed the germ of a new possibility of life and that all would come right, that we only had to wait until everything came out of the egg, etc … 'the mother and the daughter' naturally referred to the Eleusinian mysteries, and I told her about this and of the rebirth of the feminine world where the new consciousness would be a feminine consciousness, and so on. (p. 12)

Von Franz emphasized the importance for the woman in accepting that her inner world was meaningful and not simply 'crazy' – in other words, the importance of trusting in her concentric structured experience emerging from her inner world. However, concentric structured experience and creation myths as birth from a world egg are not necessarily identical with Freudian conceptions of the life drive as *Eros*. There is a need to distinguish concentric relation as foreground from concentric relation as background. The concentric background relation is a process of assumed background connection, which expresses Freud's concern with *Eros* as a unifying process. However, although concentric relation as foreground also expresses dimensions of assumed connection, the foregrounded concentric structure brings more involvement of assumed connection in movements of change and restructuring – movements that are not necessarily a binding principle, at the level of foreground structures.

Freud's death drive expresses a diametric split background itself between diametric ego structures and foreground concentric structures of experience such as projections of secure attachment and transitional objects. A life drive is movement towards a concentric background relation of assumed connection *between* diametric ego and foreground concentric projections. This gives expression to Freud's core principle of the life drive as being a uniting or binding process, while recognising that further arguments are needed beyond Freud, for an understanding of a concentric background life drive. Psychosis involves the diametric split of the death drive between concentric and diametric structured experience. In contrast, the diametric ego inversions of obsessional neurosis may still be based on a prior level of connective background relation between ego and foreground concentric structured projections in experience. The concentric background relation itself between ego and foreground concentric projections is still being maintained to a substantial degree in obsessional neurosis, whereas it has been dismantled or never came into existence in schizophrenia.

From this vantage point, two levels need to be distinguished regarding where diametric and concentric spatial structures gain expression in relation to Freud's life and death drives. Diametric and concentric spatial projections have been highlighted to be underlying systemic spaces of the unconscious, with regard to obsessional neurosis, early childhood projections and psychosis. Here they are mainly static positional spatial structures of relation being projected into experience. They are foreground spatial structures. A second background level for concentric and diametric spaces is as fundamentally dynamic interacting processes in mutual tension, in an interplay between assumed connection and assumed separation *between* the foregrounded positional structures of concentric and diametric spaces. In other words, to the extent that a background dynamic drive of diametric splitting wins out over concentric uniting in assumed connection, there is then little or no interaction between the foreground structures of diametric and concentric spaces in a person's unconscious system. On the other hand, if a concentric background life drive tends to win out, there is heightened interaction and movement between foreground concentric and diametric structured spaces of experience.

From this, it is important to distinguish a diametric space as a static positional structure, such as in ego development, from the diametric spatial process in the death drive. As a static positional structure diametricity is a reactive space to the loss or failure to establish concentric structured space, such as in early childhood attachment. In contrast, a diametric space as a dynamic directional process is an active force more than simply a reactive structure. As a dynamic directional process it gives direct manifestation to the death drive.

This dynamic background temporal process of interaction between concentric and diametric directions in the respective life and death drives also has implications for an understanding of two different kinds of death that emerge from consideration of both concentric and diametric structures as dimensions of a compulsion to repeat, insofar as they are projections. Two contrasting modes of death as a potential fragile *telos* need to be distinguished, with regard to the interplay between concentric and diametric processes of relation. One aim of life as death is the directional extremity of diametric relation. Within this extremity, death occurs as a rendering inorganic, a sealed disconnection from background stimuli. Sealed diametricity is death as the Nirvana Principle, as reduction of interactive tension constituting life to a level of annihilation. Another different aim of life as death is an implication of the process of concentric space gaining dominion over diametric spatial structures. In doing so, this connective spatial direction begins to restructure the diametric towards a concentric whole. In other words, the concentric background space lubricates the dynamic interaction between foreground concentric and diametric spaces, so that assumed connection dissolves the assumed separation built into diametric spatial positional structures. At this extreme in the direction of concentric relation, a kind of death occurs to the diametric structure which undergoes a process of disintegration and dissolution into the concentric background whole. As an expression of *Eros*, this is a numinous life-giving death, or destruction of death. In Eastern terms, it is the death of the ego, though here it is envisaged as an ongoing process of tension rather than a completed state. Thus, two modes of 'death' directions are being postulated, death as annihilation of interactive relation expressed in diametric structures and death as dissolution of diametric space into concentric relation. They are different limbs of this ambient space.

Whereas Freud (1930) refers to dissolution, 'seeking to dissolve', to describe the death drive in contrast to the life drive, dissolution is envisaged in a spatial-phenomenological sense as concentric embedded transcendence of diametric structured experience. The dissolving embraces and accommodates the diametric space within the concentric. This 'seeking to dissolve' is no longer tantamount to construal as a destructive *Thanatotic* process. Human life is the interlude between two different directions of experiential death – concentric and diametric spatial directions. Or to put this differently, it is not simply a question of a diametric split between life and death. A concentric relation between life and death places both in a relation of assumed connection. Concentric spatial relation as a directional process – as a life drive – embraces, accommodates and dissolves the diametric space within it. In doing so, this life drive brings a different kind of experiential death to the fore.

This self-referential background dimension of interaction, this unconscious of the unconscious, is further developed in subsequent chapters. It is explored as: a space of the collective unconscious, prior to myth, in Jungian terms; a spatial graphematics, prior to what Derrida exhibits as Freudian 'logocentric' repression; a background direction of being, in Heidegger's framework. Jung arguably offers more engagement with the concentric life drive dimension than Freud, whose principal concern has been seen to be with the contours of the death drive and a valiant defending of the unconscious against its excesses.

Table 3 Freud's death drive and diametric space

Death Drive	*Diametric Space*
Nirvana Principle and Decathexis	Little or no interaction between foreground and background
Compulsion to Repeat	a) Projection b) Separation from background to bring static fixed interaction with background through imposed closed system of behaviour
Tendency to Destroy and Disintegrate	Assumed separation as a process of splitting
Aim of Life as Death	Reduction of interactive tension between foreground and background so that interplay between them is annihilated

PART III

Spatial-Phenomenology as a Discourse Prior to Language and Myth through a Collective Spatial Unconscious

CHAPTER 7

Transcending Subjectivity and Myth in Search of Meaning

The work of Jung and Derrida is conjoined by a preoccupation with loss of meaning. Both respond to the crisis of meaning by interrogating a broadening of understanding beyond individual subjectivity. Less obviously, both extract key insights concerning the need to transcend myth in search for meaning. Their inquiries centrally engage with spatial themes.

A spatial-phenomenological reinterpretation of their work on the unconscious world requires straddling domains of structuralism and post-structuralism, modernism and postmodernism. It is not being sought to systematically explicate the divergent, multifarious strands within these far from monolithic abstractions, nor to bring fully to the fore tensions between conceptions of modernism and modernist movements in art and literature. A necessarily selective and somewhat fragmented exploration of these terrains is being adopted in relation to concentric and diametric spaces, and Jung and Derrida's work in particular. In doing so, it is sought to build on the strengths of aspects of these movements, while avoiding at least some of their pitfalls.

While modernist writers like Eliot and Beckett were rejecting and challenging the comforts of the edifices of myth to sustain and organize reality,[1] they emphasized the rootlessness, disintegration and wasteland

1 As Eagleton (1995) highlights, Joyce's modernist employment of myth varied between its use as a formalist device and as an ironical inversion. Joyce arguably gave expression to both Freudian and Jungian concerns in his novel *Ulysses*. In similar fashion to Freud's stage theories modelled on the human body (e.g., oral, anal, phallic, genital stages), Joyce modelled different chapters of his novel on different parts of the body. Yet Joyce's work also resonates with Jungian preoccupations with myth through

of traditional forms of meaning and the quest for existential meaning that ensues in facing up to this abyss. They were engaging in a search with analogues to the distance partially opened up by Jung and subsequently Derrida (*via* Lévi-Strauss) in relation to myths; where myths transform one into each other, the need is for some deeper structure or relation than the mythic. The question arises as to whether this space of distance from the breakdown of the essentiality of the mythic, this radical discontinuity and consequent void can stretch open, not simply into a nothingness but also into another level of relation?

The authority of myth as a source for meaning rests at least partly on a privileging of the past, preferably ancient past, as primordial. It is to be a fountain, a primordial source. A displacement of the traditional authority of the mythic coalesces with a privileging of its remnant. This privileging unobtrusively promotes a residue of this primordial truth claim situated in ancient history. What is this remnant of primordial truth as history, with the garb of traditions of myth removed? Arguably it is its mirror image. This symmetrical inversion adopts a historical approach to deconstruct truth claims as mere discourses, narratives or stories. The reversal is from truth as primordial history in myth, to history as story that provisionalizes and contextualizes a truth claim. Soft myth becomes story and claims to more fundamental experiences are lost. Far from being a neutral vantage point, the assumption of a socio-historical deconstruction of truth claims is the mirror image of a distinct starting point in the quest for primordial truth as ancient history. They are different end points along the same linear historical axis. One is a looking back from present to ancient past, the other a looking forward from past to present. Their truth goals are inversions of the other. One seeks a fundamental primordial truth, the other a provisional deconstruction of truth that abjures all grounds for fundamentality. A way out is needed beyond this diametric mirror image

---

encompassing the broader myth of Ulysses from ancient Greek times. Jung's (1932) commentary on *Ulysses* did not directly acknowledge, however, that Joyce's narrative frame merged Freudian and Jungian concerns through encompassing both a Freudian bodily schema and a more Jungian mythological one.

turn from primordiality as ancient truth *qua* myth. A way out is needed beyond simple socio-historical relativism in social constructionism, that contains within itself the seeds of its own retreat back into a nostalgia for its mirror image of traditional authority.

An exit from the confines of this particular diametric mirror image relation invites an aperture for a different relation to both primordiality and myth. This opening is not only to interrogate the diametric spatial, it is not only to problematize diametric spatial reason, diametric meaning, diametric experience. Jung and Derrida's different responses to transcending myth in search of prior meaning will be explored, not only for a symbiosis between both kinds of inquiry. A spatial-phenomenological approach is sought to uncover their unthought, blind spots, together with their direct insights into this quest for meaning prior to myth, for a way out of the *aporia* of the mirror image relation between ancient primordial truth and postmodern historical relativism.

The phenomenological resonances of Jungian themes with modernist *Angst* are a feature of his search for individuation in response to loss of meaning, a process purportedly bringing a psychic restructuring between ego and self dimensions of experience. Understanding of this restructuring necessitates clarification of the relation between the personal and collective unconscious in Jungian terms. Concentric and diametric relations will be argued to be the key unthought spatial structures and primordial discourse underlying Jung's whole framework of thought, encompassing and reframing the panorama of his core themes: archetypes of the collective unconscious, individuation, self-ego relation, the mandala central archetype, introversion and extraversion, the transcendent function, midlife crisis of meaning and projection. A spatial-phenomenological scrutiny of background spatial conditions further invites examination of blind spots regarding the relation between structure and content in Jungian projection, and the background relation between the personal and collective unconscious. Derrida postulates an array of objections to the structuralism of Lévi-Strauss, including reliance on ahistorical truth claims, a bias of presence in assumptions of centres, the subject-object dualism, simple teleology and reifications, *inter alia*. A number of these blind spots are of relevance to critique of Jung's work and will be discussed as a backdrop to reinterpretation of the Jungian unconscious world.

This section also moves onto a reinterpretation of Derrida's (1978) own widening of the unconscious beyond what he terms Freudian 'logocentric' (p. 197) repression. This quest is for a rationality described in his discussion of Foucault as one which is 'more rational than reason', where 'reason is non-meaning and oblivion' (Derrida 1978, p. 62); Derrida recognizes that 'the revolution against reason, from the moment it is articulated, can operate only within reason' (1978, p. 36) and its limits. His is not an *apologia* for the discourses of a sheer postmodern relativism. Going further, it is being argued that both Jung and Derrida offer an understanding of a primordial discourse prior to language, a spatial discourse of relation that undercuts the primacy of language-games. A rationality is required that encompasses affect and is prior to the language of diametric reason, or what Gergen (1994a) terms, 'a ferocious flattening of the world ... within terms of the binary' (p. 61).

7.1 A spatial-phenomenological reinterpretation of the central archetype of the Jungian unconscious prior to myth and individual subjectivity

Argument: That (i) the mandala structure as Jung's proposed primordial central archetype of the collective unconscious requires reinterpretation as a dynamic interactive relation between concentric and diametric spaces and (ii) concentric-diametric spatial interaction gives structural expression to the Jungian self-ego relation in the unconscious world.

A shift in primordiality in the move from myth to mandala

An exploration of explicit spatial themes in Jung's accounts of structures of the unconscious commences with a fundamental contrast, not only between his spatial understandings, but also between the implicit conceptions of primordiality that underpin them. At times, Jung harkens back to a view of the unconscious in terms of primordiality as history, as in the following analogy that he admitted was a loose one:

> We have to describe and explain a building the upper story of which was erected in the nineteenth century; the ground-floor dates from the sixteenth century, and a careful examination of the masonry discloses the fact that it was reconstructed from a dwelling-tower of the eleventh century. In the cellar we discover Roman foundation walls, and under the cellar a filled-in cave, in the floor of which stone tools are found and remnants of glacial fauna in the layers below. That would be a sort of picture of our mental structure. (Jung 1928a, pp. 118–19)

That this reliance on a historical conception of primordiality for unconscious structures was far from being an isolated example in Jung's *oeuvre* can be illustrated also by his reference to 'the collective unconscious' as 'a potentiality handed down to us from primordial times in the specific form of mnemonic images' (Jung 1922, pp. 80–1).[2] Jung was prone to refer to primordial images in the collective unconscious, though without making explicit tensions within an understanding of primordiality.

A subtle shift is manifested in Jung's understanding of primordiality of unconscious structures, the implications of which Jung himself did not seem to realize, nor address. Jung clearly grew to privilege a concentric spatial structure, the mandala, over other archetypal images that may occupy the collective unconscious, stating that the mandala 'symbolises, by its central point, the ultimate unity of all archetypes as well as of the multiplicity of the phenomenal world' (Jung 1941–54, p. 463). Jung conceived of a unity or unifying process in the psyche as being expressed through a specific spatial structure or symbol, the mandala. This synthetic or synthesizing dimension is at the level of what he termed the 'self', which he contrasted with the 'ego'.

While elsewhere he emphasised multiple disparate dimensions to the self (Jung 1951, p. 225), Jung affirmed the centrality of concentric structures with the following words about 'our Western psychology' which has 'got

2 Here Jung (1922) also claims that it has an organic foundation in the brain, a suggestion he rejected in a subsequent letter to Medard Boss (27 June, 1947).

as far as yoga in that it is able to establish scientifically a deeper layer of unity in the unconscious':

> The mythological motifs whose presence have been demonstrated by the exploration of the unconscious form in themselves a multiplicity, but this culminates in a *concentric* or radial order which constitutes the true centre or essence of the collective unconscious. On account of the remarkable agreement between the insights of yoga and the results of psychological research, I have chosen the Sanskrit term *mandala* for this central symbol. (Jung 1943, p. 573) (my italics)

This is a very large claim being made by Jung. Working through the complexity of images emerging from an individual's personal history and also the myths of the collective unconscious, there is ostensibly an underlying spatial structural unity or at least potential unity within this multiplicity. On this view, a unified meaning to experience is possible. The mandala is centrally implicated in this potential unity, though Jung also went further than simply recognizing the necessity of fragmentation, through acknowledging the need to embrace the diversity of multiple primordial images in the collective unconscious.

Any such privileging of a mode of experience or archetype as fundamental, central and unifying does not only fly in the face of the comforts of postmodern relativism. It initiates a change in conception of primordiality that drains it of the central importance of ancient history. Rather the focus on primordiality turns here with Jung towards a notion of primordiality as unity, as a unifying process. Furthermore, it is a primordiality in the sense of being more fundamental than other levels.

In the shift from the spatial theme of layers of a house to connote historical primordiality within the collective unconscious to that of the mandala spatial structure, another difference emerges. The historical primordiality view of the collective unconscious suggests a positivist view that its elements were constructed and fashioned over history, whereas the mandala structure is less evidently a positivist product of experiential input over generations.

For Jung, this spatial archetypal image of the mandala provides a level for this psychic unity or unifying process that needs to go beyond the ego level of experience. Psychic unity needs to find a source prior to the personal unconscious, and this source is in the archetypal level of the mandala in the collective unconscious. Significantly, the mandala is a level prior to myth, as a spatial structure. It is not a causal level, for Jung, but background conditions for experience.[3]

That myth cannot sustain a central archetype and requires a prior level is supported by a Freudian criticism of Jung. Bair (2004) notes that Freud:

> launched a stinging critique of Jung, saying he showed no discernment when he used mythology indiscriminately. He chastised his use of derivatives rather than originals, saying that only the originals could be subjected to 'psychoanalytic elucidation', using the Book of Genesis as a prime example of distortion through variant renderings of the same information. (p. 212)

Freud's concern with historical changeability at the level of textual versions of myths offers one basis for a critique of mythological accounts as being socially constructed. Yet this critique is further developed by Lévi-Strauss, with its meaning amplified by Derrida.

Commenting on Lévi-Strauss' critical reflection on 'his own discourse on myths', Derrida (1978) observes, 'What appears most fascinating in this critical search for a new status of discourse is the stated abandonment of all reference to a *center*, to a *subject*, to a privileged *reference*, to an origin, or to an absolute *archia*' (p. 286) (italics in original). Derrida (1978) extols the virtues of this development in Lévi-Strauss (1970), 'From the very start, Lévi-Strauss recognizes that the Bororo myth which he employs in the book as the "reference myth" does not merit this name and this treatment' (p. 286). Derrida (1978) continues:

> There is no unity or absolute source of the myth. The focus of the source of the myth are always shadows and virtualities which are elusive, unactualizable and nonexistent in the first place. Everything begins with structure, configuration or relationship. The discourse on the acentric structure that myth itself is, cannot itself have an absolute subject or an absolute center. (p. 286)

3 Jung's account of archetypes as conditions is apposite for the mandala as a spatial structural condition for experience. In a letter to Medard Boss (27 June 1947), Jung stated that 'archetypes have never been for me pure *causae* but conditions ...'.

If myths transform one into another and it is the relation or structure of myths that is more fundamental, this leaves a psychology of the collective unconscious reliant on myths in need of a deeper level of analysis for its organizing principles. Jungian emphasis on myths and primordial images needs not only to incorporate the level of relations between myths to uncover a deep connection and pattern but also to go towards what Jung conceives of as the central unifying archetype, the mandala, which is more a symbolic structure than a myth *per se* (though manifested also in myths). The question arises as to whether this mandala structure can provide this more fundamental level of relation. The accusation may remain that the role attributed by Jung to the mandala is a hyperbolic one, without at least some discourse or argument to go beyond simple assertion, to offer evidence that the mandala could provide the central unifying archetype of the collective unconscious.

7.2 A dynamic mandala underlying the unconscious world: Tension between spaces of a concentric structured self and diametric ego

The concentric spatial structure of the mandala is at first glance a static representation, so that a dimension of time is not explicitly related to it. As a visual symbol or primordial image, it expresses a stable unity rather than an emerging, dynamic, unifying process. Nevertheless, Jung (1944/1952) did refer to 'symbols of the *process* of individuation', such as the mandala, as 'the centralizing *process*' (p. 41) (my italics) and emphasized that 'the symbol of the circle is to be thought of not as static but as dynamic' (p. 192). However, space and time are not immediately interdependent within the fabric of the static mandala symbol, viewed as a visual image.

A more dynamic conception of the spatial tensions in the mandala requires exposition. This invites the question: Can the quest for the *élan vital* of the mandala can be fulfilled through the dynamic interplay of a primordial dance between concentric and diametric spaces? For present purposes, it is being argued that the mandala structure is a static simplified representation of the dynamic interactive tension between diametric (ego) and concentric (self) structures and processes.

As a projected synthetic structure that does not directly relate space and time in its visual 'image' element, as distinct from Jung's conceptualization of it as dynamic, Jung's view of the mandala arguably reveals a strong Kantian influence, emphasized more generally for Jung's thought by de Voogd (1992). Jung viewed archetypal structures in Kantian terms as '*a priori*' structures of the collective unconscious (e.g., Jung 1921, p. 400; 1951, pp. 16–17; 1938, p. 105). The mandala is similarly viewed as an *a priori* structure with a commonality among its various empirical manifestations. Kant treated space and time as synthetic grounds for the possibility of our empirical intuition. Kant's synthetic *a priori* of space and time kept space and time fundamentally separate. It is this questionable Kantian framework separating space and time that is implicitly superimposed onto the archetypal framework of Jung's understanding of the mandala.

Interpreting the mandala as a dynamic unifying process invokes temporal dimensions and has to clarify what the mandala image changes to or from. Moreover, as a purportedly fundamental unifying archetype, it must in some way incorporate not only the elements of space and time but also the relation between both. Incorporation here means that space and time are not prior to the mandala but part of it, as the purportedly fundamental unifying process to experience. Space and time are immanent in experience as interdependent structures of relation. To instill a vibrancy into this key concept of the collective unconscious, the mandala must move beyond being simply a static reified image.

Shortly after Jung's death in 1962, Lévi-Strauss (1963) highlighted cross-cultural structures of concentric and diametric relation. Despite the clear parallels between his collective structures of concentric space and Jung's notion of the mandala or self, Lévi-Strauss (1962, 1963, 1969, 1970, 1973, 1981, 1988) neither related concentric structures to the mandala, nor based his work generally on Jungian conceptions of a collective unconscious (Downes 2003). As an unveiling of dynamic interactive spatial relations, it is arguable that unbeknownst to Lévi-Strauss, his partial understanding of the relation between cross-culturally observed concentric and diametric spaces is a vital pulse to breathe life into Jung's mandala structure.

Traversing pathways beyond traditional Western subjectivity, for Jung, the self includes the collective unconscious level of the psyche to be integrated with the ego. The collective unconscious was conceived as 'a universal and homogenous substratum' (Jung 1921, p. 491) which is 'the same everywhere and at all times' ('Letter to Rhine', Jung 1945, p. 395). Jung also described the self as 'the total personality' which 'though present, cannot be fully known', the ego being 'subordinate' to the self as a part to the whole (Jung 1951, p. 5).

As a resolution within a chaotic, complex process, Jung (1959) related the mandala structure to the ego in the following way:

> Mandalas ... usually appear in situations of psychic confusion and perplexity. The archetype thereby constellated represents a pattern of order which ... is superimposed on the psychic chaos so that each content falls into place and the weltering confusion is held together by the protective circle ... I have observed these phenomena in my patients for forty years and have come to the conclusion that this archetype is of central importance, or rather, that it gains importance to the degree that the importance of the ego is lost. (pp. 162–3)

From this, a view emerges that the ego and self (mandala) are in a compensatory relationship (see also Jung 1916a, p. 85). This compensatory relation, where the self gains importance to the degree that the ego loses importance, offers support for a view of the Jungian self as a concentric projection and the ego as a diametric projected structure, where both spaces are in compensatory relation. The tension between self and ego, inherent in a compensatory relationship, is also evident in Jung's (1951, pp. 24–5) acknowledgment of the dangers that the ego either be assimilated by the self, or deny its reality. It is not a question of inevitable integration between ego and self. Rather this fragile potential for change and transformation may suffer from the buffeting forces of other diremptive trajectories. It is not a question of an integrative *telos* being expressed in its plenitude, unfettered by other regimes of influence upon subjectivity. Significantly, a compensatory relationship implies a dynamic dimension of time and change as underlying the ego and self relation.

A concentric relation allows for distinction and difference that does not have to lead to opposition. Thus, a concentric model of inwardness allows for an inner realm that is not reducible to the outer but which is in a relation of assumed connection with it. It also allows for a conception of an inner realm of experience that is not necessarily a detached abstraction from the outer in Cartesian fashion. And as the inner concentric pole within and surrounded by the outer concentric pole, the inner realm is also immanent in the external world, or what Brooke (1991, 2009) treats as 'life-world' in his exposition of synergy between phenomenology and Jungian thought. Concentric inwardness offers a response to Brooke's (2009) raising of the need for an understanding of interiority that is not reducible to the innerness of the Cartesian mind.

Brooke (1991) treats Jung's (1944/1952) description of the self as both 'centre' and 'the whole circumference' as a 'bold paradox' (p. 97), while also noting that Fordham (1963) treats Jung's definitions of self as organizing centre and totality as being mutually exclusive and a logical contradiction which cannot be masked as being simply a paradox. Fordham's position is reiterated in his later work, 'the two conceptions [of self as centre and circumference] cannot be easily reconciled' (Fordham 1994, p. 10). It is clear that the archetypal level of the self goes beyond Western diametric structured logic but this need not be a flaw for a more embracing framework of rationality that incorporates the vicissitudes of the supposedly irrational.

Jung (1935a) eschews the 'niggardly European "either-or"' mode of understanding, which he contrasts with 'a magnificently affirmative "both-and"' (p. 175) in Tibetan thought. The latter offers a harmony between two parts of relation, thereby offering a strong affinity with the bipolar relation expressed in concentric space. Jung (1929) accepts also that 'it is characteristic of the Western mind that it has no word for *Tao*' (p. 20), taking *Tao* in a psychological sense to be 'the method or conscious way by which to unite what is separated' (p. 21). For Jung, the *Tao* has close proximity to the self and mandala as a unity – or at least direction towards psychic unity, to the extent that it takes over from the ego. The *Tao*, the mandala and concentric relation tend to struggle to gain expression conceptually and linguistically in Western culture.

Brooke (1991) highlights Jung's description of the self as, 'the new centre of the psyche that emerges out of dialogue between conscious and unconscious, or ego and archetypes. The realisation of this new centre is the goal of individuation' (p. 98). Interaction between a symbol of the self such as the mandala on the one hand, and the ego level on the other hand, can accommodate a view of the self as both centre and totality, *contra* Fordham (1963, 1994). This can take place once this interaction is understood firstly in terms of *movement between* the concentric and the diametric structure – where the former is the self level and the latter is the ego level. Change from the diametric structured ego to an emerging centre rooted in the concentric structured self raises the question as to the *relation itself* between diametric and concentric structures. *Is the relation itself a diametric or concentric one?* A potentially concentric relation between these structures of relation brings *an assumed connection and interaction between them*. This also clarifies how the self is both the new centre (the first concentric structure) and also the circumference or totality, i.e., the concentric background relation which allows the diametric and concentric structures to interact.

While the first concentric level is open to direct representation in thought, the second background concentric level of the self as totality of the psyche is more the level of the unrepresentable archetype *per se* rather than its concrete manifestations (see e.g., Jung 1948/1969, pp. 123–4). The initial world egg (concentric) myth, prior to the balance between concentric and diametric structures in *yin/yang*, is one attempt to represent a *background* archetypal level. Lévi-Strauss (1963) acknowledged that a more dynamic conception of the background *relationship* between concentric and diametric structures was needed and difficult to directly represent:

> These [diametric and concentric] forms as described, do not necessarily relate to two different organizations. They may also correspond to two different ways of describing one organization too complex to be formalized by means of a single model, so that the members of each moiety would tend to conceptualize it one way rather than the other, depending upon their position in the social structure. For even in such an apparently symmetrical type of social structure as dual organization, the relationship between moieties is never as static, or fully reciprocal, as one might tend to imagine. (p. 135)

Lévi-Strauss (1963) explicitly conceived of concentric structures as offering the function of being a 'mediator' between diametric dualism and tri-adism, 'since it is through the agency of the former that the transition takes place between the other two' (p. 151). The view of concentric relation as the centre of the self also places it (*qua* centre) in the role of mediator between diametric structures and the potentially concentric background as the triadic dimension.

Diametric structures as defensive complexes such as the ego-complex: Beyond the mandala as quaternity

Despite Jung's (1943) reference to a concentric order as the core of the collective unconscious, he emphasized a different structural dimension to the mandala as a frame for understanding the psyche. He frequently reiterated the importance of the quaternity or four corners of the outer square in the mandala (Downes 2003, 2011). Jung (1921) strongly emphasized archetypal form drawn from the mandala, in his analysis of personality into four or eight psychological types, 'But whatever the criterion for a classification of types may be, a comparison of the various forms of habitual attitudes will result in an equal number of psychological types' (p. 490). His non-hierarchical quaternity of the four functions drawn from the four corners of the mandala, placed feeling diagonally opposite to thinking (Jung 1941–54, pp. 203–5), so that 'real thinking ... must rigorously exclude feeling' (Jung 1921, pp. 405–6).

Jung did, however, give a value to a relational or feeling based approach which could be interpreted as a different relational type of thinking, overcoming a rigid distinction between thinking and feeling, and thereby foreseeing Gilligan's (1982) concerns with a rationality of care prior to justice:

> If the doctor wants to guide another, or even accompany him a step of the way, he must feel with that person's psyche. He never feels it when he passes judgment ... Feeling only comes through unprejudiced objectivity. This sounds almost like a scientific concept, and it could be confused with a purely abstract attitude of mind. But what I mean is something quite different. It is a human quality – a kind of deep respect for the facts, for the man who suffers from them, and for the riddle of such a man's life. (Jung 1932, pp. 338–9)

This *value* to the rationality of feeling is to some extent evident, even in Jung (1921), as feeling is treated as a rational function.

The quaternity dimension to the mandala structure allowed for a conception of a diagonally opposed function as the unconscious undeveloped 'shadow' function, so that feeling would be the shadow function for thinking, intuition the shadow function for sensation and *vice-versa*. This whole framework for interpretation of the mandala structure relied not upon its concentric features. Rather, it interpreted the mandala as a square, where the inner circle becomes largely superfluous (except as a level of wholeness, to overcome the separate functions into a transcendent function).

Not only did this emphasis on the quaternity in the mandala amount to a neglect of the concentric dimensions to the mandala, it was an emphasis on diametric features of the mandala as a square which is made explicit in Jung's (1964) position that 'thinking and feeling are so *diametrically opposed* that thinking almost automatically throws out feeling values and *vice-versa*' (p. 90) (my italics). The diametric structure relating the Jungian functions of thinking, feeling, sensation and intuition places them very much more in the realm of the personal unconscious and the ego, than in the self of the collective unconscious. This occurs despite the derivation of their structure from the mandala. Noting that the ego is 'essentially the focal point of consciousness' (Jung 1921, p. 376), Jung relates the four functions to consciousness and hence, to the *ego* more than the self, 'the products of all functions can be conscious, but we speak of the "consciousness" of a function only when its use is under the control of the will and at the same time, its governing principle is the decisive one for the orientation of consciousness' (p. 405). Jung's reliance on purported diametric dimensions to the mandala obfuscates the concentric dimensions of the self and invites confusion between the different opposing structural levels of ego and self within the mandala.

While the mandala may be treated as a symbol of totality and hence inclusion of the ego within the self, this tends to minimize the dynamic tensions between its concentric and diametric (quaternity) dimensions. Elsewhere, Jung (1929, p. 24) did emphasize the circular rather than square dimension of the mandala, referring to the 'protective' or 'charmed' circle, though without linking the circular explicitly to the concentric dimension of the mandala. However, Jung (1944/1952) not only reiterated that mandala in Sanskrit means 'circle' and 'magic circle' but related this to its concentric feature, where 'Its symbolism includes all concentrically arranged figures, round or square patterns with a circle, and radial or spherical arrangements' (p. 42).

For Jung (1952), '... the "centre" [of the mandala] ... is simply unknowable and can only be expressed symbolically ... Among the various characteristics of the centre the one that struck me from the beginning was the phenomenon of the quaternity' (p. 292). He explicitly recognises that he is constructing an interpretation of the mandala somewhat in the dark. Despite Jung's diffidence here, this interpretative reliance on the quaternity becomes a foundation stone for many aspects of his structure of the psyche, and is vulnerable to a Derridean, postmodern and also feminist critique in terms of a false essentialism of atemporal structures.[4]

Like Freud, Jung tended to embed his theories within a distinct conceptual structure or schema. Freud (1916) adopted a schema modelled on the body to divide a child's growth into oral, anal, phallic, latency and genital stages. In humanistic psychology, Maslow (1970) employed a hierarchical schema within which to frame his Cartesian type of theory of motivation based on a mind/body split transported into psychological terminology of growth and survival needs. For Jung, this schema was drawn not from the body or a hierarchy but from archetypes such as the mandala and *yin/yang*. While the relation of the four functions based on an archetypal model of the mandala is questionable, nevertheless, the mandala provided a structural model for Jung's conception of opposition as being non-hierarchical. This is in contrast to Maslow's (1970) hierarchical divisions for motivation.

Building a postmodernist framework for developing Jungian thought, Hauke (2000) treats the quaternity as a term open to ridicule. It is evident that Jung sought to extract a fundamental principle from the mandala

4 Similarly, Jung's attempts to frame other aspects of his theories such as the anima/animus, the container and contained, and the mother archetype through a frequently implicit *yin/yang* structural frame can be criticized as giving a false substantiality and premature grounding to these aspects as atemporal claims for gender essentiality (Downes 2011).

structure as a key insight into the unconscious world. He was open about his limited awareness of what this principle could be, beyond being an emergent structure termed the self to compensate for a loss of ego relation. Referring to 'that obscure thing we call the mandala or "self"' (p. 255), Jung (1952) emphasized it was an empirical observation somewhat lacking in explanatory adequacy, 'All that can be ascertained at present about the symbolism of the mandala is that it portrays an autonomous psychic fact, characterized by a phenomenology[5] which is always repeating itself and is everywhere the same. It seems to be a sort of atomic nucleus about whose innermost structure and ultimate meaning we know nothing' (p. 257). Against this backdrop, extracting the principle of the quaternity was a limited attempt to give expression to the importance of concentric mandala spatial structures. Jung envisaged it as an initial pathway in anticipation of further understanding vis-à-vis concentric spatial structures of the unconscious world.

The four functions are founded on a prior opposition between introversion and extraversion, which Jung (1914) explicitly treats as a diametric opposition. He refers to, 'The existence of two diametrically opposed psychologies which view the same things under totally different aspects. An extravert and an introvert find it very difficult to understand each other' (Jung 1914, p. 191). Diametricity here is not incidental to Jung's view of introversion and extraversion but is a firmly held dimension for this theme. Jung (1914) consistently maintains the relation between extraversion and introversion as a diametric opposition, stating also that 'their psychology is diametrically opposed' (p. 190). Once again, in his correspondence with Hans Schmid, prior to *Psychological Types* (1921), Jung referred to 'certain controversial points in analytical psychology' illuminating two distinct 'diametrically opposed types' (Bair 2004, p. 279). For Jung, psychological growth involves a restructuring of this diametric opposition to encompass the shadow side, whether that of introversion or extraversion. This

5 Jung's use of the term phenomenology here is in a Kantian sense to contrast with a claim for noumenal truths in the archetype *per se*.

restructuring of the diametric ego is towards a holistic concentric relation *between* dimensions of introversion and extraversion.

Jung's (1955) emphasis on the role of groups in developing structures of the ego would also tend to support an identification of diametric structures with the ego rather than the self, 'The group accentuates the *ego*; one becomes braver, more presumptuous, more cocky, more insolent, more reckless; but the *self* is diminished and gets pushed into the background in favour of the average' (Letter to H.A. Illing, 26 January 1955, p. 219). Fromm (1973) observes that the easiest way to unite a group is to provide it with a common enemy – to organize the group in diametric structured opposition to an external other. The diametric structure of the group relation expresses the corresponding structure underlying the ego.

Treatment of the two levels of the self (centre and totality) as concentrically structured, interacting with the diametric structured ego, offers a step forward to Stevens (1990) question for which he says there are only 'partial answers', 'How does an archetype of the collective unconscious become a complex in the personal psyche? This is a crucial question because the answer must tell us something of how in each and everyone of us, our personal life becomes grafted ... onto the collective history of the species' (p. 32). The movement from archetype to complex can be described as that from a concentric to a diametric structure. The diametric structure at the personal level frames the particular content of the complexes. Jung (1934) describes complexes as 'split-off psychic fragments' (p. 104) and clearly emphasizes the splitting or assumed separation (diametric) feature is a reaction to traumatic events, when describing them as '"splinter psyches"' where 'The aetiology of their origin is frequently a so-called trauma, an emotional shock or some such thing, that splits off a bit of the psyche' (p. 98).

Characterizing the self and ego in terms of concentric and diametric structures respectively, also assumes that these diametric patterns are defensive, whatever the particular content of the complexes themselves. Traumatic experiential content can be anticipated to bring a structural reaction constellating diametric structured experience, as well as a diminution of concentric structured experience. Henderson (1964) cites Jung's description of the conflict between the ego and the shadow as the 'battle for deliverance' (pp. 110–11). To resolve this conflict, the very diametric oppositional tendencies constituting the relation between ego and shadow need to be challenged.

Fordham's (1974, 1985, 1994) 'defences of the self' are viewed as arising from a primitive level of psyche preceding ego development (1985, p. 214). These defences involve splitting and projective identification and thus have a diametric structure of opposition inherent in them that is non-ego. Though the ego is a product of the diametric oppositional process, diametric structures themselves are not simply reducible to the ego. Diametric structures form complexes and one of these complexes is the ego-complex. Jung (1946) emphasises that 'the egocomplex has many gradations of emphasis' as well as being a process in ongoing formation rather than a fixed structure:

> On the animal and primitive level there is a mere 'luminosity' differing hardly at all from the glancing fragments of a dissociated ego. Here, as on the infantile level, consciousness is not a unity, being as yet uncentred by a firmly-knit egocomplex ... Nor is it a fully integrated whole even at the higher and highest stages; rather it is capable of indefinite expansion. Gleaming islands, indeed whole continents, can still add themselves to our modern consciousness ... Therefore we would do well to think of egoconsciousness as being surrounded by a multitude of little luminosities. (p. 99)

Splitting and projective identification, as defences of the self in its interaction with 'not-self-objects' (Fordham 1974, p. 199; 1985, p. 159), are a movement away from the concentric structure of the self. The compensatory relation of the self and the ego implies that self and ego are not categorically distinct but are in at least potential relation. Thus, the disturbance to the concentric structure of the self in the self's defence against 'not-self-objects' leads to a diametric structure which may potentially, though not inevitably, become an aspect of egocomplex formation.

Treating concentric spatial projections as expressions of the self and diametric projections as expressions of the ego implicates concentric projection as primary and diametric projection as a defensive complex. The ego is one instance of a defensive complex. It invites interrogation of concentric and diametric spatial projections as organizing principles of myths.

Concentric space as the transcendent function in individuation

Jung's primary clinical concern was not with the complexes themselves but with their relation to the collective unconscious, i.e., 'what the *unconscious is doing* with the complexes' (Jung 1935b, p. 93). Awareness of this level of relation was, for Jung, the task of individuation, which included 'the breaking of the patient's previous personal conformity' (Jung 1916b, p. 451). Viewing diametric structured complexes as expressions of a diametric process suggests this same diametric relationship tends to exist between complexes and the collective unconscious. The process of individuation is a challenge to this diametric relation, as is implicit in Edinger's (1974) words, 'A twofold split is healed to the extent individuation is achieved; first the split between conscious and unconscious which began at the birth of consciousness, and second, the split between subject and object. The dichotomy between outer and inner reality is replaced by a sense of unitary reality' (p. 96).

A compensatory relation between ego and self implies that concentrically structured experience is an underlying potential structural *telos* for a psychological shift away from an assumption of centrality of the ego. Jung's (1944/1952) account of the mandala structure underlying a series of dreams and visions was an argument for a 'new centre' of 'mandala symbolism' (p. 41) in the psyche, where 'the central symbol, constantly renewing itself, will steadily and consistently force its way through the apparent chaos of the personal psyche' (p. 217). Individuation is the task of integrating this new concentric centre with the diametric ego. This movement from the ego level of experience in individuation presumes a sense of ultimate meaninglessness or at least dissatisfaction with the diametric mode of relation. Dreams, as a compensatory relation to ego experience (Jung 1946, p. 100), offer potential for analysis of this concentric 'centralizing process' (Jung 1944/1952, p. 41) or *circumambulatio* (Jung 1944/1952, p. 145, p. 190; Jung 1964, p. 14).

Elsewhere, Jung (1916a) refers to a second 'more important stage' beyond how the ego and unconscious shadow 'come to terms' (p. 87). This stage involves 'the bringing together of opposites for the production of a third: the transcendent function' (p. 87). The assumed separation between the shadow and ego is challenged and the reorientation of their mirror image inverted relation brings another dimension; this concentric dimension of relation is the self operating through the transcendent function. This new level of concentric self operating through the transcendent function is explicitly envisaged by Jung in terms of the mirror image entailment of diametric spatial relation, where 'the mirror-image effects, which dazzle us, would be removed, and the opposites of the two Being aspects would be shorn of their power' ('Letter to Pauli' 1957, p. 168).

Jung's (1916a) description of the transcendent function reiterates the importance of a heightened interaction or synergistic connection between previously opposing poles of relation:

> The shuttling to and fro of arguments and affects represents the transcendent function of opposites. The confrontation of the two positions generates a tension charged with energy and creates a living third thing – not a logical stillbirth ... but a movement out of the suspension between opposites, a living birth that leads to a new level of being, a new situation. The transcendent function manifests itself as a quality of conjoined opposites. So long as these are kept apart – naturally for the purpose of avoiding conflict – they do not function and remain inert. (p. 90)

When the more inert, detached relation of diametric structured opposites (the ego and shadow) is confronted by an interaction ('the shuttling to and fro'), this brings the possibility of constellating the transcendent function of '*conjoined* opposites'. Conjoined opposites are in a relation of assumed connection as expressed by concentric structures of relation. It is not simply a question of a static compromise ('a logical stillbirth') which would simply perpetuate the diametric structured relation of ego and shadow. The self or concentric relational opposition is the dynamic interactive relation of conjoined opposites, clarifying 'the archetype which it is most important for modern man to understand' (Jung 1951, p. 266).

7.3 Beyond structuralism in a spatial-phenomenological reinterpretation of the collective unconscious

Argument: That (i) a spatial-phenomenological reinterpretation of the Jungian unconscious moves beyond atomic and holistic structuralism to a focus on (ii) foreground-background interaction in projection involving a neglected structure-content relativity in its background relation.

Differences between a spatial-phenomenology and structuralism need to be cognizant of the well-known distinction between atomic and holistic structuralism (e.g., Dreyfus & Rabinow 1982). Atomistic structuralism seeks elements which are completely specified apart from their role in some larger whole.[6] In holistic structuralism, what counts as a *possible* element is defined apart from the system of elements but what counts as an *actual* element is a function of the whole system of differences of which the particular element is a part. Lévi-Strauss' holistic structuralism requires that all possible terms be identified apart from any specific system, e.g., raw, cooked, and rotten (Lévi-Strauss 1969). The specific system of terms then develops which possible terms actually count as elements.

While a spatial-phenomenological concentration on concentric and diametric spaces is potentially meaningful for a given system, the focus is less on an actuality *qua* truth as correspondence. Empirical correspondence is a further level of analysis, or frequently an initial stage before the spatial-phenomenological scrutiny. The shift from holistic structuralism is from potentiality-actuality to an interactive focus on potential background space and diverse foreground systemic dimensions. The background-foreground interaction is with a view to fluidating the sedimented assumptions of a system of thought or discourse. It is a spatial structure in dynamic interaction with the often slumbering spatial assumption structure of the text. The

6 Such as Propp's (1958) folk tale elements, and arguably Piagetian (1960) stages of cognitive development. However, Piaget (1971, pp. 6–10) explicitly resists a rigid dualism between atomism and holism.

scrutiny of wider spatial necessary and supportive conditions is to expose and awake the spatial assumption structure for interaction with the proposed primordial spatial projections of concentric and diametric relation. These sedimented spatial assumption structures are highly contextual.

Jungian reliance on the mandala structure as the central archetype of the collective unconscious has been broadened beyond the simple foundationalism of atomic structuralism. This occurs through rendering this structure dynamic and interactive in a system of relative differences between concentric and diametric spaces. In doing so, this perspective on spatial relations in the unconscious world offers more obvious resonance with features of the holistic structuralism of Lévi-Strauss. Yet this system of spatial relations prior to and also manifested in myth eludes reduction to a structuralist manifesto. In its purported transcendence of structuralism, a spatial-phenomenological approach needs to embrace a range of important criticisms of structuralism made by Derrida.

Lévi-Strauss (1963) views his structuralist anthropology as being governed by 'universal laws' (p. 59) and modelled specifically on a phonetics (p. 34) that has, 'reached beyond the superficial conscious and historical expression of linguistic phenomena to attain fundamental and objective realities consisting of systems of relations which are the products of unconscious thought processes' (p. 58). Lévi-Strauss' concern with structure, involves for Derrida (1978) 'a neutralization of time and history' (p. 291), a timeless present.

While this may be a valid criticism of Lévi-Strauss' structuralism,[7] the cross-cultural structures of concentric and diametric space require a framework which does *not* neutralize time. On the contrary, this framework explicitly incorporates time in the relation of change and dynamic interaction between concentric and diametric structures. The compensatory relation between concentric self and diametric ego assumes a concep-

7 See also Lévi-Strauss' (1962, p. 254) explicit rejection of Sartre's emphasis that all truth is historically conditioned; Jakobsen (1973, pp. 38–9) on the exclusion of time and space from Saussure's conception of linguistic system which influenced Lévi-Strauss; Hogenson (1994, pp. 102–3) for an account of Freud's view of the unconscious as timeless.

tion of time to mediate this compensatory movement. Yet this need not be everyday linear time, a point Derrida makes in relation to the Freudian unconscious and time; Derrida (1978) advocates a reading of Freud 'the way Heidegger read Kant: like the *cogito*, the unconscious is no doubt timeless only from the standpoint of a certain vulgar conception of time' (p. 215). In other words, the dynamic compensatory relation between concentric and diametric space requires a temporal framework, although this is not necessarily 'vulgar' (i.e., linear) time. The diametric opposition between historical and ahistorical truth is to be reconceptualized as involving a relation between:

a) historically constructed truths in linear time, and
b) another temporal domain of ego-self (diametric-concentric) relation.

Whereas Freud pioneered apprehension of the splintered contours of diametric spatial dynamics in the unconscious, Jung opened doors at the limits of Freud's thought, to unveil contours of concentric projections underlying the unconscious world. In doing so, he elaborated on the movements between both structures in his expansion of the domain of relevance of the unconscious beyond individual subjectivity.

Derrida (1978) introduces a historical temporal dimension to structure through criticism of the history of structure itself in Western thought, 'the entire history of the concept of structure ... must be thought of as a series of substitutions of center for center, as a linked chain of determinations of the center. Successively, and in a regulated fashion, the center receives different forms or names' (p. 279). Giving different names or forms to the versions of centre is characterized by Derrida as operating within an assumption and bias of 'presence'. This is a pervasive postmodern concern echoed also by Foucault's (1972) emphasis on a 'decentering' leaving no privilege to any centre.

In stark contrast to postmodern concerns, Jung (1944/1952) refers to the 'centralizing process' (para. 44) in the compensatory shift from ego to self as a 'new level of being, a new situation' (Jung 1916a, p. 90). This new level is described as the transcendent function. At first glance, it would seem that Jung's recentering from ego to self, as part of the process of individuation, is vulnerable to Derrida's critique of centres replacing centres, while failing to interrogate the bias of the assumption of a presence within each centre. And similarly, examination of movement from diametric to concentric structures needs to offer an explanation beyond a simple substitution of grounded centres. It cannot sustain a narrative of traditional kinds of foundations.

Derrida (1978) criticizes the assumption of a grounded centre which provides a premature 'certitude' through which 'anxiety can be mastered' (p. 279). Yet both Jung's conception of the self as circumference and consideration of *the background relation itself between* concentric and diametric spaces embrace a more uncertain truth of experience. This experiential truth provides and requires an anxiety of uncertainty as to whether there even is an interactive background relation to connect the respective concentric and diametric spaces. The possibility of a diametric non-interactive background relationship between concentric and diametric modes needs to be acknowledged, such as in ruptures of the ego-self axis (e.g., Neumann 1973; Edinger 1972).

Derrida's search for a 'play' prior to the diametric opposition between presence and absence invites exploration of the potential split or absence of relation between concentric/diametric structures.[8] The dynamic compensatory relation between the diametric ego and the concentric self is an interrelation which cannot be presumed as a certain ground, but is more an unstable potential and by no means the only pathway for experience. Jung's view of movement from diametric structured ego level experience recognizes that such movement is a *potential* process, 'you anticipate the loss of power of the mirror image – i.e., of the opposites. You know something that is a secret to everyone else – namely, that in the unconscious the Third is preparing itself and is already starting to neutralize the tension energy

8 A poststructuralist questioning of a bias of presence would question the Kantian assumption of a synthetic *a priori*, such as in Jung's view of archetypes as 'an *a priori* existing image' (e.g., Jung 1951, 'Letter to Pauli', p. 70). Yet a synthesis between concentric and diametric structures through a connective, concentric, interactive background relation is not being presumed but is only being treated as a potential.

that comes from the opposites' ('Letter to Pauli' 1957, p. 168).[9] Search for meaning in the individuation process must face up to a possible reality of meaninglessness – an absence of presence. An individual's experience cannot be presumed to reach an inevitable teleological satisfaction and resolution of the quest for meaning in the restructuring from ego dimensions of experience.

Another objection of Derrida (1978) to structuralism, that can be construed as a 'bias of presence' criticism, is to 'a "preestablished" teleological framework' (p. 25). Maranda (1972) accepts that structuralism in anthropology takes into account teleology or final causes. Moreover, Jung evidently was committed to some form of a teleological framework.[10] A compensatory relation between ego and self implies that concentrically structured experience is an underlying structural *telos* for a psychological shift away from an assumption of the centrality of the ego. However, the concentric movement from a diametric relation is not some inevitable quasi-Hegelian *telos*. Jung emphasizes the uncertainty and danger inherent in the individuation process, and this is given expression in the lack of certainty that movement from diametric towards concentric space will – as opposed to can – occur. As differential structures *of* relation *in* relation, the 'presence' is not 'in' either structure but in the difference between the two. Similarly, for Saussure (1954), meaning is not in the 'presence' of the word but in its difference from other words.

Throughout *Writing and Difference*, Derrida sees structuralism as a quest for a universality which amounts to a bias towards truth totality. Structuralism is criticized as 'as an attempt to account for the totality of a phenomenon by reduction of it to a formula that governs it *totally*' (p. xvi).

9 Elsewhere, Jung reiterates the view of archetypal reality as a potential process, while explicitly making an analogy between the probability level of quantum physics and archetypal potential, referring to 'the analogy archetype-probability. In physical terms, probability corresponds to the so-called law of nature; psychically, it corresponds to the archetype' ('Letter to Pauli' 1951, p. 70).

10 See e.g., Jung 1928 on final causes; Hogenson 1994, pp. 15–17, on Jung's teleological thinking as early as his dissertation.

Leach (1982, p. 111) observes that Jung, Freud and Lévi-Strauss all shared the feature of proposing genuine cultural universals.

Derrida (1978) resists a view of history as 'totality' but examines 'the history of the departures from totality, history as the very movement of transcendence, of the excess over the totality ...' (p. 117). The concentric mandala or self is to be viewed as a unified and unifying process *within* totality that necessarily recognizes the multiplicity and also fragmentation within totality of truth and experience. It engages in a process of modifying diametric structures prematurely grounding totality – i.e., brings departures from totality – so that the diametric can move towards a concentric relation. Jung's unifying archetype does not treat a unity within experience as *all* experience (see also, Brooke 1991, p. 96; Downes 2003b, p. 167). Allowance of a potential unity within experience gives full recognition to fragmentation within experience and arguably requires such fragmentation. A *telos* does not underlie all truths or experience, even potentially; the diverse plurality of truths and experience is not to be governed by an underlying totalizing principle or some quasiHegelian totalizing view of history as reason.

Spivak's (1997) introduction to Derrida notes that 'a structuralist statement of structuralist objectives bases itself on the distinction between subject and object' (p. lvii). Derrida (1974) questions the very framework of the subject-object dualism relied upon by Lévi-Strauss. Only some aspects of a Jungian view of projection are based within the subject-object dualism. For example, a central theme of *Psychological Types* (1921) is the examination of how the different functions, i.e., feeling, thinking (judgment), intuition and sensation, are projections of different views of reality. Projection, here, is described as occurring when 'a subjective content becomes alienated from the subject and is, so to speak, embodied in the object' (p. 457). However, the conception of the collective unconscious – and 'archetypes' introduced by Jung in 1919, allows for a transpersonal level of projection. This thereby offers a psychology of projections which goes beyond the subject-object dualism.

7.4 Structure-content relativity in projection: Concentric and diametric spatial relation as the collective unconscious background to experiential contents

A spatial-phenomenological inquiry into background spatial assumptions calls into question the background relation between structure and content of projections, and between levels of the personal and collective unconscious. Like Freud, Jung (1921) acknowledges the intimate interconnection between projection and repression, 'the repressed intuitions begin to assert themselves in the form of projection ...' (p. 365). However, the conception of the collective unconscious allows for another level of projection. Jung (1959) refers to 'different ranges' of projection emanating from 'merely personal conditions or from deeper collective ones' (p. 10).

The question as to whether projection at the collective unconscious level is a projection of content and/or structure must acknowledge, as Stevens (1982/1992) does, Jung's propensity to make 'a semantic confusion between images and archetypes' (p. 341). This ambiguity between archetypal form and content in Jung's work is also assailed by Hayman (1999), who describes Jung's 'confusing the path with the journey' (p. 228) on this issue, interpreting Jung's equivocality here as a flaw, 'he never succeeded in sorting out the muddle' (p. 229). Yet the confusion may be as much in the eye of the beholders as in what they behold in Jung's work on this point.

Relating structures of experience to content of experience invites a broadened perspective on traditional psychoanalytic concepts such as repression and displacement. This broader view treats repressed and displaced experiential contents as also being a repression and displacement of experiential structures. Assumptions of a split between content and structure are to be challenged. *Repression and displacement of foregrounded experiential contents also brings a repression and displacement to the background spatial structure within which these experiential contents are located.* Change through repression and displacement involves movement into a displaced diametric spatial background for experience; direct opened experience, namely, experience that is not repressed at least relative to other more repressed experiences, implies movement of experiential contents towards a concentric spatial background.

This focus on foregrounded experiential contents and background spatial structures of relation for these contents will be argued to unite Freudian concerns with personal history and the Jungian collective unconscious. The foregrounded experiential contents being repressed and displaced, or else opened out of repression, are the personal history level. The background spatial structures, changing through repression and displacement or opening out of a repressed state, give expression to the transpersonal collective unconscious dimension to experience. As with a Gestalt psychology figure/ground focus, the same picture or experiential contents can uncover two complementary dimensions of foreground and background, personal and collective unconscious respectively. Both dimensions can be selected for differing emphasis at a given time. Concentric and diametric spatial structures of relation provide the collective unconscious background mediating the directional change to experience – either by working through repressed contents, or on the contrary, imposing the process of repression and displacement onto experiential contents. Concentric and diametric spaces are frames for experience and experiential change.

This figure/ground relation between the personal and collective unconscious helps shed light on the relation between what poet Louis MacNeice (1987) terms 'the paradox of the individual and the impersonal' (p. 43), described by T.S. Eliot in his influential exposition on *Tradition and the Individual Talent*. Fogarty (1995) suggests that 'the trait of impersonality' which Eliot 'purportedly supports is confusingly grounded in an equally heartfelt belief in the individuality of the writer' (p. 215). Though a challenge to traditional Western either/or logic, it is not confusing phenomenologically in terms of structures of primordial experience. The trace of personal experience shapes the corresponding collective spatial experiential domain and *vice-versa*, in figure-ground relation.

Equating archetypes with the 'primordial image' (p. 377), Jung (1921) regards archetypes at an experiential level as being a *content* of experience, 'the primordial images are ... just as much ideas as feelings' (p. 387).[11] The image pertains to at least two levels. Referring to the image as a 'functional form', Jung states that it is intended to express not only the form of the activity taking place but the typical situation in which the activity is released' (Jung 1934/1954, para. 152).

Three levels of projection can thus be separated:[12] (i) projection of ego contents, (ii) projection of archetypal image as content and (iii) projection of archetypal form. Yet Jung (1964) offers another prior level for projection implicit in his words, 'the symbols are natural attempts to reconcile and reunite the opposites within the psyche' (p. 90). The symbolic level is not directly equivalent to the opposites level as the former are in the service of the latter. Von Franz (1980/1992) recognizes this distinction of levels, 'The collective unconscious appears at first to be ... the sum of archetypal structures that manifest themselves in typical mythological motifs in all human beings. Underneath these structures, however, one finds a still deeper layer that has the appearance of a unit' (p. 366). She equates this deeper layer with the mandala or self, as does Jung (1943, para. 945; 1941/54 para. 661). This fourth level of 'the opposites', namely the interaction between ego and self is the level where the self or concentric structures are projected.

Structure-content relativity and projection: Beyond reification to a background level of relation

Separation of four different levels of projection invites focus on the *interaction* between the levels. Jung (1941) described Freud as being 'essentially concretistic', whereas he himself was 'chiefly impressed by the relativity of psychological phenomena' (Jung, *Letters*, Vol. I. p. 301). Such a relativity can be applied to his understanding of projection. Interaction between projected structure and content of experience allows for structural projections

11 Gordon (1985/1992) also refers to 'archetypal contents' as 'archetypal images and affects' (p. 293).

12 See also Roth (2001) for an account of four levels of transferences, largely at the ego contents projection level. These levels are complementary to the levels being discussed here.

to be potentially contents of experience. Given the different levels of Jungian projection, it emerges that the very terms 'structure' and 'content' are *relative to the prior level of projection*. The meaning of structure and content is not absolute as a positional sense of truth but relative to a vantage point in a system of relations between projections.

Focus on interaction raises the question as to whether the relation between levels of projection is a structural or formal one. The words of Lévi-Strauss (1973) develop this important distinction generally which Jung did not clarify, 'Contrary to formalism, structuralism refuses to set the concrete against the abstract ... Form is defined by opposition to material other than itself. But structure has no distinct content; *it is content itself*, apprehended in a logical organisation conceived as property of the real' (p. 115) (my italics). On this view, *projected structures differ from projected forms because structures assume connection with content, whereas forms assume separation from content*. In projection, the structure-content relation is potentially malleable and interchangeable so that structure is basically latent content for experience. Thus, Jung's (1951) reference to the need to 'dissolve projections' (p. 10) can be understood, at one level, as advocating the need to make structural dimensions to projections a content of experience rather than just a structure for experience. On this structuralist view of projections, Jung's (1964) emphasis, that archetypal forms are 'not just static patterns' but are 'dynamic factors' (p. 64), is a view of dynamism not just *within* levels of projection. Experience itself as a content is a dynamism *between* levels as projected structure is latent content of experience.

Another level of 'dissolving' projections rather than just 'withdrawing' them is the movement from diametric towards concentric modes of relation. The diametric projection is not just an isolated ego structure but is potentially intimately interactive with the concentric self projection. This suggests that the interaction between concentric and diametric projections, as processes, is a dynamic interaction not simply at the fourth level of projection (between the opposites of self and ego) but also *between levels* of projection. The concentric structured self is the 'centre' and 'totality' where the individual and collective overlap for Jung; at the fourth level of projection the concentric structure expresses the collective dimension. The interaction of the concentric self with the ego structured diametric projection relates the individual experience to the collective and is a potentially dynamic interaction which moves *between* levels of projection. *The relative differences between the concentric and diametric structures of relation (regarding connection/separation, background interaction and symmetrical inversion) are a level where structure of experience and content of experience are in assumed connection.*

The relativism between levels of projected structure and content allows for an experiential movement between levels as *what may at one stage be a structure framing content of experience can subsequently become a content itself for experience.* A key objection to such a structuralist perspective on projection is the charge of Lamarckism, namely, the scientifically discredited assumption that experiences of ancestors can be inherited by individuals. This charge has been levelled at Jung's collective unconscious, although it was Freud, unlike Jung, who was a committed Lamarckian. Speaking the year of his own death about the Lamarckian hypothesis of mnemic inheritance, Freud (1939a) stated, 'I have no hesitation in declaring that men have always known (in this special [Lamarckian] way) that they once possessed a primal father and killed him' (p. 101). By way of contrast, Jung was at pains to emphasize that the archetype or primordial image (e.g., Jung 1921, p. 377) was an inherited deposit from past generations at the level of form only and not the content of the specific memories experienced in the past (Jung 1934/1954, p. 79; Jung 1938/1986, p. 107). This avoids the charge that Jung was a Lamarckian, believing in the inheritance of acquired characteristics (Storr 1973, Samuels 1985).

A biological role for concentric and diametric structures as inherited characteristics would have to clearly separate the levels of projection as a sharp division between form and content would be needed to avoid the charge of Lamarckism. However, the structuralist approach emphasizing potential interrelation between projected form and content, including interrelation between concentric and diametric projected structures and experiential contents must find a source for these structures not primarily in biology but elsewhere. Maranda (1972) observes that structuralism in anthropology is 'only minimally concerned with biological components' (p. 330). The framework of concentric and diametric projected structures does not exclude a role for biology with regard to projections at other archetypal (and ego) levels which can sustain an assumed separation between form and content. Yet it does postulate a fourth level of projection for the concentric self which is not reducible to a biology of archetypes[13] and is thus, in this sense, a transcendent function.

An aspect of reification criticized by Derrida (1978) is the tendency to place the idea before the experience, putting 'the notion of an Idea or "interior design" as simply anterior to a work which would supposedly be the expression of it'; this is 'a prejudice: a prejudice of the traditional criticism called idealist' (p. 11). This debate as to whether experience precedes the idea, or *vice-versa*, can be resolved in the context of diametric space by a focus on differing levels of explanation. The diametric structure at the personal level frames the particular content of the complexes (Downes 2003, pp. 66–7). This constellating of diametric structured experience in reaction to traumatic experiential content translates the personal history at the level of the contents of a complex – 'the split-off complexes' (Jung 1935, p. 188) – into the collective unconscious dimension. This translation occurs through the structural organization of these personal contents (e.g., the active sadistic aggression of the *Wolf Man* towards his father combined with an opposing tender passive attitude) into a diametric structural reaction. This framework arguably offers a way out of the problem observed by Cambray (2001) that the collective/personal unconscious dichotomy easily becomes rigid and 'polarizes the psyche' (p. 280). A diametric structured constellation to frame the contents of a personal complex allows for the personal to directly relate to the collective rather than foreclosing it from the collective unconscious.

Focus on experiential content places the experience as primary to some underlying idea or structure. Yet the experienced complexes tend to organize themselves in reactive diametric fashion (Downes 2003). This brings emergence of an underlying structure. From a different perspective, this structure becomes more primary and could be said to precede the

13 This does not exclude a fifth level, namely, the background relation itself between concentric and diametric structures. This fifth level of concentric structured self as totality expresses the *per se* level for the archetype of the self.

experience. The question as to whether the complexes' experiential content or diametric structure is to be given priority requires a both/and answer. It resonates with the Gestalt psychology view of a figure and ground; the content of the complex is to be interpreted as the foreground figure, the diametric structure of the collective unconscious as the background. Both are relevant levels of reality.

Derrida's concerns with placing a reified image before the idea are an important warning against reduction of concentric and diametric spaces to merely abstract decontextualized schemata; it is important to emphasize that these structures are inherently relational and require context, whether empirical, experiential or both, for meaning. Concentric and diametric structures are not mere logic schemas to be divorced from context of relation, whether interpersonal, intrapsychic, or beyond; they are primarily directional and differential than simply static and positional. Nevertheless, construed as images, the danger of their possible reification must be acknowledged.

While Jungian conceptions of the collective unconscious transcend the subject-object dualism through going beyond the individual subject, it is arguable that another feature of the collective unconscious is still locked within this dualism. Jung's emphasis on archetypal images – on the role of images – is a visual metaphor which *assumes an image to be viewed as an object, as well as by an observing subject*. Derrida (1978, p. 118) criticizes a metaphysics based on the metaphor of light, challenging Platonic metaphors of knowledge as sight. In similar vein, Norris (1982) notes that 'the etymological link between "theory" and "seeing" (Greek *thea* = spectacle) becomes a forgotten or sublimated metaphor underlying the certitudes of science' (p. 82).

A related objection to reification, visual metaphors and the certitudes of limited versions of science is Derrida's recognition of the limitations of positional truth claims in his discussion of *Beyond the Pleasure Principle*. This process could be termed *claritism*, namely, the neurotic desire for premature clarity, for the illusion of a closure of meaning, the shortcircuiting of a problem of uncertainty in the name of clarity. In a legal context, such claritism would subvert the goals of justice for the desire for certainty, through a clear though unjust conclusion; this claritism is where clarity becomes a defining end of itself and displaces more important goals. Claritism suppresses what Spanos (1995) would term, 'this silent realm of dreadful uncertainty' (pp. 38–9), while in jurisprudence Hart (1961) describes clarity as being merely a secondary norm in legal-decision making. In Heideggerian terms, claritists suppress the anxiety of authenticity of search for meaning; in Nietzschean garb, claritism is a promotion of a desiccated form of Apollonian certainty and parallel repression of the Dionysian propensity to break open edificial masks posturing as truths. Claritism is akin to the transparency of a Benthamite *Panopticon*, his hypothetical prison where all inmates could be seen, offering a clarity of sorts yet ultimately imprisoning a species, whether that species is truth or justice. This is obviously not a diatribe against clarity *per se* but rather against a premature clarity born of insecurity – and a recognition of the limitations of positional truth claims' seductive clarity, compared with directional, relational truth claims.

Derrida (1978) criticizes the reification of structures as 'confusing meaning with its geometric, morphological, or in the best of cases, cinematic model' (p. 16), where 'structure becomes the object itself, the literary thing itself. It is no longer … a heuristic instrument' (p. 15). Yet these criticisms apply not only to structures but to all images, including primordial images in Jung's collective unconscious. Lévi-Strauss' postulation of an interplay between structure and content, in contrast to formalism, not only advances his own position beyond a reified view of structures. It also offers a defence of Jung's unwillingness to consistently apply a rigid form/content dualism to his conceptions of archetypes.

Warnings against the dangers of reification given in analytical psychology (e.g., Samuels 1985, p. 6; Cambray 2001, p. 281; Knox 2003, p. 212) and anthropology (e.g., Caton 1987, p. 251), invite further focus on *what* is projected. Whether image, content or structure of projection, structure-content relativity implies that change can occur so that a projected structure can become a content of experience. The role of time in this change is implicated. Moreover, what is projected is not independent of the mode of relation (to the projection) of the person experiencing the projection. Projections are not just about what is projected but are also about a prior relation, namely, the relation of the projection to the person experiencing the projection. In other words, *what is a projected structure or content inheres not simply in the projected internal object but in the person's experiential relation to this object.*

Projection needs to be considered not simply as a quasi-independent object (i.e., image, structure, content) but *in relation*. The projected structures or contents at least potentially interact with the relational background of the person experiencing the projection – so that change or movement from structure to experience in structure-content relativity can take place. Acceptance of these two levels of projection (as an object and relational background to the person) highlights that *the background mode of relation is itself a projection*. As Jung highlighted, although not always consistently, with regard to the related context of dreams, it is not so much the objective dream which has meaning but the person's subjective relation to the dream through his/her associations to it. Cambray's (2001) account of subjective and objective amplification recognizes an 'increased sensitivity' (p. 300) of Jung towards subjective feeling responses from the late 1940s.

Consideration of the mode of relation to the projection as itself a projection opens the door to concentric and diametric spaces, as the key underlying structural projection for this mode of relation.

Distinctions such as being in assumed connection versus being in assumed separation to the projection are central to the person's mode of relation to their projections. Similarly, the person's angle of relation to the projection can allow them to be in an interactive background relation to the projection (a concentric relation) or a non-interactive background to the projection (a diametric relation).

This accommodation of two levels of projection – objectified and relational[14] – involves a reorientation of Jung's dichotomy between a collective

14 Relational is in the sense of relation to the projection, rather than as interpersonal. Other terminology could be used such as the foregrounded objectified projection being termed the 'proximal' projection and the background mode of relation the 'distal' projection. However, such terms are potentially misleading as what is phenomenologically i.e., experientially, proximal or more remote (distal) can change within experience. Perhaps a preferable term would be horizontal projection (for the

and personal unconscious. Jung's bifurcation is challenged by Eigen (1986) as 'the formation and operation of Freudian drives and ego is anything but "personal"', whereas 'similarly, the subject's relationship to Jungian archetypes and the archetypes themselves may be anything but impersonal (viz., a personal God)' (p. 61). Eigen (1986) continues, 'My suspicion is that Jung first went off by making his primary dichotomy the collective unconscious and the personal unconscious thus foreclosing the personal at the deepest levels of psychic life' (p. 62).

The background (concentric or diametric) mode of relation to objectified projections exists, whether the foregrounded projections are ego or archetypal projections. Images, contents and structures, as projections from the personal and collective unconscious, still potentially interact with the background mode of relation. Thus, the personal-collective unconscious dichotomy (i.e., ego-archetype dichotomy) has been preserved, although relativized, as being one part of a broader relationship. This relationship is between objectified projections on the one hand, and their relation to background *archetypal, yet personal*, structures of experience, i.e., concentric and diametric spaces.

It is to be emphasized that interaction between concentric and diametric spaces is not a proposed metanarrative (Lyotard 1984), abstracted from contextual interaction and superimposed mechanically across universal contexts. Rather this potential spatial background interacts differentially with a given context to open unthought horizons for meaning within that context and beyond. Lather (1994) asks from a postmodernist perspective about developing the framing of meaning possibilities. This spatial-phenomenological interrogation of primordial projections raises such questions of directional spatial possibilities for framing and changing meanings. It is a condition for the possibility of meaning change, rather than constitutive of meaning in causal mechanical fashion. And the directional possibilities are

---

objectified images/contents/structures) and vertical projection (for the concentric or diametric projected mode of relation to the projections) – with vertical also having connotations of being a transcendence of the horizontal.

for the goal not so much of truth as correspondence (as in structuralism), nor simple empty possibilities, but for uncovering primordial truth and experiential meaning. This goal can also be construed in scientific terms as improvement of the explanatory adequacy of a paradigm, as deconstructing blind spots in malleable experiential projections.

CHAPTER 8

Uncovering a Primordial Phenomenological Spatial Discourse Prior to Language: Examples of a Prelinguistic Spatial Discourse from Modernist Art and the *Yin/Yang* Archetypal Structure

Argument: That concentric and diametric spatial structures offer (i) a phenomenologically meaningful, prelinguistic discourse to express key aspects of modernist experience and (ii) provide a model of depth to challenge a postmodernist 'waning of affect' (Jameson 1991).

8.1 Modernism and postmodernism: Structures of desire and the waning of affect in a crisis of meaning

In Jung's account of a mid-life crisis, many people experience a loss of meaning to life, where having attained common goals such as financial security, establishment of a family and career recognition, they still feel a vacuum, 'not ... from any clinically definable neurosis, but from the senselessness and aimlessness of their lives' (Jung 1954, p. 41). In contemporary society, this crisis of meaning, requiring a restructuring within experience, arguably extends to other times of life and not simply a person's mid-life. Experience of an ossifying *ennui* to existence and a concomitant crisis of meaning is not the preserve of the middle-aged.

Jung's experiential journey towards individuation expresses a search for meaning that is by no means a postmodern 'waning of affect' (Jameson 1991, p. 15). Jung's mid-life crisis implicates a renewal from a desiccation of affect. Though more heterodox than characterized by Kvale – and with Derrida a clear exception – postmodern assumptions tend to deny any need to go beyond the surface in life, as Kvale (1992) highlights, 'Postmodern man has stopped waiting for Godot. The absurd is not met with despair; rather it is a living with what is, a making the best of it, a relief from the burden of finding yourself as the goal of life; what remains may be a happy nihilism' (p. 38). Meaninglessness in a postmodern culture is to be enjoyed and revelled in, as with Huxley's happiness pill *soma*, eerily envisaging Prozac, Ecstasy or even Viagra, in his technological dystopia *Brave New World*. But, to reassert the obvious in these rapid remarks, meaninglessness may also not be a happy nihilism.

While being cognizant of the need to avoid lapse into a lassitude of categorization that would treat postmodernism as a monolithic, unitary whole, nevertheless, a feature of postmodernist thought is its rejection of such contrasts between surface/depth, essence/appearance, as well as inner/outer. In effect, postmodernism reduces this opposition to a monism, where depth is reduced, compressed and flattened to surface and the inner is treated as expression of an outer cultural realm.

Jungian psychology stands in resolute contrast with postmodernism regarding search for wholeness. A unity within experience, balancing unconscious and conscious forces, is for Jung, both possible and desirable. This is not to say that this journey towards experiential wholeness is not an extremely difficult one, which requires a person to stake all of one's being (Jung 1939). The mandala archetypal structure embodies a contrast between inner and outer – between the space inside the circle and that outside the square. Similarly, concentric and diametric spatial structures bestow fundamental contrasts between inner and outer. However, the relations between inner and outer differ in both, as it is only in a concentric relation that the outer fully surrounds the inner as part of a whole. A diametric polarity between an inner and outer realm firmly splits one from the other. Nevertheless, the primordial structures of the mandala, and concentric and diametric spaces, all postulate an inner/outer distinction which is anathema to postmodernism.

A Jungian implication of this interplay is that through integration of ego and self levels, a potential progress towards the concentric can occur, though this is fragile and fraught with difficulty and anxiety. In contrast, a feature of Freud's life and death drives, retained in its spatial-phenomenological reinterpretation, is a challenge to Enlightenment ideals of progress in history (Brickman 1993). For Freud, there is little or no guarantee that the concentric unifying background of *Eros* will progress against that of the diametric split background of *Thanathos*.

A spatial-phenomenological engagement with structures of affect offers immediate resonance with concerns epitomized in modernism, such as with anxiety and desire. It is to these aspects that a prelinguistic space can be further apprehended through the modernist art of Munch's anxiety and Klimt's desire. In doing so, the surreptitious discourse of concentric and diametric archetypal spaces again comes to the fore to challenge a waning of affect in human experience.

8.2 Diametric and concentric archetypal spaces in the modernist art of Munch's *The Scream*

Edward Munch's masterpiece *The Scream* (1893) (see Figure 4) is an image fusing existential *Angst* with Jungian archetypal themes and structures. In the words of Eggum (1998), *The Scream* 'has become recognised as the actual mental image of the existential *angst* of civilised man ... none developed such a uniquely "private" symbolism on the basis of personal traumatic experience ... In Jungian terms he crystallises archetypal images and symbols of human existential experience, and he takes this crystallisation farthest in *The Scream*, where the almost abstract figure in the foreground makes concrete and personifies the existential *angst* of modern man' (pp. 34–6). A spatial-phenomenological account of *The Scream* invites an inquiry into the preverbal structures of space projected into the images therein, without claiming that this exhausts its meaning.

Gergen (2000) places Munch firmly in the tradition of romanticism: 'In Norway, Edvard Munch sustained the romantic tradition in his faces contorted by anxiety and anguish from an internal wellspring far removed'

Figure 4 *The Scream* (1893) by Edvard Munch.

(p. 25). Munch's art generally is described by Alexandrian (1970) as going 'far beyond expressionism ... where he gives mystical expression to love, to solitude and to primitive fears' (p. 21). *The Scream* expresses modernist themes that extend to a silent discourse encompassing diametric and concentric spaces. Jameson (1991) recognizes that Munch's painting develops 'the hermeneutic model of inside and outside' (p. 12):

> *The Scream*, is, of course, the canonical expression of the great modernist thematics of alienation, anomie, solitude, social fragmentation and isolation, a virtually programmatic emblem of what used to be called the age of anxiety ... The very concept of expression presupposes indeed some separation within the subject, and along with that a whole metaphysics of the inside and outside. (p. 11)

Jameson (1991) contrasts *The Scream* with postmodernist concerns, though any such juxtaposition needs to discriminate between different modernisms.

The bridge in *The Scream* effectuates a diametric sundering, an assumed separation between the homunculus figure and the concentric background. The overall frame of relation is a diametric spatial one, between the diametric structure of the bridge and the concentric swirling background. The bridge is a border that divides and removes from the background, though not here as an active agent of uprooting, not as a cause of rootlessness for the homunculus. This diametric split is contained additionally *within* the bridge itself, where the rectangular portions of the fence on the bridge are in a basically diametric structural relation to each other. The bridge expresses a diametric function in relation to the concentric background, while its fence also crystallizes a diametric structure. The borders of a diametric relation help found a somewhat self-contained autonomous subject, abstracted on a bridge from a background of contextual relation. Jameson (1991) comments on conceptions of the individual as a monad in modernist works such as *The Scream*:

> You constitute your individual subjectivity as a self-sufficient field and a closed realm ... Postmodernism presumably signals the end of this dilemma, which it replaces with a new one. The end of the bourgeois ego, or monad, no doubt brings with it the end of the psychopathologies of that ego – what I have been calling the waning of affect (p. 15)

In postmodern cultural theory, 'fundamental depth models' are 'repudiated' (Jameson 1991, p. 12). Such depth models include those of Jungian psychology, while Jameson (1991) highlights others, 'the Freudian model of latent and manifest' content, distinctions between essence and appearance and 'the existential model of authenticity and inauthenticity whose heroic or tragic thematics are closely related to that other great opposition between alienation and disalienation' (p. 12). Postmodernism collapses any distinctions between foreground and background. Within the hemiplegia of a postmodernist schema, the bridge and subject (homunculus) of Munch's *The Scream* would collapse into the contextual background, and the scream of anxiety as search for meaning and healing would not be heard among the cacophonous din. Or if heard, it would be dismissed, parodied out of relevance.

It is possible that the scream is being heard at a level prior to sound as the homunculus has no ears. Anxiety vibrates at a mode of experience prior to the sensual level of sound, in a crisis of space, as an aural throbbing in a space or medium of feeling more primordial than hearing. In the words of Jameson (1991):

> *The Scream* subtly but elaborately disconnects its own aesthetic of expression, all the while remaining imprisoned within it. Its gestural content already underscores its own failure, since the realm of the sonorous, the cry, the raw vibrations of the human throat, are incompatible with its medium (something underscored within the work by the homunculus's lack of ears). Yet the absent scream returns, as it were, in a dialectic of loops and spirals, circling ever more closely toward that even more absent experience of atrocious solitude and anxiety which the scream was itself to 'express'. Such loops inscribe themselves on the painted surface in the form of those great concentric circles in which sonorous vibration becomes ultimately visible. (p. 14)

Munch opens up an implied space for experience, encompassing the gasp of anxiety, in some way prior to traditional empirical senses.

From one vantage point, a condition for this anxiety is the separation of the homunculus figure on the bridge from the concentric background. On this view, the bridge is a factor in alienation and displacement from the concentric background. Alternatively, the bridge is a protective border from the swirling background so that the anxiety is one of connection with the background. This second perspective is reinforced by the location of the homunculus's head against the background not of the bridge but of the concentric swirling forces; on this view, the hands of the homunculus placed around the head are to protect from the concentric background. The background concentric space is far from benign, not of itself, but in its overpowering, unfurling relation to the homunculus. The grid of the bridge manufactures the pathway as a buttress towards a waning of affect, an attempted dulling of anxiety. It is thus is an apparent protection through disconnection. It is a disconnection that is not yet a repression, being sufficiently bereft of activity as to fail to constitute a moving process. Here hell is not so much other people as the summoning of movement, accelerated life in the concentric whirl.

The terror of possession by concentric spiraling animation is juxtaposed with the confined and defined space of the inert diametric structures of the bridge. Yet with this great anxiety, there is too much room. In the warring spaces between concentric background and passive bridge enclosed in its diametricity, though scarcely a fortress, the homunculus is caught, torn between retreat to the bridge and dissolution in the background frenzy. In a space without shadow, there is no obvious source of light.

The sway of air threatens a drowning. Beyond two remote figures walking in the background of the bridge, no one else is around, whether to help or further accentuate the anguish. Again an ambiguity is opened as to the role of isolation of the homunculus in heightening the fraught experience or necessary confrontation of the existential dilemma.

Significantly, the painting is cleft in two through the border of the bridge. Munch offers no asymptote of hope to reconcile line and circle, bridge and background, diametric and concentric spaces. Hope and space here do not rhyme. Yet there is a chiming of meaning within, across, a distinct primordial spatial discourse implicated in *The Scream*.

Boulton Smith (1977) comments on Munch's, *Self Portrait. Between the Clock and the Bed*, where Munch is a '"slippered pantaloon" almost as much a "thing" as the twin poles of his room, the clock and the bed ... Shoulders sag, arms hang limply, in a parody of the clock ... His blue and green clothes are set against the radiant orange and yellow of the background with the result that he seems to shrink still further' (p. 36). The aged man is a paltry object among objects side-by-side with each other in the room – he is a prime expression of Heidegger's (1927, p. 81) mode of side-by-sideness, being in a diametric spatial relation to other objects in the room and in assumed separation from the iridescent brightness of the background realm.

Other examples of a diametric split relation of side-by-sideness among the figures in Munch's work include *Eye in Eye* (1894), *Adam and Eve* (1909), *Old Man in Warnemünde* (1907), as well as his feeling of 'walking beside oneself' (Eggum 1998, p. 77). In *The Woman and the Heart* (1896), the heart has been moved from its concentric relation within the body to being held by the woman side-by-side with her body in a diametric relation of assumed separation. *The Sun* (1909–1916), the central painting of the Oslo University murals, is perhaps his most obvious concentric structured painting.

Ibsen was a contemporary and friend of his compatriot Munch. Eagleton (1995) describes a 'tragic' Ibsenite version of modernism where, 'The present is suspended between an unbreachable past and an unattainable future, and slowly withers to death between them' (p. 317). In contrast, Jung's journey towards individuation offers the hope that a future unification within the psyche is attainable. This hope must be distinguished from a simplistic optimism that this unification is inevitable. Jung recognizes that this crisis of meaning brings a rootlessness and sense of alienation which cannot be denied, dismissed or more subtly flattened. This experience of rootlessness and attempt to refreshen experience through and beyond myth has strong resonances with modernism. In Eagleton's (1995) words, 'The celebrated formalism and aestheticism of the modernists, their scandalous insistence that one could live inside myth or language or archetype, that the art-work was its own origin, audience and *raison d'etre*, was among other things a defiant rationalisation of their own rootless condition' (p. 300). Significantly, Munch's spatial discourse goes beyond the seductions of myth, to expose a pathway to meaning – meaning through concentric and diametric spaces that render public some of the extremes of private experience, as an expression of a distinctive axis of the unconscious world. In doing so, *The Scream* articulates not so much a primordial dance between concentric and diametric spaces, as a primordial paralysis.

A framework of interaction between concentric and diametric spaces does not treat the limitations of a diametric opposition between inner and outer as, thereby, requiring a postmodern monism between inner and outer. Inner need not be merely reduced to outer. Deconstruction of the diametric inner and outer realms need not lead to a nihilism regarding depth. It rather invites the possibility of moving to a different kind of primordial inner/outer relation in a restructuring to a concentric inner/outer space, where the inner is surrounded by and contained in the outer.

This perspective elucidates not only how a framework of interactive concentric and diametric structures differs from postmodernism; it also illustrates what it adds to modernism. The postmodernist critique of modernism is to be acknowledged regarding modernist assumptions of an autonomous inner realm, where such a realm is founded on a Cartesian diametric split between inner and outer. Jung (1939, p. 104) himself criticized the isolation of a mental sphere in Western thinking, thus eschewing a Cartesian framework for psychology. Here Jung basically challenges a diametric relation between an inner realm of experience and an outer world. A concentric movement towards assumed connection between self and world is a prior spontaneity. It occurs before diametric Cartesian suspicion, detachment and selfconsciousness gains dominion. It is not a denial of a Cartesian dimension as illusory or nonexistent, but rather a dissolving of this mirror image space of selfconsciousness into a different concentric space of experience. Brooke (1991, pp. 85–6) suggests that challenge to a Cartesian inner realm does not reduce Jungian psychology to sociology, nor general systems theory. Envisaging the shift from diametric Cartesian innerness to concentric inwardness avoids sheer reduction to societal forces. It further substantiates a challenge to Cartesian innerness.

The framework of interaction between concentric and diametric spaces adds an alternative concentric model of inwardness; this contrasts with a diametric model of an abstracted inner realm, split from the outer world. It invites a restructuring or movement from the diametric model of inwardness to the concentric mode of inward relation. Moreover, unlike postmodernism, it confronts the anxiety of this restructuring; it invites a renewal rather than waning of affect. Neither is it a mere inversion of a waning of affect. Within the reanimation of the restructuring, it encompasses the dried space of diametric projections that bring a closure, separation and waning of repressed affect. This spatial-phenomenology provides a frame for the structure of existential *Angst* in dynamic spatial terms. This restructuring involves the anxiety of a dialectical relationship between diametric and concentric spatial relations framing experience. This does not eliminate or minimize anxiety but rather invites facing up to a crisis of meaning which allows for a process of unity between conscious and unconscious levels.

8.3 Diametric and concentric archetypal spaces in the modernist art of Klimt's *The Kiss*

Eagleton's (1990) critique of the superficiality of postmodern conceptions of choice that fail to interrogate the subjective desires underlying such choices, resonates with a Jungian concern for meaning prior to the intentional, 'Interests and desires operate, in effect, if not in admission [in postmodernism] as quasitranscendental anteriorities; there can be no asking from where they derive ... [they] are simply withdrawn from the process of rational justification, as that which one can never get behind' (pp. 379–83). Criteria upon which a choice is made is viewed by postmodernism as being products of the cultural conditioning the individual undergoes; in a postmodern world the individual cannot escape his/her own culture, as there is no prior source of freedom that can serve as a source that transcends cultural relativity.

A Jungian journey towards a psychic unity, as part of the individuation process, offers the hope that the individual is not merely a product of cultural conditioning. Search for a primordial experiential unity expressed through a dynamic mandala structure is tantamount to recognition that a postmodern diversity that denies unity becomes mere frenzy, a cacophony of sounds squeezed of the juices of silence, voices that grate, blocked of air. A diversity that denies unity becomes humdrum experience, denuded truth, a cocktail of violence and indifference. A parody of experience becomes itself the only experience, in the glitz of its apparently variegated forms. A primordial experiential and truth search for unifying directions – as distinct from unity as abstraction and unity as conformity – is an interrogation of structures of desire; these are domains of the unconscious which become

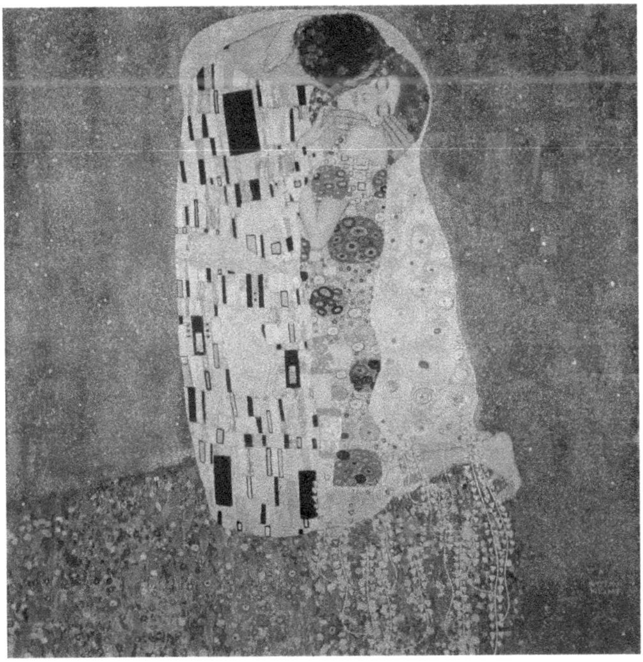

Figure 5 *The Kiss* (1907–1908) by Gustav Klimt. Belvedere, Vienna.

simply withdrawn from relevance in much of postmodernist thought. Like the ruptured cadences of unrequited love, concentric structured experience is flattened in postmodernism.

A spatial-phenomenological approach builds upon rather than ejects affect and desire articulated in modernist experience. Hoffman (1985) highlights that there is a prior, more primordial opposition than the male-female one in Gustav Klimt's modernist painting *The Kiss* (see Figure 5). Hoffman (1985) describes this opposition as being between rectangular and round patterns. In doing so, he has touched upon the contrasts between diametric and concentric structures of relation and the implicit primordial discourse within it, 'In *The Kiss* he [Klimt] has taken away the male-female tension from the two bodies and delegated it to the opposition of rectangular and round patterns. Thus, instinct and desire have been encoded in a scheme of ornamental contrasts' (p. 122). This scheme of ornamental contrasts offers a meaning as a primordial relation between diametric and concentric spaces. Hoffman did not go far enough, the opposition is not so much between rectangles and round patterns but between diametric and concentric spaces, as structures of primordial experience. An absence coexists in the presence, a chill in the kiss. Where foreground subjects unite in *The Kiss*, background spaces do not. An existential tension of relation and impenetrable distance persists.

Other commentators emphasize symbolic dimensions to *The Kiss*. For example, Whitford (1990) comments, 'The painting is not autobiographical but a symbolic, universalized statement about sexual love' (p. 118). Fliedl (2006) builds on Hoffman's point in relation to *The Kiss*:

> Because of the ornamental symbolism in the lovers' garments, the picture has often been described as symbolizing their union. However, it is precisely those ornamental elements which here distinguish male and female. Following the clichés of biologically and psychologically distinctive features, the man has been given 'harsh' forms – rectangular areas of black, white and grey – while the woman is endowed with the 'soft' features of colourful, flowery and curved elements. So although the lovers' embraces, their selfcontained shared outline, their background and their golden garments suggest a single configuration, the two figures can nevertheless be distinguished by the own specific ornaments ... Indeed it is only their ornaments which indicate, in an abstract and symbolical way the 'little difference' between them. (p. 116)

Once again with a focus on the implied discourse built into structures of relation in *The Kiss*, the contrasts between the primordial relations of concentric and diametric spaces emerge. It is important to accentuate, however, that while *The Kiss* associates the male with diametric relations and the female with concentric relations that this is not a necessary connection or inference outside of this context. Rather, a more primordial spatial opposition thrives prior to gender relations, underived from an anatomy of the body. It is also notable that, elsewhere in Klimt's work, there are strong concentric structures in *Tree of Life* (1905/6), the major motif of the stocket Frieze. Concentric and diametric structures of relation are primordial experiential relations and are prior to the reductionism of gender essentialist claims.

Fliedl (2006) notes that, 'In many works – including Klimt's earliest ones – he created tension and significance as well as particular relationships between the figures by means of empty spaces' (p. 145). Yet these voids offer distinctively different structures to embrace them. A monistic fusion and embrace of the couple in *The Kiss* must go further to dance with, what Nietzsche (1883) described as the 'terrible mistress' (p. 167) of solitude, as a space for a further level of unity of the voids and connective webs between self and other. A crisis of meaning is imported into the structures of desire. The framework of concentric and diametric relations offers models of a spatial discourse for such 'empty' spaces, physically manifested and yet irreducible to the anthropocentrism of the body.

Against the backdrop of a perceived shift historically in Western culture to a secular time and distanciation from an 'enchanted' world, Taylor (2007) asks where the equivalent forms of the crisis of romanticism are being expressed in much of Western culture today, 'Where has the set of dissatisfactions of the Romantic age gone among contemporary materialists?' (p. 391). He also emphasizes that a crisis of meaning is a historically changing mode of experience across eras, where calls of writers like Nietzsche and Camus for the courage to face the void and create meaning anew would not have been understood in prior eras, 'But how coherent is this view of the creation of meaning and value in face of the void? Certainly, as an account of what happened in the early stages of modernity, it verges on fantasy. If you had tried to explain to Locke or Grotius that this is what they were doing, they would have stared at you in incomprehension' (Taylor 2007, p. 589). A purported dance between concentric and diametric spaces is one pathway into meaning through confrontation of the void in intrapsychic and interpersonal experience. It focuses on a flattening of experiential space, in somewhat complementary fashion to a compression of lived time in Taylor (2007), though without tying such flattening to a distinct era in history in a macrostructural or causal analysis.

Table 4 The different conceptions of subjectivity in modernism, postmodernism and spatial-phenomenology

Modernism	*Postmodernism*	*Spatial-Phenomenology*
Cartesian split between inner and outer; Diametric split between inner and outer	Inner is reducible to outer; Inner/outer dualism is reduced to a monism of the cultural text	Restructuring from a diametric split between inner and outer towards a concentric relation between inner and outer
Anxiety of displacement; crisis of meaning	A 'happy' nihilism; denial of crisis	A unifying process interacting with anxiety; a direction towards concentric relation
Depth psychology	Surface realities predominate; truth is relativistic and pragmatic	Reclaiming of a depth of experience and priority for truth; beyond relativism to a primordial truth within a multiplicity of truths
Subjectivity as autonomous inner realm abstracted from outer	Death of the autonomous subject through immersion in the cultural (con)text	Primordial structures of experience prior to subjectivity

Concentric and diametric relations offer not depth of core identities, but core qualities of relation to and changes for a multiplicity of identities. Concentric spaces of assumed connection allow and provide a fluidity and mobility mediating aspects of self. The primordial relations of concentric and diametric spaces are not core 'foundations' of personal subjective identity but are potentially unifying dimensions of relation for the range of personal identities of a person. They are transsubjective structures of differential relation in a dynamic interplay with contextual complexity. Assumed connection and assumed separation, as relational differences of concentric and diametric spaces, may include interpersonal relations but are not simply reducible to them.

Gergen (2000) considers the Freudian unconscious as a combination of 'the romanticist drama of personal depth' with 'modernist demands for objective evidence' (p. 27). Moreover, Gergen (1994) highlights contrasting views of individual stability and change over time within developmental psychology, treating aspects of Freudian theory of childhood development as 'the classic exemplar of the stability orientation' (p. 148). The interplay between concentric and diametric spatial relations is not so much to favour stability over change, or change over stability, as to *mediate between* change and stability. It is the spatio-temporal background relation itself between stability and change that is being focused upon. Interplay between concentric modes of assumed connection and diametric modes of assumed separation offer a framework of potential relation between multiple sites of selves – this interplay *between* also becomes an interplay *with* these sites of selves to render them more static and/or dynamic.

Gergen's (1994) words note that 'the dialectic emphasis on ongoing change is antithetical to the mechanistic, stability orientation' (p. 159). Yet if stability is viewed as one form of change (as a static self in a dynamic environment is in effect changing in relation to that environment), the binary opposition between change/stability instead focuses on the relation *of* change and stability *between* change and stability. This is the more primordial space for play. The change/stability opposition is reorientated into a focus on the prior primordial relation of interplay between concentric assumed connection and diametric assumed separation as expressed through relations between more stable and more fluctuating dimensions of selves. This exemplifies how concentric-diametric spatial projective interaction is a discourse not only on a more primordial unifying process but also how it is a potential unifying process that requires fragmentation to become itself meaningful.

There is still a need for conceptualization of the background relation itself *between* the prematurely grounded stability of the socially constructed, categorial identity and the complexity of the hybridity of identities of self in a postmodern context (see also May et al., 2004). Again this mediating space between simplistic, categorial, social identities and a more complex, hybridity of identities of a saturated self (Gergen 2000) involves silent assumptions of connection and separation, of concentric and diametric spatial relations. A background spatial condition of concentric and diametric interaction mediates between the different initial unities and diverse fragmentations of identity in the construction of self in society.

Analysis of the existence of these diametric and concentric spaces is a somewhat different (though related) level to that of the contextual meanings of their existence in a given text. A primordially meaningful interpretation, i.e., meaningful in relation to primordial spatial structures, is not a primordial meaning or truth *per se*. Primordially meaningful interpretations can be construed as horizontal meaning, i.e., horizons of sociohistorically constructed meaning from the interaction between the contextual materials and the concentric and diametric structures. The *relative differences* between concentric and diametric spaces are being proposed to be horizons of embedded transcendence, i.e., an embedded meaning, transcendent of socio-historical horizons, a vertical meaning level as a background for horizontal meanings. This vertical meaning level is distinct from a truth as correspondence level. It is not a subterfuge imposed upon sociohistorical empirical factuality – but a space for play within the factual constructions.[1]

These proposed primordial structures of relation also offer a challenge to postmodernist theory which tends to reduce binary oppositions such as surface-depth, inner-outer to monistic priority of one pole over another, rather than conceiving these oppositions as diametric structures requiring change towards concentric spaces. Adapting the words of Stephen Daedalus, in Joyce's *Portrait of the Artist*, 'History is a nightmare from which I'm trying to awake', a spatial-phenomenology decentres the emphasis of postmodern theory on historical time to allow for a renewed focus on space and desire. This invokes a different kind of temporality from linear historical time in its conception of change between concentric and diametric space – a temporality which challenges the nightmare of the diametric binary opposition between the historical and the ahistorical.

1 A spatial-phenomenology is to be firmly distinguished from the strong social constructionist (Sayer 1997) position that treats the referents of social processes as merely ideal, or where construction is naively equated with falsity.

8.4 A spatial-phenomenological reinterpretation of the archetypal structure of *yin/yang*

Argument: That the archetypal structure of *yin/yang* offers an implied, prelinguistic discourse in terms of concentric and diametric structures.

Jung (1948) recognizes that dreams provide an expression that is 'never ... in this logical, abstract way but always in the language of parable or simile', a feature he observes it shares with so-called 'primitive languages' (p. 34). It will now be argued that the *yin/yang* structure provides a spatial discourse of implication, one that is more primordial than abstract logic. This discourse of implication is to be distinguished from the traditional associations with *yin/yang* and can serve as a precursor of the discourse of implication emerging from the relations between concentric and diametric spaces.

A first avenue for exploration of this spatial discourse of implication is recognizing that the opposition between light and dark in *yin/yang* is predominantly a complementary one, where there is a neutrality as to which is to gain priority. The very notion of balance in *yin/yang* suggests that it is a state of being in the centre between light and dark that is the basic priority – neither of the states of light or darkness themselves are to be prioritized. The very harmony and intuitive appeal of *yin/yang* is where there is an exact equivalence of light relative to darkness, rather than where one direction is winning out over the other. If one direction predominates over the other, this implies an imbalance, as it brings deviation from a neutral centre of balance. Therefore, *yin/yang* implies relativism and equality between the states of light and dark. In *yin/yan*g, if white replaced black and black replaced white, the overall pattern would not be challenged. While there is evidently some scope within *yin/yang* for a directional aspect, it is fundamentally limited as being a deviation from a positional centre.

As a symbol of harmony or synthesis, *yin/yang* may be characterized as the postmodernist *both/and*,[2] whereas concentric and diametric spaces are not simply in complementary interaction but also in dynamic tension. Concentric and diametric structures express a *both* both/and *and* either/or perspective.

The basic priority of *yin/yang* would ultimately seem to be one of convergence, of neutralizing the dynamic tensions of direction between light and dark into a static, conciliatory positional state. Thus, while both *yin/yang* and concentric/diametric structures of relation express directional and positional aspects, *yin/yang* invites ultimate favouring of position over direction through its balance at the centre. This contrasts with the proposed primordial dance between concentric and diametric spaces which treats the *directions* of concentric and diametric relation as being more primordial than static *positions*.

A spatial-phenomenological approach, developed out of concentric and diametric spaces, problematizes any basic priority of a static mediating central positional state. Unlike *yin/yang* as a visual structure, concentric and diametric structures are not in exactly the same relation and are not interchangeable with each other. *Yin/yang* does include both diametric space (the two halves of light and dark) and concentric space (the light within the dark half and the dark within the light half). However, *yin/yang* is closer to diametric space. This is because there is a fundamental neutrality (in the symbol itself, if not in Chinese culture itself) as to whether light or dark is on the right or left hand side of the opposition. Similarly, in diametric space there is a fundamental neutrality as to which half is to be on the right or left hand side. While diametric poles are interchangeable, the inner and outer circles of concentric structures are not replaceable by each other. Hence, in the tension between diametric and concentric spaces

2 Yet at another selfreferential level of implication, *yin/yang* is an *either/or* symbol. This either/or dimension is because *yin/yang prefers* both/and to either/or and preference assumes choice between (either/or) alternatives. *Yin/yang* adopts an either/or position where, in a choice between *either* both/and *or* either/or, preference is given to both/and. This is a consequence of its implicit favouring of a centre – of a balance reconciled by exact equality at a centre so both states are supported.

within *yin/yang*, it is diametric space framing the interaction which ultimately wins out. Its surface relativism masks a prior trumping of diametric over concentric space. It is this surreptitious triumph of a diametric spatial frame that is to be dethroned in a spatial-phenomenology.

The question arises as to how a transcendent relation between concentric and diametric structures could be more primordial than *yin/yang* and its relativism. How can concentric and diametric structures of relation include or incorporate *yin/yang* within them,[3] rather than be reducible to *yin/yang*? The proposed concentric and diametric structures relate to *yin/yang* not simply at the level of *yin/yang* itself but through the potential connection between the original background concentric egg structure and its later *yin/yang* form. Expanding the ambit of relevance for *yin/yang* to a spatial background focus is key to this dethroning of diametric space. *Interplay between the relativistic diametrically framed yin/yang structure and its early background concentric egg structure implies a greater priority to a concentric background.* This contrasts with the priority and dominion given in *yin/yang* to the diametric positional frame locating the two basically concentric dualisms. While diametric and concentric structures are embedded in *yin/yang*, they are not reducible to the *yin/yang* structure as they also relate to the background egg structure preceding *yin/yang*. *Yin/Yang* subsumes concentric space within a diametric structure; yet it does not go much further without taking the potential influence of the concentric egg background into account.

Leach (1965/2000) describes one of the 'fundamental peculiarities' (p. 106) of Lévi-Strauss' approach to myth, namely, that a myth is not to be considered in isolation but in relation to other myths. It is this relational or oppositional dimension to myths, going beyond simple contrasts, which D'Aquili (1975, p. 46) suggests is a Jungian influence on Lévi-Strauss. It is an archetypal dimension expressing the tendency of pairs of opposites to resolution. A relational perspective on *yin/yang* treats this symbol not just

3 See also Lakatos' (1970) characterization of the explanatory depth of a scientific theory, through contrasting a negation *monster-barring* approach to alternatives with a preferred *lemma incorporation* approach between oppositions.

as a symbol *of* relation but a symbol *in* relation – in relation to its prior concentric egg background. On this view, *yin/yang* is not to be viewed as existing as a figure against some kind of blank page background, as residing in some kind of abstract, non-interactive, Cartesian-type space. *Yin/yang* needs to move beyond being just a reified image painted upon a dull blank background.

Treating it in relation to its prior concentric egg background serves to destabilize and invite reconfiguration of the diametrically framed concentric structures constituting *yin/yang*. The tendency towards a concentric background is a movement away from the diametric structure grounding *yin/yang*. Using Jungian language, *yin/yang* is an ego resolution of concentric and diametric interaction, whereas the background concentric egg's interaction with *yin/yang* implies another mode of interaction. This other mode of interaction is an emergent level of self, where a concentric background interacts with the *yin/yang* ego resolution of the concentric and diametric interaction.

Another related difference between concentric/diametric spaces and *yin/yang* concerns movement between concentric and diametric relation, and from light to dark (or *vice-versa*). Change from diametric towards concentric relation is through reconfiguring one into the other, so that the concentric state itself is changed in quality and not simply quantity through its inclusion of the diametric structure. It includes internally the diametric structure rather than simply excluding and dominating over it. While *yin/yang* may leave open the possibility that light includes dark or *vice-versa*, so as to change the quality of light or darkness rather than simple change in quantity, its apparent emphasis is on a static central compromise. In this static central compromise, directional change is to be tolerated rather than seen as fundamental. This leaves *yin/yang* more open to the interpretation of light gaining relative to darkness or *vice-versa*. This gain is *not through inclusion but through imposition – through imposing one upon the other in order to simply negate or exclude the other.* Lévi-Strauss (1962) describes this difference between *negation/imposition* and *dissolving* generally:

> [...] I believe the ultimate goal of the human sciences to be not to constitute, but to dissolve man ... I am not blind to the fact that the verb 'dissolve' does not in any way imply (but even excludes) the destruction of the constituents of the body subjected to the action of another body. The solution of a solid into a liquid alters the disposition of its molecules. It also often provides an efficacious method of putting them by so that they can be recovered in case of need and their properties be better studied. (p. 247)

Lévi-Strauss' (1962) words offer an alternative to the light/dark *negation* by superimposing one on the other to destroy the other in *yin/yang*. This alternative is through a *dissolving* process. On this view, concentric relation needs to be able to dissolve diametric relation into itself, in order to distinguish its mode of change from the mutual negation/imposition in *yin/yang*.

Significantly, Jung's letter to Hermann Hesse (18 September 1934) describes a conception of sublimation which resonates with a process of dissolving:

> *Sublimatio* is part of the royal art where the true gold is made ... This is just about the opposite of what Freud understands by sublimation. It is not a *voluntary* and *forcible* channelling of instinct into a spurious field of application, but an *alchemical transformation* for which fire and the black *prima materiae* are needed.

A transformation through fire is one form of a dissolving process, a dissolving of a solid into the flame. Jung's *sublimatio* or dissolving process brings a transformation to an existing substance and is not just a destroying or replacing of it. Directional changes in *yin/yang* do not give expression to this Jungian sublimation of one pole into the other. This is a fundamental contrast with the interaction between concentric and diametric relation, where change to one is a Jungian *sublimatio* into the other.

Jung (1939) develops this conception of transformation for ego into self. He views transformation as an inclusion, as with a dissolving process, rather than a destroying or 'blotting out', where 'The self is a more comprehensive thing which includes the experience of the ego and therefore transcends it ... the blotting out of one picture and its replacement by another is an everyday occurrence which has not of the attitudes of a transformation experience' (pp. 142–6). *Yin/yang*'s implied discourse of change amounts to replacement of light by dark and *vice-versa*. Thus, it does not accommodate change as inclusion and transcendence as a Jungian dissolving process.

Table 5 The spatial discourse of implication in *yin/yang*

• Neutrality between light and dark • No priority, Equality, Relativism
• Balance is a positional state • Balance is at centre between light and dark
• Direction is accommodated within positional structure • Dark negates light and *vice-versa*, Change is through an imposition which negates the other rather than being a Jungian *sublimatio* or dissolving process for transcendence and transformation
• Both/And harmony; Harmony prevails over conflict; Synthesis prevails over fragmentation • Either/Or in the limited sense that it prefers the alternative of Both/And to Either/Or
• Diametric halves contain two basically concentric structures • Priority to balance at centre gives priority to a diametric relation framing the two concentric structures

It is not being argued that the *associations* historically given by *yin/yang* furnish a more primordial discourse. In ancient Chinese culture, *yin* represents feminine, dark, weak, night, moon, earth etc and *yang* represents masculine, light, strong, day, sun, sky etc. *Yin/yang* may be seen as a symbol which gives rise to certain associations. However, it is the key process of the jump from the symbol to the associations that needs to be scrutinized. There is no necessary connection between the symbol and, for example, masculinity or femininity. Nor is there a necessary connection between the associative parts themselves, e.g., femininity and weakness, masculinity and sun. However, other associations of dark and night, and hence moon, do have a publicly justifiable referential quality.

This criticism, of the links concerning *yin/yang* and (i) its associations, and (ii) between the associations themselves, is not to assert that this symbol is somehow 'wrong' or lacking in meaning for the cultural conditions in which it is expressed. These associations may make perfect sense as an expression of the socially constructed, historical reality of a particular culture, e.g., China. The associations are not being criticized for their *contextual* truth. Commitment to pluralistic truths acknowledges the experiential importance of purely contextual realities. Yet these associative realities may not translate to other cultures; the richness of the *yin/yang* symbol is not necessarily in the non-spatial associations it gives rise to. Criticism from the perspective of public justifiability of reference between the *yin/yang* symbol and its associations is for the purpose of ascertaining a more primordial, cross-cultural truth.

CHAPTER 9

Uncovering a Primordial Spatial Discourse Prior to Language: A Phenomenology of Concentric and Diametric Space as Lived Experiential Content

9.1 Beyond Foucault's structure of exclusion to a prelinguistic discourse of diametric space in Memling's *Last Judgement*: Concretizing Derrida's critique of early Foucault's historical origins

Argument: That (i) early Foucault's argument for the historical emergence of diametric structures of exclusion in the seventeenth century is untenable and (ii) Memling's pre-modern fifteenth-century painting *Last Judgement* exemplifies a phenomenologically meaningful diametric spatial projection.

An opening of Jung's collective unconscious beyond a simple origin of the mandala structure as its central archetype moves understanding of the role of the mandala beyond atomic and holistic structuralism. While amplifying the importance of the mandala to the unconscious through a spatial-phenomenological scrutiny, this discourse on the unconscious challenges simple origins. Derrida (1997) explicitly criticizes Lévi-Strauss' nostalgia for lost historical origins and assumptions of an original innocence and natural goodness in primitive tribes such as the Nambikwara. The deconstructor *par excellence* challenges the view of violence to innocence as being derivative (p. 106). Here Derrida is, in effect, avoiding a diametric oppositional split between a phase of innocence and subsequent violence.

Derrida (1974) challenges unitary conceptions of the origin across different contexts. In a liquefaction of traditional devices of meaning,

Figure 6 *Last Judgement* (1467–1471) by Hans Memling.

origins or foundations are ruptured into a chain of signifiers. Derrida (1974) develops a focus on the 'trace' rather than the simple origin, '… a meditation upon the trace should undoubtedly teach us that there is no origin that is to say simple origin' (p. 75). Elsewhere, Derrida (1978) criticizes 'the myth of a present origin' and suggests that '… it is a non-origin which is originary' (p. 203). Any such non-originary origin, or at least non-simple origin is, for Derrida, not only prior to the comforts of the mythic but also prior to a location of the originary in either a historical or causal sense. Any reconciliation with Derrida of a primordial truth dimension for the unconscious world rejects an identification of primordiality with an event of (ancient) history or causality.

In carving out a domain of relevance for understanding of primordial concentric and diametric spatial projections, further argument is needed as to their relation to history and causality. Derrida's challenge to early Foucault's attempt to situate what amount to diametric structures as originally constituted at a precise time in history is a debate that still operates within the limited frame of reference of linear time supporting a historical axis of meaning. A spatial-phenomenological reinterpretation of this debate invokes Hans Memling's painting, *Last Judgement* (1467–71) (see Figure 6), 'unquestionably the most outstanding early Netherlandish painting in Poland', according to Nuttall (1995). It provides a European case study from the fifteenth century, to concretize the concerns here of Derrida and amplify lived experiential dimensions to diametric meaning. In doing so, it is being highlighted that a spatial-phenomenological discourse is by no means confined to modernist experience and art; it is not being argued that, in some finalist or teleological perspective, a linear 'progress' in experience has taken place from this premodernist artistic example to the modernist ones of Munch and Klimt.

The Derrida/Foucault debate on the singularity of the classical moment

A bone of contention emerged between Derrida and Foucault regarding the latter's attribution of what he termed the 'structure of exclusion', containing an opposition between reason and unreason, to a distinct period in history, namely, the seventeenth century, classical Age of Reason. In developing his claims pertaining to a specific historical event in the seventeenth century, Foucault (1972) relies on art, literature, philosophical works and social history from different epochs. Foucault conceptualizes, in effect, in diametric spatial terms both regarding the 'structure of exclusion' as a structure of assumed separation furnishing mirror image inversions in 'the binary structure of classical unreason (truth and error, world and fantasy, being and non-being, Day and Night)' (p. 522). He treats what amounts to a diametric spatial structure as burgeoning at a distinct point in history, in the seventeenth century. It is this historical claim for diametric spatial projections that requires direct challenge. In doing so, it is not being viewed as a necessary condition for the primordiality of diametric spatial structures that they would exist as ancient historical structures. If such diametric spatial structures of exclusion were accepted on Foucault's argument to arise initially in the seventeenth century in European culture, this would offer an argument against its primordiality in the sense of being a spatial structure of experience that is not simply dependent on socially constructed realities in a given society. Foucault's argument would significantly undermine a role for diametric spatial projections as a fundamental, primordial structure of experience.

Before elaborating on Memling's work, three separate but related claims of Foucault require exposition in relation to the purported emergence of these dimensions in the seventeenth century. Firstly, Foucault (1972) postulates a structure of exclusion, a structural dimension that separated the supposedly mad from the apparently reasonable. Confinement was merely one dimension of this process of development of the structure of exclusion in the seventeenth century:

> Confinement was merely the visible phenomenon on the surface of this deeper process, and an integral part of the whole of classical culture. There were certain experiences that the sixteenth century had either accepted or refused, formulated or sidelined, which were now taken up by the seventeenth century and grouped together and banished *en masse*, exiling them together with madness, creating a uniform world of Unreason. (p. 82)

For Foucault (1972), the structure of exclusion arose as an invention of the seventeenth century:

> By inventing the space of confinement in the imaginary geometry of its morality, the classical age found a home-land and a place of redemption for sins of the flesh and faults committed against reason. Madness found itself side by side with sin, and it is perhaps from there that stems the immemorial linking of unreason and guilt that the alienated today still feel to be their fate ... In this artificial space created out of nothing in the mid-seventeenth century, dark alliances were created ... (p. 86)

Consideration of Memling invites the question as to whether Foucault is overstating the case to suggest that this conceptual geometry was a space that emerged *ex nihilo*. If the pervasive features of this space are already evident in Memling's *Last Judgement* then Foucault's argument is substantially deconstructed.

This structural feature of exclusion was fleshed out, by Foucault, into a second claim, that the content of this structure of exclusion involved an opposition between reason and unreason, whereby unreason only gained its identity through its relation and contrast with reason. For Foucault (1972), the seventeenth century brought an attenuated form of unreason, it became tamed of autonomous, quasi-autotelic features; it became merely the inversion of reason:

> Not so long ago it was still visible in the light of day, as in King Lear or Don Quixote, but within the space of half a century it found itself a recluse in the fortress of confinement, bound fast to Reason, to the rules of morality and their monotonous nights (p. 77)

> [...] madness and reason enter into a perpetually reversible relationship which implies that all madness has its own reason by which it is judged and mastered, and all reason has its madness in which it finds its own derisory truth (p. 28–9)

Thus, madness purportedly lost its independent force in the classical Age of Reason.

This second claim for an inverted symmetry between reason and unreason was supplemented by Foucault's third claim that the sexual became repressed and desiccated by way of this fundamental opposition between reason and unreason in the classical age, 'our culture, by a choice typical of its own form of classicism, placed sexuality on the dividing line of unreason ... it is a comparatively recent particularity of our own culture to have divided it [sexuality] so rigorously into Reason and Unreason' (p. 89).

While these key claims are at issue, this is not to suggest that this account of Foucault's arguments relating to the structure of exclusion as an opposition of inverted symmetry between reason and unreason embraces the full scope of Foucault's various historical claims regarding 'madness'. A more moderate supplementary argument of Foucault is that unreason became weakened in the classical age. Thus he asks, 'How did it end up being the case that madness was appropriated by reason, so much so that at the dawn of the classical age all the tragic images previously associated with madness suddenly passed into shadow?' (Foucault 1972, p. 28). This decline of tragic images of madness in the Age of Reason is not being contested here by examination of Memling. Rather it is Foucault's more extreme advocacy of the exclusivity of this singular event through the construction of modes of experience in the seventeenth century that is at issue.

While Foucault's multi-stranded argument wove a tapestry of claims for the structure of exclusion, focus here is on Derrida's (1978) skepticism vis-à-vis Foucault's claim that this structure of exclusion emerged at a particular, singular, moment in history, in the seventeenth century. While Derrida's skepticism here is for purposes other than a spatial-phenomenological inquiry into diametric projections, his counterarguments are important for defence of diametric spatial projection as a primordial structure. Foucault (1972a) insists that the emergence of the structure of exclusion was a sudden feature of the classical age of the seventeenth century and far from retracting this point in response to Derrida, he reasserted its centrality to his whole thesis, 'He [Derrida] does not know the category of the singular event; it is therefore pointless for him – and probably impossible – to read that which occupies the essential part, if not the totality of my book: the analysis of an event' (p. 577). Yet in developing this supposedly central argument, Foucault neither clarified the opposite to such a structure of exclusion, i.e., a structure of inclusion, nor explicitly considered other candidate structures of exclusion from other periods of history, nor cultures beyond Western ones.

Derrida offers a range of reasons for his skepticism regarding Foucault's claim. These include questioning a unitary presence prior to any such division into a structure of exclusion, as well as viewing Socrates' dialectics as incorporating a reason and unreason dichotomy prior to the Age of Reason. Derrida further explicates his objections:

> if the decision through which reason constitutes itself by excluding and objectifying the free subjectivity of madness is indeed the origin of history, if it is historicity itself … if the structure of exclusion is the fundamental structure of historicity, then the 'classical' moment of this exclusion described by Foucault has neither absolute privilege nor archetypal exemplarity. It is an example as sample and not as model. (p. 42)

In order to evoke the singularity of the classical moment, Foucault needs, according to Derrida, to historically distinguish this 'own structure of exclusion … from the others, from all others' (p. 42).

Memling's *Last Judgement* will be argued to be a radical anticipation of many of the key structural features of Cartesianism and the 'the great caesura between reason and unreason' (p. 432) in the classical age evoked by Foucault (1972), two centuries before Foucault's supposedly singular event giving birth to structure of exclusion. In doing so, a distinct diametric background spatial structure underpinning Memling's painting needs to be illuminated, as a more ancient structure of exclusion than the one posited by Foucault. Spatial features in Memling's *magnum opus*, such as the mandala structure and its diametric spatial dimensions, have been somewhat overlooked in previous commentary on *Last Judgement*. This silent discourse of spatial relation needs to emerge for a fuller understanding of Memling's themes, as well as to foster dialogue between Foucault's and Derrida's concerns.

Foucault (1972) conceptualizes in terms of a historical process of experiencing, where the structure of exclusion is a mode of experience that uniquely came to the fore in this epoch of the seventeenth century, 'It would be absurd to look for a cause in confinement, as it was precisely confinement itself, with all its strange modalities, that signalled an experience that was in the process of being constituted' (p. 103). It is the experiential more than the overt activity which is Foucault's primary concern. He interrogates *via* art, literature and historical documents, not only a kind of *Zeitgeist* but also a mode of experience, what Taylor (2007) would term the background context of the social imaginary, the largely unspoken, background understanding, rather than intentional beliefs, as such. Yet if the structure of exclusion is to be viewed as an experiential mode rather than predominantly a concrete activity, the argument applies *a fortiori* that Memling's underlying structures of experience and space in *Last Judgement* are already substantive expressions of such an experience.

Three questions are thus to be considered:

(i) Does Memling's *Last Judgement* provide evidence for or against Foucault's claim on the distinct emergence of the structure of exclusion in the seventeenth century?
(ii) Does this painting, 'generally considered Memlinc's earliest major work' and 'one of the most imposing of Memlinc's inventions' (Nuttall 1995, p. 156), offer insight into a reason-unreason relation to precede Descartes and thereby to challenge Foucault's major claims for a new epoch in the seventeenth century in relation to a reason-unreason dichotomy?
(iii) Can this painting offer support or challenge to Foucault's comprehension of sexuality within a reason-unreason dualism that was apparently constituted in the classical age?

The argument based on interpretation of Memling's *Last Judgement* is with a view to supplementing other avenues of critique of Foucault's position. These include Foucault's (1972) purported misreading of divisions within reason in Greek thought according to Derrida and, as noted by Kisiel (1993), the recognition of Dilthey and Heidegger that Augustine had anticipated Descartes' *cogito* in an arguably 'more profound' way (p. 106).[1] These would undermine the ostensible historical uniqueness of the Cartesian oppositions gaining prominence in the Age of Reason.

1 Augustine in *The City of God* (11.26) emphasized that 'I am certain that I am, that I know that I am, and that I love to be and to know' and called the object of self certainty, 'life'.

Memling's *Last Judgement*

Much discussion of Memling's *Last Judgement* highlights its early theft and disagreement on the identity of its painter for almost four centuries. There is some analysis of spatial themes but aspects of the painting's mandala structure (as a circle within a square) and its diametric underlying relation have tended to be overlooked, even in comparative perspectives.

Memling's *Last Judgement* is a three-wing altarpiece with double-side painted wings; the open altar reveals a powerful vision of the Eighth Day, with the scene of judgement in the centre and images of the redeemed on the right wing and the damned on the left. In the centre of the composition, Christ conducts the final judgment; his red robe and visible wounds evoke his sacrifice to redeem human sins. The twelve Apostles, sitting in the clouds behind the figure of Christ serve as the jury. Beneath Christ stands armoured archangel Michael weighing the souls. According to the idea that the good deeds of a lifetime are being measured, the blessed are on the heavier level of the scale compared to the damned. On both sides of the archangel the souls are leaving graves. In the scene of the fight for the souls, *Psychomachia*, the angels and the devils are in combat. Although each received a specific judgement after his or her death, now everyone takes part in the general judgement when time fulfils itself and reaches its ineluctably perfect state. Though there are some elderly men, the persons depicted are approximately the same age, according to the conviction that everyone appears at the last judgement in the corporeal state that occurred at the age of thirty-three (Groebner 1999). This displays Memling's awareness of the writings of Aquinas, who claimed that, no matter at what age people died, they all will be resurrected *in iuvenili aetate* (Przybyszewski 1979).

Memling's painting is deeply rooted in the iconographical tradition of the time and was dependent on contemporary works of leading Netherlandish painters, following written sources such as the Old and New Testament, mystic literature and pervasive fifteenth-century philosophy (Sztyber 2003, p. 2). It offers more narrative than comparable *Last Judgement* artworks by van Eyck and van der Weyden (Białostocki 1966; 1970, p. 45). Mazurczak (1985) adverts to the importance of the circular (i.e., concentric) structure, though nevertheless envisaging it as subservient to temporal thematizing influenced by Augustine's subjective conception of time, 'Both light and shadows are subordinated to the circular spatial structure of the painting and constitute a source-generating substrate for the temporal process. The cosmic chaos of the Day of Judgment on which Christ is coming is linked to the First Day of Creation' (p. 35). Białostocki (1970) observes that the structure of space, expressing the idea of cosmic rotation, was applied, by Memling, sixty years before Michelangelo, in his work of art from the Sistine Chapel in Rome.

It is notable however that none of these interpretations of space bring the structural dimension to the fore of diagonal axes expressing a mandala symbol. Jung (1936/1985) observes generally, though without explicit reference to Memling, that, 'in the Western mandalas of medieval Christendom the deity is enthroned at the centre, often in the form of the triumphant redeemer together with the four symbolical figures of the evangelists' (p. 252). It is not simply the content of who is at the diagonal points that is of interest but also for current purposes, the *structural* dimension of the mandala.

Taylor (2007) offers a perspective on fifteenth-century art, pertinent to Memling, though without any specific reference to his work, 'An art which remains within the understanding of things as *loci* of transcendent power need not concern itself with their relative placing in some coherent order ... But with the painting of the fifteenth century, with the achievement of perspective, we get object which are clearly ranged in a single coherent space' (p. 96). However, understood against this backdrop, Memling's perspective is not simply a hierarchical relative placing. As will be seen, it is a diametric structural one, giving expression to an aspect of the mandala structure.

Foucault overtly conceptualizes in terms of structures of experience and these are for him frequently spatial (see also, Elden 2001). Foucault (1972) claims to be pursuing 'the links in the chain of the fundamental structures of experience' (p. 529). In this quest, he explicitly distances his conception of unreason as a structure from Jungian notions of a collective unconscious, 'This survival is not to be explained by the properties of a collective unconscious, but rather by the structure of the domain of experience that is unreason, and by its modifications' (Foucault 1972, p. 105). Yet this rejection of the relevance of Jung may apply only to Jung's preoccupation with the level of myths and not with a prior structural level of the mandala. The mandala can be seen to speak to much of Foucault's concerns with spatial structures of exclusion and unreason, once the mandala is conceptualized as a fusion of two kinds of spaces, diametric and concentric.

Memling's *Last Judgement* and projection of diametric spatial meaning

In Memling's *Last Judgement*, the diametric oppositional feature of inverted symmetry operates to a notable degree between those going to heaven and to hell. Those entering heaven appear sober, righteous and unemotional, whereas those entering hell are characterized as grimacing, fearful, in pain. A clear juxtaposition is at play in so far as it is only those in the hellish domain who are envisaged as expressing emotion. The futural Cartesian splicing apart of reason and affect has been presaged here. The almost stoic demeanour of those entering heaven, unsmiling, uncelebratory, singularly lacking in joy, imbued at most with a serenity of sorts, offers a canvas bringing a firm inversion between reason and affect. This diametric split is already at play.

However, this has not yet reached Foucault's level of contrast in his account of the structure of exclusion between reason and unreason that is supposed to have arisen in the seventeenth century. So, for example, it is not that those within a hellish unreason in Memling's *Last Judgement* could be said to have chosen this fate, whereas on Foucault's account, one of the quintessential qualities of the classical age was precisely that unreason *qua* 'madness' was perceived, not only as a relational plaything of lost reason, but also as a chosen state. The Cartesian antinomy, between those choosing reason and the insane, prioritized a dimension of choosing which is not illuminated in Memling; it is precisely the opposite of this, those wretches damned to hell are prodded and pushed in there by dark devilish figures with forks (there are no angels with forks prodding the figures into heaven). The damned rail against their fate, rather than in Foucauldian accounts of seventeenth century madness, being perceived as reconciled to their choice. Yet against the backdrop of diametric background structural relation, this furnishes even more support for the inverted symmetry, the mirror image operating in this diametric relation.

Heaven-hell, reason-affect, choice-lack of choice are all elements of this mirror image diametricity. The stark opposition between the white flower and the red sword are clearly intended by Memling to reach a level of mirror image inversion, as they are almost identical in both length and shape, as well as concerning the angle at which they are placed to the head of Jesus. Jesus' head thereby becomes a quasi-line of symmetry between the mirror opposites of the white flower and the red sword, in diametric directional relation. These diametrically opposing forces give expression to the prior diametric oppositional extremities of heaven and hell.

A further dimension of diametric oppositions takes place in relation to the circle itself, where Jesus and his disciples are placed above, clothed, in colour, while the morass of bodies below are naked, not quite colourless but with a distinct pallor. The diametric structural features of reversal are preeminent. Other contrasts are more by virtue of their spatial location within the diametric frames than as direct mirror image inversions. These include those between the stone building sculpted in its apparent splendour as the gate to heaven and the fires of hell; stone and fire also provide the backdrop for a sense of ascension and descent. A moving upwards is through the steps or the wings in the portal of heaven. A sense of falling is as figures are upturned, lose their footing, and are seen to collapse almost in a dizzied state into the fires and furnaces which encase them.

Thus, together with the array of mirror image inverted symmetries of heaven-hell, reason-affect, choice-compulsion, above-below, ascending-falling, white flower-red sword, there are a range of ancillary oppositions. These occur between stone and fire, or possibly sculpted stone and roughly hewed rocks, between colour and pallor, clothing and nakedness. Blood is conspicuously absent from all the bodies, even those being prodded by forks and those falling on the rocks; its colour would distort the antinomy between the pallid below and the colourful apparel of the disciples above. Indeed, despite all the mayhem of the *inferno*, the only rupturing of a blood-free surface in the painting is that of the feet of the saviour figure, Jesus. The blood has been sucked out of the figures even to the extent that there is no reddening of the skin for those enveloped by the flames of damnation. It is as though a discourse of relatedness is not even allowed between the bodies and the fires.

A further diametric feature is the scale of balance, where weight and counterweight brought a *dénouement*, where one is measured as fit for heaven, the other as bound for hell. The sense of a calibration of and within opposition is at play here. There is a pellucid structure of exclusion, a diametric framed calibration underpinning Memling's work. Foucault's (1972) following words therefore need refinement:

> Confinement was an institutional creation peculiar to the seventeenth century. It immediately took on a scale that bore no relation to the practice of imprisonment in the Middle Ages ... A new sensibility had been born: a line had been drawn, a threshold established and its purpose was banishment. The society of the classical age created a neutral zone in its own concrete space ... order was no longer in a free conflict with disorder, and reason no longer attempted to find its way through places that eluded it or refused it entry. (p. 77)

As this aptly describes Memling's threshold of banishment governed by the diametric structural features of the mandala, two centuries earlier, narratives of birth of lines and thresholds and a new sensibility, though providing dramatic rhetorical effect for Foucault's story, are largely unsustainable in relation to the structure of exclusion and its reason-unreason opposition. The diametric aspects of the mandala structure offer a space, a structure for exclusion, a structure of exclusion.

Memling's painting, as both a structure of exclusion and with contents of reason and unreason within this structure, is arguably thereby a powerful form of the reason-unreason dichotomy argued by Foucault as existent uniquely from the seventeenth century. Here reason as sobriety and choice (with stoic overtones scarcely anathema to Roman Emperor, Marcus Aurelius, in his *Meditations*) operates against the counterpoint of grimacing affect and compulsion. The background conditions are already in place for Foucault's locus of madness within unreason, in contradistinction to reason. The diametric structure of exclusion predominates and animates the movements of the pictorial text. Foucault (1972) states:

> In approximate terms, it can be said that until the Renaissance the world of ethics, beyond the great division between Good and Evil, kept its equilibrium in a sort of tragic unity, that of destiny and of providence and divine will. That unity was now to disappear, broken by the definitive split between reason and unreason. A crisis in the

> world of ethics therefore came into being, and to the great struggle between Good and Evil was juxtaposed the irreconcilable conflict between reason and unreason, multiplying images of the split. (p. 104)

Yet, it is evident that the seeds of any such split, not merely between good and evil but also between reason and unreason, have already flowered in Memling, long before the classical age. Foucault (1972) does appear to recognize the structure of exclusion as tethered to ancient roots, in his reference to 'the division itself, the re-enactment of the ancient drama of exclusion' (p. 172). However, this 'drama' of exclusion is apparently different for Foucault from the more concrete visible spatial 'structure' of exclusion in the seventeenth century.

The additional step in the foreground figures is admittedly not yet there, namely, depiction of the damned as, in some way, mad. Madness and the infernal are not yet equated within unreason in Memling, even if the infernal and unreason are firmly coallied, coagulated almost, into a fused state of compression through the diametric spatial frame. The second foreground step excavated by Foucault for the Age of Reason, is in relation to a locus of sexuality within unreason in opposition to reason. By way of contrast, despite the naked torsos and the relative juvenescence of many of the figures, sexual or even sensual overtones or undertones are singularly absent from Memling's depiction. The sexual is *hors de vue*, beyond relevance for the manifestly higher concerns of learning one's fate. Touch does partially enter the arena through the hands of one of two figures ascending the stairs to *paradiso*, and the angels distributing the clothing on these stairs, yet even here the interaction is highly limited. Interpersonal relation is overwhelmingly absent, whether for heaven or hell; every figure is almost in a statue-like relation, of what Heidegger (1927) would term side-by-sideness with the other; there is no being-alongside, no warmth of eye contact, nor even hostility of eye contact. Eyes have been removed from interpersonal sight.

Madness, sexuality, sensuality and eye contact are all limbs of interaction that are consistently removed from relevance in Memling's *Last Judgement*. The figures are almost at right angles to each other, carved out upon the background and somewhat anticipating the divisionism of the work of Georges Seurat, as well as the more extreme harsh angular box-like spatial figures and backgrounds of Escher. And the further excision from the flesh is that of language; the figures, whether bound for heaven or hell, do not even attempt to talk with each other. The diametric structural feature of assumed separation pervades both sides. The diametric spatial separation pervades the foreground figures relations between themselves, as well as through the background structural relation which splices one group into *paradiso* and the other into *inferno*, as a structure of exclusion. Diametric structured exclusion is immanent in their mutual relation, in the prevailing atmosphere, as well as in the steps towards differentiation into the transcendent. One further juxtaposition – which operates in conjunction with the commonality of excisions of the sexual, sensual, linguistic and visual discourse – is that between silence and sound. Silence is diffused throughout those making their way into *paradiso*, while the infernal cries, groans and screams offer the inverted symmetry here of sound. Yet this contrast is a relative one as another can be made between harmonious music and the chaotic disorder of sounds. The angels at the top of the gate of paradise are singing and playing instruments, giving expression to the idea of music as a reflection of the harmony of the universe, rooted in Pythagorean theory and writings of Plato, known in the Middle Ages through Boetius (Purc-Stępniak 2007).

Interpreted thus, the inverted symmetry of diametric relation is the predominant spatial mode fuelling oppositions between heaven-hell, reason-affect, choice-compulsion, above-below, ascending-falling, white flower-red sword, silence-sound. A range of ancillary oppositions additionally coexist, namely, between stone and fire, or possibly sculpted stone and roughly hewed rocks, between colour and pallor, clothing and nakedness. And a further implicit space of monistic fusion is evident, through a pervasive erasure of sexual, sensual, linguistic and visual discourse. It offers a riot of stasis, a paralysis of interaction, a diametric structural mode of assumed separation between the figures. Other removals from the domain of relevance for Memling, such as madness and difference in race, are less easily construed in terms of spatialization and meaning.

It is significant that the scope of the 'judgement' dimension within Memling's *Last Judgement* is limited to a structural dimension of location within place and a range of inverted symmetries, whereas there is little moralistic comment *per se* on the damned as individuals. There is minimal attempt to seek to portray this group as deserving of their fate; if anything, it is an account of people forced into this locus of despair and damnation, not through choice, fault or any obvious 'deficit' of personal quality.

As the diametric structural features of the mandala gain dominion, they become utilized as vehicles for an oppositional structural placing as part of a judgement mode, as part of a moralistic discourse, at least at the level of structure. It is an implicit moralism built into the diametric structure of judgement. Yet it retains a distance with regard to justice as content, namely, commentary on the moral worthiness or otherwise of individuals. This is not so much a commitment to moral relativism in Memling at the level of depiction of the figures as individuals; it is more an extension of the lack of discourse for the figures, whether at a sexual, sensual, linguistic or visual level. Memling engages in a minimalist account of his own attitude to the figures as individuals, as distinct from figures in relation to a spatial background. It is a paring down of emotional interaction on a par to Beckettian minimalism with regard to language, 'As we cannot eliminate language all at once, we should at least leave nothing undone that might contribute to its falling into disrepute. To bore one hole after another in it, until what lurks behind it – be it something or nothing – begins to seep through' (Beckett 1983, p. 172). The background silence and force of the diametric space seeps through in Memling, much more than the individuality or relationality of his foreground figures – or of his individual relation to them.

Diametric inversion is a movement of opening compared to flattened monism, which Taylor (2007) suggests was the role of carnivals after the French revolution:

> The epoch of the French Revolution is perhaps the moment in which at one and the same moment anti-structure goes into eclipse ... This emerges most clearly in the attempts of the various revolutionary governments to design festivals which would express and entrench the new society ... But the nature of the enterprise was in a certain sense reversed. That is because the dimension of anti-structure was totally missing. The aim of the exercise was not to open a hiatus in the now reigning code, but to give expression to its spirit and inspire identification with it. (p. 51)

Memling's *inferno* is clearly not an expression of anti-structure. It is firmly contained within the diametric structure of exclusion; it is the embodiment of a precise structure. There is no Dionysian threat to Apollonian structure, the dominion of the image is all-powerful; structure is the enthroned god in a world of firmly arranged spatial relations. Following Christian orthodoxy in the social imaginary at that time, hell was not so much a *caveat* to a social contract for existence; it was a voracious expression of its implied terms.

From this construal of Memling, it is notable that the diametric spatial features of the mandala predominate over concentric ones, as they also tend to do in Jung's application of the mandala to the unconscious. Nevertheless, concentric structures are clearly evident in the central position of the circular rainbow, as light upon which Jesus is sitting.

Building on Kisiel's (1993) point, noted earlier, regarding the view of Heidegger and Dilthey that Augustine radically anticipated the Cartesian *cogito*, it is arguably significant that a number of features of the painting give expression to Augustinian themes. Positioning of the blessed as the heavy one on the scales of judgement, regarded as traditional by Bialstocki (1970), is rooted in Augustine's idea of the good as a quality and of evil as *privatio boni*, as a lack. Further Augustinian themes include ideas of time, as discussed by Mazurczak (1985). Thus, it would be less than surprising to view Memling as having anticipated Cartesian developments in the Age of Reason, *via* Augustine.

Despite his trenchant self-defence in response to Derrida, Foucault's work subsequent to *The History of Madness*, such as, for example, *The History of Sexuality* (1978), marks a significant distancing from the concerns of his earlier exposition with regard both to 'structure' and 'exclusion'. Foucault (1978) moves from structure and mechanism to discourses, 'We are dealing not nearly so much with a negative mechanism of exclusion as with the operation of a subtle network of discourses' (p. 72), 'power is not an institution, and not a structure' (p. 93). In contrast to the later tide of Foucauldian concern as moving away from structure and exclusion, while remaining immersed in the pivotal causal status of the seventeenth century (for constructions of madness and sexuality), the argument presented here is for a renewal of focus on projections of both structure and exclusion,[2] as well as to challenge the pivotal causal role of the seventeenth century invoked by Foucault.

These projected phenomenological structures, while prelinguistic, can, nevertheless, coexist with Foucault's later framework on discourse; they are different levels of description but not necessarily anathema to each other. The system of relations between diametric and concentric spatialization offers an assumption structure to aspects of discourse – they provide a horizon for understanding movement in experience within which a discourse is framed.

As Foucault (1972) recognizes the ancient 'drama' of division and the 'great' division between good and evil, his argument is better taken as being one where the *structure* of exclusion already existed in diametric structural form prior to the seventeenth century, and that even the diametric structured content of opposition between reason and unreason existed prior to the Age of Reason (as evident in Memling's work). It was this ancient structure of exclusion that was applied *in extremis* specifically to 'madness' and sexuality in the seventeenth century. In doing so, the wings are clipped from some of the ambition of Foucault's theory, though nevertheless supporting the importance of his framework as applied to the context of madness in the seventeenth century. This view would thus give sustenance to Derrida's (1978) critique of Foucault, that 'The free circulation of the mad ... would only be a socioeconomic epiphenomenon on the surface of a reason divided against itself since the dawn of its Greek origin' (p. 40).[3]

The more expansive claim of Foucault (1972) that there are 'fundamental structures of experience' and that the structure of exclusion is a fundamental dimension in 'the links in the chain' (p. 529) of this experience (quite apart from issues of its historical emergence) can also gain some support from Memling; diametric structures of spatialization, illuminated

2 This argument is not a bias of the present, as it is not an explicit reconstruction at the level of facts, historical events or their meaning at that time in history. It is for primordial experiential concerns not truth as correspondence concerns.

3 Nevertheless, the treatment of socioeconomic factors as epiphenomenal in relation to prior structures of thought and experience clearly depends on the goals underpinning a particular truth paradigm.

in Memling, are a different candidate for the existence of this proposed fundamental structure of exclusion. Memling's *Last Judgement* is arguably an archetypal example of diametric spatialization as a primordial structure of exclusion. As a logic of justice, it offers resonance with a diametric spatial projection uncovered in the work of Gilligan (1982). As a reference point for cultural constructions of madness, Foucault's (1972) structure of exclusion offers a vantage point for analysis of the diametric spatial projections in Western culture historically onto those perceived as 'mad', and those as 'damned'. They are paradigmatic examples of projected diametric meaning.

9.2 Beyond reification: A spatial-phenomenological reinterpretation of Derrida's deconstruction of the Western subject as it pertains to the unconscious and repression

Argument: That Derrida's (1978) proposed 'new psychoanalytic graphology' can be developed through diametric and concentric spatial movements as structures of difference in Derrida's accounts of traces in systems of repression.

In opening up a quest for a more dynamic and elusive spatial domain, Derrida (1978) proposes his distinctive concept of *différance*, as an innovative kind of question about metaphor, writing and spacing in general, 'The thinking of difference can neither dispense with topography nor accept the current models of spacing' (p. 204). He relates concerns with differential relation to those of both space and time, 'Difference is the articulation of space and time. The phonic chain or the chain of phonetic writing are always distended by that minimum of essential spacing upon which the dream-work and any formal regression in general can begin to operate' (Derrida 1978, p. 219). Undercutting the triad of subject-object-image, *différance* fuses spatial and temporal concerns, being both a differing in space and a deferral in time. Habermas (1987) recognizes a shift in origins or primordiality in Derrida towards a spatial dimension more primary than ancient history, 'What is first and last is not the history of Being, but a picture-puzzle: The labyrinthine mirror-effects of old texts, each of which points to another, yet older text without fostering any hope of ever attaining the archewriting ... Derrida clings to the dizzying thought of a past that has never been present' (p. 179).

Derrida's preoccupation with a spatial dimension has antecedents already in French phenomenology (and not only French structuralism *via* Lévi-Strauss), such as Bachelard's (1964) recognition that, 'Philosophers, when confronted with outside and inside, think in terms of being and non-being. Thus profound metaphysics is rooted in an implicit geometry which – whether we will or no – confers spatiality upon thought' (p. 212). Yet Derrida's interrogation of structures of difference goes further to seek to cast off the garb of metaphysical thought itself.

Derrida is at the threshold of an entirely other text. This text involves a spatial opening prior to language, and yet, seeped into language. A preoccupation with space encompasses not only his earlier work such as *Writing and Difference* but also later interrogations in *Archive Fever*. A common thread in these works is an engagement with interpreting Freud's conceptions of the unconscious in spatial terms. He seeks 'a new *psychoanalytic graphology*', suggesting tentatively that Melanie Klein's work 'perhaps opens the way' (Derrida 1978, p. 231, italics in original).

Derrida's (1996) concern with time, memory and the unconscious archive examines a spatial dimension, as the archive is 'already a psychic spacing' (pp. 91–2); 'The archive takes place at the place of originary and structural breakdown of the said ["spontaneous, alive"] memory' (p. 1). For Derrida (1978), understanding of the archive is key to conceptualization of repression to unlock a domain prior to 'logocentric repression' (p. 197) and purportedly antecedent to individual repression. Referring to Freud's *The Project* (1895), Derrida (1978) prioritizes focus on spatial concerns, 'we repeatedly find a persistent attempt to account for the psyche in terms of spacing, a topography of traces, a map of breaches; and we repeatedly find an attempt to locate consciousness or quality in a space whose structure and possibility must be rethought ...' (p. 205).

Derrida's discourse on the archive in the unconscious offers a challenge to a prior truth as being located in linear historical time. Though allowing for some division within repression (Freud 1926), a Derridean perspective would consider diametric spatial relation as being too static and requiring a prior background dynamism and structure of difference for the unconscious. Freud does recognize that diametric structured reversals are problematic and in need of working through for change. They are the hidden spaces of repression upon which subjectivity is constructed – a restricted space, a confined site for integration through mirror image symmetries. A Derridean critique would focus on the limitations of diametric spatial mirror image symmetry as a logocentric repression founding the construction of subjectivity.

The mirror image construction of subjectivity, as part of a Freudian logocentric repression, does not go far enough for Derrida. While diametric spatial inversions offer a step forward in providing a spatial discourse or graphematics, Derrida would accentuate the limitations of such diametric mirror image truths as being chained within a Western metaphysics of knowledge as sight going back to Plato. Mansfield (2000) locates Derrida as part of what he provisionally describes as an anti-subjective tradition that highlights the illusionary certainty of this historical construct. On this reading of diametric mirror image relations, the inverted image is a constructed truth which may be illusory. The lapse into mirror image split relations is an occlusion of a prior truth. Movement is needed from diametric mirror image inversion in excess of this restricted diametric spatial realm. This interruption of diametric mirror image space by another invites an opening towards other spaces such as concentric relations. These provide not stable fixities but rather tendencies and directions for experience within a larger fluctuating system of processes. Moreover, it is to be recognized that power is not somehow separate from or subsequent to the construction of the subject as a diametric spatial site of experience. The locus of power is built into the diametric spatial polarity itself, in the tension between both poles in mirror image inversion of the other.

A notable feature of this proposed psychoanalytic graphology is that the interplay between diametric and concentric spaces offers a movement beyond the subject-object dualism in this reconstruction of subjectivity. Exploring boundaries between subjectivity and objectivity, Derrida (1996) tentatively dances into a space before the subject-object relation, 'the pressure of the printing, the impression, before the division between the printed and the printer' (p. 18). The printer and the printed (including the image) exist against a prior background space of relation; printer and printed are arrested effects upon a prior space.

This printer-printed, footstep-substrate, subject-object relation is unfolded by Derrida (1996) through a dimension of time, the 'instant',[4] 'In the instant when the imprint is yet to be left, abandoned by the pressure of the impression. In the instant of the pure auto-affection, in the indistinction of the active and the passive, of a touching and the touched' (p. 98). Derrida (1996) conceptualizes in structural, or at least, fluid structural terms, seeking a prior 'imprint', 'At least that imprint (*Abdruck*), distinct from all the others, must be rediscovered – but this presupposes *both* memory *and* the archive' (p. 99).

Derrida searches for a language to overcome the subject-object dualism, when seeking to locate a primordial impression. Whereas Hunter (2006) argues that Derrida's structure of difference cannot be outside history, it would seem that here for Derrida, like early Heidegger (1927), there is a temporal mode prior to linear historical time. Derrida's rejection of origins is not a rejection of some spatio-temporal realm of purity, of 'pure auto-affection'. Derrida (1996) continues:

> this is the condition of singularity ... It is the condition for the uniqueness of the printer-printed, of the impression and the imprint, of the pressure and its trace in the unique *instant* where they are not yet distinguished the one from the other ... The trace no longer distinguishes itself from its substrate. No longer distinguishing *between themselves*, this pressure and this imprint differ henceforth *from all other* impressions, from all other imprints, and from all other archives. (p. 99, italics in original)

Derrida's interrogation of Freudian repression and memory seeks to go beyond the printer and the printed. The printer dimension serves as a condensed account of the causal history, the event impacting upon memory

4 In a different context of discussing Abraham and Isaac, Derrida also imports his preoccupation with the 'instant', 'for only an instant, a *no-time-lapse*, separates this from the raised arm of the murderer himself' (italics in original) (Derrida 1996a, 95).

and repression of memory in the unconscious. This shift in focus away from the printer (causal event) resonates with criticisms of psychoanalysis as being the production of a subject, in conjunction with the specific set of familial and social relations dominant in the culture of Freud's time (Olsen & Køppe 1988; Mansfield 2000). Derrida is interrogating a level prior to the external, socially constructed causal history of the printed; he is going beyond a focus on events and the reaction to the event as the 'printed' memory or repression. Another significant feature of this shift of interests beyond the causal event 'printed' in relation to repression is that neither Derrida's ambit of relevance – nor that of the proposed psychoanalytic graphology of interaction between diametric and concentric spatial relations – are confined to a Freudian preoccupation with repression and castration anxiety. Nor are they a preoccupation with other dimensions which Freud (1926) locates as central to repression (as distinct from other wider unconscious defences), such as genital fixation as causal sources of repression and the myth of the Oedipus complex in relation to repression. The graphology concerns are pre-causal and pre-mythic.

Derrida's quest is for a spatio-temporal organizing principle prior to event-memory and not simply reducible to the reactive psychic constellation of the printed. The trace of the reactive constellation of the printed engages in some key relation with what Derrida calls the 'substrate'. What is the spatial structure or structuralizing process of this unique instant and substrate? What is the rationality, if any, underlying this prior temporal and spatial relation, before the division into impression and imprint, subject and object? It is important here to draw attention to a clear difference between Derrida's and Freud's understanding of the trace; the printed differs notably from Freud's (1925) account in a *Note upon the 'Mystic Writing Pad'*. Freud (1925,) conceptualizes the traces upon the unconscious as being 'permanent' (p. 227, p. 230), as observed also in passing by Derrida (1978, p. 204). In stark contrast to this later emphasis of Freud (though not to that of Freud's 1896 letter to Fliess, which Derrida 1978, p. 206, quotes in terms of memory-traces subjected to a rearrangement), Derrida (1978) opens up a dynamic background realm of interaction with the trace to challenge its permanency, 'The trace is the erasure of selfhood, of one's own presence, and is constituted by the threat or anguish of its irremediable disappearance, of the disappearance of its disappearance. An unerasable trace is not a trace, it is a full presence ...' (p. 230). Derridean erasure of the trace is conceptualized explicitly in *structural* terms in relation to repression:

> This erasure of the trace is not only an accident that can occur here or there, nor is it even the necessary structure of a determined censorship threatening a given presence; it is the very structure which makes possible, as the movement of temporalization and pure *auto-affection*, something that can be called repression in general, the original synthesis of original repression and secondary repression, repression 'itself'. (Derrida 1978, p. 230, italics in original)

It is a structure which makes possible. The deconstructor *par excellence* allows for a dimension of purity; it contains the auto-affection dimension of the 'instant', that prior relation to the printer and printed, a mode of relation prior to the subject-object dualism. As a movement, it is a directional structure crossing out other spatial structures. The structure of *différance*, the erasure of the trace in the instant between the impression and the imprint, is an erasure of a present non-origin. This invites strong resonances with the spatio-temporal structures unseating diametric mirror image symmetry.

For Derrida (1996), the space itself of the archive is in some way divided and 'there is no archive without a place of consignation, without a technique of repetition and without a certain exterior' (p. 1). This division within memory, traces of memory and traces of the archive, 'that objectivizable storage called the archive' (Derrida 1996, p. 26), invites a concomitant focus on an absence in claims of presence. It invites further interrogation of issues of division, separation, interaction and connection, as well as repetition, both in Freudian conceptions of the unconscious and in going beyond logocentric repression to another domain of relevance. It is this dimension of separation and connection which invites a further discourse pertinent to diametric and concentric spatial relation.

The contours of a Derridean text prior to Freud's logocentric repression give expression not only to the interconnectedness of space and time as an interplay, but also bring an intensification of concentration on dimensions of rupture and connection, 'Temporality as spacing will be not only the horizontal discontinuity of a chain of signs, but also will be writing as the interruption and restoration of contact between the various depths of psychical levels: the remarkably heterogenous temporal fabric of psychical work itself' (Derrida 1978, p. 225). This focus on interruption is an expansion of the two-way repressive movements highlighted by Freud (1926) in mirror image symmetry for obsessional neurosis. Derrida seeks a wider view of systemic repression and connection, as a series of interruptions and restorations at different heterogeneous levels. This wider view gains some succour also from Freud's (1926) acknowledgement that 'instead of a single repression we have found a collection of them' (p. 107). A Derridean background questioning involves examination of the differences and connections between these systemic collections of repressions. It highlights the need for concentrating on how to relate and not relate these repressions to each other as structures of difference.

Interruption and restoration implicates both diametric spatial process dimensions of assumed separation and concentric spatial projections of assumed connection. A view of spacing as dynamic leads to the proposed psychoanalytic graphology of diametric and concentric spatial differential relation through this focus on interruption and restoration – assumed separation and assumed connection – as pervading the different heterogeneous aspects of the unconscious. Interaction between diametric and concentric spaces of assumed separation and connection respectively requires this wider systemic focus of Derrida, amplifying Freud, on background relations between collections of repressions. The divisions in these collections of repressions encompass what Derrida (1996) refers to as 'archive fever', as contradictions in a divided archive of the unconscious, what Derrida (1978) describes as 'the ungraspable and invisible difference between breaches' (p. 201) in the trace as memory.

Repression and the unconscious is for Derrida a dynamic process of archivization. Suggesting that 'the archivization produces as much as it records the event' (p. 17), Derrida (1996) argues that Freud:

> wants to exhume a more archaic impression, he wants to exhibit a more archaic imprint than the one the other archaeologists of all kinds bustle around, those of literature and those of classical objective science ... an impression that is almost no longer an archive but almost confuses itself with the pressure of the footstep that leaves its still-living mark on a substrate, a surface, a place of origin. (p. 97)

The process dimensions of concentric assumed connection and diametric assumed separation provide a level of systemic interactions between the various depths of psychic levels, whether in moving beyond the mirror image symmetries in neurosis and more radical splits of assumed separation in psychosis, or in relating constellations emerging from reactions to external events to a prior spatial organizing principle to repression in unconscious relations. They offer a spatial interplay for engaging with difference between breaches in systems of repression and memory.

Building on the edifice of Freud, Derrida (1996) describes, 'A compulsive, repetitive and nostalgic desire for the archive, an irrepressible desire to return to the origin, a homesickness, a nostalgia for the return to the most archaic place of absolute commencement' (p. 91). Whether this is equivalent with Freud's compulsion to repeat or otherwise, it bears reiteration that conceptualizing both diametric and concentric spatial structures dynamically, as projections, invokes a repetition and return taking place through such projections. The dynamic process of constructing such projections upon experience and the environment, and within the system of the unconscious, is itself a process of repetition – of repeating the structure being projected by means of the projection.

Concentric spatial structures give way to diametric ones and *vice-versa*, in a relativistic relational process. As each is a displacement and deferral of the other, the mutual tension in which they are held brings a resistance to either existing in full presence. This amplification resonates with Derrida's (1978) account that 'psychic life is neither the transparency of meaning nor the opacity of force but the difference within the exertion of forces' (p. 201). Whereas Derrida (1978) interprets Freud as wanting 'to think force and place simultaneously' and views 'differences in the work of breaching' as concerning 'not only forces but also locations' (p. 204), a basically similar concern with a simultaneous interplay between directional and positional dimensions to diametric and concentric spaces exists for current purposes. Derrida's difference goes beyond a static central ground. No simple centre is anticipated. Structure-content relativity, in a chain of differences between foregrounds and backgrounds, can be construed as a principle of difference with a structural dimension that is resonant with Derrida's *différance*. Depending on the interpretative vantage point, there is no absolute space as starting or end point. This principle of difference has already been seen to move beyond a form-content schema and to pertain to projected concentric and diametric spaces of relation. It offers a relativity between centres as foregrounds and backgrounds, structure and content of experience, that does not reduce such relativity to sheer postmodern relativism of truth or experience. Concentric and diametric spatial movements give concrete structural expression to this principle of difference in structure-content relativity.

Table 6 Key dimensions of a proposed psychoanalytic graphology

Diametric Spatial Relation	*Concentric Spatial Relation*	*Freudian Repression*	*Derridean Divided Archive and System of Traces as a Spatio-Temporal Organizing Principle Prior to Event-Memory (Printer-Printed)*
Mirror Image Inverted Symmetry	Symmetry as Unity	Wolf Man Inversions – Obsessional Neurosis Inversions a General Feature of Obsessional Neurosis (Freud 1926) Schreber Case Inversions-Psychosis (Freud 1911)	Restricted Construction of Western Subjectivity through Visual Metaphors
Assumed Separation	Assumed Connection	Repression as Splitting (Freud 1914; 1923; 1940)	Interruptions and Restorations in Breaches/ Contradictions of a Divided Archive in Collections of Repressions
Assumed Separation from Background as Noninteraction/ Relative Closure	Assumed Connection to Background as Interaction/ Relative Openness	Repression as Withdrawal of Cathexis (Freud 1924; 1926); 'Isolation' (Freud 1926); Closure of Repetitive Play/Ritual (Freud 1920; 1896)	Beyond Restricted Space of Logocentric Repression and Narrowed Construction of Western Subjectivity

Derrida (1978) focuses on the relation of sameness and difference in relationship, 'What is the division *of being between* the same and the other? Is it a division *between* the same and the other, which does not suppose, at very least, that the same is the other's other, and the other the same as oneself' (p. 127, italics in original). Concentric and diametric structures of relation offer models of sameness and otherness – of assumed connection and separation – which accommodate conceptions of sameness and difference. They offer dynamic structures of differential relation. His is a quest for a space that is non-cognitive or at least a precognitive threshold, a space always already deferred. A movement more radical than reliance on the visual, aural or haptic is needed, being neither in thrall to metaphysics, nor mourning the certainty of binary opposition.

Derrida conceptualizes the trace and archive in terms of reciprocal interaction between footstep-footprint, printer-printed, pressure and its trace, where the imprint of one shapes the other. The footprint is the inverted shape of the footstep. They are partially symbiotic. Erasure of the trace presupposes a temporal dimension that is not necessarily reducible to linear time.

Whereas Derrida refers to the structure of the instant underlying the impression and the imprint as being 'erased', there are two different kinds of erasure that can be taking place – or more precisely, that can be embracing space. There is a difference and division within erasure itself. One direction of erasure is the loss of the inverted diametric dimension into a further desiccated space without polarity. Yet a different direction of erasure of the trace of the archive of diametric space may also be possible, though not necessarily observable in any given historical context. This variant of erasure of the trace of diametric structures would be in a reverse direction towards concentric relation. It is not so much erasure of the trace of diametric relation *qua* annihilation, but as a possible directional process of dissolving, of potential change towards concentric relation. Erasure takes contrasting directions, where one direction occludes the other.

Derrida's search for a psychoanalytic graphology is a quest for a spatial membrane that is not mere matter invested with logocentric values of thingness; neither is it a conception of 'reality' opposed to the idea. Dimensions of diametric spatial relation as assumed separation and concentric spatial relation as assumed connection open up a site of interaction that is not contingent of visual metaphors of light.

Myths provide but one avenue into this spatial process of relations. In opening a space for a supposedly entirely other text, Derrida invites scrutiny of a level prior to myth. There is no myth as a still point of the turning world. There is no Archimedean point for myth. A fundamental reference point has been expelled from a mythical Eden of the mythic. If myths transform one into another and it is the relation or structure of myths that is more fundamental, this requires further interrogation of this background relation. This invites a renewed focus on spatial and temporal dimensions.

A shift from diametric spatial structures also invites the danger of a further fragmentation and splitting in this restructuring, so that the turning open toward concentric spatial relation may not necessarily come forth. It is not simply that a loss of meaning may occur in the horizon shift away from diametric spatial relation; concentric directions of opening need not be confined to injunctions towards meaning making. Whereas concentric spatial movements unsettle the fixities of diametric spatial relations, this is not reducible to a purpose of finding a different static mould or cognitive mapping for truth or experience. The directions of the contours of this different experiential angle of relation than the diametric do not map in linear fashion onto a correspondent cognitive construction of reality. As Heidegger would describe it, a questioning of being is not reducible to a mere hypostatized worldview. It is not for Derrida, a return to a simple naieve origin or home.

Derrida (1981/1995) notes that, 'My work does not ... destroy the subject; it simply tries to resituate it' (p. 175). This proposed psychoanalytic graphology engages with a presubjective expansion from repressive diametric spatial relations to challenge the construction of a restricted subjectivity. It is envisaged as a discourse pertaining to a more radical displacement and deferral than Freud's logocentric repression. A common spatial domain of relevance has been uncovered in Section B for diverse features of Freudian repression, including aspects of ambivalence in obsessional neurosis and psychosis, splitting of the ego, and withdrawal of cathexis and repetition fixation. This graphological domain has been developed through a range of dynamic interactive dimensions for diametric and concentric spatial movements, across common thematic concerns of Derrida and Freud, such as inversions, interruption and restoration, openness and closure, in their accounts of traces in systems of repression in the unconscious. This psychoanalytic graphology challenges the construction of a restricted subjectivity based on repressive diametric spatial relations. It identifies Derridean motifs as pertaining not only to deconstruction but also to the threshold of an entirely other text.

9.3 Beyond a split between sense and concept of self in Jungian psychology: A 'breathing' rather than reified mandala

Argument: That concentric structured experience is phenomenologically meaningful as lived experiential content, meditative awareness of breathing and sense of self.

Fordham (1985) distinguishes between the *sense* and *concept* of the Jungian self. He views the latter as being outside direct experience. Following this cleavage, concentric structures framing experience would be outside experience. There would be an arbitrary relation between concentric structures and experiential dimensions to the self.

A concept of self, diametrically severed from an experience or sense of self, falls into the danger of becoming a reified structure. Derrida's (1978) critique of reification and structure raises further distinctions between a) the thought of the structure itself, b) speech or language describing the structure, and c) experience of the structure, 'For the thought of the thing as *what* it *is* has already been confused with the experience of pure speech; and this experience has been confused with experience *itself*' (p. 9). Derrida's distinction between thought and experience of, for example, concentric structures, echoes Fordham's need to distinguish concept or sense of self. Nevertheless, acknowledgement of the need to distinguish conceptual and experiential levels does not mean that these levels have to be fully split from each other. It is arguable that sense and concept of self can be in a relation of assumed connection. Concentric structures of relation can be meaningful, not only conceptually, but also experientially.

Like a pulse, a heartbeat, the colour of one's own eyes, concentric space is so close it struggles to be seen. Assumed connection and separation is a distinction, which treads paths beyond the modality of sight. Shelley's words, 'Peopled by shapes too bright to see' are somewhat apt to describe a sensing of the tissue of these spatial shapes. Developing this expands Nietzsche's (1872) portrayal, in *The Birth of Tragedy*, of the dark spots on the eyes after looking at the sun, to delve into the reverse effects of bright spots emerging after glancing into the darkness of the abyss. Can concentric and diametric spaces provide such spots of brightness, without being reduced as in Nietzsche's metaphor to being merely an Apollonian mask to heal the eyes?

Recognition of the need not to conflate phenomenological experience with structure does not mean that there is simply an arbitrary relation between them. While Saussure's (1954) structuralism highlights the arbitrary relation in language between signifier and signified (e.g., word and the object to which it refers), concentric and diametric structures do not have to be reified into a split from lived experience.[5] So, for example, lived experience of 'walls', 'blockages', 'barriers', 'masks', 'defensiveness' provides a phenomenological language regarding splits within experience which bear a structural and not arbitrary relation to the assumed separation of diametric space. The sands of the walls of diametricity are dry. Similarly, experience of the unconscious as 'fluid', as 'water', highlighted in the following passage of Jung (1941–54), bears a structural and not arbitrary relation to the assumed connection and interactive background of concentric spaces:

5 A Saussurean structuralist emphasis on the arbitrary relation between signifier and signified can be given expression at the level of the *content* of the diametric relation in a given culture, e.g., lynx and coyote, in some South American myths (Downes 2003, p. 60). Even if the content is frequently arbitrary (e.g., at some dimensions of function and reference), this does not mean that it is *necessarily* arbitrary. Some contents of experience retain a basic connection to the diametric and/or concentric structure. See also Jakobsen (1973) for a challenge to Saussure's position regarding an arbitrary relation between signifier and signified.

> Water in all its forms – sea, lake, river, spring – is one of the commonest typifications of the unconscious, as is also the lunar femininity that is closely associated with water. The dissolution of the heart in water would therefore correspond to the union of the male with the female, and this in turn to the union of conscious and unconscious … (p. 272)

The wave-like dimension to experience of concentric space – expressing an assumed connection and increased background interaction of a fluid relative to a solid state – is also exhibited by Freud's (1930a) recognition of an oceanic feeling. This feeling was experienced, not by Freud personally but by his friend, Romain Rolland. It was a sense also adverted to by Primo Levi (1985), a survivor of Auschwitz. Freud (1930a) described it as 'a sensation of eternity, a feeling as of something limitless, unbounded – as it were, "oceanic" … it is the feeling of an indissoluble bond, of being one with the external world as a whole' (p. 65). Relative to concentric structures, diametric space provides an increased, tightened boundary between two domains, as diametric structures sever active interaction between its two parts. Concentric poles are distinct, but with decreased, looser boundaries compared with diametric poles because concentric distinction between the two parts is based on an assumed connection to a whole. Thus, a diametric-concentric contrast can be given expression through a solidity-fluidity contrast for experiential contents.

Freud (1900, 1915e, 1920) refers to 'free' 'mobile', in effect, fluid energy and 'bound', 'quiescent', solid energy. Eigen (1986) also highlights how conceptions of fluidity and solidity pervade Freudian thought in particular, 'For Freud, libido is both rigid and fluid. Libido is fluid and electrical in its ability to change forms and to invest a wide range of objects, but its basic functions are the same, as fixed as respiration or the circulation of the blood. It is too simple to equate rigidity with superego and fluidity with id, as is often done' (p. 346). Though linguistic and conceptual constructions expressing fluidity and solidity cannot be simplistically equated with concentric fluidity and diametric solidity, they do offer examples of potential connection between sense and concept of self. This provides a bridge between experiential and structural-conceptual concerns. Diametricity turns to flow. The hollow, dried vessel of diametric space is decompressed to a fluidity. In embedded transcendence, the concentric trajectory for change occurs to unseat the supporting conditions for diametric experience and to fluidate diametric relation into a movement towards concentric relational flow.

These silent oceanic realms of concentric experiential relation defy mapping in a one to one correspondence with exclusively one mode of experience, just as diametric spatial projections encompass a panoply of diverse states and experiences. Experience of concentric spaces cannot be reduced to a formula in its concrete manifestations as experiential contents. Nevertheless, one major aperture for exploration of concentric experiential spaces is concerning breathing and its openings in meditative experience.

A 'breathing' rather than reified mandala: Concentric and diametric relations to breathing

Movement beyond a static reified image through accommodation of a dimension of time breathes life into the mandala structure. And the idea of a breathing mandala can be developed beyond a metaphor by closer examination of contrasts between concentric and diametric modes of relation to *breathing*. A concentric relation of the breath as an inner circle within the outer circle of the body assumes a basic connection. It involves awareness of the breath in the body. A diametric relation of the breath to the body splits awareness of breathing, as a basic experience. In the words of a ten-year-old Irish girl, in a questionnaire response, 'It's good to talk about your feelings, you feel relaxed and relieved instead of holding your breath' (Downes 2004a, p. 11). Breathing is a process of relation, which can be expressed through the primordial structures of relation of concentric and diametric spaces in dynamic tension.

Meditation, as an emptying of the mind, invites a more intense awareness of the breathing process. This emphasis on breathing as part of connection to a transcendent or transpersonal level of experience (e.g., through holotropic breathing) challenges a view of spirit as mind, and reclaims the association between spirit and breath in a range of cultures. Spirit, as mind or intellect, contrasts with, for example, the Latin etymology of *spiritus* as breath and the Hebrew etymology of *ruach* uniting spirit and wind. These roots are largely lost to an English association of spirit as mind and a German, or at least Hegelian, treatment of spirit as *Geist* or self-consciousness. Nevertheless, association between spirit and breath is implicit in English terms such as *respiration*. Spirit as breath is still evident in, for example, Finno-Ugric languages. For example, spirit in Finnish is *henki* (breath) and spiritual *(hengillinen)* literally means breathful. Similarly, in Estonian, *hing* (spirit) is expressed through *hingama* (to breathe) and *hingeohk* (breath). In Russian, *Duch* means spirit, *Dusha* means soul, both of which have clear associations with *Dychanie* (breath) and *Dyshat* (to breathe). Beyond these limited European examples, Jung (1939) notes that in the East 'the psyche is … all important; it is all-pervading Breath, the Buddha-essence' (p. 110). The mandala can be interpreted as a circular space opened in the structure of the heart for the awareness of the flow of the breath. A compressed circle, in other words, a line, expresses the closure of a space giving awareness of the breath flow.

Recognition of the dimensions of breathing as a mode of awareness challenges traditional Western reliance on empirical experience through the five senses. However, Homer's *Odyssey* does furnish an indirect point of reference in traditional Western thought for associations between spirit and breath, with occasional examples of their interconnection, such as in the following passages: '… to let a coward breathe/Spirit enough to dare his brother's death?' (p. 59), 'The spirit of that little, that the whole/A sacred odour breath'd about the bowl' (p. 176), 'But deity/Hath giv'n so many other sighs and cares/ To my attendant state' (p. 270). Here again the fabric of the breath is the spatial throbbing to hold thought, as though breathing for an opened air.

Acceptance of the dimensions of breathing as a mode of awareness also challenges other Western views, which rely on assumptions of intentionality, where consciousness is assumed to have an object: meditative awareness of breathing is more an objectless experience. Despite some scepticism on his part, Jung did acknowledge accounts of the experience of *satori* in Eastern cultures, including a level of imageless experience.[6]

6 See e.g., Mansfield (1991–92) on *satori* and 'empty' consciousness, though also Jung 1939 on *satori* experience as being extremely alien to Western experience, and Jung

Jung (1931) gives an account of Edward Maitland's emphasis on 'suspension of breathing', where ordinary breathing stops and is replaced by an internal respiration, 'as if by breathing of a distinct personality within and other than the physical organism' (p. 27). However, Jung's own tendency to associate spirit with mind and abstraction is evident for example, in his letter to Wolfgang Pauli (24 October 1953).

Images as reifications locked within assumptions of a subject-object dualism invite the question as to the possibility of experience which is not simply at the level of reified images. Some forms of meditation invite an emptying of the mind for a transcendence of simply image-based experience. *Dissolving of the diametric ego into the concentric self during the process of individuation can also be interpreted as a dissolving of image based experience.* The assumed separation necessary for the subject-object relation governing the observing subject and observed image is dissolved. Thus, a realm for experience is opened that goes beyond reification.

Space and time grounding empirical experience is not necessarily transcendent of experience in Kant's sense of being impossible to experience, being beyond experience, once a prior level of awareness of breathing is accommodated. This concentric and diametric structured awareness within breathing invokes an awareness of space and time as dynamic structures of experience. Concentric and diametric structures are spatial models and their interaction offers a temporal dimension to experience. With this spatio-temporal awareness, space and time are now immanent aspects of structures of relation and do not stand abstractly outside experience. A lived connective awareness of the breath makes a dimension of space and time interdependent, as well as immanent and interactive within experience.

Unwrithing the twisted walls of the diametric relation through the breath invites a turn into the primordial rivers of concentric relation. In this transformation into embedded transcendence, the mandala structure to primordial experience breathes into an animation beyond the realm of a static image. It involves an experiential shift from the detached, observing

---

1958, 'Letter to Kirsch', pp. 466–7, for a critical account of the *satori* tradition of imageless experience.

self-consciousness of a Cartesian frozen frame of mind-body. As a breath-pulse passes through impulse, this implicates an opening to dissolve the scratched diametric spaces of a heartbeat.

An opening of a breath-affective realm for primordial experience is a level of personal transformation that need not be the preserve merely of the few. Taylor (2007) notes that:

> For spiritual outlooks of the transformation perspective, Christianity and Buddhism, say, the point where we achieve our full human capacity, beyond pathological and other confusions about our spiritual condition, is placed well beyond the level of recognized human flourishing. It is a distinctly minority phenomenon. (p. 623)

Though obviously not separate from societal conditions and opportunities, this minority phenomenon may be more malleable and ripe for expansion than stated by Taylor. An increasing openness to the possibility of experiencing embedded transcendence of diametric space has already reached popular culture in the twentieth century, through awareness of the need to confront projections and the shadow side to a person's personality, as part of personal growth. Embedded transcendence as a process has taken firm steps at this level of personal development, in moving beyond diametric splits and away to some degree from a flattened monism of homogenous space to experience.

For an *aeon* of the breath to gain further expansion in experience, the need is to continue this process of opening towards concentric modes of experience. Jung's key insight here is that search for meaning is not simply a matter of change to a person's ideas but involves a restructuring of modes of experience, as part of facing this crisis for personality. There is a need to own these structures of our primordial experience, for the dancer to dance in the spaces where both concentric and diametric spaces clash in cacophony, as a process of their ongoing resolution. A further urgent need is for a publicly defensible discourse to provide aspects of a map through this journey. An existential science of embedded transcendence can provide a discourse to engage with not only individuals' lived experiences but also with traditional cultural patterns as projections – in a dynamic dialogue.

It was noted earlier that Gilligan's work describes what amounts to a diametric structured mirror image inversion between voice and silence, as a feature of repressive cultural communication, 'Girls in the study live in a territory between voice and silence: If they continue to speak from their experience they may find that their voice is out of relationship, too loud, off key. If they remain silent they are in immediate danger of disappearing' (Taylor, Gilligan & Sullivan, 1995, p. 202). Connection in relationship is envisaged as a pathway out of such fragmentation. However, the spatial assumptions underlying this relation between voice and silence in Gilligan's work need further interrogation.

Gilligan tends to locate a diametric opposition between voice and silence, where voice is trapped and silenced into suppression. This is but one view of silence. There is a need for recognition of a different silence. A concentric relation between silence and voice accepts that they are in assumed connection, with silence in the inner circle within voice. Silence is the breath of voice. And voice needs silence to give meaning. This is not only a silence that is needed on the part of the listener for a voice to emerge and be heard. It is not only silence as a passive complement.

The danger in Gilligan's association of silence with forces of repression is that a diametric opposition becomes set up, where voice equals good and silence equals bad. While this has some force for a certain kind of fear-based, dominating silence, it is also a parody of the potential space for silence in individual and cultural experience. The silent space of breathing is much explored in meditation across a wide range of Eastern traditions. There may be different spaces of silence for a culture to foster. Much of postmodern thought has completely lost a concentric within-ness due to its rejection of the diametric structured model of within-ness. Concentric structured modes of experience become pushed beneath the radar of relevance in postmodernism. In doing so, postmodern tendencies exhibit a surreptitious concern to drown out silence in experience, through a preoccupation with language and interpersonal communication as relation. Yet a concentration on concentric spatial structures of experience brings to the fore that space itself is a relational structure and projection within experience.

Concentric spaces for experience bring a different dance between breath and voice. It is a different dancing rhythm between the tremours of silence and sound. This opening suggests there is not simply one different silence, but a panoply of different silences. Sleep is another primordial silence for experience, though not the only one. The voice is a string for the breath, a tube for the breath flow. Diametric spatial closure for experience is not only a slumber of a kind, it is a snoring disturbance within the slumber. Diametric compressed space is as a weight upon the breath, a closure of experiential tubes through the heart. It operates as a barely perceptible lump in the breath, hidden from the self.

The taut strings of diametric space furnish a fortress bridge. The wave is tightened into solidity, into a compression that becomes a frozen frame for mind. The knotted circles of displaced concentricity become tied into a tension of diametricity or its derivatives. Sealed off from primary background stimuli, the diametric vessel thirsts for compensatory stimuli to fill the self-manufactured void. This invites the animation of the inert. The diametric ego blocks out the concentric self from experience, as the artificial lights of houses and streetlamps diminish the moonlight. The opaque halls of diametric space threaten to obscure the primordial movement into concentric relation.

The existential shift to search for meaning confronts the void of meaninglessness. This void is the empty homogenous space of lived experience, before even partial expansion through diametric structured inversion. Frankl's (1959) harrowing account of his time in the Nazi concentration camps and his emphasis on search for meaning makes the vital point that an existential search is real, concrete, different and unique for each individual. The 'will to meaning' he describes can arguably operate on at least two levels, the foreground and background level. The foreground search for meaning is real, concrete, different and individual; the background level is where concentric and diametric spaces of relation for experience emerge and help develop the foreground construction of meaning. In confronting the existential void, the framing space for an experience of meaninglessness – the space frame itself structuring experience – needs to be confronted. Existential despair cannot be adequately overcome without this restructuring of experiential space, as Jung realized, from diametric ego structured experience to concentric structured self. The dynamic breathing mandala incorporates this interplay between the concentric and diametric, as part of this process of potential, though far from inevitable, restructuring. It is a restructuring underlying the wound in the breath, the cavities of the psyche or soul. Background existential structures of experience, as well as the more obvious foreground, individual concrete tasks, cannot be overlooked in this existential search for meaning. Quest for meaning needs the question and dimension of being, a quest for being. The primordial relation between concentric and diametric spaces offers a framework where the 'void' can be understood as real – the existential void is real as a flattened truth of background experience within primordial existential structures.

9.4 Concentric and diametric structures as a primordial sense beyond socially constructed language-games

Argument: That (i) a direct referential relation exists between concentric and diametric spaces as primordial structures of experience and as experiential content and (ii) this primordial experiential content is potentially cross-culturally meaningful as prior to the cultural relativity of language-games.

Challenging Fordham's (1985) view of the sense and concept of self as being in assumed separation, where the latter is outside direct experience, requires a number of steps. It implies rejection of an arbitrary relation between phenomenological experience of concentric and diametric structures and the structures as concepts. The further step arises of examining whether a *sense* of concentric and diametric relation is cross-culturally possible, so that it is not only concentric and diametric structures as concepts that are cross-cultural. In other words, can the proposed primordial structures, concentric and diametric experience, offer the potential for expression of a cross-cultural *sense* of self? Through different cultural forms of expression of solid diametric and fluid concentric relation, can it be concluded that solid diametric experience and fluid concentric experience are at least potentially universal across cultures and hence potentially primordial as a sense?

To express a primordial sense, it is arguably *not* necessary that the linguistically equivalent terms of solid(ity) and fluid(ity) be directly found in a particular culture. Berlin's (1978) recognises that linguistic and cognitive categories are not necessarily to be equated. According to Berlin (1974), if one observes that, for example, the generic term, 'plant' or 'animal', is named in some language but not in others the following question arises, 'Are there sufficient data to indicate the cognitive recognition of the category in those languages where [these categories] are not named' (p. 328). Berlin (1974; 1978) states that the answer depends on the ethnobiological facts of a particular case. In any case, the absence of direct *linguistic* cross-cultural categories of solidity and fluidity is not a criterion for falsification of the proposed primordial structures of relation as a primordial sense.

The concerns of Berlin (1974; 1978) are with recognition of factual categories by a culture. The emphasis for present purposes regarding a cross-cultural primordial sense of concentric fluidity and diametric solidity is with the *potential* for recognition of experiential solidity and fluidity by individuals in a given culture and for solidity and fluidity to be a dynamic relational opposition in a given culture's categories.[7]

Wittgenstein (1958) advocates a cultural relativity of language-games, where languages like games, follow initially arbitrary rules as social conventions. Wittgenstein's (1958) language-games perspective is an assault on claims for abstract essences of meaning, treating such ambitions as specious and reducing their scope to being truths that are socially and culturally conditioned *simpliciter*. A language-game critique would furnish the important warning against treating diametric 'solidity' and concentric 'fluidity' as fundamental reified positional states, or as abstract cognitive categories. Wittgenstein argues that even 'pain' is not a concept or word that can transfer from one culture's language-game conventions to another's (Malcolm 1995, pp. 100–2). Without invoking Wittgenstein, Hart's (1958) examination of definition and theory in jurisprudence makes a similar point on the dangers of assumptions that the same word has the same, or even comparable, meaning when transferred to another context. The apparently large coincidence or chance of transferability of a common meaning for a word or law (or structure of relation) across different contexts is a cautionary

7 This recognition issue is not equivalent to another issue of how to develop actual primordial experience in a given culture.

note in a legal context that one must be cognizant of a presumption of slippage of meaning in any such attempted transfer; Wittgenstein takes the *grand hasard* of this cautionary note and makes it ubiquitous for language.

If according to Wittgenstein, not even the concept of pain can translate from one culture's language-game conventions to another, then how could 'solidity' and 'fluidity' be even envisaged as translatable? Wittgenstein seems to reject, not only the universality of actual language-games, but also even the potential of any specific imagined (Malcolm, 1995, p. 93) language-game to translate precisely across cultures. Billig (1987, p. 49) notes the cultural and gendered constructedness of games historically. This invites a self-referential critique of Wittgenstein's language-games concept, as itself locked into language-game relativity. It, thereby, leaves a permissive space as a locus for a more primordial realm than language-games. Furthermore, Billig (1987, p. 49) observes a notable limit to the game metaphor; it deals only with rule-acceptance and not rule-generation. The tenuity of this bifurcation between rule-following and rule-generation needs to be exposed.

The primordial structures of experience, concentric fluidity and diametric solidity, do not contradict Wittgenstein's conception of language-games insofar as (i) language-games describe *non*-primordial experiences, (ii) the primordial structures express *a pre-linguistic sense stratum rather than linguistically reliant experience*. A potentially universal primordial sense stratum is not being postulated as a language-game but as being a pre-linguistic level of experience, prior to the rule-following mode of relation underlying language-games.

A transcendental language-game attacked by Wittgenstein is a very different species from a potentially transcendental sense stratum or structure of pre-linguistic primordial experience, such as that postulated by a concentric fluidity and diametric solidity. This can be illuminated through Wittgenstein's (1969) statement, 'Certain events would put me into a position in which I could not go on with the old language-game any more. In which I was torn away from the *sureness* of the game. Indeed, isn't it obvious that the possibility of a language-game is conditioned by certain facts' (p. 617). The primordial experience tears away the sureness of particular old language-games and offers a directional horizon for change to be expressed through interaction of primordial experience with previous frames for meaning. Individuation is a quest for structures of experience that can reconstitute the preexisting language-games of a culture, games experienced as desiccated and meaningless by the individual. The assumption structure underlying language-games needs to be exposed and torn open and its 'sureness' deconstructed, as part of touching the prelinguistic sense stratum of primordial experience. In doing so, the apex of relativism in Wittgenstein's linguistic relativity remains intact but operates over a smaller canvas of truth and experiential concerns.

It is being accepted that: (i) the linguistic expression of the proposed primordial sense stratum of concentric fluidity and diametric solidity may vary across culture, i.e., the type of exemplar to illustrate the primordial structure or its level of abstraction may vary, and (ii) the cultural meaning assigned to primordial experience may also vary, i.e., if it is viewed as good or bad etc. However, the primordial experience structures need not necessarily become *merely* a language-game plaything of culture.

Potential for recognition of experiential realms of diametric solidity and concentric fluidity can arguably be accepted once there are given (not necessarily linguistic) *exemplars* of solid-fluid oppositions in a culture. Exemplars of solid-fluid oppositions abound across cultures, though only a preliminary account will be provided here. A most obvious exemplar of solid-fluid opposition is that observed in the Miwok of California. As Lévi-Strauss (1963) states:

> The Miwok moieties, like those of Indonesia, express a general dual classification of objects and phenomena. The moieties are called *kikua* (of water) and *tunuka* (of land). Although all animals, plants, physical geographical features, and meteorological and astronomical phenomena are divided between the two moieties, the male and female principles are excluded from this universal dichotomy, as though the native dialectic were unable to overcome the objective consideration that men and women exist in both moieties. (p. 157)

So for primordial experience of diametric solidity and concentric fluidity in interaction to be characterized as change, between an 'of land' (*tunuka*) and 'of water' (*kikua*) experience or sense, would not so much be a small leap, as a natural continuity for the Miwok.

The Miwok's classification resists the traditional Western opposition of literal and derivative metaphorical realms. Another example of a culture where the solid-fluid opposition is viewed as fundamental, as expressed through exemplars, is that of the Osage. In Lévi-Strauss' (1962) words:

> In Osage thought, the most important opposition, which is also the simplest and has the greatest logical power, is that between the two moieties: *Tsi'-zhu*: sky, and *Hon'-ga*; subdivided into *Hon'-ga*, properly speaking: dry land, and *Wa-zha'-zhe*: water. Starting from here a complex grammar is developed by means of a system of correspondences with more concrete or more abstract domains but within which the original scheme, acting as a catalyst, initiates the crystallisation of other schemes of two, three, four or more variables. (p. 143)

There are gradations of fluidity (solid-liquid-gas) here from the solidity of dry land to water and to sky. The proposed primordial sense stratum of diametric solidity and concentric fluidity purports to express *primordial* experience – *not all* experience – and is also a *potential* experiential realm. Thus, it is not necessary for solid-fluid exemplars to exist in a culture as a universal classification of *all* reality. It need not be a *fundamental* valued opposition but simply a *recognized* one, through exemplars that need not even be linguistic. Some other examples of solid-fluid exemplar oppositions are as follows: earth/water, dry season/rainy season are opposed in Eastern Timbira (Lévi-Strauss, 1963, p. 148); a Great Lakes tribe, the Winnebago, oppose sky with earth and water in a triadic opposition (Radin; Lévi-Strauss 1963, p. 153); the Chinese *yin/yang* opposes earth and sky (Needham 1979). The fluid exemplars of fire and water are opposed to some extent by the Berber (Bourdieu 1973, p. 104).

Some obvious objections arise to the conclusion that simply search for *any* exemplar of a solid-fluid opposition in a given culture suffices for a potential *sense* of primordial experience to be cross-culturally expressable in a meaningful way. It may be objected that the leap from solid-fluid exemplars to an experience of diametric solidity or concentric fluidity, is a jump from the literal to the metaphorical that may not be possible in all cultures. Yet the governing frames of such an objection are locked into the traditional Western Aristotelian opposition between the metaphorical and literal is inadequate for the pervasiveness of the *kikua* (of water) and *tunuka* (of land) opposition for the Miwok.[8] Jahoda's (1982) general words are pertinent, 'Since people themselves do not attach such labels as "symbolic" and "non-symbolic" to their classification, such a property has to be inferred or attributed' (p. 251). This is tantamount to stating that a Western mindset would have to be imposed on experiences which are not broken down into literal/metaphorical categories.

It is not only the Miwok who have little difficulty in using symbol or metaphor to describe features of their experienced world. Ellen's (1977) review of anatomical classifications, drawing on various research traditions, found not merely communalities and variations in body taxonomy, but also concluded that the symbolic and metaphoric use of the human form is probably universal. Furthermore, Needham's (1979) cross-cultural review suggested (in effect, echoing Lévi-Strauss 1962, 1963) that any classification can take on a symbolic aspect. As an example, he referred to the spatial groupings of occupations in towns; from one perspective classification may be regarded as being of practical convenience (e.g., butchers or cloth merchants all clustered in particular areas) and from another, as a form of symbolic ranking which divides 'good' and 'bad' parts of a town. Streicker's (1997) research on gender and space symbolism in Cartagena, Columbia, supports this. Thus, a leap from a solid-fluid exemplar to treating this as a description of a primordial experience – diametric solidity becoming, for example, 'earth' or 'dry land' experience, concentric fluidity becoming, for example, 'water' or 'fire', 'rain', 'blood', 'sky' experience – is a descriptive realm that is cross-culturally possible. In doing so, this is not to equate the (public) language of private experience with private experience.

This important problem of the relation between structure and content in image schemata is adverted to by Johnson (2005) concerning the difficulty of integrating lived feeling with a structural approach, 'There is a "down side" to our standard way of describing image schemas ... if you attend only to *structure*, you necessarily ignore the nonstructural, more

8 A range of empirical research in cognitive psychology also suggests that a rigid distinction between literal and metaphorical levels is not a meaningful distinction for cognitive processing, even in Western cultures (see e.g., Gibbs 1993).

qualitative aspects of meaning and thought … The human experience of meaning concerns *both* structure *and* quality' (pp. 27–8). Suggesting that there 'may be no way around this problem', Johnson (2005) does 'not envisage a different way of speaking about image schemas that would someday successfully incorporate qualities of experience' (p. 27–9) (see also Johnson 2007, p. 71). The split between structure and experience content is here in some contrast to schema structure-content relativity, where the interchangeability of structure and content for experience is not so fundamentally cleft in two. And for primordial experience, the projection of concentric and diametric spatial structures invites at least some continuity with experiential content. Projection implies a referential continuity. Structure-content relativity brings structure and life-world together.

It may be further objected that while diametric solid-concentric fluid opposition exemplars abound across all cultures, a dynamic relational opposition may not. Here the key feature that would need to be retained cross-culturally for a potential *sense* of primordial experience to be expressed through the concentric fluidity and diametric solidity is simply the notion of *change* – change towards solidity (e.g., earth, dry land) and change towards fluidity (e.g., water, fire, sky). Thus, before the possibility of a cross-culturally meaningful primordial experiential *sense* of concentric and diametric spaces could be refuted or falsified, a culture would be needed that: (i) has no concept of change, and hence no concept of time, death nor movement, or (ii) does not recognize a solid-fluid exemplar opposition, or (iii) has no symbolic or metaphorical capacity.

The relative differences between concentric and diametric spaces, and their continuity between experiential structure and content (structure-content relativity), offers a primordial discourse for cross-cultural dialogue. However, the discourse of implication for concentric and diametric spaces is not a metalanguage for all language-games to make them commensurate. It is a language to bridge private primordial experience with public narratives and meaning.

This phenomenology *through* space is to be distinguished from Bachelard's (1964) evocative phenomenology *of* space and of objects in space. Bachelard's lens of concentration is mainly upon physical perceptual spaces in a 'phenomenology of images' (p. 112), whereas a phenomenology through space is a spatial-relational concern with unconscious structures projected into experience.[9] The very basis for experiential contents of solidity and fluidity does not come from empirical experience of everyday solids and fluids – it comes from the differential relation between diametric and concentric spaces as dynamic directions of primordial experience. This point is absolutely vital as the primordial experience fragments are a directional relation of difference, and not simply positional as everyday solids and fluids. Thus, Bachelard's (1962) example of a concentric object, a snail's shell, or even shell-symbolism (p. 116) is not a basis for inferences about relative differences between concentric and diametric spatial relations. Nor is Thoreau's (2005) association of 'many concentric layers of woodenness' with 'the dead dry life of society' (p. 198), derived again from an object, a basis for entailments of concentric or diametric space. It is not the surface feature of objects or entities that is the basis for primordial inferences but rather the relational differences between concentric and diametric spaces – structures of relation in relation.

Other examples of how meanings are associated with or superficially derived from imagined or apparently empirical features of concentric structures that are to be contrasted with a more primordial *a priori* questioning, include the attribution of an outer concentric ring to Moslem religion in Dante's *Divine Comedy*. This is aptly criticized by Said (1978), '"Maometto" – Mohammed – turns up in canto 28 of the Inferno. He is located in the eighth of the nine circles of Hell ... Mohammed thus belongs to a rigid hierarchy of evils, in the category of what Dante calls *seminator di scandalo e di scisma*' (p. 68). A related association is that of outer layers of concentric structured space with a loss of power due to distance from the centre. Lévi-Strauss (1963) draws this conclusion from empirical observation of given concentric societal spatial arrangements, 'the opposition is, with regard to social and/or religious prestige, necessarily unequal' (p. 139). He provides

9 With implicit reference to Heidegger's existential-phenomenology, Bachelard (1964) acknowledges that 'Such formulas as being-in-the-world ... are too majestic for me and I do not succeed in experiencing them ... I feel more at home in miniature worlds' (p. 161).

the following rationale for his conclusion, 'In the case of concentric structures, the inequality may be taken for granted, since the two elements are, so to speak, arranged with respect to the same point of reference – the center – to which one of the circles is closer than the other' (p. 140). In a jurisprudential context, analysing legal conventions founding law, Marmor (2001) draws on a similar association, 'the image I suggest is a division of labour taking place in concentric circles: the closer one is to the centre, the greater effect one has on what the convention is – and vice versa' (p. 210). These interpretations of particular examples of concentric structures are a) not a *necessary* entailment of concentric space relative to diametric space. They also b) thwart the connectivity in a primordial concentric relation, as they treat the inner concentric circle as exclusionary of what is in the outer concentric layers – rather than the outer circle as *also* occupying the space of the inner circle. The inner concentric pole is treated here by Dante, Lévi-Strauss and Marmor, as more like a fortress abstracted and excised from a common space than as a common space embedded in assumed connection for each of its surrounding layers. It twists a concentric space of assumed connection into a hierarchy. These examples offer a cautionary note against premature inferences based on concentric space harnessed to, at best, culturally meaningful associations, and at worst, the function of a premature ground for manipulation based on power.[10] Understanding of concentric and diametric spatial projections can also be compressed and distorted through a diametric splitting projection in interpretation of concentric spatial relation as hierarchy.

10 While Nietzsche and Foucault question how any truth claim can escape power relations, a primordial truth claim as an *a priori* structure seeks to interrogate a dimension of purity from the subjectivity of power relations and wider societal systems in its challenge to solely socially constructed truths. Nevertheless, such a primordial questioning inevitably engages with power relations, especially as it moves into truth as correspondence issues. And at a level prior to truth as correspondence claims, this is by no means to equate a possible horizon of purity with actual purity in a given contextual questioning. A primordial questioning requires facing up to the dangers of a flattening into inauthenticity in such a seeking. Any such spatial-phenomenological seeking is always in any given context to be a provisional arriving and not a dogmatic slumber.

PART IV

Primordial Structures Prior to Subjectivity: Projections of a Dynamic *A Priori* Structure

CHAPTER 10

Early Heidegger's Search for Concrete, Dynamic *A Priori* Structures of Being-in-the-World

A broadening of the unconscious world has already been observed to take place through a scrutiny of not only concentric and diametric spatial structures but also of the dynamic background relation between these spaces. This background level moves the unconscious beyond anthropocentrism, while being resonant with a reinterpretation of the Freudian life and death drives, the Jungian self as circumference and dynamic mandala, and Derrida's erasure of the trace of unconscious imprints. This dynamic background level of interactive relation, allied with foregrounded concentric and diametric spaces, will now be argued to pertain to Heidegger's (1927) structures of being-in-the-world. Heidegger's (1927) structures of being are purportedly primordial, *a priori* transcendental structures of relation. Understanding of these unthought concentric and diametric spaces can revitalize early Heidegger's transcendental project, one that was subsequently abandoned by him.

Early Heidegger's question of being sought a primordial structure of relation, a holistic (though not simple), background structure of primordial experience and truth, transcendent of linear time. Heidegger (1924) refers to 'the dangerous threat of relativism' (p. 20E) and for Heidegger (1927), 'the structure of existentiality lies *a priori*' (p. 69), with his search being for 'not just any accidental structures, but essential ones' (pp. 37–8). Early Heidegger is not to be marshalled into a postmodernist straitjacket. The question arises as to how a structure of being-in-the-world may be a unity and yet be multi-membered. In confronting this issue, the relevance of concentric and diametric spatial structures for this complex unified structure needs to be brought to the fore.

Heidegger rejects a conception of structure as that of empirical objectification, 'being and the structure of being lie beyond every entity and every possible character which an entity may possess' (p. 62). These purported structures of being are ontological, *a priori* projected structures, and not simply epistemologically *a priori* in a Kantian sense.[1] Thus, as ontological, *a priori* truth claims, these go further than those postulated by Freud and Jung regarding unconscious structures.

For Heidegger (1927), 'being alongside the world ... is an *existentiale* founded upon being-in. In these analyses the issue is one of *seeing* a primordial structure of Dasein's being – a structure in accordance with whose phenomenal content the concepts of being must be articulated' (p. 81, italics in original). This seeing is a phenomenological disclosure that includes sight but is not simply reducible to the visual (Heidegger 1927, p. 48). In the words of Henrich (1994):

> When abstracting from the richness of phenomenological analyses and focusing solely on the scaffolding of the progression of thought in *Being and Time*, one immediately recognizes that its driving force is the question concerning the unitary structure of the original totality of Dasein ... Yet how is this concept of the ontological structural unity of Dasein different from the speculative interpretations of subjectivity? (p. 48)

For Heidegger (1927), there is a primordial structural totality of being-in-the-world, prior to predicative assertion, that encompasses Dasein's spatial structures but somehow extends beyond them; it is less a process of abstracting structures than uncovering them in their surreptitious immanence. Primordial structures of being-in-the-world are irreducible to derivative subjective unconscious structures.[2]

1 Heidegger sought to radically reinterpret Kant's *Critique of Pure Reason* as an ontological quest. As Henrich (1994) observes, this is not tenable from a Kantian perspective. Henrich (1994) also emphasizes that Heidegger's attempt to incorporate Kant's transcendental imagination as the dynamic synthesizing background realm to pure intuition and pure understanding was by no means a novel interpretation of Kant.

2 As *a priori* entailments, the relative differences between concentric and diametric spaces have already been firmly distinguished from Lévi-Strauss' anthropology and its empirical objectivist paradigm, drawn from phonetics invoking structures as

That search for *a priori* structures or structuration is pivotal to early Heidegger's question of being is evident from Kisiel's (1993) account of Heidegger's Ontoeroteric draft, *The History of the Concept of Time*, Summer Semester, 1925:

> The formally indicative 'magnet word' in the entire gloss, and beyond, is in fact 'structure': the structurations of being itself, in multiplying beings into manifold senses, in providing the apriori structures in and by which beings appear, in articulating different regions, sciences and logics; in turn, the articulation itself is obviously a structuration calling for examination; the structure of comportment, perception, the perceptual assertion, consciousness, encounter, aroundness, worldhood, in-being and so on. (p. 372)

Again Heidegger sought, in his Winter Semester 1925–26 course, what Kisiel (1993) describes as a 'preintuitional substructure', 'to get at a deeper structure of presence, immediacy, and givenness than the structure of immediacy offered by intuition' (p. 400). Heidegger's pervasive structural preoccupation occurs at an ontological level purportedly prior to the *reason* of Kantian *a priori* truths; it is antecedent to a *ratio* as synthesizing representations into judgments, Kantian categories or even antinomies of pure reason.

As Kisiel (2006) notes, as early as 1919, in the *Kriegsnotsemester* course in Freiburg, the 'breakthrough' occurred for Heidegger's phenomenology defined as 'the pre-theoretical originary science of original experience' (p. 276). Heidegger accommodates an *a priori* discourse on aspects of affect that are absent from Kant. Heidegger's (1927) purportedly primordial structures of relation include 'being-alongside' as 'being-in', both modes 'equiprimordial' with 'being-with' (p. 187). He juxtaposes the primordiality of 'being-with' and the purportedly unprimordial mode of empathy (p. 163). Similarly, fear is envisaged as being derivative from *Angst*, which *'first makes fear possible'* (Heidegger 1927, p. 230). This *modus operandi* of identifying prior primordial structures of relation, which purportedly

communication. This is not to deny some commonalities between Lévi-Strauss' structuralism and Heidegger, such as search for transsubjective background relations prior to causality and intentionality. As Culler (1976) highlights, structuralist explanations tend to resist causal explanations.

integrate affective qualities, also extends to other emotions. Thus, Heidegger (1927) treats 'will, wish, addiction and urge' as being derivative, 'founded upon' (p. 227) and 'modifications of' (p. 254) care. Through probing for a more primordial truth than Cartesian-like bifurcation between reason and affect, Heidegger persistently interrogates a unitary background structure, including being-alongside, *Angst* and care, to contrast with foregrounded and derivative emotional states. *Being and Time* embraces an array of affective terms. This is far from the lethargy of a postmodern 'waning of affect' (Jameson 1991, p. 15). While Heidegger contrasts a primordial background state of being-in and being-with, with a panoply of apparently derivative affective states, this invites scrutiny of background unconscious structures projected into foregrounded states, to embrace spaces of and for affect. His exploration of a precognitive background relation is envisaged as being prior to traditional Western assumptions of a subject-object dualism and challenging a model of detached subjectivity instantiated through the *cogito* of Cartesian self-consciousness. Heidegger's ontological difference, between being and human beings, invites a broadening of traditional conceptions of the unconscious to embrace this ontological structural level.

It is clear that Heidegger (1927) sought to uncover specific, concrete, *a priori* spatial ontological structures and did not succeed in doing so. His project lies incomplete. Whereas Tugendhat (1967) has already been observed to highlight the lack of criteria for truth primordiality in Heidegger's argument, more recently, Malpas (2008) in his discussion of the pervasiveness of spatial concepts across a panorama of Heidegger's lifework, raises the related problem of the lack of clarity in Heidegger's distinction between what is primordial and derivative. Again the spectre of (spatial) criteria for primordiality rears its head. In the absence of any proposed specific candidate spatial structure underlying the assumption structure of *Being and Time* – and none has been concretely proposed by Malpas, nor others who have emphasized spatial, structural dimensions to Heidegger – this important problem of conceptualizing the relation between primordiality and derivativeness involves a project that is left somewhat groping in the dark. Filling this vacuum has brought importation of a Wittgensteinian schema of shared background practices onto background contexts of being

(Guignon 1983, 2006; Dreyfus 1993; Malpas 2008) and an Aristotelian schema of spatial containment as *topos* (Malpas 2008).

A further difficulty in uncovering primordial spatial structures arises through an ambivalence running right through *Being and Time*, between structures of primordiality in an ontological sense and a historical sense. A tension arises between the conclusion of *Being and Time* that primordial temporality is prior to linear time as the transcendental horizon for the question of being and the very first sentence of Section I of the book, 'This question has today been forgotten' (p. 21). A forgetting implies a nostalgia for a past historical era of remembering. Yet if, as Heidegger (1927) concludes, linear historical time is derivative and inauthentic compared with authentic primordial temporality, uncovering spatial structures of being becomes not so much an undoing of a forgetting in linear time, as a search for spatial structures of primordial experience through a more authentic avenue than the ancient past. This other avenue is given emphasis somewhat by early Heidegger (1928), in his recognition of transcendence in *Being and Time* as radically different from traditional approaches, '[the task of a] more originary conception of intentionality and transcendence, a basic determination of *Dasein*'s whole existence [is] a central problem that has remained *unknown to all previous philosophy*' (p. 162) (my italics). Primordiality must go beyond Heidegger's vacillation between historical and ontological primordiality. This conflation haunts the text of *Being and Time*.[3] There is a questionable groupthink in both Heidegger and Jung (*via* Nietzsche) that quests for a primordial truth predominantly in the ancient. Waves crashed against rocks many ages ago. Yet waves still crash against rocks with vibrant intensity of immediacy today. Even for an ontology that is purportedly prior to nature, inauthentic historical time is an impoverished site for primordial lived experience.

Thomson (2011) subtly interprets later Heidegger's tendency to extol an 'ancient ideal' as not being a call for 'the impossible revival of the lost

3 Guignon (1983) treats both meanings of primordiality as not only complementary but that they '*amount to the same thing*' (p. 78). Such a view amounts to a relegation of Heidegger's transcendental project to the historical.

Greek past' (p. 76) and being more than a nostalgia for the past. Yet its fundamental orientation is past-based, even if it moves from the past to reconstruct new futures, going beyond mere reproduction. Whether claimed as an ideal (problematically tethered to an ideal-real dualism), a model, or a necessary condition for future opening, these distract somewhat from a lived experiential truth as dis-closure of being. A weaker claim that the ancient provides supportive clarifications of potential is a more convincing one, but even here a broadening of pathways is needed.

Any talk of new renaissances based on classical thought, *via* later Heidegger, is still filled to some degree with the hot air of nostalgia for origins, and for Eurocentric origins at that. Again it rests within the chamber of a largely unquestioned association of the primordial with the ancient. Primordiality needs to emerge from its childhood and adolescence to confront modes of primordial experience that are not simply enchained within the simplicities of reliance on ancestral vestiges (however, rich these remnants may be). In doing so, it must neither jettison the past, nor commit to the Enlightenment trajectory of necessary, as distinct from possible, progress in history. It is the mode of reliance itself that must be challenged.

A spatial-phenomenological reinterpretation of *Being and Time* goes further than engagement with Heidegger's explicit spatial themes to unthought spatial structures pervading a wider range of its key concepts. These basic concepts will be seen to include: (i) Dasein's existential spatiality as being-in, being alongside, directionality, deseverance and encountering, contrasting with the extended space of categories. It also embraces central concepts in Heidegger (1927) of (ii) *Angst* of authenticity, (iii) phenomena and appearances, unconcealment, (iv) care as an *a priori* structure and primordial temporality as a transcendental horizon. Initially, the focus is on uncovering the existence of concentric and diametric structures as the unthought of central concepts of Heidegger, rather than as a specific defence of his claim that these are *a priori* structures of being-in-the-world. Nevertheless, it is to be emphasized that in a claim for the primordiality of these dynamic spatial structures, the *a priori* feature of primordiality is a truth claim being made by Heidegger (1927). Any focus on spatiality in *Being and Time* needs to recognize the obvious point that spatial structures are still subordinated, in early Heidegger, to the overall structure of temporality as the transcendental horizon for the question of being. For current purposes, it is not being sought to privilege space over time, but rather to develop an argument in relation to spatial structures that leads to wider temporal transcendental concerns.

Exposure of the proposed structure of concentric and diametric spaces requires elucidation additionally of the significance of a distinction between primordiality and authenticity, made by Heidegger (1927), to explicate how a dimension of inauthenticity may still be comprehended as a primordial level of experience and truth. An understanding of primordiality in relation to structures of authenticity resists reduction of authentic experience to a public, social realm and defends a site of freedom in inner experience that is not reducible to Cartesian detachment from the outer. An *aporia* in Heidegger's argument is that his core concept of care, pivotal to Dasein and the transcendental temporal horizon, does not at first sight appear to be granted an opposite.[4] This understated opposite to care must be brought to the fore through an understanding of the background to concentric and diametric spaces.

Focus for present purposes is less on Heidegger's accounts of equipmental space, of the contrast between being ready-to-hand (*zuhanden*) and present-at-hand (*vorhanden*). This level is less fundamental than other ontological spatial concerns, as Malpas (2008, p. 96) also recognizes, and is arguably less original than other aspects of Heidegger's work.[5] Neither is it

4 Crowell (2007) recognizes the important point that Heideggerian care is in contrast to Kantian reason. This is not to invite importation of a diametric projection of a rational-irrational opposition onto care in relation to reason – that would classify care as irrational. Whereas Habermas (1987) characterizes 'being' in later Heidegger as an undermining of reason, this would be a massive simplification for interpreting early Heidegger.

5 While Habermas (1987) characterizes this account in sections 14–24 as 'not really an advance beyond what was elaborated in Pragmatism from Peirce to Mead and Dewey' (p. 148), this is somewhat an oversimplification as Heidegger cannot be reduced to being a pragmatist (Norris 1997; Blattner 2000), a point Dreyfus (2000) now concedes. Moreover, Habermas overlooks here the distinctive insights into Dasein's existential spatiality in sections 23–4, though he does acknowledge the significance of Heidegger's critique of Cartesian consciousness. Other aspects of

an inquiry into place [*Platz, Ort*] in Heidegger (1927). It bears reiteration that this uncovering of concentric and diametric spatial structures is not reducible to structuralism, nor is it a conflation of levels between ontology and psychology or anthropology.

10.1 Dasein's existential spatiality in contrast to categories: Early Heidegger's being-in and being-alongside as a concentric spatial projection and extended categorial space as a diametric projection

Argument: That the interplay between concentric and diametric spaces offers a framework for understanding of Dasein's existential spatiality in its dynamic interaction with extended space.

A distinctive feature of *Being and Time* is the opening up of a realm of Dasein's existential spatiality. Existential language came late in the genesis of *Being and Time*, and is 'totally absent' from the penultimate, ontoeroteric draft (Kisiel 1993, p. 394). It is the primordial spatial dimension to this existential spatiality that is pivotal to this work. Heidegger contrasts 'the primordial spatiality of being-in' (p. 141) with measured distances of things or entities. A focus on measured distances is an appearance in which this primordial space is 'concealed' (p. 141). The spatial phenomena of 'existential spatiality' (p. 155) are an opening:

Heidegger's understanding of space are more primordial, innovative and radical than the *vorhanden, zuhanden* distinction emphasizing background contexts of meaning. Even schema explanations in cognitive science encompass a purposive conception of an in-order-to (Davies 1994; Anderson 2000), as do Gibson's (1966) *affordances* in perception, and von Uexkull's (1934/1992) evaluative perception in biosemiotics (Kull 2001; Downes 2010).

> When being-in-the-world is exhibited phenomenologically, disguises and concealments are rejected *because* this phenomenon itself always gets 'seen' in a certain way in every Dasein. And it thus gets 'seen' *because* it makes up a basic state of Dasein, and in every case is already disclosed for Dasein's understanding of being, and disclosed along with that being itself. (p. 85)

This emphasis on *seeing* a primordial structure (through a disclosure for Dasein) is combined with an allusion to the contrasts between phenomena and appearances that disguise and conceal such phenomena.

Acceleration of focus on implicit spatial assumptions underlying Heidegger's (1927) being-alongside, one of the 'fundamental characteristics of Dasein's being' (p. 293), helps furnish a structural discourse of differential relation for integration of being and domains of affect. De-severance is central to this being-alongside and '*Dasein is essentially de-severance – that is, it is spatial*' (p. 143, italics in original). A recurrent spatial theme within *Being and Time* is the tension between loss of interactive relation and an overcoming of this loss. Some typical examples of this tension between two modes, an interactive, connective, involved mode and a detached, severed, non-relational mode, respectively, occur in the context of the purported spatiality of being-in-the-world. Heidegger refers to the relational state of de-severance, '"De-severing" amounts to making the farness vanish – that is, making the remoteness of something disappear' (p. 139). This is thoroughly consistent with a movement from a mode of assumed separation or severance within diametric structures of relation, to a spatial mode of assumed connection summoning concentric structures of relation, '*The circumspective de-severing of Dasein's everydayness reveals the being-in-itself of the "true world" – of that entity which Dasein, as something existing, is already alongside*' (p. 141, italics in original). Being-in gives expression to the 'true' authentic world of its existential space through de-severance, which brings a return to an already being-alongside, to a concentric assumed connection.

As a feature together with the 'directionality' of the spatiality of being-in-the-world (p. 138),[6] Heidegger (1927) treats de-severance as movement

6 Dreyfus (1991) seeks to replace a translation of directionality with that of 'orientation' but this loses a connotation of dynamic movement.

towards a more connective state, 'Every bringing-close has already taken in advance a direction towards a region out of which what is de-severed brings itself close' (p. 143). This connective state of de-severing reveals a being already alongside (p. 141). Loss of interactive relation is highlighted in Heidegger's words, 'The spatiality of what is ready-to-hand within-the-world loses its involvement character ... the world loses its specific aroundness' (p. 147). As already outlined, in concentric space, the outer pole surrounds or is around the inner pole, a feature lost to diametric space; in concentric relation, one part is always 'in' the other, unlike diametric relation. A concentric structure is a mode of being-in, and, for Heidegger, '... Being-in is not a "property" which Dasein sometimes has and sometimes does not have' (p. 84); it is a fundamental feature of Dasein's existence. The inner concentric circle is interpretable as being in a mode of 'being-in' the outer. The 'spatially encountered' (p. 143) being-alongside is a concernful, connective (de-severant), concentric mode, which is subject to a displacement or 'falling' (p. 237), where Dasein can become 'rid of its being-alongside'. In other words, the concentric being-alongside can be displaced into a diametric relation, where its relation to Dasein's 'ownmost potentiality-for-being is an issue' (p. 225).

Spatiality of being-in-the-world is expressly linked in Division One, III, 21c of *Being and Time* with the earlier discussions of being-in and the two modes of 'categories' and 'existentialia'. Seeking to transcend the nature-culture binary opposition in his conceptualization of space, Heidegger develops these contrasting modes of spatial relation. Traditional Western conceptions of 'world' oversimplify this existential conception of being-in. Being-in, as a *category*, is like water in a glass or a dress in a closet, whereas the *existential* mode of Being-in-the-world is a different spatial mode of being-in, which overcomes a distance or remoteness within the categorial mode of being-in. Existential remoteness is not something measurable in terms of objective spatial distances of objectively present entities, as Heidegger (1927) explicates, in a well-known passage:

> 'The table stands "by" ["*be*"] the door' or 'the chair "touches" ["*beruhrt*"] the wall'. Taken strictly, 'touching' is never what we are talking about in such cases, not because accurate reexamination will always eventually establish that there is a space between

> the chair and the wall, but because in principle the chair can never touch the wall, even if the space between them should be equal to zero. If the chair could touch the wall, this would presuppose that the wall is the sort of thing 'for' which a chair would be encounterable. An entity present-at-hand within the world can be touched by another entity only if by its very nature the latter entity has being-in as its own kind of being ... (pp. 81–2)

Relations between solid objects in space are diametric, as there is a basic assumed separation between each object as an object. Both objects exclude each other from occupying the same space. This assumed separation means they are not 'encounterable'; encountering overcomes the remoteness of assumed separation and is a concentric possibility which Dasein as being-in-the-world possesses. Heidegger (1927) explicitly equates the 'touch' of encountering with the mode of being-alongside (pp. 81–2). For Heidegger, entities such as a table, chair cannot even *potentially* be encounterable.

Heidegger challenges the primacy of 'side-by-side-ness' or the separation built into two entities in order for them to be 'side-by-side'. He overcomes a diametric relation between Dasein, being and 'world' in his description of 'being-alongside' the world, 'There is no such thing as the "side-by-side-ness" of an entity called "Dasein" with another entity called "world"' (p. 81). *Diametric space is where both parts are side-by-side.* For a mode of 'being-alongside' the world, a different mode of assumed connection is needed, which is not a diametric 'side-by-side' relation. Concentric space expresses a concomitant 'being-alongside' model of relatedness, where one pole dwells within and alongside the other, surrounded and in assumed connection. The smaller, inner pole within concentric space is far from being a mere bungalow annex to the larger pole. Rather it dwells centrally within the other larger pole, immersed within it inextricably, in complementary fashion. Concentric spatialization offers an existential structural relation which overcomes the remoteness and non-involvement within diametric space. Furthermore, it offers a spatial relation, where one pole is 'in' the other, and hence, is a being-in. 'Being-alongside' is founded upon 'being-in' for Heidegger (1927, p. 81).

De-severance is an active process of interaction for Dasein who 'cannot wander about with the current range of its de-severances; it can never do more than change them' (p. 143). Dasein's primordial connective space undoes the assumed separation in its engagement, what Heidegger calls 'encountering', 'Dasein is spatial in that it discovers space circumspectively, so that indeed it constantly comports itself de-severantly towards the entities thus spatially encountered' (p. 143). It is evident that for Heidegger an interaction takes place between this primordial spatial relation and that space of entities diametrically side-by-side each other which is, thereby, changed through this interaction, what Heidegger also terms 'directionality' (p. 143). They are not simply two spaces divided into existential and 'objective' space, spliced apart from each other, as Dreyfus (1991) envisages. To do so, would be to reimport a subject-object dualism through a kind of subjective versus objective space, very much contrary to the project of Heidegger.

The very distinction of subject-object, challenged by Heidegger in his spatial conception of *Dasein*, can also be viewed as a challenge to a relation of assumed separation built into the subject/object distinction founding the metaphor-literal relation and the 'literal' Cartesian subject. In effect, Heidegger's task is to assault the diametric structural relation that frames the subject/object relation. Thomson (2011) succinctly summarizes Heidegger's insight into this assumed separation, 'As Heidegger frequently points out, in the modern, post-Cartesian world, an "object", *Gegenstand*, is something that "stands opposite" a human subject, something *external* to subjectivity' (p. 49). Diametric spatial relation is such a standing opposite; the diametric poles are opposite each other. Ricoeur (1981) refers to distanciation as establishing the relation between subject and object. He treats distanciation as the reflective, critical or suspicious moment within consciousness. While the assumed separation of diametric relation is not to be equated with Ricoeur's concept of distanciation, nevertheless, both perspectives on the subject/object relation recognize a fundamental distance or separation, as the basis for the subject/object dualism.[7] Challenging the assumed separation within the subject-object

7 Ricoeur (1981) explicitly appeals to Heidegger's being-in-the-world as the basis for a contrast to distanciation – a contrast which Ricoeur terms 'belonging' (p. 110/51). Ricoeur treats belonging as an immediate or unreflective relation 'correcting'

frame opens up a pathway beyond experiences tethered to the husk of diametric reason and linear time. In doing so, it carves out a space for recognition of the ontological unconscious,[8] the unconscious level of being, a primordial spatial unconscious.

Characterizing the spatial contrast in terms of existential and 'objective' space is unhelpful not only because it minimizes scope for interaction between them and the ontological quality for Heidegger of this so-called objective space, as a 'category'. Dreyfus' (1991) characterization also underplays that there are many kinds of objective spaces (such as contrasts between Newtonian space, Einsteinian space of special relativity and general relativity, quantum physics etc) and that cognitive psychology has long recognized the constructive and developmental dimensions to spatial perception (Neisser 1967; Gibson, Piaget & Inhelder 1956). Much of this challenges the exclusive 'objectivity' of the Euclidean extended space that Dreyfus is basically invoking.

Heidegger (1927) summarizes the contrast of 'Dasein with a way of being in space which we call "insideness" [*Inwendigkeit*]. This expression means that an entity which is itself extended is closed round [*umschlossen*] by the extended boundaries of something that is likewise extended. Yet even if we deny that Dasein has any such insideness in a spatial receptacle, this does not in principle exclude it from having any spatiality at all …' (p. 134). This closure of entities, a sense of being sealed off through the extended boundaries, is explicated through specific examples of water in a glass and a garment in a cupboard, 'the kind of being which an entity has when it is "in" another one, as the water is "in" the glass, or the garment is "in" the cupboard. By this "in" we mean the relationship of being which two entities extended "in" space have to each other with regard to their location in that space. Both water and glass, garment and cupboard, are "in" space and "at" a location, and both in the same way' (Heidegger

distanciation and a concretizing of the universality of distanciation. However, the metaphysical poles of abstract-universality versus concrete-singularity are inconsistent with Heidegger's concerns with a more primordial truth.

8 A term employed also by Stolorow (2007).

1927, p. 79). The specific phrase 'closed round' [*umschlossen*] in extended space is susceptible to more than one interpretation in relation to concentric and diametric structures. This association of closure brings particular resonance with diametric more than concentric structures, as discussed in entailment three of the relative differences between both spaces. Yet an association of roundness in relation to closure invites an interpretation more of concentric roundness surrounding the inner pole with the outer. Elsewhere, as noted, Heidegger emphasizes the primordial spatial world as featuring an 'aroundness'. In arguing for an association of 'closed round' in this context with diametric rather than concentric spatiality, it is important to contextualize that this closure 'round' refers not to existential aroundness – but rather to the closure round of entities in 'extended' space of measured distances and things. This contextualizing of the term *umschlossen* to 'boundaries' in 'extended' space very much prioritizes the emphasis here to be on the closure, and on the sealed dimension to such closure rather than on roundness.

Far from rejecting this mode of extended space as irrelevant to ontology, Heidegger (1927) explicitly describes this 'definite location-relationship with something else which has the same kind of being' as 'ontological characteristics' termed the 'categorial'; 'they are of such a sort as to belong to entities whose kind of being is not of the character of Dasein' (p. 79). The categorial 'in' is still part of an ontological world, though not of Dasein. While Dreyfus (1991) and Malpas (2008) prefer to term this kind of space, an 'objective' or 'container' space, it is vital to reassert that this space is ontological as a categorial space. Malpas (2008) explicitly interprets Heidegger's text here through an Aristotelian schema of space as a container. What is less explicit in the account of Malpas is that this importation of the term 'container' to characterize Heidegger's ontological mode of categorial space, in order to explicate a conception of 'insideness' in measured space of extended things and entities, amounts to an interpretation of Heidegger's text, where Heidegger nowhere employs the term 'container' or 'containing'. Heidegger's (1927) words again are explicit that this 'insideness' is a *category* state, 'the ontological difference between being-in as an existentiale and the category of the "insideness" which things present-at-hand can have with regard to one another' (p. 82).

Both Dreyfus (1991) and Malpas (2008) endeavour to extract a key concept or principle underlying Heidegger's account of extended space, to contrast with existential space. Relying on Heidegger's account of extended space as 'insideness' to characterize what the existential space of Dasein is not, Dreyfus abstracts a purportedly core concept of 'inclusion' to characterize this extended space, though this term does not appear in *Being and Time*. Malpas relies on a twin argument to import a core concept of 'containment' space, i.e., being contained in space, into Heidgger's (1927) text. Malpas (2008) cites an earlier 1925 summer semester lecture of Heidegger which uses the water in glass, garment in wardrobe examples but which explicitly uses the term 'contains'.[9] He combines this with recognition of an Aristotelian account of a spatial *topos* as one of space as a container. Though he also aptly recognizes that Heidegger is less concerned with Aristotle than with Descartes' conceptions of space as being extended and measurable, he suggests that Aristotelian space as a container was integrated into Cartesian spatial accounts that Heidegger is contrasting with existential space. While the passage from the 1925 lecture is a clear precursor to that in *Being and Time*, it could equally be argued that the apparently deliberate omission of explicit reference to this space as a container, in the passage as it appears in *Being and Time*, is because Heidegger is wary of not wanting to convey a sense of an Aristotelian *topos* as container for space; the more complex and convoluted phrase in *Being and Time* of a 'insideness in a spatial receptacle' (p. 134) is precisely because Heidegger is going out of his way to resist commitment to an Aristotelian spatial *topos*, contingent on the bounding inner surface of a container.[10] This is because his empha-

9 'When we try to give intuitive demonstration of this [nonexistential] "in", more accurately to the "something-in-something", we give examples like the water "in" the glass, the clothes "in" the closet, the desks "in" the classroom. By this we mean that one is spatially contained in another and refer to the relationship of being with regard to place and space of two entities which are themselves extended in space' (Heidegger 1925, pp. 157–8).

10 There is a certain plausibility to Malpas' (2008) invoking an Aristotelian schema for this non-existential space given that Heidegger treated Aristotelian time, characterized as a succession of nows, as a feature of derivative, inauthentic temporality.

sis in the concrete examples provided is not on the containing aspect as such, but on another aspect of this kind of relation. Even the 1925 passage explicitly emphasizes that this is for the context of 'things', of 'something-in-something', and reiterates that this context of 'containment' is for *entities*, later given further distinction by Heidegger (1927) as entities side-by-side.

These examples of entities such as water in a glass and garment in a cupboard, and reference to 'insideness in a spatial receptacle' (p. 134), are confined to entities with clear boundaries in an extended space, where both entities are closed off from each other, so that they do not fundamentally 'touch'. This does not preclude a feature of containment being part of a different primordial space than one of extended measured space for entities side-by-side with each other with clear boundaries. Key features of this extended space explicitly observed by Heidegger (1927) are a) its side-by-sideness, b) its inability to 'touch' and 'encounter', c) its relative closure between entities, d) its lack of connective involvement between entities. All of these are thoroughly consistent with a diametric spatial relation through its entailments of assumed separation and relative closure from background environment.

The concentric background structure of being-alongside, as a mode of being-in, is projected into the foregrounded emotional and interpersonal relational states through Heidegger's (1927) interpersonal connective mode of being-with, namely, solicitude, 'Being-with the Dasein-with of Others as we encounter it within-the-world could be taken as *solicitude* [*Fürsorge*]' (p. 237). Heidegger (1927) explicitly relates *Fürsorge*, as a dimension of care [*Sorge*], with encountering. In other words, a concentric spatialization emerges at the 'being-with' assumed connection level of encountering others (including others 'only privatively', pp. 238–9).

Nevertheless, if Heidegger was seeking to treat space here through an Aristotelian lens, he would presumably state, on such a fundamental point, that he was doing so, as he did for time. A counterargument here is that throughout *Being and Time*, Heidegger makes unattributed allusions to the thoughts of others. For example, the following passage makes only implicit reference to 'drives' as Freudian and 'will' as Schopenhauerian, 'Nor is resistance experienced in a drive or will which "emerges" in its own right. These both turn out to be modifications of care' (p. 254).

Heidegger (1927) envisages this encountering or touching as a distinct existential spatiality, involving an affective dimension, 'Letting something be encountered is primarily circumspective; it is not just sensing something, or staring at it. It implies circumspective concern, and has the character of becoming affected in some way [*Betroffenwerdens*]' (p. 176); 'what touches them shows itself in an affect' (p. 177). Following on from a characterizing of encountering as 'something that matters to us', Heidegger states that 'Indeed from the ontological point of view we must as a general principle leave the primary discovery of the world to "bare mood"' (p. 177). Again, disclosure of being-in-the-world is described as an ontological state that centrally encompasses an affective orientation. This is not to reduce this affective dimension in being-in-the-world to simple subjective feeling, 'Any cognitive determining has its existential-ontological constitution in the state-of-mind of being-in-the-world; but pointing this out is not to be confused with attempting to surrender science ontically to "feeling"' (p. 177). Foreground affective states are characterized as deriving from a more primordial structural relation, whether of being-in, being-with, being-alongside or *Angst*.

For Heidegger (1927), 'Dasein takes space in; this is to be understood literally' (p. 419). This assertion of Heidegger's can be construed beyond the phenomenological content of a literal taking in of space as a breathing process. Neither does it require a reimportation of the traditional metaphysical distinction between the literal and the metaphoric. The taking in of diametric space into Dasein's existential spatiality is a more radical step than simply movement towards a concentric space; it is a restructuring, a modification of the diametric space, so that it is taken in by or dissolved into the concentric holistic space. Insofar as diametric space is engaged with 'objective' extended space, its being-taken-in through interaction with concentric space becomes a process of literal change to this relation in extended space. The interaction with concentric structured space brings literal effects in extended space, influences mediated through the ablutions of concentric spatial openings.

This characterization of existential space as a concentric structure and of extended space as a diametric structure offers a number of advantages over the interpretations of Dreyfus and Malpas. It provides domains of interaction between both spaces as envisaged by Heidegger. Treating both spaces as part of the ontological structure of being-in-the-world paves the way not only for their interaction but also for a view of them as key to Heidegger's transcendental project – as the relational interaction between *existentialia* and categories is viewed by Heidegger (1927) as key to the transcendental horizon for the question of being, 'The connection between these two modes of the characters of being [*existentialia* and categories] cannot be handled until the horizon for the question of being has been clarified' (p. 71). While Malpas (2008) does centrally acknowledge the need for uncovering a primordial spatial structure, the specific concrete structures of concentric and diametric spaces go further than simply an assertion of the need for such primordial spatial structures. The interpretation of existential spatiality as a concentric mode of spatial relation and extended space as a diametric mode of spatial relation is arguably highly consistent with Heidegger's (1927) account.[11] Nor does it treat Heidegger's spatiality of being-in-the-world as fundamentally confused (Dreyfus 1991, p. 129).

Existential spatiality of Dasein's being-in is a concentric spatial structure of assumed connection. Dasein's existential spatiality is a dynamic process of taking space in, it is a directional movement towards concentric structured space. This concentric directional movement belongs to being-in and its equiprimordial dimensions of being-alongside and being-with that involve directionality and de-severance. All are part of the same concentric spatial movement.

11 It is highly consistent once concentric and diametric spaces are recognized as *a priori* structures, prior to their projection into anthropological contexts observed empirically by Lévi-Strauss, and prior to psychological understandings of the unconscious as simple subjectivity.

10.2 Concentric and diametric projections as a structural expression of Heidegger's *Angst* of authenticity

Argument: That the interplay between concentric and diametric spaces offers a framework for understanding the primordial *Angst* of authenticity and thereby resists reduction of authenticity to a public, social realm.

Complementary with interpretation of Munch's primordial scream of anxiety in a spatial-structural sense, Heidegger's (1927) existential-phenomenological account of *Angst* goes further to give expression to a concentric and diametric spatial interplay as dynamic, purportedly *a priori* structures. Heidegger (1927) notes that the mode of 'being-in' was defined as 'residing alongside' and contrasts this state with the displacement through the 'uncanny' of being-in entering into the existential 'mode' of the 'not-at-home' (p. 233). In anxiety, the being-alongside of concentric relation 'falls' into an uncanniness of the not-at-home, assumed separation, of diametric space. The assumed connection of the poles in concentric spatial relation is the home or intimate dwelling that is displaced in the uncanny [*Unheimlichkeit*] state of *Angst*'s not-being-at-home.

Angst is ontologically prior to fear, for Heidegger. It is painted with a Kierkegaardian and Freudian hue, as anxiety, unlike fear, is envisaged as not being in relation to a specific other. Anxiety is, for Heidegger (1927), a central dimension of the 'the primordial structural totality' of care (p. 238), as being-in-the-world. On this proposed reading of early Heidegger's conceptions of encountering and being-alongside, as projections of concentric existential structures in contrast with diametric structures, *Angst* can be examined as the process of openness to movement – of openness to change from and between concentric and diametric spatial modes of relation structuring experience.

For Heidegger (1927), 'The turning away of falling is grounded rather in anxiety, which in turn is what first makes fear possible' (p. 230). Diametric structures involve a turning away from concentric spatialization. This turning away uncovers the dynamic compensatory interaction between concentric and diametric structures of experience, mediated through *Angst*. Similarly, being-alongside undergoes a 'falling' which again illustrates this directional movement, as the being-alongside of concentric spatialization turns away towards a diametric mode.

Section I.6 § 40 of *Being and Time* is entitled, 'The Basic State-of-mind of Anxiety as a Distinctive Way in which Dasein is Disclosed' (p. 228). Anxiety provides an aperture for a disclosure of projected possibility for primordial experience, as movement between distinctive concentric and diametric spaces, 'Anxiety individualizes Dasein for its ownmost Being-in-the-world, which ... projects itself essentially upon possibilities ... anxiety discloses Dasein as *Being-possible* ... Anxiety makes manifest in Dasein its *Being towards* its ownmost potentiality-for-Being' (p. 232) (italics in original).

Angst, as the dynamic component of change and movement between concentric and diametric spaces, brings a focus on change and transformation within experience; this can take place in concentric modes of encountering and being-alongside. These primordial structures also encompass a falling, fleeing, turning away dimension into inauthenticity, as a direction towards diametric space. This structural interplay explains how inauthenticity can still be a primordial state of relation; falling, fleeing inauthenticity is implicated in its directional movement away from concentric structures and towards diametric space. Heidegger (1927) observes the possibility of Dasein 'becoming ... rid of its being alongside' (p. 216), so that a radical shift from concentric to diametric structures would occur.

This apprehension of 'the possibility of authenticity and inauthenticity' is reiterated as being associated with *Angst*, with an additional emphasis that this awareness of these possibilities becomes 'shown, with a primordial elemental concreteness' (Heidegger 1927, p. 236). A primordial elemental concreteness to authenticity and inauthenticity invokes the phenomenological seeing of a specific spatial structural relation – such as that of concentric and diametric spatial structures, as the horizons of possibility within which Dasein experiences anxiety. A Heideggerian futural directional-truth focus is not mere 'subjective discretion' (p. 270). Freedom for movement between these concentric and diametric spaces describes an opening for a choosing and freedom that is not mere subjectivity, nor subjective discretion. However, as a precognitive movement, it projects into a pluralism of possible cognitive states framed through this spatial movement; the movement does not fixate onto one, given, cognitive worldview in a static one to one correspondence. It evades reduction to the monotony of a prepackaged, programmed construction of meaning.

Heidegger (1927) explicitly relates *Angst* to being 'ahead-of-itself-in-already-being-in-a-world' (p. 236). This requires acknowledgment of a futural dimension to any proposed primordial spatial structure encompassing *Angst*. *Angst* invokes a futural direction of possible movement towards authentic concentric spatialization, through modifying diametric structures – through modifying a state of assumed separation into a state of separation on the basis of assumed connection. This sense of directional movement, towards the 'aroundness' of concentric relation, gains indirect support from Christenson's (2007) examination of the translation of Heidegger's (1927) understanding of purpose, in his phrase '*etwas, um zu*'. While MacQuarrie & Robinson (1962, p. 98) note the dual meaning of *um* as 'around' and 'in order to', Christenson (2007) amplifies this point:

> The German phrase *etwas, um zu* ..., which MacQuarrie and Robinson translate as 'something-in-order-to', is, while not ungrammatical, certainly unusual; one would normally speak of *etwas zum*, as in *etwas zum schreiben*, i.e., something for writing. This indicates that Heidegger is placing weight on what the expressions in the phrase individually mean. In particular, he is placing weight on the meaning of the word *um*. In German this word doubles as a preposition meaning 'around', as in *um die Ecke* ('around the corner') and as a prefix meaning 'surrounding', as in *Umwelt*. (p. 165)

A key distinguishing feature of concentric from diametric space is that, in the former, the outer pole 'surrounds' and is 'around' the inner, in a relation of assumed connection – a dimension which is not obtainable in diametric relation. Purpose, envisaged as directional change towards concentric spatialization of surrounding and being around, is thus consistent with Christenson's (2007) conclusion, regarding Heidegger's emphasis on '*um*', 'It is thus reasonable to conclude that Heidegger is using the unusual phrase *etwas, um zu* ... in order to exploit, on the one hand, the meaning of the whole phrase *um-zu* as expressing purpose, and, on the other, the meaning of the component word um as expressing aroundness' (p. 165). Concentric spatial projection is a directional movement towards aroundness.

Directionality is not akin to mere instrumentality and concentric structures of relation become a horizonal schema, in Heidegger's terms.[12] Whereas directionality, a key aspect of Heidegger's existential spatiality, includes movement towards concentric relation in being-alongside, *Angst* involves the possibility of movement between concentric and diametric directions of primordial experience. It provides recognition of the 'leeway' or space for play in the directional movement between both spatial structures, 'a leeway which has been opened up for it in directionality and de-severance' (p. 420). Dasein, 'in existing ... has already made room for its own leeway' (p. 419), thereby inviting an anxiety associated with experience of this freedom for movement within the space for play of the leeway between concentric and diametric spaces structuring primordial experience. A primordial questioning provoked by the *Angst* of collapse of simplified diametric meanings penetrates not only through the husk of diametric reason, but also to the husk of diametric experience. It involves a search for sources prior to these edifices imposed not only upon the mind but also as gates upon experience. These sources are arguably intimately related with the onrushing spaces of concentric relation. Concentric openings involve a breakdown of everyday compressed diametric meaning and reality constructions, where diametric framed truths run dry and their hollowness invites failed attempts to stuff this space with vitality.

Modification between authentic and inauthentic structures (of understanding) is explicitly described in terms of change to projections, 'Understanding is either authentic ... or inauthentic ... Because understanding, in every case, pertains rather to Dasein's full disclosedness as being-in-the-world, this diversion of the understanding is an existential modification of projection as a whole' (p. 186). Diversion into inauthentic

12 See also, Heidegger's (1927) words, 'Dasein, as being-alongside, is at the same time making present. The horizonal schema for the Present is defined by the "in-order-to"' (p. 416).

diametric structures is a modification of concentric projected structures, and *vice-versa*, as part of a change to this whole structural interaction.

A number of features of the authentic-inauthentic relation invite analysis in terms of the third entailment of the relation between concentric and diametric spaces, namely, that concentric spatial structures are relatively more open with the background and that diametric spatial structures are relatively more closed and sealed off from the background. Heidegger (1927) observes that 'the authenticity of being-one's-self has of course been closed off and thrust aside in falling' (p. 229). This emphasis on a closing off in the movement from authenticity to inauthenticity resonates with a shift from concentric space to the relatively more closed off structures of diametric space. This is characterized as a 'privation' of a 'disclosedness' (p. 229); diametric space is a structural modification of concentric space that amounts to a privation of the concentric, and a 'fleeing in the face of' (p. 229) concentric structured existence. Again, while referring to 'a disclosure of spatiality as the being of the "there"', Heidegger (1927) highlights that Dasein 'carries in its ownmost [i.e., most authentic] being the character of not being closed off' (p. 171). The clearing of dis-closure is a challenge to the diametric structure of experience as being closed off from background interaction, at least relative to the greater openness and interaction with background of concentric space.

Heidegger (1927) contrasts a 'transparency', as part of the 'clearedness' and 'disclosedness' of authentic existential 'seeing', with an 'opaqueness' of inauthenticity (pp. 186–7). The relative closure of diametric structures to their background environment stimuli and relative openness of concentric structures invite an association of relative opaqueness for diametric space and relative transparency and clearedness for concentric interaction. Firmer compressed boundaries of diametric structures tend to inhibit a light from passing through. It is important to reiterate that the entailments of the relational differences between concentric and diametric spaces are relative claims of one aspect being more/less interactive than the other rather than an absolute claim to associate, for example, diametric space with closure, opaqueness and nonpermeability.

This diametric closure off from background stimuli in inauthenticity is described through another feature of 'tranquilizing' (p. 222). A tranquilized stasis of interaction with a primordial background is a diametric spatial closure, also described by Heidegger (1927) with regard to inauthenticity as 'alienating' (p. 222).[13] Heidegger portrays tranquilizing as a diametric relation of inversion with 'tempting' (p. 222) as two aspects of this alienating inauthenticity. Tempting tranquilizing feeds off itself to aggravate the existential falling into inauthenticity. The mirror image inversion between tranquilizing and tempting is treated as a common process, where the tempting occurs through tranquilizing and tranquilizing through the tempting. This is one of the exceptionally rare examples of an opposition in *Being and Time* being basically a binary inversion; the mirror image diametric structure appears to be treated as a unified complex with two composite parts of tranquilizing and tempting. This somewhat obscures the active/passive contrast in this association, where tempting is an active part of a more passive tranquilizing state. Both could be said to motivate the other; tempting is for the purpose of tranquilizing, tranquilizing paves the way for and is instrumental to tempting in the they-self [*das Man*]. They coexist as diametric mirror image inversions in a structure of inauthenticity. Heidegger emphasizes the tranquilizing dimension more than the 'tempting' dimension in relation to being-towards-death, where the 'they' provides a '*constant tranquilizing about death*' (p. 298, italics in original). A concentric opening towards authenticity does not crack the mirrors of diametric relation, even as it induces its destabilization. For the more fluid concentric space to even enter the more solid diametric spatial surface, the diametric space must be opened and this is a dimension of being-towards-death – towards the death of diametricity.

While the issue of being-towards-death has been adverted to for Dasein's anxiety, being ahead-of-itself and tranquilizing, it is evident that, for Heidegger, there is a further problem that needs examination. This is the issue of authenticity for being-towards-death as one's ownmost possibility,

13 Another feature of inauthenticity as an alienating described briefly by Heidegger (1927) is an 'entanglement' (pp. 222–3) in oneself through a kind of splitting process associated with a diametric spatial projection – what Heidegger names as a 'self-dissection', and a categorizing into a kind of diametric side-by-sideness of 'characterologies' and 'typologies' (p. 222).

where authenticity would relate to the 'full' aspect of Dasein, and not simply be in an interplay with inauthenticity, 'With death, Dasein stands before itself in its ownmost potentiality-for-being ... If Dasein stands before itself as this possibility, it has been *fully* assigned to its ownmost potentiality-for-being' (p. 294, italics in original). The emphasis here on 'fully' is significant and is related to the question, 'But can Dasein also exist *authentically* as a whole?' (p. 277, italics in original). In other words, can Dasein modify its inauthentic diametric structures fully into authentic concentric space, as distinct from simply moving into the authentic space without major change to the inauthentic space? Heidegger treats this issue as being fundamentally related to being-towards-death, where 'the existential structure of such being proves to be the ontologically constitutive state of Dasein's potentiality-for-being-a-whole' (p. 277). So the question arises as to how being-towards-death is to be expressed regarding this interplay between Dasein's concentric (authentic) and diametric (inauthentic) spaces?

Heidegger (1927) also highlights that this being ahead-of-itself of Dasein is, from another vantage point, a prior 'not-yet' (p. 303). This is not simply a matter of a preexisting spatial structure, such as concentric relation, being the not yet, even if viewed in potential terms as a modification of diametric space. In Heidegger's words, 'the "not-yet" which belongs to Dasein, however, is not just something which is provisionally and occasionally inaccessible to one's own experience or even to that of a stranger; it is "not yet" actual at all' (p. 287). A more primordial relation again is envisaged. This parallels the recognition that the ontological whole of care is a more primordial structural whole than simply that of Dasein. In an important statement of this problem of the 'not-yet', Heidegger raises the issue that a bias of presence cannot be assumed for this fragile possibility, 'Our problem does not pertain to getting into our grasp the "not-yet" which is of the character of Dasein; it pertains to the possible being or not-being of this "not-yet"' (p. 287). This unstable possibility highlights not only that it is not a matter of a preestablished *telos* to be reached in this not-yet; it is not a notion of a fixed, preestablished potential, such as in reductionist assumptions of an IQ test, or of stage theories in psychology which describe an edifice of potential steps awaiting actualization, like some virtual staircase or carpark level. This move is to a dimension of not only engaging in an authentic concentric spatial structure of experience and to modify inauthentic diametric spaces in doing so. A fuller holistic spatial integration in 'full' authentic existence 'as a whole' is sought. A more primordial dynamic spatial-structural process is required that gives expression to being-towards-death – and to care, emphasized as being a 'not simple' structure (Heidegger 1927, p. 240). It is part of this shift to the wider question of a fundamental ontology rather than simply the existential analytic of Dasein.

Heidegger (1927) underlines the uncertainty of such a being 'grounded', as it is an 'awaiting', 'The self-directive discovery of a region is grounded in an ecstatically retentive awaiting of the "hither" and "thither" that are possible. Making room for oneself is a directional awaiting of a region, and as such it is equiprimordially a bringing-close (de-severing) of the ready-to-hand and present-at-hand' (p. 420). It is a directional awaiting through an interplay between a possible movement between a 'hither' and 'thither'. In other words, the background relation between concentric and diametric space brings a possible mutual interplay, if it is a concentric one of assumed connection rather than a diametric split background of assumed separation. This awaiting of a possible interplay treats this background as not necessarily inevitably arriving to make the hither of concentric space interact with the thither of diametric space.

For Heidegger's *Angst* of futurity, a questing underlying questioning, it is this ache that fuels the resoluteness of hoping. The anxiety of authenticity reveals the possibility of moving from diametric structures (a category mode of experience) in a direction towards concentric space. From this perspective, authenticity occurs in the modification of diametric structures of experience towards concentric, existential 'being-in' structures. In Heidegger's (1927) words, 'Authentic being-one's-self does not rest upon an exceptional condition of the subject, a condition that has been detached from the "they"; it is rather an existentiell modification of the "they" – of the "they" as an essential existentiale' (p. 168). In his influential commentary on *Being and Time*, Dreyfus (1991) requires that this modification of the 'they' self or 'one' must still have a cultural source, as Heidegger is not equating authenticity with nature and as 'authentic existence is not something which floats above falling everydayness' (p. 179). Moreover, for

Dreyfus (1991), this supposedly cultural source to modify inauthenticity treats 'the social context as the ultimate foundation of an intelligibility' (p. 7), Dasein being 'somehow dependent upon shared social practices' (p. 14). Modifying diametric towards concentric structures acknowledges that concentric spaces do not have to be reduced to nature; neither are they a detachment from diametric structures but a modification of them through their mutual interactive tension. However, primordial *a priori* diametric and concentric structures directly bring challenge Dreyfus' social constructionist requirement and posit a search prior to the nature-culture diametric opposition itself.

Dreyfus (1991) does acknowledge that examples of 'shared [social] background practices' are nowhere to be found in *Being and Time*, 'Since the notion that our social practices embody an ontology is an unfamiliar idea, we need a specific illustration. Because Heidegger does not provide one, we have to bring one in from outside' (p. 144). Heidegger does not provide any examples of background social practices because this background is primordial temporality not historical society. As a purportedly *a priori* structure, it is thus, for Heidegger, prior to derivation from the social. Historical society is treated, by Heidegger (1927), as a derivative linear time which is inauthentic, in contrast to authentic primordial temporality, where 'the primary meaning of existentiality is the future' (p. 376, see also pp. 185–6). To be compatible with Division Two of *Being and Time*, culture would have to be futural and existentially prior to linear historical time. Dreyfus (1991) explicitly acknowledges the tension between his social constructionist reading and Division Two of *Being and Time* (p. viii). In contrast, a futural direction of movement towards concentric structures, through modifying diametric structures, does not require that Division Two be sundered from Division One. It must also be noted that Heidegger's exploration of *Angst* in Division One provides no suggestion that the *Angst* of authenticity is founded on language as a necessary condition for the possibility of experience of that *Angst*.

Without acknowledging explicit criticisms of interpreting Heidegger in terms of public, social practices (Olafson 1994; Arisaka 1995; Ewing 1995), Guignon (2006) reasserts this schematic imposition onto early Heidegger, referring not only to 'the public context [which] provides the medium of intelligibility' (p. 279), but that 'taking the familiar demands of the public world as of consummate importance – as "the only game in town"' (pp. 279–80). Guignon (2006) draws an implicit diametric split between Heideggerian authenticity and an inner world, 'authenticity has nothing to do with such romantic ideals as getting in touch with a deep inner self' (p. 281). Again primordial experience is colonized by publicness as a radical foreclosing of experiential possibility. The encrustations of an orthodoxy on this issue need to be desedimented.

A danger with Dreyfus' assumption that the inauthentic they self (or 'One') is modified by a cultural source is that this may lead to the conclusion that the 'dictatorship of the they' self (Heidegger 1927, p. 164) is the primary source of its own modification. Heidegger's authentic self, which is not detached or floating above the inauthentic self, can still retain a realm distinct from inauthenticity if the relation is viewed in terms of a concentric relation, where the authentic is the inner circle surrounded by and immersed in the outer inauthentic pole, yet still differentiated from it. Dreyfus vaporizes private experience. Even its possibility is excised. The framework for his assault on a non-social authenticity rests on the necessary condition of the authentic-inauthentic relation as a diametric opposition, where, given the inability of the authentic self to be detached from the inauthentic, all that is left is to reduce the authentic to the inauthentic part of the opposition. Dreyfus, in effect, does this through relying on the social as the source of authenticity. Reduced to public language games, private experience is sacrificed to the behemoth of the social in paradigmatic postmodern fashion, not even reaching the dizzy heights of being a 'deformed' 'private language' on Habermas' (1972, p. 228) view. Derrida (1974) similarly struggles to conceptualize the relation between primordial and derivative truth as anything more than being metaphysical (p. 63); in effect, he treats the primordial/derivative distinction as a diametric opposition instead of investigating possibilities for this distinction being meaningful if envisaged as a concentric relation, where the derivative is in an assumed connection with the primordial.

Angst needs to be construed as experiencing a potential *telos*, an unstable fragile opening, in the direction of concentric spatial structures – and away from the levelled certainties of the premature grounds of diametric space. This *Angst* is one of recognizing the potential to resist the relative closure offered by diametric space. Yet in doing so, the pathways towards a concentric opening are fraught with difficulty and uncertainty. There are no guarantees that an opening from diametric space will inevitably bring a concentric connective horizon. The modification of diametric space is not a naïve breaking off from this space into a free-floating void, while this loss of meaning into a nothingness is an experiential possibility.

It is important also to draw a distinction between these concentric authentic and diametric inauthentic primordial spatial projections and Lafont's (2007) characterization of Heidegger's *a priori* projections as being 'historically alterable' 'cultural projections' (p. 110). Historically alterable is not to be reduced to linear historical time, as Heidegger's primordial time is a significantly different temporal dimension within which the *a priori* projections exist. While the concentric and diametric spaces of projection are not merely cultural projections, they nevertheless frame understandings at a cognitive and constructivist level that do amount to historically alterable cultural projections. The primordial projections are not reducible to a constructed worldview, though they are conditions of the possibility for such historico-cultural constructions. It is by no means a matter of a simple cognitive switching between concentric and diametric spaces. The key experiential structural movement occurs at a precognitive level.

Rather than *objects* being projected at a primordial level, as Lafont (2007, p. 117) envisages, projection occurs as spatial structures. Such structures of being are, for Heidegger, beyond any entities or objects. Dasein's concentric existential spatiality is part of a wider structure of interactive elements of being-in-the-world. This being-in-the-world is a structural whole. It includes the spatial movement from concentric being-in. It is the spatial movement from concentric relation towards diametric assumed separation and side-by-sideness. Both concentric and diametric space are primordial, whereas the concentric is authentic and diametric is inauthentic. Anxiety is the awareness of the individualizing possibility for movement between both concentric and diametric spaces, in the existential leeway for Dasein. *Angst* is that of the potential for the hither and thither of concentric and diametric spatial structures of experience. *Angst* encompasses a concentric connection to a falling direction of diametric space. Authenticity involves a movement towards concentric spatial structures of experience; this movement is an existential modification of the structure of diametric space of inauthenticity. *Angst* presupposes an existential freedom for primordial movement as a space for play between authentic concentric structured spaces and inauthentic diametric structured spaces.

Yet a further feature of *Angst* as being-towards-death involves not only authenticity as a directional movement but as a full concentric space. Such a full concentric space rather than a partial concentric movement towards that space requires not only a restructuring of diametric space but a death of that space in its dissolution into concentric space. This full concentric space is a not-yet, it is not a preexisting structure but emerges from the modification and restructuring of diametric space, at an extreme in the death process of diametric space. This interactive movement between concentric and diametric space in being towards death invites focus on the background structure and dynamic of such an interaction.

Dreyfus (1991) dissects discussion of authenticity into structure and motivation, and treats these as being contradictory in Heidegger's account. While this may be a legitimate distinction generally, the spatial-phenomenological reinterpretations of Freud and Jung have already argued for an intimate relationship between concentric and diametric spaces and motivation, in particular unconscious motivation. Structure and motivation can be reconciled in these contexts. Rather than pit structure against motivation, a task has been to uncover these spatial structures of motivation additionally in Heidegger's account of authenticity and affect, to interrogate their significance in this specific context of Dasein's existential anxiety, fleeing and choosing.

Heidegger's account of authenticity falling into inauthenticity treats both aspects as primordial. They are both primordial spatial structures. As structures of experience prior to subjectivity and intentionality, it is not a question of labeling a person as 'authentic' or 'inauthentic'. Authentic modes and structures of experience are more subtle contours than the jargon of authenticity (Adorno 1973) which places an essentializing label onto a person's identity, like Holden Caulfield's 'phonies' in Salinger's, *Catcher in the Rye*. Heidegger's account of authenticity, as a structural modification of inauthentic structures, allows an interplay between both spatial levels. The inauthentic diametric structure serves as a resistance to authentic concentric spatial possibility. The structural modification of inauthentic diametric space to authentic concentric space can work both ways.

10.3 Transcending the horizon of diametric space in *Being and Time*: Phenomena and appearance

Argument: That the pivotal phenomena/appearance relation in Heidegger (1927) implicates a spatial structural discourse going beyond a diametric projection of binary opposition between both levels.

Though largely neglected in Malpas' (2008) spatial analysis of *Being and Time*, Heidegger's oppositions between phenomena and appearance, together with authenticity and inauthenticity are pivotal to the whole work, including a comprehension of the unthought spatial structures projected into Heidegger's text. For Heidegger (1927), phenomena are structural, 'We have formally defined "phenomenon" in the phenomenological sense as that which shows itself as being, as a structure of being' (p. 91). Through their interaction with 'appearance', the phenomena are structural and spatial.

Heidegger's (1927) discussion of the relationship between phenomena and appearance express his attempts to go beyond dualisms of surface/depth and inner/outer, based on Cartesian ontology. Thus, when he states that the focus of phenomenology is on 'something that lies *hidden*, in contrast to that which ... for the most part does not show itself' (p. 59), he needs a conception of hidden that does not mean hidden in inner Cartesian space. Heidegger's notion of hiddenness is strongly resonant with the potential concentric spatial relation that is latent within diametric space, as part of a directional movement towards concentric space.

Phenomena are projected into appearance but some loss occurs in this projective process, 'Phenomena are *never* appearances though on the other hand every appearance is dependent on phenomena' (Heidegger 1927, p. 53). Such a relation goes beyond the alternatives postulated by Malpas (2008) for derivation and foundedness, where a relation is to be viewed as either hierarchical or mutually dependent. Hierarchical priority versus mutual equality invokes a binary opposition that Heidegger is studiously trying to avoid in his interactive dimensions to originary phenomena and derivative appearance. These pathways of hierarchy and mutual dependence understate the *structural* aspect to these relations between phenomena and appearance; the concentric phenomena are structurally modified in their turn towards diametric spatial appearance. In this way, they can give rise to appearance, as a ground for appearance, and are partially expressed through appearance. Derivation here places the diametric space as being a projected, displaced, fallen structure from the more originary concentric space. In other words, the structural-spatial emphasis needs to go further than in Malpas' account here, though, nevertheless, recognizing that Malpas has frequently emphasized a structural-spatial dimension as pervading *Being and Time*. For example, Malpas (1997) recognized that, '[Heidegger's] transcendental-ontological project is essentially concerned with "laying out" a structure that is already present in our being the kinds of beings we are; that is already present in the possibility of experience' (p. 12). It is this interactive dimension between phenomena and appearance as spatial structures, between the ontological *a priori* and the projected ontic structures, that requires further explication.

Though the concentric structured phenomena are hidden, Heidegger (1927) states, 'but at the same time it is something that belongs to what thus shows itself, and it belongs to it so essentially as to constitute its meaning and its ground' (p. 59). If concentric fluidity is the source of diametric solidity and appears as solidity through compression out of its fluid state, it could be said to belong essentially to solidity and to be its ground as its original source. Heidegger adds further emphasis to a fundamental dependence of a solidity or appearance on its concentric fluidity or phenomenal source, 'Yet that which remains *hidden* … or which relapses and gets *covered up* again, or which shows itself only "in disguise", is not just this entity or that, but rather the being of entities …' (p. 59) (italics in original). Similarly,

Heidegger (1927) scrutinizes the 'phenomenal basis' for 'pure space', 'pure spatial being' that remains 'concealed' (p. 147).

This covering up pertains to a process of compressed closure through diametric space as a direction. The primordial interactive concentric and diametric spatial relations undergo this diametric projection process of closing to compress their structural whole into a 'disguise' or changed state of fragmented split relations. When Heidegger (1927) states that 'Appearance is a *not-showing-itself*' (p. 52), this may be interpreted in terms of the proposed primordial spatial structure as how concentric space does not show itself when compressed into its diametric state of appearance. In *Being and Time*, all appearance and appearing is an ineluctable concealing. Once again, Heidegger (1927) goes to almost tortuous lengths to escape a traditional dualism, this time of presence/absence:

> [...] appearance, as the appearance 'of something', does not mean showing itself, it means rather the announcing-itself by [*von*] something which does not show itself, but which announces itself through something which does show itself. Appearance is a *not-showing-itself*. But the 'not' we find here is by no means to be confused with the privative 'not' ... (p. 52)

The absence in the appearance is by no means a total absence; it is not a binary inversion. Heidegger here uses the aural metaphor of announcing to describe relations between phenomena and appearance.

An apposite visual metaphor is that of blood being exposed to air, where the phenomenon upon being uncovered undergoes a hardening and drying into appearance. The appearance of the hardened crust of blood contains much of the blood flow in the showing of itself, though there is also a necessary loss in the movement from the flowing blood 'phenomena' in the body and its congealing upon the skin. Similarly, compression of concentric space does not mean that the more fluid state of concentric relation is completely absent in the more solid diametric spatial relation but is still in intimate relationship with it. This view of concentric space as expressing phenomena and diametric space as appearance also pertains to Heidegger's (1927) words on a directional process of closure, '*Dasein*'s kind of being thus demands that any ontological interpretation which sets itself the goal of exhibiting the phenomena in their primordiality, *should capture the being of this entity, in spite of this entity's own tendency to cover things up*' (p. 359). This 'cover[ing] things up' again involves compression out of a state of more fluid concentric space due to increase in the more solid diametric spatial direction over the concentric. Like water turning to ice, the gelid frame of diametric space defies expansion in its anti-thirst for closure. *Dasein*'s tendency to cover things up relates to this state of inauthenticity. This invites examination of *Dasein*'s inauthenticity as the appearance in a diametric spatial domain, and authenticity as the phenomenal, hidden concentric spatial realm.

A tendency in the commentary on Heidegger has been to project a diametric spatial structure, an implicit binary logic, onto hermeneutic efforts. Thus, debate on *Being and Time* becomes framed in terms of Dasein as subjectivity versus antisubjectivity (Carman 1994), temporality as ahistorical versus historical (Guignon 1983; Rorty 1991; Dreyfus 1991),[14] authenticity as inner and private versus social and public, Dasein as individualist or antiindividualist (Carman 1994), as well as Habermas' (1987) characterization of Heidegger's challenge to traditional truth foundations as, thereby, constituting an inverted foundationalism. Heidegger's holism presents an exhortation to de-sever binary divisions. Kisiel (1993) summarizes early Heidegger's (1920) position in his Summer Semester course on the phenomenology of intuition and expression, revealing Heidegger's longstanding preoccupation with refashioning the Kantian *a priori*, 'Is the opposition of absolute-relative, apriori-history, irrational-rational, really a genuine one? Placing the schema itself in question and perhaps dissolving it is to be realised with the help of critical destruction, a basic aspect of the phenomenological method' (p. 125). Significantly, this is a direct questioning of diametric structured spatial oppositions as a schema in traditional Western thought, whether between a priori-historical truth realms, or otherwise. At this stage it appears more as an outright rejection of diametric

14 Jung (1987) highlights this diametric projection in commentary on *Being and Time*, 'they misunderstand – each in a diametrically opposing way – Heidegger's conception of historicity (*Geschichtlichkeit*): one ignores it as the redemption of eternity, while the other as the recovery of time' (p. 218).

spatial projections than a view that they need to undergo a modification process, as part of a wider spatial whole of being-in-the-world.

Like a glass window pane, the domain of diametricity is a barrier, a membrane against touching more subtle contours of experience and truth. A rationality prior to diametric reason is needed – it is a rationality that renounces such stilled space, and yet, in shifting away from its glassy features, it extracts a truth from its illusionment. The contrast with Heidegger's own challenge to a diametric spatial oppositional logic requires greater recognition in his whole phenomenological framework of appearance and phenomena, together with authenticity as a structural modification of inauthenticity and a temporal transcendence prior to linear history. In doing so, the cloth of critics wrapping debate on Heidegger in terms of inversion and diametricity must be, not so much cut, as torn asunder.

The analytic of Dasein's existentiality, already prior to intentionality, is envisaged by Heidegger as preparing the way for fundamental ontology. Heidegger asks a vital question about the relation between, on the one hand, the basic spatial structural interaction of authenticity-inauthenticity in Dasein's existence and, on the other hand, phenomena and appearances, 'Does our present approach *via* the existential analytic provide us an avenue for arriving at this being phenomenally?' (p. 226). In other words, do the spatial structures of (authentic) concentric relation and (inauthentic) diametric spatial relation provide an avenue for arriving at a spatial structure for unveiling of the phenomena-appearance relation? Heidegger confronts this issue with the following statement:

> The being of Dasein, upon which this structural whole as such is ontologically supported, becomes accessible to us when we look all the way *through* this whole *to a single* primordially unitary phenomenon which is already in this whole in such a way that it provides the ontological foundation for each structural item in its structural possibility (p. 226, italics in original).

The italics here are important for interpretation of this account. *Through* this whole of Dasein's structure of existence as authentic/concentric-inauthentic/diametric spatial structures, there is a passage to the wider whole of the primordial unitary phenomenon of being-in-the-world. 'Already in this whole' of concentric-diametric spatial interaction for Dasein's authentic-inauthentic structures of existence is the ontological foundation for each aspect of the overall primordial structure. Thus, on this reading – building on the response of Heidegger here to his question of the relation between the existential and phenomenal – concentric and diametric spatial structures provide the ontological foundation for a single primordially unitary *phenomenon* of being-in-the-world. The relation between phenomena and appearance is centrally dependent on these primordial concentric and diametric spaces.

Heidegger (1927) moves from this conclusion to the issue of Dasein's phenomenal seeing, reiterating his earlier emphasis on seeing a primordial structure in a special phenomenological way, 'The way of disclosure in which Dasein brings itself before itself must be such that in it Dasein becomes accessible as *simplified* in a certain manner. With what is thus disclosed, the structural totality of the being we seek must then come to light in an elemental way' (p. 226). It is through the 'whole' of Dasein's structures of existence (i.e., through the interplay between authentic-concentric and inauthentic-diametric structures), that the disclosure of the wider structural totality of being-in-the-world is to be revealed as coming to the fore in phenomenological seeing. Heidegger states that this 'seeing' of the phenomenal structure must allow for a simplification, for an elemental whole to be seen. The concentric and diametric spatial structures of relation offer such a simplification and elemental whole for phenomenological seeing. It can be concluded that an implication of the fusion of the existential and the phenomenal is that the structures of authentic-inauthentic existence (concentric-diametric spatial existence) are revealed not only to be part of the wider phenomenal world as a single unitary whole. They are further to be the ontological foundation of this wider phenomenal world.

Crowell (2000) highlights a letter of Heidegger to Karl Löwith (20 August 1927) which states that 'ontology can only be founded ontically' a fact which 'no one before me has explicitly seen or stated'. Furthermore, as Crowell (2000, p. 322) aptly recognizes, what Heidegger (1928) says of Kant arguably expresses his own position, 'Ontology is grounded in the ontic, and yet the transcendental problem is developed out of what is thus grounded, and the transcendental also first clarifies the function of the ontic' (p. 164). The empirical, or at least the ontic, is to be a starting point for modification towards the transcendental. The direction of inference is from projections into the ontic empirical-historical materials towards the transcendental. A displaced, refracted dimension of the transcendental reveals itself in the ontic, historical projection. Heidegger's discourse on phenomena and appearances comes to the fore again here. The appearance exhibits grains of truth as a projected residue or seed of the phenomena. The process of inference is based on potential modification of projection, of projected manifested structures of relation.

The ontic projection is an inauthentic starting point for modification towards the ontological-transcendental. The projection into the ontic is no bedrock, even as it overcomes a diametric opposition to the ontological. Transcendence is embedded in displaced form in the appearance of the ontic-historical. Heidegger's direction of transcendence is from the ontic-historical but is not *of* the ontic-historical. The structures of concentric and diametric spaces are the ontic starting point in appearance for the modification through the transcendental horizon of their temporal interaction.

This view of falling concentric and diametric structures as ontic provisional grounds to be modified by the ontological temporal background relation amounts to a rejection of the view, expressed by later Heidegger, and summarized by Crowell's (2000) words that 'the ontic ground of ontology is understood precisely as something the recognition of which undermines the project of ontology, signaling the end, the collapse, of *Being and Time*' (p. 329). On a spatial-phenomenological interpretation, a collapse does occur in the fallingness of the primordial structures of concentric and diametric spaces. However, this collapse, far from portending the end of transcendental structures, is rather a starting point in experience for assembling a potential directional expanse towards the gambolling spaces of these primordial structures.

On this reading of the unthought in Heidegger (1927), there is a whole series of interconnected levels at which concentric and diametric spaces interact. These include the horizontal level of authentic-inauthentic movement, and the falling level between the primordial phenomena and appearances. This falling between phenomena and appearances enters the dimensions of *a priori* projections broken in their movement into the empirical-ontical-historical. The prevailing account is of an ongoing falling, covering up, directional process which can in glimpses be reversed through an unconcealment, as a counterdirectional opening.

Truth as unconcealment of phenomena, as *alētheia* exemplified by Dasein's disclosedness, is a presencing given structural expression again in this opening from the more rigid, impermeable, closed boundaries of diametric space to the clearing of concentric space. This structural movement brings about a change to an obscuring concealment for particular beings and the phenomenal whole of being-in-the-world. Diametric spatial exclusion and noninteraction is a deprivation of *alētheia*, a spatial tightening that covers up a more open and opening space. The uncovering of concentric space offers a stratum of permeability for primordial experience.

Interpreting authenticity and inauthenticity as concentric and diametric spaces recognizes that both are still primordial. Phenomena and appearances involve a primordial ground and its derivative, respectively. As primordial phenomena, both concentric and also diametric spaces get displaced and compressed into appearances. They are both projected into appearances. There is a compression of the structural whole into broken fragments in appearance; fragments or traces of the phenomena of concentric (authentic) and diametric (inauthentic) primordial spaces are in the projected appearance. This site of fragments is the threshold of differentiation between the primordial ontological and the compression into the ontic appearances. A distinction here is between the authentic and inauthentic spaces as primordial structures (of Dasein) and the relation between phenomena and appearances. A focus needs to be retained on both the spatial structures and a dynamic process of diametric splitting of a phenomenal whole (of being-in-the-world) into ontic appearances.

10.4 Care and the temporal horizon of transcendence in early Heidegger: The background relation between concentric and diametric spatial structures

Argument: That concentric and diametric spaces and their background relation (i) encompass early Heidegger's search for a non-simple structural whole of care and a transcendental horizon of temporality, including non-being, and (ii) interpretation of concentric and diametric spaces as dynamic directional projections explicates key features of Heidegger's primordial and derivative temporality.

Soffer's (1996) illustrative criticism of the 'dense cloud of ambiguity' (p. 568) in Heidegger's treatment of temporality is acknowledged somewhat by Heidegger's (1927) own admission that his account of transcendental temporality was an 'incomplete ... preparatory procedure' (p. 38), being only 'a path' (p. 436), where 'the question of the meaning of being remains unformulated and unclarified' (p. 437). Again, without elucidation of a concrete, elemental spatial structure of relation, the account of temporality and care struggles to gain breath.

A key part of this problem of the obscurity of the relationship between the (ontological) transcendental horizon and the (ontical) historical is the relationship between Heidegger's 'authentic temporality' (p. 378–9) as the transcendental horizon of being and ordinary Aristotelian 'inauthentic' (pp. 374, 379), 'derivative' (p. 374) linear time, which is, for Heidegger, 'secondarily' (p. 433) historical. The relation between primordial and derivative time is intertwined with the authenticity/inauthenticity relation. As has been argued, this authenticity/inauthenticity relation is given expression as a dynamic spatial structure of concentric and diametric relation. The question thus arises as to how concentric and diametric spatial relation, conceived of with regard to authenticity and inauthenticity, can pertain to primordial and derivative time as part of the transcendental horizon for Heidegger's question of being?

Having characterized the unthought of Heidegger's *Angst*, authenticity and inauthenticity in spatial structural terms, as the anxiety of possible movement towards concentric or diametric structured primordial experience, a further layer must be scrutinized for this proposed *a priori*, ontological realm. This layer explicated by Heidegger, at least provisionally, is that of care and primordial temporality. It is apparent that again, for Heidegger (1927), both care and primordial temporality must be interpreted in structural terms, 'the care-structure does not speak against the possibility of being-a-whole but is the condition for the possibility' (p. 365) of this potentiality, 'the ontological meaning of "care" is temporality' (p. 416) and his search is for 'the *temporalization-structure* of temporality' (p. 381) (italics in original).[15]

For Heidegger (1927), the care structure is not simple, though it is central to the question of the unity of the structural whole of Dasein, as 'Dasein can *be* spatial only as care' (p. 419). Care embraces the contours and structures of Dasein's existential spatiality, but goes further. Heidegger's being-in is treated as being equiprimordial with being-alongside and being-with. As seen, these features all give expression to a common structural dimension of assumed connection argued to constitute a spatial projection of concentric relation underlying these phenomena. Heidegger explicitly questions whether care as being-in, being-ahead-of-oneself, and being alongside requires a 'still more primordial phenomenon which provides the ontological support for the unity and the totality of the structural manifoldness of care?' (p. 241).[16]

Heidegger's (1927) inquiry into 'the meaning of care' asks '*what makes possible the totality of the articulated structural whole of care*' (p. 371). Is there a background relation engaging with the structure of care? This focus on a more primordial dimension than concentric (authentic) and diametric (inauthentic) spaces invites a questioning of the background spatial relation

15 Kisiel (1993) highlights that Heidegger never calls temporality an existential and that care is the 'master existential' (p. 419). It is not, however, reducible to the anthropocentrism of 'an existentially *a priori* anthropology' (Heidegger 1927, p. 227).

16 In 1929, Heidegger sought to interpret care through a Platonic lens of transcendence as a 'beyond beings'.

itself between concentric and diametric spaces. Is this background spatial relation between concentric and diametric spaces itself a concentric one of assumed connection or a diametric one of assumed separation? A diametric spatial relation between concentric and diametric spaces would be a split between both spaces to minimize their interaction. The connective feature of care is a background spatial movement of concentric spatial direction towards unifying the foreground spatial structures of concentric and diametric spaces. However, this background is in an ongoing dynamic tension between a connective care as a concentric spatial direction, on the one hand, and an assumed separation, a diametric split in the background itself between concentric and diametric spaces, on the other hand. The direction of connective concentric care, as a background relation between Dasein's concentric and diametric structures of existence, is not static; nor is it the only possible direction. Care encompasses both the background connective relation between Dasein's concentric and diametric structures and these structures of Dasein themselves; it becomes *both connective background and the totality of the foreground spatial structures.*

As a basic existential phenomenon, for Heidegger (1927), care encompasses Dasein's authenticity (p. 369), while in 'the temporality of care ... Dasein's inauthenticity may be made visible in its own specific temporality' (p. 380). Although care expresses concentric structured authenticity, the contrary space of diametric inauthenticity is made visible as a potential structure. Like *Angst*, care includes an awareness of the potential for movement between authenticity and inauthenticity, between concentric and diametric spaces. However, care goes further than *Angst* to a prior connective directional level. For this possibility of movement between concentric and diametric spaces, a prior background temporal dimension is a necessary condition, '*Temporality reveals itself as the meaning of authentic care ... the primordial unity of the structure of care lies in temporality*' (Heidegger 1927, pp. 374–5) (italics in original).

Is there a background relation to concentric and diametric space in interaction? It is this temporal interplay between care and a diametric splitting non-relation in the background to the being-in-the-world of Dasein's concentric and diametric spatial structures of existence that is the candidate temporal transcendental horizon for the question of being. The questioning of being at this level is as to the concentric, directional temporal dimension of care coming to an opening, to an unconcealment, rather than a concealing split of non-being governing the interactive relations between authentic concentric spaces and inauthentic diametric spaces. As Richardson (1974) highlights, it is a *question* of being:[17] 'It is only when we comprehend the horizon of transcendence as both the unifying dynamism of sheer presence and as non-being that we understand it properly' (p. 148). Both Richardson and this self-referential questioning of the background relation to concentric and diametric spaces accommodate this background as both a unified structure and possible non-unity. It is neither a bias of presence, nor a bias towards a necessarily synthetic *a priori*. It is not a presumption of continuity over rupture. A 'neutral' (or actively) non-interactive background space between diametric and concentric spaces itself preserves a diametric relation between the two structures themselves. On this reading, authentic primordial temporality is the concentric connective direction of care, though this falls into a split background direction of inauthentic diametric time.

What is the opposite to care? This question, though not asked directly by Heidegger, brings the following spatial-phenomenological response: Care as the assumed connective dynamic background relation between concentric and diametric foreground spatial structures, encompassing also these *a priori* foreground structures, is met with its opposite as a diametric split in the background between foreground concentric and diametric structures. The opposite to care is this dynamic, directional background movement of diametric relation as the strife of an assumed separation of non-being. This reading also views care as not being a derivative structure, as Malpas (2008, p. 117) has emphasized. Moreover, it gives recognition to a fundamental ontological uncertainty and instability in the movement at this background level.

17 As already discussed, the uncovering of concentric and diametric spatial structures in dynamic interaction requires a contextual questioning for its meaningfulness in a spatial-phenomenology. Though providing an 'answer' to the question of Heidegger's search for concrete, *a priori* structures of transcendence, this answer is itself a structural questioning. Moreover, the dynamic, unstable interplay between concentric and diametric spaces can constellate a plurality of positional regional ontologies.

The opposition between authenticity and inauthenticity has been characterized already as concentric and diametric spaces in dynamic interaction and tension. This can be further developed concerning authentic and inauthentic temporality, as the key, for Heidegger, to interaction between the ontological and ontical-historical realms. When Heidegger (1927) refers to a 'primordial temporality [that] has been levelled off' (p. 377), this echoes the 'levelling down' of the 'they' – as compression of concentric fluidity into diametric solidity. Heidegger (1927) emphasizes this 'levelling off' does not mean reduction to a state of nothingness, of non-entity, 'But this very levelling off, in accordance with its existential meaning, is grounded in the possibility of a definite kind of temporalizing, in conformity with which temporality temporalizes as inauthentic' (p. 377). It is a levelling to down to a diametric structure of temporality. This requires further articulation.

Three distinct levels emerge in relation to concentric and diametric spatial structures:

(i) The primordial foreground level of interaction between concentric and diametric spaces, in the *Angst* of Dasein's authenticity and inauthenticity.
(ii) The prior background level, the phenomenal level prior even to Dasein's existential spatiality. This background level involves, in effect, a self-referential questioning of whether the relation itself, between concentric and diametric spaces, is a concentric or diametric one. This dynamic, directional tension between the positional structures of concentric and diametric spaces presupposes a temporal dimension.
(iii) The falling away from primordial spatial structures (of concentric and diametric spaces). The compression, splitting, breaking of the primordial spaces brings them into derivative modes as fragments. This is again a self-referential process where the foreground fragments emerge from the background direction of a diametric splitting process. This collapse of the primordial structures implicates a different realm of movement and time. It

> implicates the ontic-historical,[18] what Heidegger (1927) characterizes as derivative, inauthentic linear time. That it does so still requires explication in spatial-structural terms.

Heidegger (1927) discusses these different levels of temporality in marginally different terms from above. He describes a futural, past and present orientation (for modes of time as its ecstasies). Heidegger (1927) refers to 'The schema in which Dasein comes towards itself *futurally*, whether authentically or inauthentically …' (p. 416). Movement between authentic concentric and inauthentic diametric spaces is futural. It is a *Spielraum* corresponding with (i) above. Thus, authentic temporality is a key dimension of a wider primordial [*ursprünglich*] temporality.

Heidegger (1927) further explicates 'The schema in which Dasein is disclosed to itself … as thrown' is 'the horizonal schema of *what has been*' (p. 416). The thrown projection of the primordial fragments of concentric and diametric structures, revealed in the appearance of the ontic-historical-empirical, involves a search for these past fragments or traces. These fragments or traces involve the entailments of the relative differences between the broken, thrown, projected primordial spaces of concentric and diametric relation. It corresponds with (iii) above.

Somewhat less impressively in terms of a phenomenology of lived experience in dis-closure of the present, Heidegger (1927) offers the following account, 'In existing for the sake of itself in abandonment to itself as something that has been thrown, Dasein, as being-alongside, is at the same time making present. The horizonal schema for the *Present* is defined by the "*in-order-to*"' (p. 416). From the starting point of these fragments of primordial structures, lived experience of these structural fragments in the

18 It is this realm of compressed fragments of primordiality that is the ontic level, to be distinguished from the ontological. It is at this ontic level that fragments of relations between concentric and diametric spaces coalesce with empirical observation in domains such as the regional sciences of psychology and anthropology. On occasion, dimensions of psychology, such as a dynamic space prior to the mandala and a preanthropocentric background life and death drive, are movements towards ontological concerns.

content of experience involves an experience of the present, a primordial experiential engagement that is also directional as an 'in-order-to'; it is a directional experience towards embracing the primordial structural spaces of concentric and diametric relation. Primordial experience is a moving of the projected trace of structure in experiential content into an assumed connection with its primordial structure. Heidegger (1927) relates a loss of the present to fear, 'fear springs from the lost Present, of which it is fearfully apprehensive, so that it falls prey to it more than ever' (p. 395). This closure from interaction with present stimuli in fear resonates with a diametric spatial projection (see entailment three). Yet the present here opens up lived experience of the primordial experiential levels of diametric space, as well as concentric space. It is an opening to primordial experience as presence, and in doing so, the absence in presence becomes apparent. The in-order-to in present experience is a directional engagement with primordial structures of experience.

The objection could be made that it is not logically necessary that concentric space would be associated with authenticity and diametric space with inauthenticity. Could a case be made for the reverse? A view of authenticity, not primordially, but as an expression of subjectivity would seem to incorporate at least some scope for assumed separation, a detachment fuelling honest conflict in 'authentic' communication. A preference for authenticity as assumed connection and holism needs to be justified, a) more generally, and b) for Heidegger's (1927) text.

a) In previous sections, structural accounts of unconscious structures have associated concentric spaces with accentuated interaction and integration, over the splitting of diametric space. Concentric space is treated as an overcoming of key aspects of obsessional neurosis and psychosis, and associated with the life drive. In doing so, authenticity as an *a priori* concentric structure framing experience is not being reduced to subjective honesty, nor even sincerity, with their assumptions of intentionality. As a connective directional background process, in tension with a direction of diametric splitting, care fulfils a dimension similar to Freud's background life drive. Both are a concentric directional background process. The need to distinguish between (i) diametric space as a reactive displacement from concentric dimensions, as a position and structure, and (ii) diametric relation as an active process and direction was already highlighted at a preontological level regarding Freud's death drive. The implications for Heidegger's transcendental horizon of an *a priori* diametric spatial relation feeding off itself, dissected from concentric spaces, need to encompass this space as a shadow of a shadow. Through the spatial-phenomenological understanding of diametric and concentric spatial projections, Freud and Jung's personal and collective unconscious levels lead to the horizon of the ontological unconscious. In doing so, they provide at least indirect support for an association of authenticity with concentric spaces and inauthenticity with diametricity.

b) In Heidegger's (1927) text, authenticity is directly associated with primordial temporality, whereas inauthenticity is attributed to linear time, 'inauthentic temporality has its source in temporality which is primordial and authentic' (p. 374). The question arises as to how this claim by Heidegger can relate in a structural sense to concentric space as primordial temporality and diametric space as linear time. This invites renewed focus on each structure as a directional projection. A diametric spatial structure is both a positional and directional truth. As a directional truth and process of projection, the diametric space feeds off itself. Whether as a rectangle, square or circle divided in half, each projective movement in diametric space follows a distinctive trajectory – a linear path. Diametric directional projection ineluctably occupies a linear space in its movement to recreate itself. In contrast, the concentric structure, in pure form as a circle within a circle occupying the same central point, brings a projective directional movement outwards to create a further wider circle. Its projective directional movement is in circular expansion to recreate its own structural form. Expressed in terms of entailments of relative differences between diametric and concentric spaces as dynamic directions, a fourth entailment of the relative differences between diametric and concentric space is that a diametric spatial structural projection moves in a more linear direction and a concentric spatial structural projection expands in a more circular direction.

This fourth entailment of the relative differences between diametric and concentric spaces entwines diametric spatial movement with that of a linear movement, and hence, a linear temporal dynamic. This brings a consistency between inauthenticity, time and diametric spatial movement. It does not mandate a conclusion that concentric spatial movement is thereby an authentic primordial temporality. However, it does offer some support for a conception of the temporal movement in concentric spatial projection as more primordial than diametric linear time. This is in so far as a circular outward movement is more primordial as a more unifying direction, and arguably is more fundamental than a linear direction. The collapse of a circle, the flattening of a circle, leads to a line. Like a punctured lung, the flattened line is derivative from the circle. A line requires additional resources to emerge to be a circle. A circle contains the potential of a line within itself, as a loss of its circularity, whereas a line does not contain the potential of a circle within itself, without addition. In this spatial logic, a circle is more fundamental or primordial than the line.

Diametric space as a projective process is a linear direction. Diametric structured time as inauthentic time is a linear projective spatial movement. On this reading, the interplay between authentic, concentric directional space-time of background care and inauthentic, diametric directional space-time, in the transcendental horizon of temporality, brings a temporality that is falling into linear diametric structures – to the extent that the diametric direction is triumphing over concentric care. Primordial temporality is not so much a ground for care as a wider world within which care is one fundamental direction of authentic temporality – and where care also embraces the foregrounded concentric and diametric spatial structures of Dasein for their interaction.

The falling into linear, inauthentic diametric structured space-time is the dynamic counterpoint to the authentic, concentric structured space-time. That the concentric structured background space-time can exist in this directional horizon, as a transcendental spatio-temporal movement to contrast with falling into linear diametric space-time, is the horizon for the question of being. As with the authentic-inauthentic relation in Dasein, this suggests two phases, one of the existence of authentic concentric spatial movement, another as a 'full' authentic concentric spatial movement which would dissolve the diametric space-time falling, into the authentic concentric space-time.

In summary, on this interpretation, authentic primordial temporality is the concentric connective direction of care, though this falls into a split background direction of inauthentic diametric time. Diametric space as a projective process is a linear direction. Diametric structured time as inauthentic time is a linear projective spatial movement. The interplay in the transcendental horizon of temporality between authentic, concentric directional space-time of background care and inauthentic, diametric directional space-time, means that, in Heidegger's words, 'Temporality is essentially falling, and it loses itself in making present' (p. 421). The transcendental horizon of temporality is not simply the concentric, authentic primordial temporal direction but rather its unstable dynamic interplay with diametric, inauthentic linear temporality. That the dance of a dynamic interaction occurs between both temporal dimensions is a question, arguably the horizon for the question of being. This corresponds with level (ii) above.

Though 'Dasein's specific spatiality must be grounded in temporality', Heidegger (1927) envisages this grounding as being neither a deduction of space from time, nor a dissolving of space into 'pure time' (p. 418). The proposed temporal background bringing interaction between concentric and diametric spaces, as positional structures, treats the temporal dimension as immanent directional movements in the spaces and affecting the spaces. This is neither a deduction of the spatial from the temporal, nor a dissolving of all spatial structural positionality into the directionality of the temporal. It is not a question that 'the spatiality of being was sacrificed [by Heidegger 1927] to the wish to ground existence on temporality' (Elden 2001, p. 82). The very directionality of the temporal is also spatial.

Here Heidegger's (1927) 'demonstration' (p. 418) is simply assertion of space being contingent on time, and is an assertion rejected by later Heidegger (1972) who, abandoned the transcendental project, 'The attempt in *Being and Time*, section 70, to derive human spatiality from temporality is untenable' (p. 23). However, derive here does not mean deduce, but means simply to be dependent upon temporality. On a view of concentric and diametric projections being primarily directions over positional structures, spatiality can be said to depend on temporality. Furthermore, even the continuity of a spatial structure, whether concentric or diametric, presupposes a prior temporal background.[19] Though by no means a complete account of all the contours of *Being and Time*, nor an addressing of much of his later work that drew back from early Heidegger's transcendental project, this spatial-phenomenological inquiry integrating core themes of the concrete, *a priori* structure of Dasein's existential spatiality, *Angst* and authenticity, as well as care and primordial temporality, offers an array of steps developing an argument that there is a need to stall the timorous retreat from a horizon of transcendence.

This conception of primordial temporality is not reducible to a view of time as offering a fundamental unity and space as the fundamental principle of differentiation, as tentatively explored in Malpas (2008, p. 261).[20] Concentric space offers a spatial conception of a fundamental unity through assumed connection. A background of temporality allows for the possibility of a split relation between concentric and diametric spaces, in the uncertainty of their interaction. Primordial temporality as only a unity would thereby provide a certainty that would become reducible to simple teleology. This would remove the need for *Angst* and runs counter not only to Heidegger's existential and structural concerns. It would amount to a revision of Heidegger's phenomenal concerns regarding the loss of the phenomena in appearance. Though this is not a total loss, a temporal horizon assumed to be simply a unity would import the possibility of a complete presence of phenomena in appearance. It filters any sense of loss or displacement in the projection of structures. Such a view is untenable for a transcendental existential-phenomenology emerging from a spatial-phenomenological approach interrogating a phenomenology *through* space.

19 Significantly, Kant (1770) recognizes that the law of non-contradiction regarding A and non-A presupposes a temporal condition of simultaneity, i.e., that A excludes non-A for a subject at the same time (para. 406). This insight regarding a background temporal condition of simultaneity also applies to diametric space, in so far as one pole excludes the other through a relation of assumed separation, on the assumption of a prior temporal relation of simultaneity.

20 In seeking to distinguish his position from the image schemata and conceptual metaphors of Johnson (1987), Malpas (2008) again relies on a conception of space as 'differentiation' and a dynamic 'differ-ing', though here also apparently recognizing a 'unifying' aspect of space, at least in its 'essential reference to the temporal' (p. 374).

CHAPTER 11

A Space Prior to Subjectivity as Cognition and Pure Reason

11.1 Diametric spatial projection as an ontology underlying cognitive science and Kant's Third Antinomy of causality and freedom: A self-referential questioning to uncover a primordial precognitive space

A key claim in Heidegger (1927) is that the uncovered structures of being-in-the-world and the transcendental horizon of primordial temporality provide a fundamental ontology prior to the ontologies of the regional sciences. If dynamic, *a priori* structures of concentric and diametric space are pivotal to such a fundamental ontology, on the proposed reading of the unthought in Heidegger's transcendental project, at least two related issues need to be addressed.

Firstly, if concentric and diametric spaces are precognitive structures as phenomena projected into appearances, how do they relate to regional ontologies, such as in cognitive science's purported structures of cognition? In what way do these prior primordial spaces manifest themselves as projections into structures of cognition, such as in those examined in cognitive science? There is a need to concretize a Heideggerian attack on the 'mental' to pave the way for concentric and diametric spaces as primordial structures of experience, prior to mind. Dreyfus (1991) emphasizes the incompleteness of Heidegger's Cartesian critique:

> The Cartesian ontologist, like the modern cognitivist,[1] would answer that it is not enough to *say*, as Heidegger does, that such an ontology must fail in the attempt to put the whole together out of elements … The cognitivist would hold that he has merely patiently to spell out the relation of each type of equipment [i.e., cognitive structure] to other types of equipment and thus gradually build up a representation of the equipmental whole … How can Heidegger *argue* against this claim? (p. 116)

How can an argument be developed, internal to the empirical data and computer models of cognitive science, in order to challenge as unprimordial this psychology founded on Cartesian-like abstraction and subject-object divisions, and to argue for a publicly justifiable ontological realm?

This argument needs to be taken up through interrogation of key background spatial assumptions in the problem-space models of cognitive science, abstracted in Cartesian fashion from the body and from emotion. In doing so, a spatial-phenomenological amplification of Heidegger's ontological critique offers resonance with the words of Johnson (1987) in cognitive linguistics, in anticipating, in a general sense, this blind spot of space in classical cognitive science, 'Our schemata for spatial and temporal orientation are so pervasive and so constitutive of our ordinary experience that they are taken for granted (and thus overlooked) in standard accounts of meaning and understanding' (p. 31). Johnson (1987) and Lakoff & Johnson's (1999) framework of image schemata can, with some modifications, offer a key ally for a spatial-phenomenological approach, in concretizing Heidegger's critique of the hidden ontological assumptions underlying accounts of cognitive structures of mind.

Secondly, a claim for a fundamental ontology invites challenge to a Kantian *a priori* realm of pure ideas as being fundamental. While this is a huge task, one aspect of this realm of pure ideas, Kant's Third Antinomy of freedom and causality will be interpreted, for current purposes, at least provisionally, in relation to concentric and diametric spatial structures as

1 This point is well taken, once it is recognized that many functionalists advocating the cognitivist computer metaphor of mind, nevertheless, tend to reject a Cartesian substance dualism (though advocating a realm of the 'mental' as Descartes did), through a property dualism that mental properties are determined by, or supervenient on, underlying physical properties (Kim 2000; Ross & Spurrett 2003).

a more fundamental ontology. To pave the way for such an interpretation, Kant's *a priori* categories, particularly in relation to the synthetic category of cause-effect, require critique from the vantage point of primordial spatial structures. Johnson (1987) and Lakoff & Johnson (1999) have developed some pathways into such a critique with their understanding of image schemata. However, the focus of their critique needs to be redirected to the level of Kant's *a priori* pure ideas more than Kantian *a priori* categories.

In developing a spatial-phenomenological approach to these two issues, another latent dimension in Heidegger (1927) requires illumination for primordial truth claims. This is the role of self-referential questioning in uncovering a background context for inquiry into primordial truth. A level of *spatial* self-reference was identified, in chapter 10, for the centrality of concentric and diametric spaces to a primordial temporality. Such self-reference involves concentric and diametric space in a movement a) to its own background of potentially dynamic interaction in the transcendental horizon for the question of being and b) to its foreground of a diametric splitting of these primordial spaces themselves into fragments and traces. Self-reference implicates a range of foreground-background interactions, where foreground or background is relative to the level of description. This primordial spatial self-reference level can be closely linked with other aspects of self-referential truth claims.

A potential ally to bridge concerns between ontology and cognition is Hofstadter's (1979) emphasis on self-referential truth claims as being at a level not only of language but of concepts.[2] Hofstadter (1985) describes self-reference in terms of a 'healthy sentence' or truth claim which 'practices what it preaches, whereas a neurotic sentence is one that says one thing while doing its opposite' (p. 33). At the *sentence* description level, this point of self-referential consistency can be clarified by examples given by Hofstadter (1979):

2 See also Rogers & Molzon (1992) on self-reference, mathematics and the law, Hofstadter (1979; 1985) on the self-referential mathematics of Gödel's theorem.

a) 'This sentence no verb',
b) 'is a sentence fragment',
c) 'This sentence has five words'.

Here sentence structure and content are a consistent whole, in contrast to the following examples of Hofstadter (1979), that go back to classical recognition of paradoxes attributed to the Megarian logician Eubulides of Miletus:

a) 'This sentence is false',
b) 'I am lying'.

If the sentence is true it is false, and if it is false it is true – a paradox, i.e., sentence structure and content are divided from each other.

An example of self-referential inconsistency at the *conceptual* rather than linguistic (sentence) level is provided by Fletcher & Haig's (1989, p. 117) criticism of Gergen's (1973) argument that all social psychological 'laws' are historical. They ask if this 'law' that everything is historical is *itself* susceptible to historical change. If it is not historically changeable, its content violates its structure, thereby splitting one level of abstraction from its relatively more concrete counterpart. A similar splitting occurs if this 'law' is viewed as historically changing.

Heidegger's questioning of being is a self-referential questioning of the background-foreground relation of a truth claim. Heidegger (1927) focuses on a prior realm to the idea/word and the 'objective' referent, 'With regard to what do *intellectus* and *res* agree? In their kind of being and their essential content do they give us anything at all with regard to which they can agree?' (p. 258). He clarifies this question, 'This relationship ... pertains to a connection between an ideal content of judgment and the real thing as that which is judged about. *Is this agreement real or ideal in its kind of being or neither or these?*' (p. 259) (my italics). This 'being' question is basically a self-referential one, to inquire into the relational background for correspondence truth statements. For Heidegger (1927), traditional truth as correspondence between word and world is limited at the self-referential level, as it does not clarify the domain over which the word-world correspondence relation *itself* corresponds. A variant of this self-referential questioning of the background to the ideal-real opposition is Rumelhart's (1993) conclusion that there is a continuum from the literal to the metaphorical. This invites the question as to whether this continuum is itself literal or a metaphor; the attempted explanation of the question becomes displaced and substantially unanswered. Heidegger (1927) states, '... to clarify the structure of truth it is not enough simply to presuppose this relational totality, but one must go back and inquire into the context of being which provides the support for this totality as such' (pp. 258–9).

Heidegger asks the question of the conception of temporality underlying time itself. In one way this question is quite unremarkable as Aristotle asked a similar question of space, in his *Paradox of Place*, '... if everything that exists has a place, place too will have a place, and so on ad infinitum' (209a, 25). Heidegger asks self-referential questions regarding time, referring to 'The historizing of history ...' (1927, p. 440), and giving emphasis to the question of 'How is this mode of the temporalizing of temporality to be interpreted? Is there a way which leads from primordial time to the meaning of being?' (1927, p. 488). This self-referential interaction between different conceptual levels treats the two levels as distinct but on the assumption of an assumed basic connection to a whole. It is not a diametric split relation between two levels – the interaction is one of active common relation. They share a common basic concentric structure of assumed connection in the self-referential interaction between foreground content and background structure. The interactiveness of the two levels occurs, whether the self-referential relation is consistent or inconsistent. Even a split non-interaction is itself a mode of interaction.

This opening up of a self-referential questioning can be applied to both cognitive science's regional ontology and a Kantian *a priori*. For classical cognitive science, this brings a) a self-referential spatializing of cognitive science's space in its problem-space models and b) a self-referential questioning of the schematizing underling schema explanations in cognitive science. In other words, what is the background spatial assumption structure in cognitive science's problem-space models? What is the background schema underlying cognitive science's schema-based explanations? A self-referential questioning of the cause-effect category in Kant is one that Kant anticipated. It involves the background cause underlying a cause-effect series. This background questioning Kant answered as the Third Antinomy of freedom and causality, as an *a priori* pure idea.

11.2 The silent projection of a necessary condition of diametric, noninteractive space in cognitive science: The primordial blind spot in Newell and Simon's information processing paradigm

Argument: That cognitive science (i) ignores its foundational spatial assumption structure and (ii) this structure is a projection of diametric, noninteractive space pervading computational models of the mind, as a necessary condition gluing together cognitive science's whole framework.

A spatial-phenomenological reinterpretation of cognitive science hones in on the unthought, blind spot of space that silently binds the whole framework of its computational models. The problem of space will be raised here for cognitive science's problem-space framework governing its information-processing paradigm. Though frequently employed linguistically, for example, in problem-space theories such as Newell & Simon's (1972) General Problem Solver which 'became practically the Bible of information processors' (Hearnshaw 1985, p. 275), it will be argued that the *concept* of space has tended to be neglected and in doing so, cognitive science's overwhelming reliance on a diametric spatial projection has been obscured. A diametric assumed separation between the foreground contents in the space and the space itself leaves the space as a diametric noninteractive background in computational models. Spatial conditions have been either ignored or removed from the domain of relevance for cognitive science's view of symbolic processes. The key entailments of the relative differences between diametric and concentric spaces that are focused upon here are that of diametric space as one of assumed separation, and noninteraction between foreground and background.

The computer metaphor of mind: The centrality of space as a necessary 'primitive' condition neglected in Newell and Simon

Newell's (1990) Soar problem-search computer model, developed from Newell & Simon's (1972) problem-space model, is a fundamental framework adopted within cognitive science's problem-solving and expertise contexts. Newell's (1990) Soar model seeks to incorporate a feature absent from Newell & Simon (1972), namely, domain specific knowledge. Newell (1990) views Soar as a candidate cognitive architecture (i.e., as a general framework for characterizing all of cognition). Holyoak (1995) describes Newell & Simon's (1972) problem-space search, upon which Newell's (1990) Soar is fundamentally based, as drawn from an everyday metaphor, 'This conception of problem solving as search in a metaphorical space ... has been elaborated to provide a rigorous theoretical framework for the analysis of problem-solving' (p. 269). It is on this assumption of a metaphorical space that Newell's (1990) 'primitive functions' (p. 161), which in turn ground Soar, are founded.

Newell's (1990) four primitive functions of his problem-space architecture are a) selection of a problem space; b) selection of a state from those directly available; c) selection of an operator and d) application of the operator to obtain a new state. Operators are actions to be taken in the metaphorical space in order to alter the current state of the problem. In Newell's (1966) words, 'The key constraint is that all changes in the knowledge state (as defined for the problem space) that are detectable in the protocol must come about through one of the operators of the problem space' (p. 34). That this supposedly metaphorical space is the glue holding together Newell's (1990) four primitive functions is clear from his words:

> *But if the problem space is the basic organisation, in that nothing but operation in problem spaces occurs*, then the primitive functions can be those of ... [the four functions outlined above] without ever dropping into another computational engine organized in some other way. The four functions ... must be genuinely primitive; and much of the rest of architecture is devoted to accomplishing these functions. (p. 163) (my italics)

The so-called 'primitive' functions rest on the more primitive notion of space[3]

Newell (1990) states that 'this uniform use of problem spaces as the task representation is called the problem space hypothesis' (p. 163). The supposed metaphor of space is the foundation for Newell's (1990) emphasis on search as the core of his candidate cognitive architecture, 'Search is fundamental for intelligent behaviour. It is not just another method or cognitive mechanism, but a fundamental process. If there is anything that AI has contributed to our understanding of intelligence, it is discovering that search is not just one method among many that might be used to attain ends but is the most fundamental method of all' (p. 96). He does acknowledge, however, in a footnote that 'a case can be made that pattern-match processes are equally fundamental' (p. 96). Simon & Kaplan (1989) likewise conclude that 'the principal mechanism of intelligence observed in people and computers operating in problem environments is heuristic search' (p. 39) in space, while Simon (1996) summarizes his research on expertise with the conclusion that heuristic search and pattern recognition are the two fundamental principles. Search governs the computational model of mind; this model of computer systems and the mind is based on a more primordial condition of space in order for search itself to take place.

For the problem of space to emerge as a fundamental issue within problem-space computer models of the mind, space itself needs to be more than just metaphorical but must also be central to causal explanations in cognitive science. Fodor (1976) outlines his requirement of purely causal explanations for cognitive science, 'what it [cognitive science] talks about is at most mental states that have mental causes. It may be that we are labouring in quite a small vineyard, for all that we can't now move out of its borders' (p. 202). He accepts that 'Nothing principled precludes the chance that highly valued mental states are sometimes the effects of (literally)

3 See also, Simon & Langley's (1981/1989) references to the need for 'depth of explanation' (p. 105), and to avoid 'shallowness in explanations' (p. 106). However, they do not refer to a shallowness of explanation in relation to space itself.

nonrational causes' (p. 202). Fodor's rigid projection of a diametric spatial relation between causal mental states as 'the domain of explanatory mechanisms' (p. 202) and non-explanatory 'nonrational' causal states is too crude and itself unprincipled. There is a need to go beyond a narrow and flawed division between mental causes and nonrational causes to focus on conditions necessary for causal relations (Mill 1872; Rutter 1985). And it is here that the fundamental role for space emerges. Space is to be viewed not as a mere metaphor irrelevant to causal explanation but as a necessary condition upon which the causal relations of computer simulations of the mind hinge.

Characterizing space as metaphorical removes it from the domain of relevant phenomena for observation and justification. No argument is presented for why it is less literal than the search operators in it. Moreover, an assumption of a rigid dualism between a literal and metaphorical realm is itself quite unsatisfactory (Lakoff & Johnson 1980; Lakoff 1987, 1993; Gibbs 1993; Ortony 1993). The depiction of space as metaphorical, and as implicitly removed from the need for public justification, neutralizes in Cartesian (and Newtonian[4]) fashion, the importance of the glue for Newell's whole framework. Descartes (1954) referred to 'empty space, which almost everyone is convinced is mere nonentity' (p. 200). Within cognitive psychology, Neisser (1967) acknowledged that space itself was a concept that could be problematized in the realm of perception, 'Space is another cognitive dimension which is important but not as "primitive" as is sometimes supposed … Position on the retina is an important source

4 For a more detailed related extension of this argument, that cognitive science's computational models rely on outmoded Newtonian spatial assumptions, see Downes (2006, 2010, 2010a), Kinsella (2008). Flat Euclidean space is not being treated as equivalent with diametric space. Euclidean space is a positional extremity of diametric space. Diametric space is a directional process, the limit of which is Euclidean space. The diametric spatial relation is inferred in its relative differences with concentric space. It is relatively more closed and noninteractive with background stimuli. In cognitive science's models, this closure brings an extremity of noninteraction and a diametric space that is in no interaction at all with background materials and in radical split assumed separation even within the space of its internal opposition.

of stimulus information, but it is not directly represented by a position in cognitively elaborated space' (pp. 291–2). This view implicitly echoed that of Piaget and Inhelder (1956) who argued that Euclidean space was a developmental construction in a child's capacity for perception and representation, observing that drawings of children aged on average 3.6–4 years revealed that 'euclidean relationships [were] ... completely ignored' (p. 52). Piaget and Inhelder (1956) criticized a position that is 'confused after the manner of elementary text-book authors who start out by treating distances and simple euclidean figures as if they constituted real "elements" in the construction of space' (p. 45). In its spatial understanding, cognitive psychology is in significant tension with the basic spatial concept underpinning cognitive science.

A problem-search which constructs its space

Newell (1990) might object that his conception of space is not static and is interactive. He describes, after all, a 'problem search' that 'constructs its space' (p. 100) and continues:

> The only states that exist as declarative data structures are the current one, plus possibly, some that were generated in the search up to the current moment and have been saved to be accessed by memory operations. Each new operator application generates a new state, which has never been seen before by the agent. The problem space is necessarily combinatorial (with greater or less branching factor). Its topology could be reduced in dimension only if new states converged back on one another. (Newell 1990, p. 100)

The problem search 'constructs its space', the spatial dimension itself does not construct the search in a two-way interaction; the space itself has no active shape. This construction of space is where *only the contents in the space are relevant, not the space itself*; the space itself is viewed as a neutral, *blank page*, as a passive permissive vehicle for the interaction of objects within it. It is the operators' applications that generate new states, not the space itself which affects new operators or states – so construction is that of an essentially static, independent space.

Movement across the expanse of a neutral, noninteractive diametric space is precisely what Newell (1990) is assuming when he describes the movement of the Soar searcher, 'We now have seen how Soar performs – by using problem spaces and moving through them to attain its tasks, detouring as necessary to resolve whatever impasses arise' (p. 185). This movement is through the four supposedly primitive functions (i.e., selection of a problem space), selection of a state from those directly available, selection of an operator, and application of the operator to obtain a new state. When Newell (1990) refers to application of operators (p. 100, p. 185), *apply* is conceived of as a force – not as an interactive, non-diametric space between operator and state.

Knowledge-search space

Even the supposedly 'radically' different (Newell 1990, p. 99) knowledge search space, akin to a schema storing long-term knowledge, is locked into a fundamental view of space as a frozen and noninteractive, side-by-side diametric relation. Newell (1990) argues that, 'knowledge search occurs in a fixed, preexisting structure. The items being sought (the analog of the states in the problem space) preexist as data structures. The structure of the space (its connectivity and how paths through it are described) is preconstructed. Indeed, it is preconstructed to facilitate the search' (p. 100).

The connectivity referred to here by Newell is not that between space and its constituents. When he refers to the connective 'structure of the space', this structure is that defined by connection and relation between the objects (data structures and operators) in the space. It is a connection between the figures in the space, not between figures and the ground. Moreover, Newell's (1990) numerous diagrams show this space to be the blank part on the page upon which he portrays the constituent states' and operators' interaction. A central aim of Soar, namely to transform aspects of problem search into knowledge search aspects (p. 193), in order to obtain pattern recognition, does nothing to change the fundamentally diametric, non-interactive side-by-sideness of the most primitive reality construct that glues his and classical AI's framework, namely, space itself.

Simon's (1996) emphasis on the searched rather than the searcher

It might be suggested that Simon's (1996) inversion of the subject-object relation through emphasis on the searched rather than the searcher in a problem space incorporates the dynamism of a more interactive concentric spatial concept. Simon (1996) describes the story of the ant, 'We watch an ant make his laborious way across a wind- and wave-molded beach. He moves ahead, angles to the right to ease his climb up a steep dunelet, detours around a pebble, stops for a moment to exchange information with a compatriot. Thus, he makes his weaving, halting way back to his home' (Simon 1996, p. 51).

Simon asks how to understand the complexity of the ant's path and suggests that the complexity lies in the terrain, not the ant. The ant is a quite simple mechanism moving over an intricate topography. Moreover, Anderson's (1996, p. 364) ACT-R theory is in basic agreement with Simon's ant metaphor, while Perkins (1995) suggests that Simon's basic focus on the searched can be extended to the general idea of search in possibility spaces:

> The possibility spaces of chess play, poetry writing, or other pursuits are complex, whereas the basic mechanisms of human behaviour, Simon urges, are rather simple, We need to understand the complexity of the paths people trace as they think, not so much in terms of complex psychological mechanisms as in terms of the topography of the possibility spaces through which they search. (p. 512)

However, any simple reversal of the subject-object, searcher-searched relationship in space, such as in Simon (1996), misses the subtlety of the assumed connection and interactive dynamism between a concentric type of space and its objects. Simon's (1996) emphasis on the searched terrain is basically that of Newell's (1990) 'connectivity' (p. 100) of the knowledge-search preexisting data structures, discussed above. The searcher and searched are both still figures side-by-side against a passive ground. Barrow's (1992) concrete example of the effects of Einstein's theory of gravitation can be used to clarify this point as an example of a more concentric interactive space than in diametric or Newtonian spaces, 'the Sun creates a large ditch in the space near the Earth, and the Earth moves around the inside surface of that ditch. This path we call its orbit. There are no gravitational "forces" acting between distant objects. Everything takes its marching orders from the spatial topography of its immediate locale' (p. 81).

The difference distinguishing this spatial topography between sun and earth from Simon's (1996) emphasis on the complex topography of the searched terrain acting upon the ant must be made clear despite the potentially confusing use of the common term *topography*. There is no obvious space actively mediating the interaction between ant and terrain. Attributing the term *'topography'* to Simon's terrain would be equivalent to attributing the term *topography* to the sun and not the space between sun and earth. It is his key aspect of an interactive concentric mediating space that neither Newell's nor Simon's problem-spaces can get at, in the addiction of cognitive science to the glue of a diametric space binding the whole framework of information-processing.

While it may be difficult to envisage the meaning of an interactive spatial background if one takes cognitive science as the fundamental starting point, conceptualization of an interactive space is facilitated if one takes other starting points, whether a spatial-phenomenological one, or one from a PostNewtonian physics challenging Euclidean space or even if one takes the cognitive psychology of Piaget as a starting point, given that he had no problem in recognizing the distinction between a noninteractive Euclidean space and a prior non-Euclidean space. The precise difficulty in conceptualizing an interactive, non-diametric, non-Euclidean space for computer models in cognitive science is to be emphasized, as it highlights that such cognitive science models are locked utterly within highly narrow, diametric side-by-side spatial assumptions.

An infinite regress of If-Then statements

While Kvale (1992) examines 'abandoning the cognitivist tyranny of the rule' (p. 50), expert production systems such as Newell's (1990) Soar illustrate the centrality of If-Then rules or condition-action pairs to production system models of mind. The *If* or condition part specifies the circumstances under which the rule will apply. The *Then* or action part specifies what to do in that circumstance. Newell gives the following example, 'If the problem-space is simple-blocks-world, and the state is one proposition different from the goal, and the state has block 1 and block 2 clear, and block 1 is on the table, and the desired state has block 1 on block 2, then make a best preference for the operator that moves block 1 onto block 2' (p. 189). Such If-Then rules, with some modifications, are at the core of the production system model of mind generally.

The problem of the homunculus will be considered with regard to If-Then production rules to highlight the absence of an active mediating space in production systems. The problem of the homunculus, or tangled hierarchy (Hofstadter 1979), is basically the selfreferential question of what rules govern the application of particular rules, and what rules govern the higher rules' application themselves? A potentially infinite chain of rules for rules for rules is set up.

Newell & Simon (1972) describe this problem in their problem-space, Problem-Solver:

> Up to this point none of the components – the operators or the selection and evaluation processes – have been spelled out in detail. It may be that the essential problem solving is done 'inside' one or more of these. If this were so the problem space would have to be termed superficial, since although a true enough description, it would not explicate the important processing steps. (p. 186)

Newell & Simon (1972) continue, 'Note that the basic issue is not how much selection is performed within the components (e.g., by the operator-selection process) but *whether the selection requires problem solving*: either search in another space or some as-yet-unspecified intellectual process' (p. 186, my italics).

Resonant with Derrida's questioning of centres replacing centres in substitutions of meaning, the question arises, Do spaces of If-Then rules need prior spaces of If-Then rules or something more? At the higher problem space levels, Newell & Simon (1972) refer to the possibility of:

> imposition of a priority ordering on the set of production [if-then] rules We can attempt to impose a linear ordering on the productions, always placing production rules j above production i, if the (i j)th entry is greater than the (j i)th entry ... In general this can lead to difficulties if there are intransitivities in the data, so that i precedes j and j precedes k but k precedes i. However we do not in fact meet this

> problem [in the specific cryptoarithmetic problem space their Problem Solver was dealing with], since there are no intransitivities in the data. (p. 199)

Newell & Simon (1972) do admit that there is to some extent a top-down imposition of the abstract (If-Then) production rules onto the concrete data, 'The transitivity of the ordering does not imply that the priority system fits the data perfectly' (p. 199).

Newell (1990) and the homunculus regress 'resolved' through a non-interactive space assumption

Newell (1990) no longer sees the self-referential homunculus problem of infinite regress as being problematic:

> It might seem that there is an infinite regress here, because there is need for a composable scheme to compose the transformations, which requires its own medium, hence yet another level of transformations, and so on. But this regress stops immediately when the same medium is used for the transformations [operators] as for the representations [states]. Then, it is all one medium and so there is self-application. (pp. 64–5)

Newell's approach to the homunculus chain is to resolve it implicitly using Peirce (1960) or Wittgenstein's (1958) approach of clarity through pragmatic action. Newell (1990) states, 'The transformations are expressed in some medium, which need not be the same as the medium used for the representation, though it might be ... Its key property is executability [i.e., capacity for effectiveness of action]' (p. 64). He continues, 'problems of conception that would have been substantial fifty years ago are now of no moment because of the computerized world we live in, which makes familiar all these ideas and their basic consequences' (p. 65). Newell's brave new world has not offered some new conception of the homunculus problem. He is simply implicitly adopting the advised resolutions of Peirce and Wittgenstein, namely, of ending the infinite chain of rules for rules through pragmatic action.

Newell's (1990) position is a similar strategy to that of behaviorism with regard to this problem. Skinner (1974) also advocates clarity for action (what Newell calls executability) to deal with the homunculus problem:

> It has been objected that we must stop somewhere in following a causal chain into the past and we may as well stop at a psychic level. It is true that we could trace human behavior not only to the physical conditions which [cause it] but also to the causes of those conditions and the causes of those causes, almost *ad infinitum* but there is no point in going back beyond the point at which effective action can be taken. That point is not to be found in the psyche. (p. 210)

The contrast between Newell and Skinner is that the former is arguing that points in the psyche, or at least mind, are not epiphenomena.

When Newell (1990) uses the term *medium*, mentioning that it can be active or passive (p. 64), his conception of medium is not of some potentially interactive background concentric or at least non-diametric space but of *objects* as mediums. Thus, when he notes that the medium 'that is to be processed must have adequate variety. Even more, it must be capable of being in combinatorially many states' (p. 63), he discusses an object or entity like flowers and their combinatorial range of colour, height, movement – 'swaying in the breeze' on a hot or cold day – and changing over time (p. 63).

There are other points where Newell (1990) makes it clear that his approach to the homunculus problem is one is one of pragmatic clarity for action. Whereas Newell & Simon (1972) tended to impose a linear priority ordering on a choice of If-Then production rules, Newell (1990) describes a conflict impasse:

> One production can provide a preference that operator o1 is better than operator o2, and another production can provide a preference that operator o2 is better than operator o1. And when the smoke clears that is all that is left. Since no constraint exists on what preferences are generated, such an eventuality can certainly happen (although in our experience it does so only rarely). Given the semantics of preferences, there is no way to proceed, hence an impasse occurs. (p. 176)

He continues:

> impasse does not mean that Soar is stymied and therefore halts. Soar responds to an impasse by creating a sub-goal to resolve it ... it must include some preferences that make the decision occasion that produced the impasse now yield a *clear* choice. *This does not require any formulation of the set of possibilities for what could resolve the impasse. The decision procedure itself determines that.* (pp. 176–7, my italics)

The sub-goal used to choose the preferred rule does so not by any high-level principle but by testing the consequences of a production rule that can have a clear procedure for application (see also, Downes 2003b, p. 162). Thus, the (limited) dynamism described by Newell for the paraphernalia of the Soar architecture concerns sub-goals but not a dynamism concerning high-level procedures of evaluation or problem framing, 'The Soar architecture creates the goals dynamically as it goes along. This is an important feature of Soar that contrasts substantially with the current state of the art. In essentially all AI systems, subgoals are created dynamically, but only as predetermined and stored in memory' (Newell 1990, p. 174).

The importance of higher level evaluation strategies

That the dynamism at lower sub-goal levels is far less important than dynamism at the higher goal levels is acknowledged by Newell's (1990) own words, 'Any change in a goal at some level – a change in problem space, state or operator completely pre-empts all changes about subgoals, because these latter were all created in response to the impasse at this higher level' (p. 175). The decisive animating rationality at the highest levels of strategy choice is dealt with, by Newell (1990), only by indifference as to choice of strategy to be tested. This choice can be made only by effectiveness of consequences at a lower level.[5] While this may be of limited consequence for solving routine, closed problems, it gains significance for thought processes requiring a reframing of problems – for more open problems of greater complexity that require construction of more innovative meanings.

Eysenck & Keane (1990, p. 135) suggest that the inflexibility of spatial metaphors for memory is an underemphasis on the *processes* operating on those memorial representations. Yet these more abstract processes, for example, within problem-search and schema explanations, still presuppose

5 See also Simon's (1977) description of 'an action space' and 'a state space' as being based on design of planning and performance programs governed by the criterion of 'efficiency of search' (p. 174). Thus, it offers nothing regarding quality of framing of choice alternatives, apart from efficiency considerations.

a silent centrality of basic spatial constructs that are being argued to be diametric, noninteractive modes of assumed separation. Without a capacity for frame change, for movement from the fundamental underlying diametric spatial projection, the lower-level logical applications limp along in a litany of monotony.

Constructive pictorial versus formalist explanations

It might further be objected that a space and search type of explanation is simply a metaphor to make Newell's (1990) theories more accessible to a layperson but is not the essential part of Newell's (1990) 'scientific' explanation. This invites further focus on the scope of explanations in cognitive science. Such a position that the pictorial part of a scientific explanation is somehow inessential would presumably reject, for example, Cushing's (1991) argument, based on historical examples from explanations in physics, that 'understanding of physical processes must involve picturable physical mechanisms and processes that can be pictured' (p. 341). Einstein (1954) distinguished picturable scientific theories from simply formal explanations:[6]

> We can distinguish various kinds of theories in physics. Most of them are constructive. They attempt to build up a picture of the more complex phenomena out of the materials of a relatively simple formal scheme from which they start out ... When we say we have succeeded in understanding a group of natural processes, we invariably mean that a constructive theory has been found which covers the processes in question. (p. 288)

This synthetic aspect to most scientific theories contrasts with, what Einstein (1954) terms, *principle theories* employing the analytic rather than

6 The different role of mathematics in the explanations of, for example, physics and cognitive science must not be overlooked. A linear equation in physics may lead to non-linear real world events – the mathematical structure or equation is not the real world event in an explanation in physics. In contrast, the computer simulation in cognitive science is supposedly a direct simulation of real world mental processes and is the actual event which is being claimed to be taking place (or it is in direct syntactical relation to the real, for Fodor, 1976). See Downes (2006) for a critique of Simon's conflation of these levels.

synthetic method. If a cognitive scientist emphasizes the formal aspect of an explanation of mind and treats the pictorial or constructive aspect as inessential, this clearly reduces the scope and ambition of cognitive science's explanation of mind. Moreover, it is not a case where a pictorial explanation is not available due to the complexity of the formalism (i.e., the computer simulation). *A pictorial or constructive explanation is directly available and explicitly offered by both Newell (1990) and Simon (1996)*, in terms of search through noninteractive, static space. It is the diametric spatial projection underlying this constructive explanation which is being highlighted here.

James' (1890) conception of mind as a river, actively influencing what is within it, also contrasts a foreground of objects with the need to recognize a neglected dynamic interactive background:

> Traditional psychology talks like one who should say a river [stream of association] consists of nothing but pailsful, spoonsful, quartpotsful, barrelsful and other moulded forms of water. Even were the pails and the pots all actually standing in the stream, still between them the free water would continue to flow. It is just this free water of consciousness that psychologists resolutely overlook. (p. 255)

Saturated with diametric side-by-side spatial assumptions, it is questionable whether the passivity of Newell's (1990) background space has gone any further than the 'traditional psychology' for 1890.

The functionalist perspective dominating cognitive science (e.g., Fodor 1976; Newell & Simon 1972; Newell 1990; Simon 1996) treats the symbol system underlying human intelligence as being disembodied. Once the computational properties of this system are characterized successfully, it can be implemented in other physical systems, such as computers. Thus, functionalism implies that the computational system can be understood independently of the human body. *Removing space from the domain of relevance for causal events is a necessary condition for this disembodied, as well as nonphenomenological approach*; the negating of space itself is the very path that paves the way for the disembodiment assumption and a related excision of space from a phenomenological analysis in experiential terms. As a diametric spatial projection, cognitive science's purported mental processes are contingent on distinct experiential, existential states – diametric structured experience allied with the reduced world of means-end, instrumental reason. Even the potential for a thought as an expression of concentric structured experience is foreclosed. A prior rationality of frames requires elbow room within diametric reason for its reconstruction beyond the differentiation membrane of diametric space. The classical cognitive science paradigm excludes even the potential for a broader space than a diametric one.

11.3 Developing a space for more primordial structures than mind: Uncovering a schema structure-content relativity principle to deconstruct a key pillar of classical cognitive science

Argument: That cognitive science (i) overwhelmingly relies on schema type explanations that are hierarchically structured and (ii) this leads to an untenable division between deterministic schema structure and undetermined schema content: a principle of schema structure-content relativity emerges to deconstruct this basic concept of classical cognitive science. That (iii) a *prima facie* case can be made that the entailments image schemata, apparently the most fundamental concept in cognitive linguistics, are traces or a residue of more primordial concentric and diametric spaces.

The problem of 'being' a schema structure of mind

Heidegger's (1927) search for a level of 'being' prior to mind and cognition invites the suggestion that another blind spot occurs in a basic concept of cognitive science, the schema. Eysenck & Keane (1995) acknowledge that 'schema theories ... remain the most overarching set of proposals on the structure and organisation of knowledge in long-term memory' (p. 268), while Markus & Sentis (1982) describe schemata as 'the central cognitive units in the human information processing system' (p. 43).

A questioning of being would interrogate what it is 'to be' a cognitive structure or schema. Shanon (1993) touches upon this point generally, 'before one studies the underlying mechanisms of memory one should define what memory, and in particular human memory (as distinct, for instance, from computer memory), actually *is*. In their haste to focus on the question of mechanics, cognitive scientists often overlook this' (p. 332) (my italics). Neisser (1967, p. 8) does at least ask 'but what kind of thing is a schema?', responding that 'memory consists of transformations', so that a schema is the 'structured pattern' of information transformations. Discursive and narrative psychology (Harre & Gillett 1994; Bruner 1990) envisage the schema as a social construct rather than internal structure of mind. However, there is a need for an argument internal to the logic of cognitive science, drawing on its own empirical research to highlight why schema dimensions are a social construct, rather than simply a prior commitment treating schemata as social constructs, such as that adopted in discursive and narrative psychology.

Schema structure as hierarchy

The hierarchical underpinning of the schema concept needs to be recognized, as does the extent to which schema based explanations are a key pillar widely employed in cognitive science, whether implicitly or explicitly. This hierarchical feature, together with the explanatory poverty of the schema concept, has implications for extraction of the schema structure-content relativity principle. The schema explanation is a hypothetical construct supposedly inferred from empirical data. Whether called 'frames' (Minsky, 1975), 'story grammars' (Rumelhart 1975) underlying most stories helping their comprehension, or 'scripts' (Schank 1982), schema-based explanations offer a framework that guides new 'processing' by predicting what is to be expected and looked for, and by filling in gaps in the currently available information. Schema-based approaches draw upon Bartlett (1932) in suggesting how our knowledge of the world is organized into packets of information, structured clusters of concepts, generic knowledge and experience of events, sequences of events and situations. Bower et al. (1979) found that people tend to reorganize information to fit with their script-based expectations and to introduce errors into stories that would be derived from the usual script but that were not in the actual story as heard.

There is an overwhelming reliance on schema-based explanations in research on expertise in cognitive science. For example, Green & Gilhooly (1992) summarize research results in five maxims:

(i) experts remember better,
(ii) experts' superior performance is founded on knowledge not on some basic capacity,
(iii) experts become expert through extensive practice,
(iv) experts employ different problem-solving strategies to novices in that they work forwards to solutions on the basis of their acquired knowledge,
(v) experts have better and more elaborated problem representations.

Better memory in (i) presupposes better access to schemata in long-term memory, more knowledge in (ii) relies on this knowledge being located in schemata. Extensive practice (iii) is to provide more information to be stored in schemata. These first three findings provide explanations that are only as satisfactory as the schema foundation they presuppose. Experts' reasoning forwards (iv) from information possessed in long-term memory is also a schema dependent explanation. Better, more elaborated problem representations (v) may at first glance suggest an explanation that does not need such a past based schema approach. However, the aim of expert production systems is precisely to move away from active high-level reasoning involving problem framing towards more past based, knowledge and hence schematic ways of processing.

Domain specific knowledge in long-term memory was emphasized by de Groot (1946). He observed that chess grandmasters perceived and recognized the characteristics of a chess position and evaluated possible moves by relying on their extensive experience, rather than by uncovering those characteristics by calculation and evaluation of move possibilities. He argued that his theory extended beyond the context of chess to shoemaking, painting and building. De Groot's emphasis on complexes (or chunks) in long-term memory is fundamentally a schema-based explanation, though

Sweller's (1994) characterization of Miller's (1956) concept of chunks as equivalent to schemata (p. 297) must be resisted as Miller dealt with short-term not long-term memory.

Schemata embody knowledge *at both more concrete and more abstract levels*. Abstract design schemata containing If-Then rules, such as in Ball et al.'s (1994) engineering design production system, contain strategic knowledge which need not necessarily relate to any specific design problems. Charness (1991) observes the need for more abstract schemata in the endgame in chess to encompass 'major classes and heuristics of play' (p. 51) rather than brute memory of every single endgame position and their appropriate methods of play. So, while the schema concept is used, for example, by Neisser (1976), as a perceptual schema (p. 54), schemata in the expertise context are more abstract than the purely perceptual. This more abstract level rather than memory of every concrete situation has been found to stretch across numerous expertise domains from physics (Chi, Feltovich & Glaser 1981), to X-ray diagnosis (Lesgold et al., 1988), computer programming (Soloway & Erlich 1984), electronic engineering (Ball et al., 1994) and mathematical problem solving (Novick & Holyoak 1991). Yet breadth of domain of research must not obscure shallowness of explanation.[7]

Just as Newell's If-Then production rules are embedded within a hierarchy of various levels of abstraction of problem spaces, Rumelhart (1980) has proposed a hierarchical organization of embedded schemata at all levels of abstraction and has suggested that in many contexts higher-level schemata may invoke lower-level ones when they are needed. This hierarchical structuring is a central implication of schema theories generally.

Markus & Sentis (1982) point out that schemata have a dual nature within a hierarchy, being both a structure and a process, method and content, actor and acted upon. This is a consequence of the hierarchical embedded nature of schemata. Bartlett's (1932) words similarly conceive of schemata as actors and acted upon, 'An organism has somehow to acquire

7 The prototype theory of categorization initiated by Rosch (1978) is also a schema-based explanation (see also Harley 2001, p. 288).

the ability to turn round upon its own 'schemata' and to construct them afresh' (p. 206).

Schank's (1982) script based theory of supposedly dynamic memory similarly proposed hierarchical levels of schemata. He argued for one long-term memory level called 'scenes', 'a scene consists of a generally defined sequence of actions' that 'transcend the specifics of a situation so they capture generalities' (p. 16). He divided them into three kinds: (1) physical scenes, (2) societal scenes, namely, 'a social relationship that obtains between two people for some particular purpose' (p. 96) and (3) personal scenes which are 'one's private plans to achieve goals' (p. 97). At the next level, he proposed memory organisation packets (MOP's): 'MOP's do not explicitly contain memories. Rather they organise scenes that contain memories' (p. 95). Schank then postulates a metaMOP which 'organises entities that organise scenes' (p. 99) and describes Thematic Organisation Points (TOP's) less tied to a particular set of situations and which could generally apply to the theme of whole sequences of episodes. For Schank (1982), 'MetaMOP's describe ordered progressions of abstract generalised scenes. As such they provide the stuff out of which MOP's are made. They do not actually contain memories' (p. 100). Schank does not develop the implications of his theory of metaMOP's. Once one metaMOP is introduced the question must then be asked as to what organizes that which organizes *ad infinitum*.

An explanation based on experience masks the need to examine the processes involved in de Groot's 'experience'. Furthermore, the broad term 'experience' masks the possible overlap between de Groot and hierarchical schema theories such as Schank's (1982). Experience of past chess board positions seem to be basically equivalent to Schank's framework of scenes, MOP's, and metaMOP's. Just as scenes are to some extent abstract in that they transcend the specifics of a situation, in chess there is a quite abstract process involved in simply seeing the position of the pieces to be remembered because the meaning of the pieces concrete positions depends on knowledge of the rules of chess. Memory of chess positions would not simply be limited to physical scenes, but also seem to correlate with the personal scenes of Schank (1982) as regards plans for possible future moves. Selection of past board positions to be oriented towards a present goal correlates with Schank's MOP's level. Organising the processes that organise the selection of scenes from past games directly relates to Schank's meta-MOP's level. So, like Schank (1982), de Groot's implicitly tiered concept of experience as the basis of chess expertise is also only as dynamic an explanation as its resolution of the infinite regress problem allows it to be.

Meaningfully related configurations of chess pieces and appropriate methods and moves were also at the heart of Simon and his associates' view that more expert chess players were able to recognize more complex 'chunks' of information. Complex chunks are described by Ericsson & Smith (1991) as 'chunks with a larger number of chess pieces per chunk' (p. 11). They do not refer to the possibility that complexity might also be pertinent to the more abstract level of the 'global and integrating encodings' (p. 24) which relate chunks to each other at different hierarchical levels – a global and integrating level which they do acknowledge in the context of de Groot's work. Hofstadter (1979) refers to higher-level 'superchunks' (p. 292). Chunks, like de Groot's experience, are *hierarchical* concepts (see also Newell 1990 on the 'chunk hierarchy', p. 206).

Davies' (1994) theory of salient programming structures incorporates a hierarchical structure *within* a schema and not simply between schemata. Importance, and not quantity of information, is pivotal to this view of internal differentiation within a schema.[8] 'Schema structures' are not 'flat undifferentiated chunks of knowledge' (Davies 1994, p. 720). Thus, a hierarchical structure would operate both inside a schema and outside it in its interactions with other schemata. Indeed, a common hierarchical structure would seem to challenge any rigid dichotomy between inner and outer. This observation arguably remedies somewhat the criticism leveled at other schema models of problem-solving (e.g., Johnson-Laird 1983), where it is difficult to know how action arises if there is equality of access to all components within a schema.

From this overview of empirical research in cognitive science, it is evident that schemata are consistently conceptualized, whether implicitly or

8 See also Anderson (2000) on a 'part hierarchy' p. 15, and 'generalization hierarchy' p. 156, for schemata.

explicitly, in hierarchical terms. Yet the implications of this have remained buried within the foundations of cognitive science, just as the spatial assumptions founding cognitive science have tended to be hidden (Downes 2006).

'To be' a schema structure: structure is content

Recognition of the hierarchical structure of schemata tends to obfuscate a key question of what is structure and what is content in the hierarchy. This is no trivial matter for cognitive science. A container-contained view of schemata, though assumed in cognitive science explanations that refer to 'storage' in long-term memory schemata, is challenged by Neisser (1967), 'It probably is unwise to think of them [schemata] as filing systems into which specific memories can be put; they are integral parts of the memories themselves' (p. 287–8). A filing systems or general container function separates the container from the contained, yet Neisser views schema structure and content as being *integrally* connected. So a fundamental question becomes: how do schema structure and content interact?

While Markus & Sentis (1982) observe that a schema is both a structure and a process, Sweller (1994) observes that each schema is a structure at one level of abstraction and a content at another. It is a part-whole relation. A schema element can itself be a schema for other elements; *while not all schema content is a schema structure at a more abstract level, all of the schema structure is itself a content viewed from a subsequent higher level.* In similar vein, Newell describes 'data structures' (p. 100) and states, 'The descriptions of computer systems form a hierarchy of levels, because each higher level description is *both* an abstraction and a specialization of the one below it' (p. 48) (my italics). This dual nature of schemata as structure and content is a consequence of the embedded hierarchical nature of schemata. While the hierarchical aspect has been highlighted in the cognitive sciences' literature, the implications of this structure-content hierarchy have not been. A structure *is* a content in the schema explanation. *If the very conception of cognitive structure and content is relative to the level of description in a schema and the schema is the supposed foundation for explanation in expertise, foundational cognitive structures cannot be attained in this context*; no abstract schema structure can avoid immanence as a content and hence these structures cannot avoid relativism. Like the emperor with no clothes this point is so obvious it can be missed.

This relativist chain of structure-content causal sequences requires that a schema structure can gain its meaning as a structure, not through some positive absolute identity, but only in its contrast and differentiation from a lower level content. A schema structure's identity as a structure is totally contingent on its *relationship* with other schema levels that are themselves structures and contents relative to other structures and contents. This hierarchical schema network of structures and contents means that any one structure is only negatively defined as a structure by its place in the system of structure-contents. There are no schema structures abstractable from the structure-content relativity chain. In describing his schema based computer model, OCCAM, Pazzani (1990) accepts that 'The distinction between a specialisation and a generalisation is somewhat fuzzy' (p. 48).[9] The fuzziness that he and other cognitive scientists do *not* seem to see is their fuzziness as to the meaning of the structure-content relationship. Even Neisser's (1976) words, highlighting the connection between schema form and content, do not go far enough, 'real formats and plans incorporate a sharp distinction between form and content, but this is not true of schemata' (p. 55–6). Not only is there no *sharp* distinction there is *no real distinction*, schema form and content are not simply connected they are basically *equivalent*.

Lévi-Strauss (1962) states generally that 'science ... is based on a distinction between levels: only some of these admit forms of determinism; on others the same forms of determinism are held not to apply' (p. 11). If schema structure cannot be abstracted from a structure-content network, a distinction of levels where structure is determined but content is not, cannot be maintained. It is notable that an independent finding that definitive cognitive *structures* cannot be abstracted from a network of content-structure chains echoes the structuralism of linguist Saussure.

9 'For example, the kidnapping schema is a specialization of the coercion schema. The kidnapping schema is also a generalisation of several kidnapping incidents' (Pazzani 1990, p. 48).

Saussure's (1954) structuralism provided a similar relativistic insight in linguistics. He emphasized that a word cannot have meaning, in an absolute abstract sense, but is reliant on its contrast and difference from other words; meaning is relative to the chain of differential relations of a word. This chain of differences is infinite as any other word/meaning can be invoked as a contrastive reference point. Saussure gave the example of a game of chess, where what constitutes the game's viability is the differential relationship between the pieces, and not their intrinsic value. Thus, words (and chess pieces) are not absolute or abstracted from a network, and similarly, aspects of schemata that describe themselves as fundamental structures are only structures relative to a certain level of abstraction in that network and are not absolute structures. Similarly, the structure-content relativity of schema structures means that no single schema structure exists independently as a structure, nor is a fundamental starting point in a causal top-down chain. There is a triple loss of foundation: (1) there is no abstract ground to start a schema hierarchical chain, (2) there are no autonomous structures because schema structures are also reducible to content, (3) a distinct deterministic realm separating schema structure and content cannot be maintained.

It must be noted that it is not necessarily being claimed that the structure-content relativity to schemata makes schemata equivalent to the phenomenon of language. The structure-content relativity pervading the schema concept is not being *derived* from a structuralist assumption of Saussure (nor from Derridean difference). Furthermore, the argument being made is not being made primarily on the basis of some loose analogy with Saussure. Structure-content relativity in schemata is a fundamental implication once the embedded hierarchical dimension to schemata is recognized.

This structure-content relativity of schemata finds that structures are contents if viewed from a different level of abstraction; it requires not merely that there are no such things as content-autonomous schema structures, but that there are no autonomous schema structures abstractable from the system of structure-contents. Schema structures are not simply dependent on content; they are the content.

This structure-content relativity of schema hierarchies is not an argument that all hierarchical models are necessarily structure-content relative, but that schemata hierarchies are relative because of the causal claims being placed on them in the deterministic cognitive sciences. This point can be clarified by Gillespie's (1984) description of Hegel's insight into chains of cause-effect:

> Cause is formally differentiated from effect as the original and active element, the free element from which motion arises. Substantively, however, the cause is not distinguished from the effect and in fact is and can only be a cause in becoming an effect, just as the effect is and can only be an effect because it was a cause. The cause becomes the effect and the effect thus becomes the cause (of the next effect). Moreover, this transformation of each into its opposite, i.e., of cause into effect and of effect into cause, is necessary, for each only has meaning in relation to the other ... (pp. 52–3)

Higher level schema structures (causes) organizing lower-level schema content (effects), in a causal manner, are transformed one into the other. While this point concerning cause-effect is well-recognized – its translation into structure-content relativity and the structuralist implications of this have not been in cognitive science. Barsalou (1987), for example, rejects the notion of actual fixed schematic structures. However, he is not highlighting the necessary poverty of the schema explanatory claim to be a structure of mind.

Structure-content relativity is not merely the idea that structures are viewable as content, as where structures of the body can be seen as parts/content of the body. It is not simply in the observer that structure-content relativity occurs. Structure-content relativity occurs in the observed – in the object or referent. The referent is changed.

Structure-content relativity for schemata challenges causal explanations

The causal claims for schema content can now be seen to become problematic for cognitive science, as schema structure-content relativity undermines its need to distinguish a level of deterministic structure from non-deterministic content. On later Wittgenstein's (1958) conception of language, and also, Saussure's view of language as a social system, it could be assumed that the *content* of thought needs to be ascertained by public interpersonal criteria in order to be communicated at least in language. If the *content* of thought is necessarily socially constructed and is 'out there' in the world of culture, this would create an obvious clash with a view of schema structure as internal and individual, as the structure-content relativity of the schema hierarchy requires all structure to be also content; it would place structure as well as content 'out there' in the culture so that schemata were no longer located in an inner realm.

Cognitive science does not claim to be seeking scientific regularities in the precise content of individual's thought *qua content*, but is examining *structures* and processes of thought. Regularity is itself a claim at the level of *structure* or processes of thought, not content. Cognitive science is not supposed to be a science of factors governing thought *content* control.

It might be questioned whether *all* thought content is culturally 'caused'. However, even if it were accepted that at some stage physiological, neural factors or some other non-cultural factors causally determined a given thought content, this would not adequately counter the conclusion that schema structure-content is cultural. This is because the past-based focus on causality of thought content cannot be the sole factor of relevance. Even if original 'causes' of thought content were non-cultural and non-social, it is scarcely deniable that present and future maintenance of that thought content requires communication and hence immersion in culture. *Focus on content does not privilege causality*. As Culler (1976) notes, Saussure among others de-emphasized the relevance of the past causal realm in finding adequate explanations.

Even if a schema *structure* is *caused* by non-cultural factors, its structure-content relativity makes it at least potentially a *content* as well as a structure; it *becomes* a content as maintenance over time takes force. As a content it is cultural and hence, given structure-content relativity, the structure is also thereby cultural. The question arises as to what is there then left for the cognitive science's assumption that cognitive structures, such as schemata, are inner and individual (von Eckardt 1993; Shanon 1993)?

Interchangeability of schema content and structure, depending on the level of abstraction, leaves the inner spatial structures of the hypothesized schema without an anchor outside the structure-content network. This point can be clarified by Shanon's (1993) words:

> On the one hand, the cognitive approach advocates the modeling of psychological processes by means of symbolic representations and computational operations that apply on them. On the other hand, this approach stipulates that between the phenomenological level of folk psychology and that of the underlying neurophysiological substrate there is another, *distinct autonomous level – the cognitive*. What characterizes this level is that it is both internal and mental. (p. 311) (my italics)

This is the cognitive level at which schema reliant theories are sought to operate.

If all schema structure is also content and hence cultural, the cultural domain of phenomenological folk psychology and the cognitive domain cannot be separate. As there are no schema structures abstractable from the structure-content relativity to bring autonomous structures, the schema cannot serve as a concept at a distinct, autonomous level called the cognitive. If a cognitive realm is to retain its claim to distinctiveness and autonomy from the phenomenological folk psychology realm immersed in culture, it will need to do so on the basis of a concept that is not a schema based explanation. In the expertise and problem-solving context, this would seem to require revision of all the schema-reliant explanations which research in cognitive science has produced.

Location of deterministic schemata 'out there' in the culture raises concerns for individual autonomy. As Lechte (1994) states, concerning Saussure's structuralism, 'Probably the main objection that can be raised against the translation of Saussure's emphasis on structure into the study of social and cultural life, is that it does not make sufficient allowance for the role of practical and individual autonomy' (p. 152). It must be noted that a social, cultural view of schemata content-structures is invited by the structure-content relativity central to the internal logic of the schema notion itself; it cannot simply be dismissed or overlooked because of its agency implications. Structure-content relativity to schemata also has significant implications for human agency once one is committed, like Fodor (1976), to seeking only mental causes in cognitive psychology. If schema structures are causally determined then the schema content, or at least those parts that can become equivalent to the structures must also be so determined – so if the schematic structures of our thoughts are not free, neither are much of the schematic contents.

Though this precise structure-content relativity rationale for the schema, as fundamentally a cultural content phenomenon and not an inner one, has not been highlighted in cognitive psychology, Lévi-Strauss' (1973) structuralism has made the general point that in anthropological studies of societies, structure *is* content, 'Contrary to formalism, structuralism refuses to set the concrete against the abstract ... Form is defined by opposition to material other than itself. But structure has no distinct content; *it is content itself*, apprehended in a logical organisation conceived as property of the real' (p. 115) (my italics). Perhaps it is cognitive science's proximity to Piagetian and Chomskian basically atomic structuralism, whose theories – alone of the major structuralists – are in tension with a view of meaning as a differential chain of contrasts, that has led to the relativistic problems in the structure-content relation to be obscured. Cognitive science explanations founded on the schema concept may be characterised as being pre-structuralist in scope and ambition.

It might be argued that there is no need to go beyond shallow causal explanations into the complexities of what a schema is because the causal chain of schemata implemented in expert production systems has been shown to 'work'. 'Working', in Boden's (1988) words, means to be an 'effective procedure' (p. 5). Similarly, Ericsson & Simon (1993) claim that computer implementation refutes the behaviorist epiphenomenality claim concerning causality of cognitive processes, 'If we can show that the information processes that are needed to reproduce the verbalized information are also required and/or sufficient to generate the answer or solution, the argument for epiphenomenality is essentially refuted' (pp. 170–1). Cognitive processes are held clearly distinct from 'the products of the cognitive processes' (Ericsson & Simon 1993, p. xxxix) which are examined in the realm of judgment and decision making. For example, mathematical regression models are products (content), whose structures are assumed not to be derived from an inner cognitive space, but from the cultural environment. Products are 'out there' in the world, while cognitive processes are 'inside' the space of the cognitive mind according to this view of Ericsson & Simon (1993).

Table 7 Schema structure-content relativity

Focus on 'to be' a schema structure and its hierarchical nature leads to a conclusion of structure-content relativity in this causal chain	No autonomous schema structures can be abstracted from content
No different level of description between structure and content, where structure is viewed as deterministic and content as non-deterministic is possible	If schema content is overwhelmingly culturally determined then so must be all schema structures as they are equivalent to content
Interchangeability of schema content and structure depending on the level of abstraction leaves the inner spatial structures of the hypothesized schema without an anchor outside the structure-content network	If schema structure is causally determined then schema content that is also structure is also causally determined and cognitive psychology is thereby implicitly seeking to find an invariance in thought content; in effect, it is a 'science' of how thought contents are controlled (not simply structures) and issues of power and knowledge need to be made more explicit
To the extent that cognitive sciences' explanations are founded on schema concepts, there is no autonomous cognitive realm in psychology as distinct from the folk psychology level of explanation	Structure-content relativity overlaps with Saussure, but is neither derived from structuralism, nor necessarily assuming equivalence between language and schemata.

The computer metaphor is often justified by the analogy that computer implementation offers the stringency of precise justification for psychological theories which mathematics does for the sciences. Mandler (1984) opines, 'as keeper of the computational grail, the AI community may well turn out to be for the cognitive science what mathematics has been for all the sciences. If mathematics is the queen of the sciences, AI could earn the mantle of the Prince of Wales of the cognitive sciences' (p. 307). Yet this link of the computer metaphor to mathematics ignores the proximity of mathematical regression models in decision-making and computer implementation in cognitive psychology. This proximity links both as products 'out there' and not as internal processes. The mathematical regression models of judgment do not claim their functional efficacy, i.e., their 'working', to be internal processes any more than telephone companies claim phones which work to be akin to ears. A computer implementation is an attempt to show that mental events are not a byproduct. *Yet this only displaces the byproduct question from concentration on CAUSAL processes to concentration on causal PROCESSES.* The instantiated processes as internal mental products is thereby called into question.[10] Cognitive science's schema hierarchy based data has crossed into Saussurean type structuralism of the mental as a cultural system, unless cognitive science wishes to maintain a position of deterministic mental *content* in the schema.

Interchangeability between schema content and structure depending on the level of abstraction leaves the spatial structures of cognitive science's schemata without an anchor outside the structure-content network. This lack of anchor is a rejection of a positively defined schema structure in an absolute space; a structure is only a structure relative to another reference point in the structure-content network and not by reference to any absolute reference point such as fixed absolute space. Absolute here means being positively defined as existing within a privileged frame of reference against a fixed background space, rather than attaining its identity merely in a relativistic way of its differences/contrasts with other states and background spaces. There is no neutral abstract transcendent position from which to view something as a schema structure rather than content. This argument offers concretization of Heidegger's (1927) rejection of 'the facile schema of content and form' (p. 108) in going beyond 'a network of forms'

10 Von Eckardt's (1993) attempt to sustain a clear inner/outer distinction for cognitive science again exposes the centrality of the reliance of cognitive science on a separation that structure-content relativity undermines, 'To clearly distinguish such behaviors [Newell's behaviour of a process] from external behaviors, I shall talk about execution behaviors of a process'. (p. 291). Interpreting cognitive structure-content as behavior, where individual schema structures are causes rather than aspects of a *system* of structure-contents, is a simplification within cognitive science.

(p. 417) for a precognitive realm.[11] Schema structure-content relativity is a necessary background spatial condition and blind spot regarding a basic concept in cognitive science.

Structure-content relativity and Lakoff and Johnson's image schemata

Beyond classical cognitive science, Johnson (1987) outlines an important spatial logic in image schemata, 'It is a matter of great significance ... that patterns [of image schemata] which exist preconceptually in our experience, can give rise to rational entailments (which we describe propositionally)' (p. 22). Examples of image schemata include the container schema, and the source-path-goal schema. Lakoff & Johnson (1999) make explicit the 'built-in spatial "logics"' of the container schema, namely, that 'Given two containers, *A* and *B*, and an object X, if *A* is *in B* and X is *in A*, then X is *in B*' (p. 31). They expand on the dimensions of this cross-modal image schema that is conceptual and yet can be physically instantiated, 'A container schema has the following structure: an inside, a boundary, and an outside ... the parts make no sense without the whole. There is no inside without a boundary and an outside, no outside without a boundary and an inside, and no boundary without sides' (p. 32). This is *de facto* an interpretative approach interrogating spatial dimensions to experience.

Whereas image schemata are described by Zlatev (2005) as 'what appears to be the most fundamental notion in cognitive linguistics' (p. 225), the scope of their discourse can extend to an obvious affinity with diametric

11 Philipse (2007) raises the question, 'Is the idea that science essentially has metaphysical presuppositions, which are *a priori* and cannot be tested empirically, not part of an outdated foundationalist view of science?' (p. 192). A focus on premature spatial grounding is without having to commit to simplistic all-or-nothing foundational conceptions of falsification or confirmation that does not recognize a wider systemic conception of understanding empirical feedback (see Quine 1961; Kuhn 1970). Nor does it overlook the provisionality of scientific foundational proofs (Feyerabend 1988). A spatial-phenomenological focus is by no means ignoring systemic interconnections between prior concepts, while treating certain concepts pertaining to space as basic within such system.

and concentric structures (Downes 2010). Schema structure-content relativity would predict that the image schema is not a fundamental ground (whether conceived as being in the body as a product of sensorimotor experience or otherwise). As well as potentially structuring modes of experience, an image schema is also an experiential content that has itself a prior background structure. The question thus arising from schema structure-content relativity is what are the identifiable features of any such background structure to foregrounded image schemata. A second inference from schema structure-content relativity is that any such prior background space for image schemata is itself relative to another prior structural level that needs recognition.

Lakoff and Johnson (1999) observe that conceptual metaphors, including image schemata, may not be consistent:

> It is not consistent to conceptualize ideas as both locations you can be at and objects you can manipulate or transfer. Nor is it consistent to conceptualize ideas as objects you manufacture and food you consume. Moreover, the entailments that ideas are produced by thinking and exist independently of thinking are inconsistent. Such inconsistency across different metaphors is normal in human conceptual systems. (p. 248)

From this inconsistency at the level of image schemata, the question arises whether they can be interpreted as being traces or residues of a prior system of spatial structures – that they are in some way a displaced or split form of prior background spatial structuring modes of experience.

As Strauss and Quinn (1997) observe, it is far from clear that the examples of image schemata and conceptual metaphors, highlighted by Lakoff and Johnson, serve to provide a *structuring* role to experience and thought. Strauss and Quinn argue that at least some of these image schemata are a means to a prior conceptual goal, 'speakers do select their metaphors to match the points they are developing or have already made' (p. 157). Thus, image schemata and conceptual metaphors may be illustrative contents of prior abstract concepts.

Lakoff and Johnson (1980) refer to structural constraints to image schemata, termed 'entailments'. Such entailments are proposed as consequences or implications of the internal structures of image schemata.

Strauss and Quinn (1997) highlight that Lakoff and Johnson's conceptual metaphors and image schemata are 'placing such inferential weight on linguistic forms' as structural entailments; their critique of the 'assumption that metaphor "structures" or provides the "model for" the understanding that it captures' (p. 144) opens up the chasm of the background relation between structure and content for schemata.

A further interchangeability along a chain of structure-content relations is evident in the implicit binary structure of diametric opposition between a range of image schemata outlined by Lakoff and Johnson, including schemata of up versus down, front versus back. Similarly Zlatev (2005, p. 329) describes image schemata of 'contrastive pairs' (p. 329) (such as containment) including: move/stay, go/come, put/get out, bring/take, up/down, on/off, in/out, over/under, here/there. Once again the question arises as to whether structure at one level is content viewed from a different level and whether such structure-content relativity for schemata is inescapable. This prior binary structure to image schemata illustrates the requirement of interrogation of a background structural relation to image schemata, what Heidegger would term a background context of being in asking what an image schema *is*. Perhaps the closest Johnson comes to recognizing a structure-content relativity principle for schemata is in referring to 'the centre-periphery schema', where he highlights that 'what is "figure" or "foreground" at one moment may become "background" at another as we move perceptually through our world' (Johnson 1987, p. 124). Moreover, Johnson (1987) commits to a view that 'schemata are definite structures' though 'they are dynamic patterns rather than fixed and static images' (p. 29). It is a small step further for his image schemata to be dynamic in the sense of a dynamic relation between being in a structural role for experience and as a content for experience.

A *prima facie* case can be made that the entailments of image schemata are traces or a residue of concentric and diametric spaces. This occurs through a strong structural resemblance between image schema structures and the entailments of diametric and concentric spaces in their holistic interaction.

Table 8 The entailments of diametric and concentric spaces in relation to image schemata

Diametric Spatial Schema	*Concentric Spatial Schema*	*Image Schema Structure*
Assumed Separation	Separation on the Basis of Assumed Connection	Containers (Interior, Boundary, Exterior); Boundedness, Differentiation
Assumed Separation and Noninteraction between Foreground Diametric Poles and Background Space	Assumed Connection and Interaction between Concentric Poles and Background Space	Centre-Periphery; Foreground-Background; Part-Whole Relation; Object-Location Dual
Mirror Image Inverted Symmetry	Symmetry as Identity	Contrastive Pairs As Opposites/Inversions

These structural features of image schemata are all shared with concentric and diametric spaces. This opens the door to a conception of image schemata as derivative modes of experience from primordial spatial structures, along a chain of structure-content relativity relations.

A self-referential focus on diametric and concentric spaces invites at least three different levels of analysis. Recognition of the prior background space dimension to diametric and concentric spaces raises the question as to whether their relation to each other is *itself* a diametric one, or a more concentric one of connection and interaction. In addition to the level of the diametric and concentric spatial structures, there is also a further possibility of displaced forms of this spatial relation, as in image schemata in language. Diametric and concentric structures are relative to each other, as part of a holistic interactive system, and thereby provide a more interactional mode of relation than image schemata's engagement with each other. While Lakoff and Johnson (1999) highlight the 'gestalt structure' dimension to container image schemata 'in the sense that the parts make no sense without the whole' (p. 32), a holistic focus is similarly required for understanding the meaning of diametric spatial relations as part of a wider systemic relation of relative differences from concentric spatial schemata.

Schema structure-content relativity requires a referential continuity from primordial spaces to image schemata to language.

11.4 Uncovering a primordial spatial structure prior to Johnson and Lakoff's image schemata to challenge key aspects of a Kantian *a priori* of pure reason

Argument: That (i) a primordial spatial background exists prior to image schemata to challenge aspects of a Kantian *a priori* of pure reason (categories and pure ideas) and that (ii) Kant's Third Antinomy of causality and freedom is not a primitive ground of pure ideas but is contingent on a prior projection – a diametric spatial projection.

Classical cognitive science employs a schema concept not in a Kantian *a priori* sense, not as a transcendental schema. It treats schemata as both images and as layers of abstraction prior to images, while maintaining their empirical veracity as a dimension of cognition. Johnson's (1987) image schemata, beyond classical cognitive science, are not confined to Kantian schemata but to a wider range of Kant's purportedly *a priori* dimensions of mind. Johnson challenges their *a priori* claim. Johnson (2007) contrasts his paradigm of conceptual metaphors and image schemata expressing bodily experience with Kantian formal structures, 'Kant famously argued for a "pure reason" that generates formal structures that are supposedly not based on anything empirical and thus are in no way dependent on our embodied, phenomenal selves' (p. 7). These Kantian structures include forms of sensibility, categories, schemata relating concepts to images and percepts, while involving applications of the categories in the principles of pure understanding. Kant's (1787) 'Table of *A Priori* Categories' is classified into those of quantity, quality, relation and modality (B106). Focus for current purposes is on one of his categories of relation – causality and dependence (cause and effect).

For Johnson, an aspect of the Kantian category of relation, cause and effect, is challenged by a scrutiny of conceptual metaphors for causality. Lakoff and Johnson (1999) offer a wide range of conceptual metaphors as illustrative examples of the constructedness of the relation between cause and effect. These include causality as:

> Location: Causation Is The Forced Movement Of An Entity (The Affected Entity) To A New Location (The Effect) …
> Object: Causation is the Transfer of A Possessible Object (The Effect) To Or From An Entity (The Affected Entity) (p. 199)

Other examples include causation as direction, 'Changing Is Turning' (e.g., 'the milk *turned* sour', 'he *turned* the lead *into* gold'), causation as shapes, 'States Are Shapes' (e.g., 'She's a *reformer*', 'Meditation *transformed* him into a saint'), as well as causation as progeneration (e.g., 'Necessity is the mother of invention', 'The seeds of World War II were sown at Versailles') (Lakoff & Johnson 1999, pp. 207–9). Their focus of critique is on deconstruction of literal event to event cause-effect, what Lakoff and Johnson (1999) describe as the 'Theory of the One True Causation' (p. 223), as part of their critique of objectivist metaphysics.

Johnson (2007) observes an extreme cleavage between Kantian *a priori* structures and embodied experience,[12] as part of his challenge to dualism:

> The source of Kant's problem is a fundamental dualism that runs through his entire philosophical system. Here it is manifested as a dualism of concepts (as part of thought) versus feelings (as tied to the body). Concepts are supposedly formal and not intrinsically related to the body, whereas feelings are obviously and inescapably perturbations of the body. (p. 216)

However, Lakoff and Johnson overstate the significance of locating a wide range of conceptual metaphors as purportedly underpinning conceptions

12 Concentric and diametric spaces are projected structures of primordial experience. Such experience is an embodied one but this is not equivalent to all bodily experiences. Allinson (2003) *inter alia* highlights the need to go beyond Kantian *a priori* assumptions, including that space and time are not interconnected. See also, Downes (2005), for a critical review of aspects of Allinson's account.

of causality. They treat this evidence as challenging Kantian conceptions of cause-effect as a prior rational category, independent of experience.

Johnson (1987) consistently refers to Kant's opposition between the sensible and the intelligible world, treating it as a 'rigid separation' (p. xxi) and referring to Kant's system of 'rigid dichotomies' (p. 168). Yet this is a simplification of Kant's position at least in the self-styled thorny paths of his *Critique of Pure Reason* (1781A, 1787B) and *Prolegomena* (1783), if not in his earlier *Inaugural Dissertation* (1770). Whereas Kant's *Inaugural Dissertation* juxtaposes sensations with pure intuition, i.e., intuition empty of sensations (so, for example, the concept of space is treated as a pure intuition, as a singular concept not put together from sensations), it does not do too much violence to Kant's *Critique of Pure Reason* and *Prolegomena* to state that they operate a tripartite rather than dual distinction – between sensation, 'categories' of pure understanding as a condition for empirical experience (i.e., sensible intuition) and 'Ideas' of pure reason that are not purportedly connected to experience. As Kant (1781) states, 'This dialectical doctrine [of pure reason] will not refer to the unity of the understanding in concepts of experience, but to the unity of reason in mere Ideas' (A 450). Thus, when Johnson (1987) describes schematism as categories and pure concepts (p. 152) in their application to sensible intuitions, it needs to be recognized that categories such as cause-effect are not for Kant (after the *Critique of Pure Reason*) simply pure concepts *per se* but pure concepts of *understanding*, to be distinguished from the conceptualizing of 'Ideas' as pure reason. The key difference here is that it is only pure reason that is purportedly independent of experience – and not pure concepts of understanding, such as cause-effect. Kant does not propose that the categories yield knowledge independently of their application to objects of sensibility.

Moreover, Kant was well aware of Hume's arguments of causality being reducible to merely contingent experience. His critique was in response to Hume and fully acknowledged an experiential role for causal type explanations, while nevertheless extracting a category of relation of cause and effect as a supposedly pure concept of synthesis belonging to the understanding *a priori*. Concepts such as cause-effect are a purported ground of the possibility of experience. With such categories experience becomes possible; they are, for Kant, the conditions of thought that make experience possible. While the relation of cause and effect, as a Kantian category of understanding synthesizing experience, is not derived from nor originating in experience, nevertheless, it is not refuted as a Kantian category, as Lakoff and Johnson claim, through illustrating the diversity of embodied expression of relations between cause and effect in conceptual metaphors in language.

Lakoff and Johnson seek to, in Kant's (1770) words, 'contaminate' intellectual knowledge by the sensitive (para 411), through excavating conceptual metaphors and image schemata giving expression to bodily experience based thought. In Johnson's (2007) words, they 'must recover the embodied meaning that Kant's formalism let behind' (p. 234). Yet illustration of experiential exemplars of cause and effect (whether through language or otherwise) is not directly pertinent to Kant's *Critique of Pure Reason*, as it does not comment on the *necessary* relation, or otherwise, between cause and effect; rather it is only a comment on habitual relations. Within Kantian terms, Lakoff and Johnson's diverse range of conceptual metaphors for cause and effect only illustrates *habituality* of relation through linguistic repetition and is a different domain of relevance from commentary on the reality or otherwise of cause and effect as a necessary synthesizing relational concept for experience. It is difficult to accept how Lakoff and Johnson's position on the drawing of conceptual inferences from linguistic statements has direct applicability to supposedly challenge Kant's different truth concerns of a category of cause-effect.

Kant's (1781) words regarding space and time, also apply to the category of cause and effect, as he notes that the scope of his discussion here applies to all concepts:[13]

13 See also, for example, Kant's (1783) recognition that 'our pure concepts of the understanding as well as our pure intuitions extend to nothing but objects of possible experience, consequently to mere things of sense; and as soon as we leave this sphere, these concepts retain no meaning whatsoever' (para 315). Thus, cause and effect, as a concept of pure understanding for Kant, retains no meaning, unless related to sense experience.

> Even space and time, however pure these concepts may be of all that is empirical, and however certain it is that they are represented in the mind purely *a priori*, would nevertheless lack all objective validity, all sense and meaning, if we could not show the necessity of their use with reference to objects of experience. Their representation is a mere schema, always referring to that reproductive imagination which calls up the objects of experience, without which objects they would be meaningless. The same applies to all concepts whatsoever. (A195)

Cause-effect was a Kantian category of understanding that explicitly draws upon empirical experience; it is not a Kantian idea of pure reason which is supposedly independent of experience. Thus, the aggregation of diverse experiential samples of metaphors of causality by Lakoff and Johnson does not refute a Kantian category of causality as unifying experience, as cause-effect is a category of understanding reliant on empirical experience for its meaning; experiential exemplars in language of cause and effect as conceptual metaphors do not negate this Kantian category but rather support Kant's view, as experiential illustrations are to be treated as an important condition for the relevance of such categories (as in the quote above in relation to space, time and other concepts). Diverse conceptual metaphors of causal relations simply exemplify, for Kant, the relevance and meaningfulness of their use with reference to objects of experience.

Furthermore, Kant's work illustrates a more heterogenous conception of causality than that attributed to him by Lakoff and Johnson. One of Kant's conceptions in the *Third Analogy of Experience* is of causality as mutual interaction for knowledge of the simultaneity of the states to be possible. In other words, it is a two-way causal relation for Kant, as Watkins (2007) emphasizes, though this relation is not a symmetrical one. Watkins (2007) also highlights that the conception of causality in Kant's better known *Second Analogy of Experience* is remarkably open-ended, as 'it requires neither that a cause be an event, nor that it be prior to its effect, nor even that it have any specific empirical characteristics' (p. 223). Much of the critique by Lakoff and Johnson of supposedly literal cause-effect models, including the 'Theory of the One True Causation' (p. 223), pertains more to a view of causality expressed more in Hume's discrete event model of cause-effect than to Kant's more complex models of causality.[14]

Rather than seeking to defend Kantian *a priori* categories of cause-effect against Johnson's (1987; 2007) challenge,[15] the goal of this argument is to highlight the need to extend Johnson's argument for at least some kinds of embodied experience and image-type schemata further back into the traditional Kantian domain of pure reason and its antinomies, as part of a claim for concentric and diametric spaces to pertain to a fundamental ontology. Lakoff and Johnson's attempts to locate a domain of experience to challenge Kantian rationalism for schemata is an important project, once this is extended not so much to Kantian categories of understanding but rather to Kantian Ideas of supposedly pure reason – as it is the latter which exist for Kant (1781) totally beyond empirical experience, 'beyond the boundary of experience' (A449). It is this arena of purportedly pure reason that can be invaded by primordial experience, mediated through concentric and diametric structures of experience.

Schematism for Kant (1787) involves explanation of the circumstances under which his categories (such as causality) are employed in concrete contexts, with each pure category granted its own particular schema in the sensible conditions of its application. Whereas pure concepts of the understanding (the categories) and empirical intuitions are 'quite heterogenous' (B117), the 'third thing' to relate both is the schema. The 'transcendental schema' (B117) is to bridge the intellectual and sensible.[16] Walsh (1967) treats this mediating role as an 'artificial solution' (p. 71), stating that 'it was

14 For further arguments that Humean concerns with abstract event to event causality is a different domain of relevance from Kantian conceptions of causal grounds and relations, see Watkins (2007), Johnston (2007).

15 Neither is this challenge to a Kantian *a priori* an attempt, *via* Heidegger, to turn Kant's own position into an ontological argument, as Heidegger (1929) tries to do in a violent and questionable way (Henrich 1994). Put simply, Heidegger extracted, from Kant's doctrine of schematism, a connection between the traditional problem of being, namely, the problem of categories, and the phenomenon of time. In doing so, Heidegger sought to invoke Kant as advocating the question of being.

16 Walsh (1967) and Dahlstrom (2010) (the latter *via* Heidegger's reading of Kant) also observe an ambiguity in Kant's (1787) text as to whether schemata are simply

to deal with this problem of the meaning and reference of *a priori* ideas, left conspicuously vague in the inaugural Dissertation, that the doctrine of schematism was devised' (p. 74). There is an ambiguity in Kant's discussion of the sense or significance conferred on categories as to whether this includes simply logical significance, wider construction of meaning or also aboutness, namely, referential meaning.

Both Guyer (2010, p. 136) and Watkins (2010) suggest that Kantian schemata or contextual time-determinations are 'in effect, spatio-temporal meanings' (p. 151). Concerning a schema as a spatial meaning, Walsh (1967) comments, 'Kant himself stated, in a passage added in the second edition of the Critique (B291), that to demonstrate the objective reality of the categories we need "not merely intuitions, but intuitions that are in all cases outer intuitions". This suggests that he may have thought at one point of recasting the Schematism argument in a fundamental way, by substituting space for time' (p. 81). Even accepting a pivotal role for space in Kantian *schemata* (in addition to Kantian categories), this does not imply that Kant treated his ideas of *pure reason* structurally in spatial terms.[17] Ideas of pure reason (as distinct from categories) are treated by Kant as organized not by schemata but by symbols. Walsh (1967, p. 85) questions Kant's apparent assumption that the process of schematization of categories can only be carried out in one way, though 'we need to know what an alternative set of schemata would be like' (p. 86).

Rukgaber (2009) seeks to develop 'the bodily basis of *a priori* intuition' (p. 167) in Kantian thought, through a spatial focus on figure-ground understandings that he purports to extract from Kant's own words. He seeks a 'phenomenologically present' *a priori*, structural 'spatial frame'

---

a priori or also empirical concepts, citing also passages where a schema is viewed as an image for a concept (B118), and on the contrary, where it is not an image (B119).

17 However, a key dimension to Kant's (1781/1787) analytic (as distinct from synthetic) claims is that of concept containment, which implies a prior spatial projection, 'Either the predicate B belongs to the subject A as somewhat which is contained (though covertly) in the conception A; or the predicate B lies completely out of the conception A ...' (B30). See also e.g., Anderson (2010) on containment in Kantian understanding of analytic claims.

(p. 178). This offers a promising commonality of concern with *a priori* spatial-phenomenological structures and image schemata. However, his argument appears to seek consistency with a Kantian *a priori*, even in its broadening to the body. In contrast, Johnson (1987) envisages the spatial structures of image schemata as challenging a Kantian *a priori*, through their being rooted in bodily experience. A spatial-phenomenological focus on concentric and diametric spaces in relation to a Kantian *a priori* accepts Johnson's position of challenging a Kantian *a priori* outside experience but relocates this challenge to ideas of purportedly pure reason, rather than simply Kantian categories. And it seeks to locate (at least an example of purportedly) pure reason against a spatial backdrop of projected structures of a primordial experience which is not all experience, nor reducible to all embodied experience.

Can image schemata, or a variant of them, challenge Kantian 'Ideas' of pure reason, through excavation of a domain of experience as underlying this purportedly pure reason? In other words, were a variant of image schemata to be uncovered as underlying any of Kant's antinomies of pure reason (prior to Kantian schemata and categories), this would undermine the purity of Kant's reason 'uncontaminated' by experience. Interaction between diametric and concentric spaces offers a framework for challenging traditional dualisms and thereby expanding Johnson's concern with *nondualism* into a *postdualism* framework; nondualism seeks to eliminate dualism, whereas postdualism offers paths towards recognition of diametric dualism to develop movement from them, towards concentric spaces.

It is perhaps significant that Johnson's challenge to dualism is allied with his rejection of Kantian pure reason outside experience – a Kantian realm of pure reason displays this necessary condition of dualism in his four antinomies. Seeking to move beyond dualism, through a postdualism rather than nondualism focus, requires not so much an *a priori* commitment to nondualism; it rather requires expression of the horizon of diametric spatial structures and then to challenge its inevitability through examination of possible movement towards concentric structures. A postdualistic approach requires engagement with Kant's prior level, the antinomies as pure ideas of his transcendental dialectic.

It is being argued that Kant's (1781) Third Antinomy of causality and freedom is not a primitive ground of pure ideas but is contingent on a prior projection – a diametric spatial projection. Key aspects of this argument can be restated more specifically:

- That the Third Antinomy of the Kantian Transcendental Dialectic regarding *a priori* ideas of pure reason involves a prior projection of a diametric spatial mirror image inversion. This occurs at the level of the described relation between freedom and causality.
- That the Kantian conception of cause-effect in the Third Antinomy assumes a prior diametric spatial projection (i) in the mirror image relation between cause and effect in an infinite causal sequence (additional to the inverted symmetrical structure of the antinomy itself), (ii) in the relative closure from background interaction of the cause-effect series that tends to exclude scrutiny of key background conditions sustaining the causal dynamic, and (iii) in the assumed separation between cause and effect.

Kant's (1781) antinomies of pure reason are expressed as a thesis and antithesis, for example, his Third Antinomy: Thesis – There are in the world causes through freedom. Antithesis – There is no freedom, but all is nature. The structure of this dialectic, this antinomy, is not itself characterized by Kant as a schema.[18] Kant, as seen, employs the term schema in a narrower sense. For Kant, both sides of the antinomy can be equally permitted to stand on their own terms.

In explicating his Third Antinomy, Kant (1781) outlines the well-known self-referential problem[19] of infinite regress in causal explanations

18 See Walsh (1967, p. 84) for an account that it is a symbol for Kant rather than a schema.

19 Moore (2010) identifies a different self-referential problem in Kant's synthetic *a priori* claims, 'Consider the very judgment that we have a synthetic *a priori* knowledge. This must itself, presumably, count as an item of synthetic *a priori* knowledge. And yet, precisely in registering the non-analytic character of the knowledge in question, does this not also have some claim to being, at least to that extent, the very thing that

for empirical realism, 'The causality of a cause, therefore, through which something takes place is itself an event which, again according to the law of nature, presupposes an anterior state and its causality, and this again an anterior state, and so on' (A474). According to the laws of nature, there will never be a 'first beginning' and the series is incomplete.[20] Kant (1781) thus asks about a counterpole to causality as part of this antinomy, 'is it not possible that empirical causality itself could nevertheless without in the least breaking its connection with natural causes, be an effect of a nonempirical, intelligible causality?' (A572). This proposed intelligible ground of a transcendental cause as freedom concerns 'thought in the pure understanding' (A574), where 'The causality of reason in its intelligible character does not arise or begin to be at a certain time in order to produce an effect; for in that case it would be subject to the natural law of appearances' (A580).

Kant (1781) treats freedom as a transcendental 'idea', as the counterpole to empirical causality:

> Reason, therefore, acts freely, without being determined dynamically in the chain of natural causes by external or internal conditions earlier in time. That freedom must then not only be regarded negatively, as independence of empirical conditions ... but should be defined positively also, as the power of beginning spontaneously a series of events. (A582)

Reason is not to be regarded as a 'concurrent agency only, but as complete in itself' (A583). On this view, reason is '*determining*, not *determined*' (A583) (italics in original).

Kant's Third Antinomy of pure ideas, namely, freedom and natural law, gives expression to the diametric structured mirror image symmetry, underlying Kant's whole framework of pure reason as antinomies. Transcendental idealism is viewed, by Kant, as coexisting with empirical realism in different domains, in a mirror image relation of inversion as antinomies in the transcendental dialectic. Postulating a prior background projection implies

---

an item of synthetic *a priori* knowledge supposedly cannot be – namely, a judgment about things in themselves?' (p. 325).

20 See Wood (2010) for a discussion of different kinds of infinite series and questioning if incompleteness is problematic.

a subversion of these mirror image inversions between transcendental idealism and empirical realism, and, for example, its Kantian application as transcendental freedom and empirical causality. The question arises as to how this more primordial truth than causality and diametric spatial projection can be apprehended in terms of a spatial-phenomenological approach to Kant's Third Antinomy between transcendental freedom and empirical causality. What is the relation between the 'appearance' of a cause-effect sequence (in its application to objects of sensibility) and primordial spatial phenomena?

Gillespie's (1984) description of Hegel's insight into chains of reciprocity of cause-effect bears reiteration in the context of Kant's infinite regress in his Third Antinomy:[21]

> Cause is formally differentiated from effect as the original and active element, the free element from which motion arises. Substantively, however, the cause is not distinguished from the effect and in fact is and can only be a cause in becoming an effect, just as the effect is and can only be an effect because it was a cause. The cause becomes the effect and the effect thus becomes the cause (of the next effect). Moreover, this transformation of each into its opposite, i.e., of cause into effect and of effect into cause, is necessary, for each only has meaning in relation to the other ... (p. 52–3)

In a causal series, this transformation of cause into effect is a *movement of inversion*. It is a diametric spatial projection of the entailment of this space as a mirror image inverted symmetry. The mirror image inversion between cause and effect infiltrates this whole cause-effect sequence,[22] as a kind of shadow-structure or whisper-structure, that is a necessary condition for the sequence rather than being epiphenomenal.

21 See also the Kantian (1787) Category of Relation, of Community, referring to reciprocity between the active and the passive. This is again a diametric mirror image inversion.

22 While it has already been recognized that Kant's analysis of the cause-effect relation was more complex than one model of relation, the account of chains of cause-effect relations above is pertinent to the issue of infinite causal regress as a sequence, as discussed in Kant's (1781) Third Antinomy.

An infinite series of cause-effect relations postulated in Kant's Third Antinomy rests somewhat surprisingly here on a limited conception of causality that tends to minimize or even negate the role of supporting and necessary conditions for any given aspect of the causal sequence. As discussed earlier, Mill (1872) highlights that every causal consequent is preceded by, not simply one antecedent, but a range of them. The antecedent background conditions buttressing the causal series of relations become filtered out in a view of cause-effect as a simple infinite regress. The causal chain is no longer envisaged as dynamically interacting with background conditions. It is this *dynamic interaction with background (conditions) that is resisted in the closed structure* of diametric space. Again the silent dominion of diametric spatial projection pervades traditional cause-effect sequences.

Though envisaged as *a priori* and not susceptible to empirical influences, nevertheless, a Kantian sequence of cause-effect in the antinomy tends to operate within a Newtonian billiard-ball conception of causality,[23] described by Toffler (1980):

> For Newton, causes were the 'forces impressed upon bodies to generate motion'. The conventional example of Newtonian cause and effect is the billiard balls that strike one another and move in response to one another. This notion of change, which focused exclusively on outside forces that are measurable and readily identifiable, was extremely powerful. (pp. 124–5)

Built into this cause-effect type of explanation (at least the Newtonian billiard ball type explanation) is the necessary condition of an assumed separation between cause and effect. It is the action of an external force upon the other; externality presupposes a basic and ongoing separation prior to and during the collision between the causal force and that which it acts upon. There is a diametric spatial projection of assumed separation built into the structure of cause-effect relations that rely on the action of external 'outside forces'; causality rests on a prior spatial frame of diametric relation of assumed separation between entities.

23 This is not to equate a Kantian understanding of space and causality generally with Newtonian theory (see e.g., Carrier 1992).

For the three entailments (mirror image symmetry, non-interactive closure from background, assumed separation), the diametric spatial structure accompanies each link in this causal chain, and not as a passenger, not as an epiphenomenon. Diametric space is a necessary condition for the cause-effect relation as an infinite regress. It governs the whole causal framework of the infinite regress in Kant's (1781) empirical causality. The malleability of this necessary condition is at issue. As a projected spatial structure framing the cause-effect relation, change to this necessary condition brings the potential to transport determined cause-effect relations into a more open dimension. It is not a question of a mirror image split for transcendental freedom in diametric assumed separation from empirical causality, as envisioned by Kant. A site for movement and alteration to a given series of cause-effect relations is opened up, in a spatial interplay implicating this necessary condition of diametric space. Diametric spatial projection is not the only possible trajectory, even as it underpins cause-effect sequences.

Does this whisper-structure dance? An interplay between diametric and concentric spatial projections, as a movement of the foundational necessary condition of diametric space gluing the cause-effect sequence, serves as a pathway for a different opening or freedom, compared to Kant's freedom as a transcendental cause of reason. This spatial-phenomenological movement is beyond freedom as reason. It moves to a conception of freedom as a potentiality for primordial experiential structural movement that operates as a background spatial condition framing modes of experience and framing cognitive choosing. Yet the movement itself between diametric and concentric spaces is much more fundamental than being itself a merely subjective cognitive choosing.

Movement of a supposedly foundational necessary condition for a given cause-effect sequence, radically unseats this sequence. Yet this deconstruction of the causal sequence is not a breaking of the diametric spatial necessary condition; it is a reconstruction of the diametric condition along a distinctive potential trajectory. The impact of moving this diametric spatial condition towards concentric spaces is a contextual one, for any given sequence. The impact is differential, it is not a homogeneity of impact, even if it is a common structural shift towards concentric space. If Kant's

Third Antinomy in the realm of pure ideas and the category of cause-effect are viewed as being along a plane of Kantian *a priori* claims as reason, the diametric spatial projection as the background to these claims (at least for these examples of Kantian antinomies and categories) can be examined in its potential dynamic movement and interplay with concentric spatial projections. As primordial experiential structures, they transcend the horizon of a Kantian *a priori* pure reason through their potentially dynamic spatial movement.

References

Adorno, T. (1973). *The jargon of authenticity*. Evanston: Northwestern University Press.

Ainsworth, M.D.S., Blehar, M.C., Waters, E., Wall, S. (1978). *Patterns of attachment.* Hillsdale, NJ: Erlbaum.

Alexandrian, S. (1970). *Surrealist art*. London: Thames & Hudson.

Alford, F. (1987). Habermas, post-Freudian psychoanalysis and the end of the individual. *Theory, Culture and Society*, 4, 3–29.

Allinson, R.E. (2002). *Space, time and the ethical foundations*. Aldershot: Ashgate.

Amaya, A. (2011). Legal justification by optimal coherence. *Ratio Juris*, 24, 304–29.

Anderson, J.R. (1996). ACT: A simple theory of complex cognition. *American Psychologist*, 51, 355–65.

Anderson, J.R. (2000). *Cognitive psychology and its implications.* 5th edn. New York: Worth.

Anderson, R.L. (2010). The introduction to the *Critique*: Framing the question. In P. Guyer (ed.), *The Cambridge companion to Kant's Critique of pure reason*, 75–92. New York: Cambridge University Press.

Appignanesi, L. & Forrester, J. (2005). *Freud's women*. London: Phoenix.

Arisaka, Y. (1995). Heidegger's theory of space: A critique of Dreyfus. *Inquiry*, 38, 455–67.

Aristotle. *Physics*. Trans. R. Waterfield. Oxford: Oxford University Press.

Bachelard, G. (1964). *The poetics of space*. Boston: Beacon Press, 1994.

Baddeley, A. (1990). *Human memory: Theory and practice.* London: Erlbaum.

Bair, D. (2004). *Jung: A biography*. London: Little, Brown.

Bakan, D. (1958). *Sigmund Freud and the Jewish mystical tradition*. New York: Dover Publications, 2004.

Ball, L.J., Evans, J. & Dennis, St. B.T. (1994). Cognitive processes in engineering design: a longitudinal study. *Ergonomics*, 37, 1753–86.

Barrow, J.D. (1990). *Theories of everything: The quest for ultimate explanation.* London: Vintage, 1992.

Barsalou, L.W. (1999). Perceptual symbol systems. *Behavioral and Brain Sciences*, *22*, 577–609.

Bartlett, F.C. (1932). *Remembering: A study in experimental and social psychology.* Cambridge: Cambridge University Press.

Beauvoir, de S. (1949). *The second sex*. New York: Vintage, 1989.

Beckett, S. (1983). *Disjecta: Miscellaneous writings and a dramatic fragment.* Ruby Cohn (ed.). London: John Calder.

Benhabib, S. (1987). The generalized and the concrete other: The Kohlbergian-Gilligan controversy and feminist theory. In S. Benhabib & D. Cornell (eds), *Feminism as critique.* Oxford: Basil Blackwell.

Bentham, J. An introduction to the principles of morals and legislation. In M.D.A. Freeman (ed.), *Lloyd's introduction to jurisprudence*, 6th edn. 1996, 229–32. London: Sweet & Maxwell.

Berlin, B. (1974). Further notes on covert categories and folk taxonomies: A reply to Brown. *American Anthropologist*, 76, 327–9.

Berlin, B. (1978). Ethnobiological classification. In E. Rosch & B.B. Lloyd (eds), *Cognition and categorisation.* Hillsdale: Lawrence Erlbaum.

Bettelheim, B. (1983). *Freud and man's soul.* London: Hogarth Press.

Bhaskar, R. (1989). *Reclaiming reality: A critical introduction to contemporary philosophy*. London: Verso.

Bhattacharyya, N.N. (1999). *History of the Tantric religion.* Second Revised Edition. New Delhi: Manohar.

Białostocki, J. (1966). Les Primitifs Flamands, I. *Corpus de la peinture des ancien Pays Bas Meridionaux au quinzième siècle 9.* Les Musem de Pologne (Gdańsk, Kraków, Waszawa), Bruxelles.

Białostocki, J. (1970). Sąd Ostateczny' Hansa Memlinga. Spostrzeżenie i analizy w oparciu o badania technologiczne. *Rocznik Historii Sztuki*, t. VIII.

Billig, M. (1987). *Arguing and thinking: A rhetorical approach to social psychology*. 2nd edn, 1996. Cambridge: Cambridge University Press.

Blattner, W. (2000). The primacy of practice and assertoric truth: Dewey and Heidegger. In M. Wrathall & J. Malpas (eds), *Heidegger, authenticity and modernity: Essays in honour of Hubert L. Dreyfus*, 231–50. MIT Press.

Blattner, W. (2007). Ontology, the a priori, and the primacy of practice: An aporia in Heidegger's early philosophy. In S. Crowell & J. Malpas (eds), *Transcendental Heidegger*, 10–27. California: Stanford University Press.

Boden, M. (1988). *Computer models of mind.* Cambridge: Cambridge University Press.

Bollas, C. (1999). Dead mother, dead child. In G. Kohon (ed.), *The dead mother: The work of Andre Green.* London: Routledge.

Boss, M. (1957). *Analysis of dreams.* London: Rider.

Boulton Smith, J. (1977). *Munch*. London: Phaidon Press.

Bourdieu, P. (1971). The Berber house. In M. Douglas (ed.), *Rules and meanings*, 1973, 98–110. Harmondsworth: Penguin.

Bower, G.H., Black, J.B. & Turner, T.J. (1979). Scripts in memory for texts. *Cognitive Psychology*, 11, 177–220.

Bowlby, J. (1973). *Separation: Anxiety and anger*. London: Pimlico, 1988.
Breger, L. (2009). *A dream of undying fame: How Freud betrayed his mentor and invented psychoanalysis*. New York: Basic Books.
Bretherton, I., Ridgeway, D. & Cassidy, J. (1990). Assessing internal working models of the attachment relationship: An attachment story completion task for 3-year-olds. In M. Greenberg, D. Cicchetti & M. Cummings (eds), *Attachment in the preschool years: Theory, research and intervention*, 273–308. Chicago: University of Chicago Press.
Breuer, J. & Freud, S. (1893a). *Preliminary communication*. SE 2, 11–13.
Brickman, C. (2003). *Aboriginal populations in the mind: Race and primitivity in psychoanalysis*. New York: Columbia University Press.
Brooke, R. (1991). *Jung and phenomenology*. London: Routledge.
Brooke, R. (2009). The self, psyche and the world: A phenomenological interpretation. *Journal of Analytical Psychology*, 54, 601–18.
Brown, L.M. & Gilligan, C. (1992). Meeting at the crossroads: Women's psychology and girls' development. Cambridge, Mass.: Harvard University Press.
Brumariu, L.E. & Kerns, K.A. (2010). Parent-child attachment and internalizing symptoms in childhood and adolescence: a review of empirical findings and future directions. *Development and Psychopathology*, 22, 177–203.
Bruner, J.S. (1990). *Acts of meaning*. Harvard University Press.
Buber, M. (1910). *Zhuangzi*. Leipzig, Insel-verlag.
Buber, M. (1923). *I and Thou*. 2nd edn. New York: Scribners, 1958.
Burman, E. (1994). *Deconstructing developmental psychology*. London: Routledge.
Buzzoni, M. (2001). The operationalistic and hermeneutic status of psychoanalysis. *Journal for General Philosophy of Science*, 32, 131–65.
Cambray, J. (2001). Enactments and amplification. *Journal of Analytical Psychology*, 46, 275–303.
Cambray, J. (2002). Synchronicity and emergence. *American Imago*, 59, 409–34.
Carman, T. (1994). On being social: A reply to Olafson. *Inquiry* 37, 203–23.
Caropreso, F. & Simanke, R.T. (2008). Life and death in Freudian metapsychology: A reappraisal of the second instinctual dualism. *International Journal of Psychoanalysis*, 89, 977–92.
Carr, D. (2007). Heidegger on Kant on transcendence. In S. Crowell & J. Malpas (eds), *Transcendental Heidegger*, 28–42. California: Stanford University Press.
Carrier, M. (1992). Kant's relational theory of absolute space. *Kant Studien*, 83, 399–416.
Cassidy, J. (1994). Emotion regulation: Influences on attachment relationships. In N.A. Fox (ed.), *The development of emotion regulation: Biological and behavioral considerations*. Monographs of the Society for Research in Child Development. Vol. 59. (Serial No. 240).

Caton, S.C. (1987). Contributions of Roman Jakobsen. *Annual Review of Anthropology*, 16, 223–60.

Charness, N. (1991). Expertise in chess: The balance between knowledge and search. In K.A. Ericsson & J. Smith (eds), *Toward a general theory of expertise: Prospects and limits*, 39–63. Cambridge: Cambridge University Press.

Chase, W.G. & Simon, H.A. (1973). Perception in chess. *Cognitive Psychology*, 4, 55–81.

Chi, M.T.H., Feltovich, P.J. & Glaser, R. (1981). Categorization and representation of physics problems by experts and novices. *Cognitive Science*, 5, 121–52.

Conquergood, D. (1994). For the nation: How street gangs problematize patriotism. In H.W. Simons & M.Billig (eds), *After postmodernism: Reconstructing ideology critique*. London: Sage.

Costall, A. (1991). Frederic Bartlett and the rise of prehistoric psychology. In A. Still & A. Costall (eds), *Against cognitivism: Alternative foundations for cognitive psychology*, 39–54. Hemel Hempstead: Harvester Wheatsheaf.

Coupe, L. (1989). Freud's interpretation of dreams and modern hermeneutics. In L. Spurling (ed.), *Sigmund Freud: Critical approaches*, Vol. III, 340–53. London: Routledge.

Crowell, S. (2000). Metaphysics, metontology, and the end of *Being and Time*. *Philosophy and Phenomenological Research*, LX, 307–32.

Crowell, S. (2007). Conscience and reason: Heidegger and the grounds of intentionality. In S. Crowell & J. Malpas (eds), *Transcendental Heidegger*, 43–62. California: Stanford University Press.

Coleman, J. (2001). Incorporationism, conventionality and the practical difference thesis. In J. Coleman (ed.), *Hart's postscript: Essays on the Postscript to the Concept of Law*, 99–148. Oxford: Oxford University Press.

Culler, J. (1975). *Structuralist poetics: Structuralism, linguistics and the study of literature*. London: Routledge, 2002.

Culler, J. (1976). *Saussure*. London: Fontana.

Cushing, J.T. (1991). Quantum theory and explanatory discourse: Endgame for understanding? *Philosophy of Science*, 58, 337–58.

D'Aquili, E. (1975). The influence of Jung on the work of Claude Lévi-Strauss. *Journal of the History of the Behavioral Sciences*, 11, 41–8.

Dahlstrom, D. (2010). The critique of pure reason and continental philosophy: Heidegger's interpretation of transcendental imagination. In P. Guyer (ed.), *The Cambridge companion to Kant's Critique of pure reason*, 380–400. New York: Cambridge University Press.

Dalal, A.K. & Misra, G. (2010). The core and context of Indian psychology. *Psychology and Developing Societies*, 22, 121–55.

Davies, S. (1994). Knowledge restructuring and the acquisition of programming expertise. *International Journal of Human-Computer Studies*, 40, 703–26.

Derrida, J. (1972). *Margins of Philosophy*. Trans. A. Bass. Chicago: University of Chicago Press, 1982.

Derrida, J. (1973). *Speech and phenomena and other essays on Husserl's theory of signs*. Trans. D. Allison. Evanston: Northwestern University Press.

Derrida, J. (1974). *Of grammatology*. London-Baltimore: John Hopkins University Press.

Derrida, J. (1978). *Writing and difference*. Trans. A. Bass. London: Routledge & Kegan Paul, 1981.

Derrida, J. (1981). Deconstruction and the Other. In R. Kearney, *States of mind: Dialogues with contemporary thinkers in the European mind*. Manchester: Manchester University Press, 1995.

Derrida, J. (1988/1990). Heidegger's silence. In G. Neske & E. Kettering (eds), *Martin Heidegger and National Socialism*. 1990 New York: Paragon House.

Derrida, J. (1995). *Points ... Interviews, 1974–1994*, E. Weber (ed.). Trans P. Kamuf. Stanford, Stanford University Press.

Derrida, J. (1996). *Archive fever: A Freudian impression*. Trans E. Prenowitz, Chicago: University of Chicago Press.

Derrida, J. (1996a). *The gift of death*. Trans. D. Wills. Chicago: University of Chicago Press.

Descartes, R. (1954). *Descartes: Philosophical writings*. Trans. E. Anscombe & P.T. Geach. London: Nelson.

Donnet, J.L. & Green, A. (1973). *L'enfant de ca. La psychose blanche*. Paris: Editions de Minuit.

Dooley, L. (1941). The concept of time in defence of ego integrity. *Psychiatry*, 4, 13.

Donnelly, J. (1990). Traditional values and universal human rights: Caste in India. In C.E. Welch & V.A. Leary (eds), *Asian perspectives on human rights*, 55–90. Oxford: Westview.

Downes, P. (2003). Cross-cultural structures of concentric and diametric dualism in Lévi-Strauss' structural anthropology: Structures of relation underlying the self and ego relation? *Journal of Analytical Psychology*, 48, 47–81.

Downes, P. (2003a). *Living with heroin: Identity, social exclusion and HIV among the Russian-speaking minorities in Estonia and Latvia*. Tallinn: Legal Information Centre for Human Rights.

Downes, P. (2003b). The relevance of early Heidegger's radical conception of transcendence to choice, freedom and technology. In M. Breen, E. Conway, B. McMillan (eds), *Technology and transcendence*. Dublin: Columba Press.

Downes, P. (2004). School promoted beauty contests in Poland and Estonia: A risk factor for anorexia and bulimia nervosa, and contrary to the UN Convention on the elimination of all forms of discrimination against Women? *Kwartalnik Pedagogiczny*, 193, 125–43.

Downes, P. (2004a). *Voices of children: St. Raphaels primary school, Ballyfermot.* Dublin: URBAN, Ballyfermot.

Downes, P. (2005). Review of 'Space, Time and the Ethical Foundations', by R.A. Allinson, *The Philosopher*, LXXXXIII, 20–1.

Downes, P. (2006). Newtonian space: The 'blind spot' in Newell and Simon's information processing paradigm. *Cybernetics and Human Knowing*, 13, 25–55.

Downes, P. (2007). Intravenous drug use and HIV in Estonia: Socio-economic integration and development of indicators regarding the right to health for its Russian-speaking population. *Liverpool Law Review*, 28, 271–317.

Downes, P. (2007a). Why SMART outcomes ain't always so smart ... In P. Downes & A-L. Gilligan (eds), *Beyond educational disadvantage*, 57–69. Dublin: Institute of Public Administration.

Downes, P. (2008). The international right to the highest attainable standard of physical and mental health: A key legal framework for human trafficking? In P. Downes, A. Zule-Lapimaa, L. Ivanchenko & S. Blumberg (eds), *Not one victim more: Human trafficking in the Baltic States*, 278–89. Tallinn: Living for Tomorrow.

Downes, P. (2009). Prevention of bullying at a systemic level in schools: Movement from cognitive and spatial narratives of diametric opposition to concentric relation. In S.R. Jimerson, S.M. Swearer, D.L. Espelage (eds), *Handbook of bullying in schools: An international perspective*, 517–33. New York: Routledge.

Downes, P. (2009a). Cultural conformity within Vygotsky's paradigm for education: A critique from the perspective of early Heidegger. *Kwartalnik Pedagogiczny*, 212, 97–114.

Downes, P. (2010). Newtonian space in Newell and Simon: Reply to Kinsella's (2008) response to Downes (2006). *Cybernetics and Human Knowing* 17: 191–200.

Downes, P. (2010). Schema structure-content relativity: Part II, From image schemata to background spatial schemata of diametric and concentric relation. *Cybernetics and Human Knowing*, 17, 25–43.

Downes, P. (2011). Concentric and diametric structures in *yin/yang* and the mandala symbol: A new wave of Eastern frames for psychology. *Psychology and Developing Societies*, 23, 121–53.

Downes, P. & Gilligan, A-L. (eds) (2007). *Beyond educational disadvantage*. Dublin: Institute of Public Administration.

Downes, P. & Maunsell, C. (2007). *Count us in: Tackling early school leaving in South West Inner City Dublin, An integrated response*. Dublin: South Inner City Community Development Association (SICCDA).
Downes, P., Zule-Lapimaa, A., Ivanchenko, L. & Blumberg, S. (eds), *Not one victim more: Human trafficking in the Baltic States* (2008). Tallinn: Living for Tomorrow.
Downes, T. (1993). *Pedagogy of the processed*. MA thesis, NUI Maynooth.
Downes, T. & Downes, P. (2007). *Pedagogy of the processed*. In P. Downes & A-L. Gilligan (eds), *Beyond educational disadvantage*, 24–38. Dublin: Institutute of Public Administration.
Dostal, R.J. (2006). Time and phenomenology in Husserl and Heidegger. In C. Guignon (ed.), *The Cambridge companion to Heidegger* (2nd edn). Cambridge: Cambridge University Press.
Dreyfus, H.L & Rabinow, P. (1982). *Michel Foucault: Beyond structuralism and hermeneutics*. New York: Harvester Wheatsheaf.
Dreyfus, H.L. (1991). *Being-in-the World: A commentary on Heidegger's Being and Time Division I*. MIT Press.
Dreyfus, H.L. (2000). Responses. In M. Wrathall & J. Malpas (eds), *Heidegger, authenticity and modernity: Essays in honour of Hubert L. Dreyfus*, 305–41. MIT Press.
Duhem, P. (1905/1954). *The aim and structure of physical theory*. Trans. P.P. Wiener. Princeton, NJ: Princeton University Press.
Eagleton, T. (1990). *Ideology of the aesthetic*. Oxford: Blackwell.
Eagleton, T. (1995). *Heathcliff and the Great Hunger: Studies in Irish culture*. London: Verso.
Eckardt, von B. (1993). *What is cognitive science?* Cambridge MA: MIT Press.
Edinger, E. (1972). *Ego and archetype: Individuation and the religious function of the psyche*. Baltimore: Penguin, 1974.
Eggum, A. (1998). Edvard Munch as a painter. In *Munch at the Munch Museum, Oslo*. Oslo: Scala Books, The Munch Museum.
Eigen, M. (1986). *The psychotic core*. London: Karnac Books, 2004.
Eigen, M. (1996). *Psychic deadness*. London: Karnac Books, 2004.
Einstein, A. (1954). *Ideas and opinions*. Trans. S. Barmann. New York: Bonanza Books.
Elden, S. (2001). *Mapping the present: Heidegger, Foucault and the project of a spatial history*. London: Continuum.
Ellen, R. (1977). Anatomical classification and the semiotics of the body. In J. Blacking (ed.), *The anthropology of the body*. London: Academic Press.
Ericsson, K.A & Simon, H.A. (1993). *Protocol analysis: Verbal reports as data*. Cambridge: MIT Press.
Erikson, E.H (1968). *Identity: Youth and crisis*. London: Faber & Faber.
Erricker, C. (1995). *Buddhism: An introduction*. London: Hachette, UK.

Ewing, E. (1995). Authenticity in Heidegger: A response to Dreyfus. *Inquiry* 38, 4, 469–87.

Eysenck, M.W. & Keane, M.T. (1990). *Cognitive psychology: A student's handbook* (1st edn). London: Erlbaum.

Farias, V. (1989). *Heidegger and nazism*. Philadelphia: Temple University Press.

Fechner, G.T. (1873). *Einige Ideen zur Schopfungs und Entwickelungsgeschichte der Organismen*. Leipzig: Breitkopf und Hartel.

Feyerabend, P. (1975). *Against method*. Revised edition. London: Verso, 1988.

Fingleton, L. (2003). *ListenB4ILeave: Early school leavers in the Canal Communities area and their experiences of school*. Dublin: Canal Communities Partnership.

Fisher, S. & Greenberg, R.P. (1996). *Freud scientifically reappraised: Testing the theories and therapy*. New York: Wiley.

Fletcher, G. and Haig, B. (1989). *The layperson as 'naive scientist': An appropriate model for personality and social psychology*. Unpublished paper, University of Canterbury, New Zealand.

Fodor, J.A. (1976). *The language of thought*. Hassocks, Sussex: Harvester Press.

Fogarty, A. (1995). Gender, Irish modernism and the poetry of Denis Devlin. In P. Coghlan & A. Davis (eds), *Modernism and Ireland: The poetry of the 1930s*, 209–31. Cork: Cork University Press.

Follesdahl, D. (2001). Hermeneutics. *International Journal of Psychoanalysis*, 82, 375–9.

Fordham, M. (1963). The empirical foundation and theories of the self in Jung's works. In M. Fordham, R. Gordon, J. Hubback, K. Lambert, M. Williams (eds), *Analytic psychology: A modern science*. London: Academic Press 1980.

Fordham, M. (1974). Defences of the self. *Journal of Analytical Psychology*, 19, 192–9.

Fordham, M. (1978/1986). *Jungian psychotherapy: A study in analytical psychology*. London: Karnac Books.

Fordham, M. (1985). Explorations into the self. *The Library of Analytical Psychology, Vol. 7*, M. Fordham, R. Gordon, J. Hubback & K. Lambert (eds). London: Academic Press.

Fordham, M. (1994). *Children as individuals*. London: Free Association Books.

Foucault, M. (1972). *History of madness*. J. Khalfa (ed.). London & New York: Routledge, 2006.

Foucault, M. (1972a). Reply to Derrida. In M. Foucault *History of madness*, Appendix III, J. Khalfa (ed.). London: Routledge, 2006.

Foucault, M. (1977). *Discipline and punish: The birth of the prison*. Trans. A. Sheridan. London: Penguin.

Foucault, M. (1978). *The history of sexuality*, Vol. 1, An Introduction. Trans. R. Hurley. London: Penguin.

Frankl, V. (1959). *Man's search for meaning*. Boston: Beacon Press.

Freeman, D. & Garety, P.A. (2003). Connecting neurosis and psychosis: The direct influence of emotion on delusions and hallucinations. *Behaviour Research and Therapy*, 41, 923–47.
Freeman, L. (2011). Reconsidering relational autonomy: A feminist approach to selfhood and the other in the thinking of Martin Heidegger. *Inquiry*, 54, 361–83.
Freud, S. (1896). *Further remarks on the neuro-psychoses of defence*. SE 3: 159–85.
Freud, S. (1900). *The interpretation of dreams*. SE 4.
Freud, S. (1909d). *Notes upon a case of obsessional neurosis*. SE 10, 155.
Freud, S. (1911c). *Psycho-analytic notes on an autobiographical account of a case of paranoia (Dementia Paranoides)*. SE 12: 3–79.
Freud, S. (1910a). *Five lectures on psycho-analysis*. SE 11: 3–55.
Freud, S. (1911/2002). *The Schreber case*. Trans. A. Webber. London: Penguin.
Freud, S. (1912–13). *Totem and taboo*. SE 13: 1–161.
Freud, S. (1914). *History of the psycho-analytic movement*. SE 14: 11.
Freud, S. (1914c). *On narcissism: An introduction*. SE 14: 67–102.
Freud, S. (1915). *The unconscious*. SE 14: 161–204.
Freud, S. (1915c). *Instincts and their vicissitudes*. SE 14: 117–40.
Freud, S. (1916–1917). *Introductory lectures on psycho-analysis*, Part 3. SE 16.
Freud, S. (1919e). *'A child is being beaten': A contribution to the study of the origin of sexual perversions*. SE 17: 177–204.
Freud, S. (1920). *Beyond the pleasure principle*. SE 18.
Freud, S. (1921c). *Group psychology and the analysis of the ego*. SE 18: 65–143.
Freud, S. (1923). *The ego and the id*. SE 19: 3–59.
Freud, S. (1924). *The economic problem of masochism*. SE 19: 155–70.
Freud, S. (1924). *Neurosis and psychosis*. SE 19: 149–56.
Freud, S. (1925). *A note upon the 'mystic writing pad'.* SE 19: 227–34.
Freud, S. (1925). *An autobiographical study*. SE 20: 7–74.
Freud, S. (1926). *Inhibitions, symptoms and anxiety*. SE 20: 77–172.
Freud, S. (1930). *Civilization and its discontents*. SE 21: 64–145.
Freud, S. (1933a). *New introductory lectures on psychoanalysis*. SE 22: 1–182.
Freud, S. (1937). *Analysis terminable and interminable*. SE 23: 209–53.
Freud, S. (1939a). *Moses and monotheism: Three essays*. SE 23: 3–137.
Freud, S. (1940). *Splitting of the ego in the process of defence*. SE 23: 271–5.
Freud, S. & Breuer, J. (1895d). *Studies on hysteria*. SE 2: 48–106.
Freud, S. (1974). *The Freud/Jung letters*. W. McGuire (ed.). Trans. R. Manheim & R.F.C. Hull. London: Hogarth Press.
Frith, C.D. & Done, D.J. (1989). Towards a neuropsychology of schizophrenia. *British Journal of Psychiatry*, 153, 437–43.
Fromm, E. (1942). *The fear of freedom*. London: Routledge.

Fromm, E. (1959). *Sigmund Freud's mission: An analysis of his personality and influence.* London: Bradford & Dickens.
Fromm, E. (1977). *Anatomy of human destructiveness.* Harmondsworth: Penguin.
Frosh, S. (2006). *For and against psychoanalysis.* London: Routledge, 2nd edn.
Garfinkel, H. (1967). *Studies in ethnomethodology.* Englewood Cliffs, NJ: Prentice Hall.
Gellner, E. (1981). General introduction: Relativism and universals. In B. Lloyd & J. Gray (eds), *Introduction to universals of human thought: Some African evidence.* Cambridge University Press.
Gergen, K.J. (1973). Social psychology as history. *Journal of Personality and Social Psychology* 26, 309–20.
Gergen, K.J. (1992). Toward a postmodern psychology. In S. Kvale (ed.), *Psychology and postmodernism.* London: Sage.
Gergen, K.J. (1994). *Toward transformation in social knowledge.* 2nd edn. London: Sage.
Gergen, K.J. (1994a). The limits of pure critique. In H.W. Simons & M. Billig (eds), *After postmodernism: Reconstructing ideology critique.* London: Sage Publications.
Gergen, K.J. (2000). *The saturated self: Dilemmas of identity in contemporary life.* New York: Basic Books.
Gergen, K.J. (2009). *Relational being: Beyond self and community.* Oxford: Oxford University Press.
Gergen, K.J., Gulerce, A., Lock, A. & Misra, G. (1996). Psychological science in cultural context. *American Psychologist,* 51, 496–503.
Gibbs, R.W. (1993). Process and products in making sense of tropes. In A. Ortony (ed.), *Metaphor and thought.* Cambridge: Cambridge University Press.
Gibson, J.J. (1966). *The senses considered as perceptual systems.* Boston: Houghton Mifflin.
Gillespie, M.A. (1984). *Hegel, Heidegger and the ground of history.* University of Chicago Press.
Gilligan, C. (1982). *In a different voice.* Cambridge, Mass.: Harvard University Press.
Gilligan, C. (1986). Reply. *Signs,* 11, 324–33.
Gilligan, C. (1988). Prologue: Adolescent development reconsidered. (vii–xxxix). In C. Gilligan, J.C. Ward, J. McLean Taylor, B. Bardige (eds), *Mapping the moral domain: A contribution of women's thinking to psychological theory and education.* Cambridge, Mass.: Harvard University Press.
Gilligan, C. (1988a). Remapping the moral domain: New images of self in relationship (3–20). In C. Gilligan, J.C. Ward, J. McLean Taylor, B. Bardige (eds), *Mapping the moral domain: A contribution of women's thinking to psychological theory and education.* Cambridge, Mass.: Harvard University Press.
Gilligan, C. (1988b). Exit-voice dilemmas in adolescent development. In C. Gilligan, J.C. Ward, J. McLean Taylor, B. Bardige (eds), *Mapping the moral domain:*

A contribution of women's thinking to psychological theory and education, 141–58. Cambridge, Mass.: Harvard University Press.

Gilligan, C. (1990). Preface. In C. Gilligan, N.P. Lyons & T.J. Hanmer (eds), *Making connections*. Cambridge, Mass.: Harvard University Press.

Gilligan, C. (2011). *Joining the resistance*. Cambridge: Polity Press.

Gilligan, C. & Attanucci, J. (1988). Two moral orientations. In C. Gilligan, J.C. Ward, J. McLean Taylor, B. Bardige (eds), *Mapping the moral domain: A contribution of women's thinking to psychological theory and education*, 73–86. Cambridge, Mass.: Harvard University Press.

Gilligan, C, Lyons, N.P. & Hanmer, T.J. (1990). *Making connections*. Cambridge, Mass.: Harvard University Press.

Gordon, R. (1985/1992). Losing and finding: The location of archetypal experience. In R.K. Papadopoulos (ed.), *Carl Gustav Jung: Critical assessments*, Vol. II. London: Routledge.

Green, A. (1983). The dead mother. In A.Green, *On Private Madness*. London: The Hogarth Press and the Institute of Psychoanalysis, 1986, 222–53.

Green, A. (1999). The Greening of psychoanalysis: Andre Green in dialogues with Gregorio Kohon. In G. Kohon (ed.), *The dead mother: The work of Andre Green*. London: Routledge.

Green, A.J.K. & Gilhooly, K.J. (1992). Empirical advances in expertise research. In M.T. Keane & K.J. Gilhooly (eds), *Advances in the psychology of thinking*, 45–70. New York-London: Harvester Wheatsheaf.

Groebner, V. (1999). *Inside out: Dissimulation, and the arts of accounting in the autobiography of Matthäus Schwarz, 1496–1574*. Representations, LXVI, s. 104.

Groot, de A. (1946). *Thought and choice in chess*. 1978. The Hague: Mouton.

Grünbaum, A. (1984). *The foundations of psychoanalysis: A philosophical critique*. Berkeley: University of California Press.

Grünbaum, A. (1986). Précis of 'The foundations of psychoanalysis: A philosophical critique'. *Behavioral and Brain Sciences*, 9, 217–84.

Grünbaum, A. (1994). *Psychoanalytic theory and therapy after 100 years, and its future*. Geneva: Fondation Latsis Internationale.

Grünbaum, A. (1998). A century of psychoanalysis: Critical retrospect and prospect. In M.S. Roth (ed.), *Freud conflict and culture*. In association with the Library of Congress. New York: Knopf.

Grünbaum, A. (2006). Is Sigmund Freud's psychoanalytic edifice relevant to the 21st century? *Psychoanalytic Psychology*, 23, 257–84.

Guignon, C.B. (1983). *Heidegger and the problem of knowledge*. Indianapolis: Hackett Publishing.

Guignon, C. (2006). Authenticity, moral values and psychotherapy. In C. Guignon (ed.), *The Cambridge companion to Heidegger*, 2nd edn, 268–92. Cambridge: Cambridge University Press.

Guyer, P. (2010). The deduction of the categories: The metaphysical and transcendental deductions. In P. Guyer (ed.), *The Cambridge companion to Kant's Critique of pure reason*, 118–50. New York: Cambridge University Press.

Gyatso, G.K. (2001). *Introduction to Buddhism: An explanation of the Buddhist way of life*. 2nd edn. Ulverston, UK: Tharpa publications.

Habermas, J. (1972). *Knowledge and human interests*. Cambridge: Polity Press, 2007.

Habermas, J. (1987). *The philosophical discourse of modernity*. Cambridge: Polity Press.

Harley, T.A. (2001). *The psychology of language: From data to theory*. 2nd edn. Hove, UK: Psychology Press.

Harre, R.& Gillett, G. (1994).*The discursive mind*. London: Sage.

Hart, H.L.A. (1954). Definition and theory in jurisprudence. *Law Quarterly Review*, 70, 37–60.

Hart, H.L.A. (1961). *The concept of law*. Oxford: Oxford University Press.

Hauke, C. (2000). *Jung and the postmodern: The interpretation of realities*. London: Routledge.

Hayman, R. (1999). *A life of Jung*. London: Bloomsbury.

Hearnshaw, L.S. (1987). *The shaping of modern psychology*. New York: Routledge.

Hegel, G.W.F. (1830/1831). *The philosophy of history*. New York: Dover Publications 1956.

Heidegger, M. (1919/2000). The idea of philosophy and the problem of worldviews. Kriegsnotsemester (KNS). In Martin Heidegger, *Towards the definition of philosophy*. Trans. T. Sadler. London: Athlone Press.

Heidegger, M. (1920). *Phenomenology of intuition and expression: Theory of philosophical concept formation*. Summer Semester 1920. Trans. T. Colony, 2010. London: Continuum.

Heidegger, M. (1924). *The concept of time*. Trans. by W. McNeill. Blackwell Publishers 1992.

Heidegger, M. (1927). Letter to Karl Lowith (20 August 1927). In *Zur Philosophischen Aktualitat Heideggers*, vol. II (ed.) D. Pappenfuss and O. Poggeler. Frankfurt: Vittorio Klostermann.

Heidegger, M. (1927). *Being and Time*. Trans. J. MacQuarrie & E. Robinson, 1962. Oxford: Basil Blackwell.

Heidegger, M. (1927a/1982). The basic problems of phenomenology. Trans. Albert Hofstadter Bloomington: Indiana University Press.

Heidegger, M. (1928/1984). *Metaphysical foundations of logic*. Trans. M. Heim. Bloomington: Indiana University Press.

Heidegger, Martin. (1929/1993). *What is metaphysics?* In *Basic writings*, D.F. Krell (ed.). New York: Harper Collins.
Heidegger, M. (1949). *Uber den Humanismus*. Frankfurt am Main: Klostermann, 1975.
Heidegger, M. (1972). *On time and being*. Trans. J. Stambaugh. New York: Harper & Row.
Hellberg-Hirn, E. (1998). *Soil and soul: The symbolic world of Russianness*. London: Ashgate.
Henderson, J.L. (1964). Ancient myths and modern man. In C.G. Jung (ed.), *Man and his symbols*. New York: Laurel.
Henrich, D. (1994). *The unity of reason: Essays on Kant's philosophy*. Cambridge, Mass.: Harvard University Press.
Hofstadter, D.R. (1979). *Godel, Escher, Bach: An eternal golden braid*. New York: Basic Books.
Hofstadter, D.R. (1985). *Metamagical themas: Quests for the essence of mind and pattern*. New York: Basic Books.
Hoffmann, W. (1985). Das Fleisch erkennen. In A. Pfabigan (ed.), *Ornament und Askese im Zeitkeist des Wien der Jahrhundertwende*, Vienna. Trans. G. Fliedl, in *Gustav Klimt 1862–1918: The world in female form*. London, LA: Taschen, 2006.
Hogenson, G.B. (1994). *Jung's struggle with Freud*. Illinois: Chiron Publications.
Hohmann, J.M. (2010). Visions of social transformation and the invocation of human rights in Mumbai: The struggle for the right to housing. *Yale Human Rights and Development Law Journal*, 13, 135–84.
Holbrook, D. (1971). *Human hope and the death instinct*. Oxford: Pergamon Press.
Holyoak, K.J. (1995). Problem solving. In E.E. Smith & D. Osherson (eds), *An invitation to cognitive science. Vol. 3. Thinking*, 2nd edn. Cambridge MA: MIT Press.
Homer. *The Odyssey*. Trans. G. Chapman (2002). Hertfordshire: Wordsworth Editions.
Hume, D. (1777). Enquiry concerning human understanding. In *Enquiries concerning human understanding and concerning the principles of morals*. L.A. Selby-Bigge (ed.), 3rd edn. Revised by P.H. Nidditch. Oxford: Clarendon Press, 1975.
Husserl, E. (1900–1901). *Logical investigations*. Trans. J.N. Findlay. New York: Humanities, 1970.
Inada, K.K. (1990). A Buddhist response to the nature of human rights (91–103). In C.E. Welch & V.A. Leary (eds), *Asian perspectives on human rights*. Oxford: Westview Press.
Ivers, J. & Downes, P. (2012). A phenomenological reinterpretation of Horner's fear of success in terms of social class. *European Journal of Psychology of Education*, 27, 369–88.
Jahoda, G. (1982). *Psychology and anthropology: A psychological perspective*. London: Academic Press.

Jakobsen, R. (1973). *The science of language.* London: William Clowes Ltd.
James, W. (1890). *The principles of psychology*. New York: Holt.
Jameson, F. (1991). *Postmodernism: Or the cultural logic of late capitalism.* London: Verso.
Johnson, M. (1987). *The body in the mind.* Chicago: University of Chicago Press.
Johnson, M. (2007). *The meaning of the body: Aesthetics of human understanding.* Chicago: University of Chicago Press.
Johnson-Laird, P.N. (1983). *Mental models*. Cambridge: Cambridge University Press.
Johnson-Laird, P.N. & Byrne, R.M.J. (1991). *Deduction*. Hove and Hillsdale: Erlbaum.
Johnston, D.K. (1988). Adolescents' solutions to dilemmas in fables: Two moral orientations-two problem solving strategies. In C. Gilligan, J.C. Ward, J. McLean Taylor, B. Bardige (eds), *Mapping the moral domain: A contribution of women's thinking to psychological theory and education*, 49–72. Cambridge, Mass.: Harvard University Press.
Jones, E. (1957). *The life and work of Sigmund Freud. Vol. 3: The last phase, 1919–1939*. London: Hogarth Press.
Jung, C.G. (1911–12/1952). *Symbols of transformation*. C.W. 5.
Jung, C.G. (1907). *The psychology of dementia praecox*. C.W. 3.
Jung, C.G. (1914). *On psychological understanding.* C.W. 3.
Jung, C.G. (1916a). *The transcendent function*. C.W. 8.
Jung, C.G. (1916b). Adaptation, individuation, collectivity. In *The Symbolic Life*. C.W. 18.
Jung, C.G. (1921). *Psychological types*. C.W. 6.
Jung, C.G. (1928). On Psychic Energy. In *On the nature of the psyche.* Guernsey: Guernsey Press, 1969.
Jung, C.G. (1928a). *Contributions of Analytical Psychology*. Trans. H.G. and C.F. Baynes. New York: Harcourt, Brace.
Jung, C.G. (1929). Commentary on 'The secret of the golden flower'. *Alchemical studies*. C.W. 13.
Jung, C.G. (1931). *The aims of psychotherapy*. C.W. 16.
Jung, C.G. (1934/1954). Archetypes of the collective unconscious. In C.G. Jung, *The Archetypes and the Collective Unconscious.* C.W. 9 Part I.
Jung, C.G. (1935a). Psychological commentary on 'The Tibetan book of the dead'. In *Psychology and Religion: East and West.* C.W. 11.
Jung, C.G. (1935b). Tavistock Lectures. In *Analytical psychology: Its theory and practice*. London: Ark.
Jung, C.G. (1936). Individual dream symbolism in relation to alchemy. In C.G. Jung, *Dreams*. London: Ark, 1985.

Jung, C.G. (1938). Psychological aspects of the mother archetype. In C.G. Jung, *Aspects of the Feminine*. London: Ark, 1986.
Jung, C.G. (1939). What India can teach us. In *Psychology and Religion: West and East*. C.W. 11.
Jung, C.G. (1939). Foreward to Suzuki's 'Introduction to Zen Buddhism'. In *Psychology and Religion: West and East*. C.W. 11.
Jung, C.G. (1939b). *On the psychogenesis of schizophrenia*. C.W. 3.
Jung, C.G. (1941–1954). *Mysterium Coniunctionis*. C.W. 14.
Jung, C.G. (1942/1948). A psychological approach to the dogma of the Trinity. In *Psychology and Religion: West and East*. C.W. 11.
Jung, C.G. (1943). The psychology of Eastern meditation. In C.G. Jung *Psychology and Religion: West and East*. C.W. 11.
Jung, C.G. (1944/1952). *Psychology and alchemy*. C.W. 12.
Jung, C.G. (1946). Analytical psychology and education. In C.G. Jung, *The Development of Personality*. C.W. 17.
Jung, C.G. (1948). *On the Nature of the Psyche*. Guernsey: Guernsey Press, 1969.
Jung, C.G. (1948). General aspects of dream psychology. In C.G. Jung, *Dreams*. London: Ark edition, 1985.
Jung, C.G. (1941–1954). *Mysterium Coniunctionis*. C.W. 14.
Jung, C.G. (1951). *Aion*. C.W. 9. Part II.
Jung, C.G. (1952). *Synchronicity: An acausal connecting principle*. C.W. 8.
Jung, C.G. (1952). Individual dream symbolism in relation to alchemy. In C.G. Jung, *Dreams*. London: Ark edition 1985.
Jung, C.G. (1954). *The practice of psychotherapy*. C.W. 16. New York: Pantheon Books.
Jung, C.G. (1959). *Flying saucers: A modern myth of things seen in the sky*. London: Ark Books.
Jung, C.G. (1964). Approaching the unconscious. In C.G. Jung (ed.), *Man and his symbols*. New York: Laurel.
Jung, C.G. (1975). *Letters*. 2 vols (eds) G. Adler & A. Jaffe. Princeton, NJ: Princeton University Press.
Jung, C.G. (2001). *Atom and archetype: The Pauli-Jung letters 1932–1958*, C.A. Meier (ed.), Trans. D. Roscoe. London: Routledge.
Jung, H.J. (1987). Heidegger's way with Sinitic thinking. In G. Parke (ed.), *Heidegger and Asian thought*. 217–44. Honolulu: University of Hawaii Press.
Kagan, J. (1989). *Unstable ideas: Temperament, cognition and self*. Harvard University Press.
Kahn-Freund, O. (1974). On uses and misuses of comparative law. *Modern Law Review*, 37, 1–27.
Kahn-Freund, O. (1977). *Labour and the law*. 2nd edn. London: Stevens & Sons.

Kant, I. (1770). On the form and principles of the sensible and intelligible world (The inaugural dissertation). Trans. J. Handyside & L.W. Beck. In L.W. Beck (ed.), *Kant: Selections*, 49–76. New York: Macmillan, 1988.

Kant, I. (1781A). *Critique of pure reason*. 1st Edition. In L.W. Beck (ed.), *Kant: Selections*, 85–148. New York: Macmillan, 1988.

Kant, I. (1787B). *Critique of pure reason*. 2nd Edition. Trans. J.M.D. Meiklejohn, 1934. London: Dent & Sons.

Kant, I. (1783). Prolegomena to any future metaphysics which will be able to come forth as a science. Trans. P. Carus & L.W. Beck. In L.W. Beck (ed.), *Kant: Selections*, 149–234. New York: Macmillan, 1988.

Kapp, R.O. (1931). Comments on Bernfeld and Feitelberg's 'The principle of entropy and the death instinct'. *International Journal of Psychoanalysis*, 12, 82–6.

Kasworm, C. (1984). Review of 'In a Different Voice'. *Adult Education Quarterly*, *34*, 247–9.

Kellogg, R. (1979). *Children's dreams, children's minds*. New York: Avon.

Kelly, J.M. (1992). *A short history of western legal theory*. Oxford: Clarendon Press.

Kelsen, H. (1945). *General theory of law and state*. Trans. A. Wedberg. Cambridge: Harvard University Press.

Kerenyi, C. (1976). *Dionysos: Archetypal image of indestructible life*. New Jersey: Princeton University Press.

Kernberg, O. (2009). The concept of the death drive: A clinical perspective. *International Journal of Psychoanalysis*, 90, 1009–23.

Kim, J. (2000). *Mind in a physical world: An essay on the mind-body problem and mental causation*. MIT Press.

Kimura, B. (2005). *Kankei tositeno jiko* [The self as relationships]. Tokyo: Misuzu syobo.

Kinsella, S. (2008). Reconciling Newtonian and Simonian Concepts of Space. *Cybernetics and Human Knowing*, 15, 69–74.

Kisiel, T. (1993). *The genesis of Heidegger's Being and Time*. Berkeley: University of California Press.

Kisiel, T. (2006). Recent Heidegger translations and their German originals: A grass-roots archival perspective. *Continental Philosophy Review*, 38, 263–87.

Klein, M. (1946). Notes on some schizoid mechanisms. In *Envy and gratitude and other works (1946–1963)*. London: Vintage, 1997.

Klein, M. (1948). On the theory of anxiety and guilt. In *Envy and gratitude and other works (1946–1963)*. London: Vintage, 1997.

Klein, M. (1952). The origins of transference. In *Envy and gratitude and other works (1946–1963)*. London: Vintage, 1997.

Knox, J. (2003). Trauma and defences: Their roots in relationship. *Journal of Analytical Psychology*, 48, 207–33.

Kockelmans, J.J. (1972). Language, meaning and ek-sistence. In J.J. Kockelmans (ed.), *On Heidegger and language*. Evanston, IL: Northwestern University Press.
Kohlberg, L. (1976). Moral stages and moralization: The cognitive-developmental approach. In T.Lickona (ed.), *Moral development and behavior: Theory, research and social issues*. New York: Holt, Rinehart and Winston.
Körner, S. (1967). The impossibility of transcendental deductions. *Monist*, 51, 317–31.
Kotoh, T. (1992). Language and silence: Self-inquiry in Heidegger and Zen. In C. Macann (ed.), *Martin Heidegger: Critical Assessments*, Vol. III, 39–49. London: Routledge.
Krabbendam, L., Janssen, I., Bak, M. et al. (2002). Neuroticism and low self-esteem as risk factors for psychosis. *Social Psychiatry and Psychiatric Epidemiology*, 37, 1–6.
Kriiska, A., Lougas, L. and Saluaar, U. (1997). Archaeological excavations of the Stone Age settlement site and ruin of the stone cist grave of the Early Metal Age in Kasekula. In U. Tamla (ed.), *Archaeological field works in Estonia*. Tallinn: Muinsuskaitseinspektsioon.
Kronenfeld, D. & Decker, H.W. (1979). Structuralism. *Annual Review of Anthropology*, 8, 503–41.
Kuhn, T. (1970). *The structures of scientific revolutions*. 2nd edn. Chicago: University of Chicago Press.
Kvaerne, P. (1975). On the Concept of Sahaja in Indian Buddhist Tantric Literature. *Temenos*, XI, 88–135.
Kvale, S. (1992). Postmodern psychology: a contradiction in terms? In S. Kvale (ed.), *Psychology and postmodernism*. London: Sage.
Lacan, J. (1949). The mirror stage as formative of the function on the I as revealed in the psychoanalytic experience. In J. Lacan, *Ecrits: A selection*. London: Tavistock, 1977.
Lacan, J. (1968). *Speech and language in psychoanalysis*. Trans. A. Wilden. Baltimore: Johns Hopkins.
Lafont, C. (2007). Heidegger and the synthetic a priori. In S. Crowell & J. Malpas (eds), *Transcendental Heidegger*, 104–18. California: Stanford University Press.
Laing, R.D. (1959). *The divided self*. London: Tavistock.
Laing, R.D. (1961). *Self and others*. London: Tavistock.
Laing, R.D. (1967). *The politics of experience*. London: Penguin.
Laing, R.D. (1982). *The voice of experience*. London: Allen Lane.
Laing, R.D. & Esterson (1970). *Sanity, madness and the family*. New York: Routledge, 1999.
Lakatos, I. (1970). *The growth of knowledge*. Cambridge: Cambridge University Press.
Lakoff, G. & Johnson, M. (1980). *Metaphors we live by*. Chicago: University of Chicago Press.

Lakoff, G. (1987). *Women, fire and dangerous things.* University of Chicago Press.

Lakoff, G. (1993). The contemporary theory of metaphor. In A. Ortony (ed.), *Metaphor and Thought.* Cambridge University Press.

Lakoff, G. & Johnson, M. (1999). *Philosophy in the flesh: The embodied mind and its challenge to Western thought.* New York: Basic Books.

Lancy, D.F. (1980). Play in species adaptation. *Annual Review of Anthropology*, 9, 471–95.

Lane, S. (1997). The sexual abuse cycle. In G. Ryan & S. Lane (eds), *Juvenile sexual offending: Causes, consequences and correction*, 2nd edn. San Francisco, Ca.: Jossey-Bass.

Lather, P. (1994). Staying dumb? Feminist research and pedagogy with/in the postmodern. In H.W. Simons & M. Billig (eds), *After postmodernism: Reconstructing ideology critique.* London: Sage Publications Ltd.

Leach, E. (1965/2000). Claude Lévi-Strauss: Anthropologist and philosopher. In *The essential Edmund Leach, Vol. I, Anthropology and society*, S. Hugh-Jones & J. Laidlaw (eds). New Haven: Yale University Press.

Leach, E. (1970). *Lévi-Strauss.* London: Fontana.

Leach, E. (1982). *Social anthropology.* London: Fontana.

Lear, J. (2009). Technique and final cause in psychoanalysis: Four ways of looking at one moment. *International Journal of Psychoanalysis*, 90, 1299–317.

Leary, V.A. (1990). The Asian region and the international human rights movement (13–27). In C.E. Welch & V.A. Leary (eds), *Asian perspectives on human rights.* Oxford: Westview Press.

Lechte, J. (1994). *Fifty key contemporary thinkers: From structuralism to postmodernism.* London: Routledge.

Leidy, D.P. (2008). *The art of Buddhism: An introduction to its history and meaning.* Boston: Shambhala Publications.

Lesgold, A., Rubinson, H., Feltovich, P., Glaser, R., Klopfer, D. & Wang, Y. (1988). Expertise in a complex skill: diagnosing x-ray pictures. In M. Chi, R. Glaser & M.J. Farr (eds), *The nature of expertise*, 311–42. Hillsdale NJ: Erlbaum.

Levi, P. (1985). *The voice of memory: Interviews, 1961–1987.* M. Belpoliti and R. Gordon (eds). New York: New Press, 2002.

Lévi-Strauss, C. (1955). *Tristes tropiques.* Trans. J. Weightman, D. Weightman. New York: Atheneum, 1973.

Lévi-Strauss, C. (1962). *The savage mind.* Trans. G. Weidenfeld, 1966 Nicolson Ltd. Chicago: Chicago University Press.

Lévi-Strauss, C. (1963). *Structural anthropology: Vol. 1.* Trans. C. Jacobsen & B. Grundfest Schoepf. Allen Lane: Penguin.

Lévi-Strauss, C. (1969). *The elementary structures of kinship.* Boston: Beacon Press.

Lévi-Strauss, C. (1970). *The raw and the cooked: Introduction to a science of mythology I.* London: Jonathan Cape.

Lévi-Strauss, C. (1973). *Structural anthropology: Vol. 2.* Trans. M. Layton, 1977. Allen Lane: Penguin Books.

Lévi-Strauss, C. (1981). *The naked man.* Trans. J. Weightman & D. Weightman. London: Jonathan Cape.

Lévi-Strauss, C. & Eribon, D. (1988).*Conversations with Claude Lévi-Strauss.* Chicago: University of Chicago Press, 1991.

Levinas, E. (1969). *Totality and infinity.* Trans. A. Lingis. Pittsburgh: Duquesne University Press.

Levinas, E. (1986). Admiration and disappointment. In G. Neske & E. Kettering (eds), *Martin Heidegger and national socialism,* 149–53, 1990. New York: Paragon House.

Lewis, I.M. (1977). Introduction. In I.M. Lewis (ed.), *Symbols and sentiments: Cross-cultural studies in symbolism.* London: Academic Press.

Lewis, I.M. (1985). *Social anthropology in perspective: The relevance of social anthropology.* 2nd edn. Cambridge University Press.

Likacheva, V. (1981). *The art of Byzantium 4th to 15th Century.* Moscow: Art. Original in Russian.

Luhmann, N. (1994). Speaking and silence. *New German Critique,* 61, 25–39.

Luhmann, N. (1995). Why 'systems theory'? *Cybernetics and Human Knowing,* 3, 3–10.

Lyons, N.P (1988). Two perspectives: On self, relationships and morality. In C. Gilligan, J.C. Ward, J. McLean Taylor, B. Bardige (eds), *Mapping the moral domain: A contribution of women's thinking to psychological theory and education,* 21–48. Cambridge, Mass.: Harvard University Press.

Lyotard, J-F. (1984). *The postmodern condition: A report on knowledge.* Trans. G. Bennington & B. Massumi. Minneapolis: University of Minnesota Press.

Macquarrie, J. (1977). *Principles of Christian theology.* Revised edn. London: SCM Press.

Main, M. & Solomon J. (1986). Discovery of a new, insecure-disorganized/disoriented attachment pattern. In T.B. Brazelton, M.V. Yogman (eds), *Affective development in infancy,* 95–124. Ablex: Norwood, 1986.

Malcolm, N. (1995). *Wittgensteinian themes: Essays 1978–1989.* New York: Cornell University Press.

Malpas, J. (1997). The transcendental circle. *Australasian Journal of Philosophy,* 75, 1–20.

Malpas, J. (2008). *Heidegger's topology: Being, place, world.* Cambridge, Mass.: MIT Press.

Mandel, M. (1984). *Minevikult tanapaevani.* Estonia: Eesti raanat.

Mandler, G. (1984). Cohabitation in the cognitive sciences. In W. Kintsch, J.R. Miller & P.G. Polson (eds), *Method and tactics in cognitive science.* Hillsdale, NJ: Erlbaum.

Mansfield, N. (2000). *Subjectivity: Theories of the self from Freud to Haraway.* New York: New York University Press.

Mansfield, V. & Spiegelman, J.M. (1991–1992). The opposites in quantum physics and Jungian psychology Part 1: Theoretical foundations. *Journal of Analytical Psychology*, 36–7, 267–88.

Maranda, P. (1972). Structuralism in cultural anthropology. *Annual Review of Anthropology*, 1, 329–48.

Markus, H. & Sentis, K. (1982). The self in social information processing. In J. Suls (ed.), *Psychological perspectives on the self.* Vol. 1. Hillsdale, NJ: Erlbaum.

Marmor, A. (2001). Legal conventionalism. In J. Coleman (ed.), *Hart's postscript: Essays on the Postscript to the Concept of Law*, 193–218. Oxford: Oxford University Press.

Maslow, A. (1970). *Motivation and personality.* New York: Harper & Row.

Masuda, T. and Nisbett, R.E. (2001). *Culture and attention to object versus field.* Unpublished manuscript, University of Michigan.

Mazurczak, U. (1985). The structure of time in Hans Memling's Last Judgment. *Gdańskie Studia Muzealne*, 4, 9–34. Muzeum Narodowe w Gdańsku.

Meier, C.A. (2001). Preface. *Atom and archetype: The Pauli-Jung letters 1932–1958.* Trans. D. Roscoe. London: Routledge.

Melikian, S. (1998). *International Herald Tribune*, June 6–7.

MacNiece, L. (1987). Poetry today. In A. Heuser (ed.), *Selected literary criticism of Louis MacNiece*, 10–44. Oxford: Clarendon Press.

May, R. (1996). *Heidegger's hidden sources: East Asian influences on his work.* Trans. G. Parkes. New York: Routledge.

May, S., Modood, T. & Squires, J. (2004). Ethnicity, nationalism, and minority rights: Charting the disciplinary debates. In S. May, T. Modood & J. Squires (eds), *Ethnicity, nationalism, and minority rights*, 1–26. Cambridge: Cambridge University Press.

Mehta, J.L. (1987). Heidegger and Vedanta: Reflections on a questionable theme In G. Parkes (ed.), *Heidegger and Asian thought*, 15–45. Honolulu: University of Hawaii Press.

Midgley, M. (1988). Teleological theories of morality. In G.H.R. Parkinson, T.E. Burke, J.G. Cottingham, M.A. Proudfoot & J.E. Tiles (eds), *An encyclopedia of philosophy*, 541–67. London: Routledge.

Mill, J.S. (1869). *On liberty.* London: Longman, Roberts & Green.

Mill, J.S. (1872). *A system of logic.* In R.F. McRae (ed.), Collected Works, Vol. VII, Books I, II, III. Toronto: University of Toronto Press, 1973.

Miller, G.A. (1956). The magical number seven, plus or minus two,: Some limits on our capacity for processing information. *Psychological Review*, 63, 81–97.
Miller, J.G. (1984). Culture and the development of everyday social explanation. *Journal of Personality and Social Psychology*, *46*, 961–78.
Minsky, M. (1975). A framework for representing knowledge. In P.H. Winston (ed.), *The psychology of computer vision.* New York: McGraw–Hill.
Mitchell, J. (1974). *Psychoanalysis and feminism.* London: Allen Lane.
Mizen, R. (2003). A contribution towards an analytic theory of violence. *Journal of Analytical Psychology*, 48, 285–305.
Mizoguchi, K. (1987). Heidegger's Bremen lectures: Towards a dialogue with his later thought (187–99). In G. Parkes (ed.), *Heidegger and Asian thought.* Honolulu: University of Hawaii Press.
Modell, A.H. (1999). The dead mother syndrome and the reconstruction of trauma. In G. Kohon (ed.), *The dead mother: The work of Andre Green.* London: Routledge.
Moi, T. (1981). Representation of patriarchy: Sexuality and epistemology in Freud's Dora. *Feminist Review*, 9, 60–74.
Monzani, L.R. (1989). *Freud: O movimento de um pensamento* [Freud: The movement of a thought]. Campinas Brazil: ed. Da Unicamp.
Montesquieu (1749). *De L'Esprit des Lois.* Livre I. J.P. Mayer & A.P. Kerr (eds). Gallimard, 1970.
Moore, A.W. (2010). The transcendental doctrine of method. In P. Guyer (ed.), *The Cambridge companion to Kant's Critique of pure reason*, 310–26. New York: Cambridge University Press.
Moran, D. (2007). Heidegger's transcendental philosophy in the light of Husserl's project of first philosophy. In S. Crowell & J. Malpas (eds), *Transcendental Heidegger*, 135–50. California: Stanford University Press.
Morioka, M. (2007). Commentary: Constructing creative appropriations. *Culture & Psychology*, 13, 189–96.
Mulla, Z.R. & Krishnan, V.R. (2008). Karma-Yoga, the Indian work ideal, and its relationship with empathy. *Psychology Developing Societies*, 20, 27–49.
Needham, R. (1973). *Right and left.* Chicago: University of Chicago Press.
Neisser, U. (1967). *Cognitive psychology*. New York: Appleton-Century-Crofts.
Neisser, U. (1976). *Cognition and reality.* San Francisco: W.H. Freeman & Co.
Neske, G. & Kettering, E. (eds) (1990). *Martin Heidegger and National Socialism.* New York: Paragon House.
Neumann, E. (1973). *The child: Structure and dynamics of the nascent personality.* Trans. R. Manheim. London: Hodder & Stoughton.
Newell, A. & Simon, H.A. (1972). *Human problem solving.* Englewood Cliffs, NJ: Lawrence Erlbaum Assoc.

Newell, A. (1980). Physical systems. In *Cognitive Science.* Vol. 4, 135–83. Hillsdale, NJ: Erlbaum.
Newell, A. (1990). *Unified theories of cognition.* Cambridge, MA: Harvard University Press.
Nicholas, B. (1961). *An introduction to Roman law.* Oxford: Oxford University Press.
Nichols, R. (1990). *The book of druidry.* J. Matthews & P. Carr-Gorman (eds). London: Thorsons.
Nietzsche, F. (1872/2000). *The birth of tragedy.* Trans. D. Smith. Oxford: Oxford University Press.
Nietzsche, F. (1883/2003). *Thus spoke Zarathustra.* Trans. R.J. Hollingdale. London: Penguin.
Nisbett, R.E, Peng, K., Choi, I., and Norenzayan, A. (2001). Culture and systems of thought: Holistic versus analytic cognition. *Psychological Review*, 108, 291–310.
Norris, C. (1982). *Deconstruction: Theory and practice.* London: Methuen.
Novick, L.R. & Holyoak, K. (1991). Mathematical problem solving by analogy: *Journal of Experimental Psychology: Learning, Memory and Cognition*, 17, 398–415.
Nuttall, P. (1995). Memling's Last Judgement, Angelo Tani and the Florentine colony at Bruges. In F. Ames-Lewis (ed.), *Responses to French art and architecture. Contrasts and similarities*, 155–65. London: Department of History of Art, Birkbeck College.
Olafson, F.A. (1994). Heidegger à la Wittgenstein or 'coping' with Professor Dreyfus. *Inquiry*, 37, 45–64.
Olsen, O. and Køppe, S. (1988). *Freud's theory of psychoanalysis.* New York: New York University Press.
Ortony, A. (1993). Metaphor, language and thought. In A. Ortony (ed.), *Metaphor and thought.* Cambridge University Press.
Osgood, C.E. (1979). From *yang* and *yin* to and or but in cross cultural perspective. *International Journal of Psychology* 14, 1–35.
Oslisy, R. (1996). The rock art of Gabon: Techniques, themes and estimation of its age by cultural association. In G. Pwiti, R.C. Soper (eds), *Aspects of African archaeology: Papers from the 10th Congress of the PanAfrican Association for Prehistory and Related Studies*, 361–70. Zimbabwe: University of Zimbabwe Publications.
Ott, H. (1993). *Martin Heidegger: a political life.* Trans. A. Blunden. London: Harper Collins.
Parkes, G. (1987). Thoughts on the Way: *Being and Time* via Lao-Chuang. In G. Parkes (ed.), *Heidegger and Asian thought.* Honolulu: University of Hawaii Press.
Parkes, G. (2006). Rising sun over Black Forest: Heidegger's Japanese connections. A complementary essay. In R. May, *Heidegger's hidden sources: East Asian influences on his work.* Trans. G. Parkes. London & New York: Routledge.

Pazzani, M.J. (1990). *Creating a memory of causal relationships: an integration of empirical and explanation-based learning methods.* Hillsdale, NJ: Erlbaum.

Pauli, W. (2001). *Atom and archetype: The Pauli-Jung letters 1932–1958.* C.A. Meier (ed.). Trans. D. Roscoe. London: Routledge.

Peirce, C.S. (1960). *Collected papers of Charles Sanders Peirce.* Cambridge Mass.: Harvard University Press.

Penrose, L.S. (1931). Freud's theory of instinct and other psycho-biological theories. *International Journal of Psychoanalysis*, 12, 87–97.

Perkins, D.N. (1995). Insight in minds and genes. In R.J. Sternberg & J.E. Davidson (eds), *The nature of insight.* Cambridge: London.

Philipse, H. (2007). Heidegger's 'Scandal of philosophy': The problem of the *Ding an sich* in *Being and Time.* In S. Crowell & J. Malpas (eds), *Transcendental Heidegger*, 169–98. California: Stanford University Press.

Piaget, J. (1932). *The moral judgment of the child.* New York: The Free Press, 1965.

Piaget, J. (1960). *The child's conception of the world.* London: Routledge.

Piaget, J. (1962). *Play, dreams and imitation in childhood.* Trans. G. Gategno & F.M. Hodgson. New York: Norton.

Piaget, J. (1971). *Structuralism.* London: Routledge & Kegan Paul.

Piaget, J. & Inhelder, B. (1956). *The child's conception of space.* London: Routledge & Kegan Paul.

Popper, K. (1959). *Logic of scientific discovery.* London: Hutchinson.

Prentky, R., Knight, R., Straus, H., Rokou, F., Cerce, D. & Sims-Knight, J. (1989). Developmental antecedents of sexual aggression. *Development and Psychopathology*, 1, 153–69.

Propp, V. (1958). *Morphology of the folktale.* The Hague: Mouton.

Przybyszewski, B. (1979). *Sąd Ostateczny Jana Memlinga w Muzeum Pomorskim w Gdańsku.* 'Nasza Przyszłość. Studia w dziejów Kościoła i kultury katolickiej w Polsce, vol. LII, 107–66.

Purc-Stępniak, B. (ed.). (2007). Usłyszeć obraz. Muzyka w sztuce europejskiej od XV do początku XX wieku. Gdańsk: Muzeum Narodowe.

Quine, W.V.O. (1961). *From a logical point of view.* 2nd edn. New York: Harper.

Rachlin, H. (1984). Mental yes. Private no. *Behavioral and Brain Sciences*, 7, 566–7.

Rajneesh, B.S. (1979). *The way of Tao.* Poona: Rajneesh Foundation.

Reddy, M.J. (1993). The conduit metaphor: a case of frame conflict in our language about language. In A. Ortony (ed.), *Metaphor and thought.* Cambridge University Press.

Reichenbach, H. (1938). *Experience and prediction: an analysis of the foundations and the structure of knowledge.* Chicago: University of Chicago Press.

Ricoeur, P. (1963). Symbole et temporalité. *Archivo di Filosofia*, Nos 1–2. Rome.

Ricoeur, P. (1981). *Hermeneutics and the human sciences.* Trans. J.B. Thompson. New York: Cambridge University Press.

Richardson, W.J. (1974). *Through phenomenology to thought.* 3rd edn. The Hague: Martinus Nijhoff.

Roberts, A. (2002). Introduction to Homer. *The Odyssey.* Trans. G. Chapman. Hertfordshire: Wordsworth Editions.

Rogers, J.M. & Molzon, R.E. (1992). Some lessons about the law from self-referential problems in mathematics. *Michigan Law Review*, 90, 992–1022.

Rorty, R. (1991). *Essays on Heidegger and others: Philosophical papers 2*. Cambridge University Press.

Rosch, E. (1978). Principles of categorisation. In E. Rosch & B.B. Lloyd (eds), *Cognition and categorisation*. Hillsdale, NJ: Erlbaum.

Roskill, M. (1997). *The Grolier Multimedia Encyclopedia*. New York: Grolier.

Roth, P. (2001). Mapping the landscape: Levels of transference interpretation. *International Journal of Psychoanalysis*, 82, 533–43.

Rossi, I. (1974). Intellectual antecedents of Lévi-Strauss' notion of the unconscious. In *The unconscious in culture: The structuralism of Claude Lévi-Strauss in perspective*, I. Rossi (ed.). New York: E.P. Dutton & Co.

Rumelhart, D.E. (1975). Notes on a schema for stories. In D.G. Bobrow & A. Collins (eds), *Representation and Understanding*. New York: Academic Press.

Rumelhart, D. (1980). Schemata: the building blocks of cognition. In R.J. Spiro, B.C. Bruce & W.F. Brewer (eds), *Theoretical issues in reading comprehension*, 33–58. Hillsdale, NJ: Erlbaum.

Rumelhart, D.E. (1993).Some problems with the notion of literal meanings. In A. Ortony (ed.), *Metaphor and Thought.* Cambridge University Press.

Rutter, M. (1985). Resilience in the face of adversity: Protective factors and resistance to psychiatric disorder. *British Journal of Psychiatry*, 147, 598–611.

Safranski, R. (1998). *Martin Heidegger: Between good and evil.* Trans. E. Osers. Massachusetts: Harvard University Press.

Sallis, J. (1992). Language and reversal. In C. Macann (ed.), *Martin Heidegger: Critical assessments*. London: Routledge.

Said, E.W. (1978). *Orientalism*. London: Routledge & Kegan Paul.

Samuels, A. (1985). *Jung and the Post-Jungians*. London: Routledge & Kegan Paul.

Sartre, J.-P. (1943). *Being and nothingness: A study in phenomenological ontology*. Trans. H.E. Barnes. New York: Philosophical Library, 1953.

Saussure, de F. (1954). Notes inédites de F. de Saussure. *Cahiers Ferdinand de Saussure* 12.

Sayer, A. (1997). Essentialism, social constructionism and beyond. *The Sociological Review*, 45, 454–77.

Scales, A.C. (1986). The emergence of feminist jurisprudence: an essay. In M.D.A. Freeman (ed.), *Lloyd's introduction to jurisprudence*, 6th edn. 1996, 1048–61. Sweet & Maxwell.

Scardamalia, M. & Bereiter, C. (1991). Literate expertise. In K.A. Ericsson & J. Smith (eds), *Toward a general theory of expertise: prospects and limits.* Cambridge: Cambridge University Press.

Schank, R.C. & Abelson, R. (1977). *Scripts, plans, goals and understanding.* Hillsdale, NJ: Erlbaum.

Schank, R.C. (1982). *Dynamic memory.* Cambridge: Cambridge University Press.

Scholes, R. (1985). *Textual power.* New Haven, CT: Yale University Press.

Schön, D. (1993). Generative metaphor: A perspective on problem setting in social policy. In A. Ortony (ed.), *Metaphor and thought.* Cambridge University Press.

Shanon, B. (1993). *The representational and the presentational: An essay on cognition and the study of mind.* New York: Harvester Wheatsheaf.

Sharma, A. (2006). *Are human rights Western? A contribution to the dialogue of civilizations* New Delhi: Oxford University Press.

Sherwood, M. (1969). *The logic of explanation in psychoanalysis*, New York: Academic Press.

Simon, H.A. (1955/1979). A behavioral model of rational choice. In H.A. Simon, *Models of thought.* New Haven & London: Yale University Press.

Simon, H.A. (1977). *Models of discovery and other topics in the methods of science.* Boston Studies in the Philosophy of Science, Vol. LIV, R.S. Cohen & M.W. Wartofsky (eds). Boston: Reidel.

Simon, H.A. (1969). *The sciences of the artificial* 2nd edn, 1981, 3rd edn, 1996. Cambridge: MIT Press.

Simon, H.A. & Chase, W.G. (1973). Skill in chess. *American Scientist*, 61, 394–403.

Simon, H.A. & Kaplan, C.A. (1989). Foundations of cognitive science. In M.I. Posner (ed.), *Foundations of cognitive science.* Cambridge: MIT Press.

Simon, H.A. & Langley, P. (1981/1989). The central role of learning in cognition. In H.A. Simon, *Models of thought, Vol. II.* New Haven: Yale University Press.

Sincoff, J.B. (1992). Ambivalence and defense: Effects of a repressive style on normal adolescents' and young adults' mixed feelings. *Journal of Abnormal Psychology*, 101, 251–6.

Skinner, B.F. (1974). *About behaviorism.* London: Cape.

Skinner, B.F. (1972). *Beyond freedom and dignity.* London: Cape.

Soloway, E. & Ehrlich, K. (1984). Empirical studies of programming knowledge IEEE *Transactions on software engineering*, 10, 595–609.

Soffer, G. (1996). Heidegger, humanism and the destruction of history. *Review of Metaphysics*, 49, 547–76.

Spanos, W.V. (1995). The detective and the boundary. In P.A. Bové (ed.), *Early postmodernism: Foundational essays*. Durham: Duke University Press.

Spivak, G.C. (1997). *Translator's Preface to 'Of Grammatology'*. Corrected Edition. Baltimore: John Hopkins University Press.

Spring, N. (2007). Tracing the language of educational disadvantage. In P. Downes & A-L. Gilligan (eds), *Beyond educational disadvantage* (2007). Dublin: Institute of Public Administration.

Stadlen, A. (1989). Was Dora ill? In *Sigmund Freud: Critical assessments* Vol. II, L. Spurling (ed.), 196–203. London: Routledge.

Stambaugh, J. (1987). Heidegger, Taoism and the question of metaphysics. In G. Parkes (ed.), *Heidegger and Asian thought*, 79–91. Honolulu: University of Hawaii Press.

Stevens, A. (1982/1992). Archetypes and behaviour. In R.K. Papadopoulos (ed.), *Carl Gustav Jung: Critical assessments*, Vol. II. London: Routledge.

Stevens, A. (1990). *On Jung*. London: Routledge.

Stolorow, R.D. (2007). *Trauma and human existence*. New York: The Analytic Press.

Stolorow, R.D. (2011). *World, affectivity, trauma: Heidegger and PostCartesian psychoanalysis*. New York: Routledge.

Stolorow, R.D., Atwood, G.E. & Orange, D.M. (2010). Heidegger's nazism and the hypostatization of being. *International Journal of Psychoanalytic Self Psychology*, 5, 429–50.

Storr, A. (1972). *Human destructiveness*. London: Chatto & Heinemann for Sussex University Press.

Storr, A. (1973). *Jung*. London: Fontana.

Storr, A. (1997). *Feet of clay: A study of gurus*. London: Harper Collins.

Strange, J.F. (1995). The art and archaeology of ancient Judaism. In *Judaism in Late Antiquity: Part one, the literary and archaeological sources*, J. Neusner (ed.). Netherlands: E.J. Brill, Leiden.

Strauss, C. & Quinn, N. (1997). *A cognitive theory of cultural meaning*. Publications of the Society for Psychological Anthropology 9. Cambridge University Press.

Streicker, J. (1997). Spatial reconfigurations, imagined geographies and social conflicts in Cartagena, Columbia. *Cultural Anthropology*, 12, 109–28.

Suler, J.R. (1991). The T'ai Chi images: a Taoist model of psychotherapeutic change. *Psychologia*, 34, 18–27.

Sulloway, F. (1979). *Freud: Biologist of the mind*. London: Burnett Books.

Sutherland, E. (1939). *Criminology*. 3rd edn. Philadelphia: J.B. Lippincott.

Sweller, J. (1994). Cognitive Load Theory, Learning Difficulty and Instructional Design. *Learning and Instruction*, 4, 295–312.

Sztyber, B. (2003). *Średniowieczny traktat teologiczny czyli sąd ostateczny Hansa Memlinga*. Gdansk: Muzeum Narodowe.

Tajfel, H. (1978). *Differentiation between social groups*. London: Academic Press.

Tang, P.C.L. (1997). On the special logic thesis in Chinese philosophy. *Metaphilosophy*, 28, 371–84.

Taylor, C. (1989). *Sources of the self: The making of modern identity*. Cambridge, Mass.: Harvard University Press.

Taylor, C. (1991). *The ethics of authenticity*. Cambridge, Mass.: Harvard University Press.

Taylor, C. (2007). *A secular age*. Cambridge, Mass.: Harvard University Press.

Taylor, J., Gilligan, C., Sullivan, A.M. (1997). *Between voice and silence: Women and girls, race and relationship*. Cambridge, Mass.: Harvard University Press.

Teo, T. & Febbraro, A.R. (2003). Ethnocentrism as a form of intuition in psychology. *Theory & Psychology*, 13, 673–94.

Teo, T. (2008). From speculation to epistemological violence in psychology: A critical-hermeneutic reconstruction. *Theory and Psychology*, 18, 47–67.

Thomson, B. (2000). *Impressionism: Origins, practice, reception*. London: Thames & Hudson.

Thomson, I.D. (2011). *Heidegger, art and modernity*. New York: Cambridge University Press.

Thoreau, H.D. (2005). Conclusion. In R.G. Geldard (ed.), *The essential transcendentalists*. NewYork: Penguin.

Toffler, A. (1980). *The third wave*. London: Pan/Collins.

Tong, R. (1989). *Feminist thought: A comprehensive introduction*. Oxon, UK: Unwin Human Ltd.

Tribe, L.H. (1988). *American constitutional law*, 2nd edn. New York: Foundation Press.

Tribe, L.H. (1990). The curvature of constitutional space: what lawyers can learn from modern physics. *Harvard Law Review*, 103, 1–39.

Tugendhat, E. (1967). *Der Wahrheitsbegriff bei Husserl und Heidegger.* Berlin: de Gruyter.

Van der Wal, M.F., Cees, M., de Wit, A.M. & Hirasing, R.A. Psychosocial health among young victims and offenders of direct and indirect bullying. *Pediatrics*, 111, 1312–17.

Vedru, G. (1997). New archaeological data of the prehistory of Lake Kahala area. In U. Tamla (ed.), *Archaeological field works in Estonia*. Tallinn: Muinsuskaitseinspektsioon.

Volk, T. (1995). *Metapatterns: Across space, time and mind.* New York: Columbia University Press.

Von Franz, M-L. (1975). *Creation myths.* New York: Spring Publications.

Von Franz, M-L. (1980/1992). The hypothesis of the collective unconscious. In R.K. Papadopoulos (ed.), *Carl Gustav Jung: Critical assessments*, Vol. II, 271–84. London: Routledge.

Voogd, de S. (1992). Fantasy versus fiction: Jung's Kantianism appraised. In R.K. Papadopoulos (ed.), *Carl Gustav Jung: Critical Assessments* Vol. I, 27–53. London: Routledge.

Wallace, E.R. (1989). Pitfalls of a one-sided image of science: Adolf Grünbaum's 'Foundations of Psychoanalysis'. *Journal of the American Psychoanalytic Association*, 37, 493–529.

Wallerstein, R.S. (1990). Psychoanalysis: The common ground. *International Journal of Psychoanalysis*, 71, 3–20.

Walsh, W.H. (1967). Schematism. In R.P. Wolff (ed.), *Kant: A collection of critical essays*, 71–87. London: Macmillan.

Ward, J.V. (1988). Urban adolescents' conceptions of violence. In C. Gilligan, J.C. Ward, J. McLean Taylor, B. Bardige (eds), *Mapping the moral domain: A contribution of women's thinking to psychological theory and education*, 175–200. Cambridge, Mass.: Harvard University Press.

Watkins, E. (2007). Kant's model of causality: Causal powers, laws and Kant's reply to Hume. In K. Brinkmann (ed.), *German idealism: Critical concepts in philosophy*, Vol. 1, 217–63. London: Routledge.

Watkins, E. (2010). The system of principles. In P. Guyer (ed.), *The Cambridge companion to Kant's Critique of pure reason*, 151–67. New York: Cambridge University Press.

Watson, J. (1914). *Behaviorism*. New York: Holt.

Weiser, M., Reichenberg, A., Rabinowitz, J. et al. (2001). Association between non-psychotic psychiatric diagnoses in adolescent males and subsequent onset of schizophrenia. *Archives of General Psychiatry*, 58, 959–64.

White, D. & Woollett, A. (1992). *Families: A context for development.* Basingstoke: Falmer.

Whitford, F. (1990). *Klimt*. London: Thames & Hudson.

Widom, C.S. (1996). Childhood sexual abuse and its criminal consequences. *Society*, *33*, 47–53.

Wilhelm, H. (1977). *Heaven, earth and man in the Book of Changes.* University of Washington Press.

Williams, L.M. (1995). *Juvenile and adult offending behaviour and other outcomes in a cohort of sexually abused boys: Twenty years later.* Philadelphia: Joseph J. Peters Institute.

Winnicott, D.W. (1966). The location of cultural experience. *International Journal of Psycho-Analysis*, 48, 368–72.

Winnicott, D.W. (1971). *Playing and reality*. London: Tavistock.

Winnicott, D.W. (1977). *The Piggle: An account of the psychoanalytic treatment of a little girl.* Harmondsworth: Penguin.

Witherspoon, G. & Peterson, G. (1995). *Dynamic symmetry and holistic asymmetry in Navajo and Western art and cosmology*. New York: Peter Lang.

Wittgenstein, L. (1958). *Philosophical investigations*. Oxford: Blackwell.

Wittgenstein, L. (1969). *On certainty*, Oxford: Blackwell.

Wohl, R. & Trosman, M. (1955). A retrospect of Freud's Leonardo: An assessment of a psychoanalytic classic. *Psychiatry*, XVIII, 27–39.

Wood, A.W. (2010). The antinomies of pure reason. In P. Guyer (ed.), *The Cambridge companion to Kant's Critique of pure reason*, 245–65. New York: Cambridge University Press.

Young, C. and Brook, A. (1994). Schopenhauer and Freud. *International Journal of Psychoanalysis*, 75, 101–18.

Yuasa, Y. (1987). The encounter of modern Japanese philosophy with Heidegger. In G. Parkes (ed.), *Heidegger and Asian thought*, 155–74. Honolulu: University of Hawaii Press.

Zabriskie, B. (2001). Introduction, Jung and Pauli: A meeting of rare minds. In C.A. Meier (ed.), *Atom and archetype: The Pauli-Jung letters 1932–1958*. Trans. D. Roscoe. London: Routledge.

Zimmerman, M.E. (2006). Heidegger, Buddhism and deep ecology. In C. Guignon (ed.), *The Cambridge companion to Heidegger*, 2nd edn, 293–325. Cambridge: Cambridge University Press.

Zlatev, J. (2005). What's in a schema? Bodily mimesis and the grounding of language. In B. Hampe (ed. with J.E. Grady), *From perception to meaning: Image schemas in cognitive linguistics*, 313–42. Berlin: Mouton de Gruyter.

Index of Subjects

Index of Names

Lightning Source UK Ltd.
Milton Keynes UK
UKHW020658231020
371957UK00014B/364

9 783034 307604